Peoples and Cultures
of the World

Edward F. Fischer, Ph.D.

THE
GREAT
COURSES·

PUBLISHED BY:

THE GREAT COURSES
Corporate Headquarters
4840 Westfields Boulevard, Suite 500
Chantilly, Virginia 20151-2299
Phone: 1-800-832-2412
Fax: 703-378-3819
www.thegreatcourses.com

Edward F. Fischer, Ph.D.

Associate Professor of Anthropology, Vanderbilt University

Edward F. Fischer was educated at the University of Alabama at Birmingham and Tulane University, where he received his Ph.D. in Anthropology in 1996. His research focuses on the modern Maya peoples of highland Guatemala and the ways that they have revitalized their culture as they have become integrated in the global economy.

Professor Fischer is the author of numerous professional articles and several books, including *Pan-Maya Activism in Guatemala* (co-edited with R. McKenna Brown), *Cultural Logics and Global Economies*, *Tecpán Guatemala: A Modern Maya Town in Local and Global Context* (co-authored with Carol Hendrickson), and *Pluralizing Ethnography* (co-edited with John Watanabe). He is currently studying Maya farmers who grow broccoli for export to the United States and working on a project comparing economic attitudes in Guatemala, Germany, and the United States.

Professor Fischer has received grants from the John D. and Catherine T. MacArthur Foundation, the Inter-American Foundation, the Wener-Grenn Foundation, and others. Since 1996, he has taught at Vanderbilt University, where he is Associate Professor of Anthropology and Director of the Center for Latin American and Iberian Studies. In 2002, he received the Jeffrey Nordhaus Award for Excellence in Teaching, and in 2004, he received the Ellen Gregg Ingalls Award for Excellence in Classroom Teaching.

Table of Contents
Peoples and Cultures of the World

Table of Contents
Peoples and Cultures of the World

Peoples and Cultures of the World

Scope:

What do we as humans share and what makes us different? What sorts of behavior are acceptable and what are not in different societies? What can this tell us about ourselves as human beings? This course addresses such questions by examining a wide range of cultural diversity. In looking at cultures around the world, we show how anthropology acts as a "mirror for humanity," teaching us about ourselves and about others.

Built around compelling examples of exotic customs, this course shows how cultures differ (from religious beliefs and marriage practices to political organization and economics) and addresses the question of why such differences exist and persist in the modern world. Studying cultural diversity also allows us to look at our own customs in a new light, and, in so doing, stimulates creativity.

We begin with a brief overview of the four subfields of anthropology: physical anthropology, archaeology, linguistics, and cultural anthropology. Physical anthropology defines our field of inquiry (what makes us biologically human) and shows how our evolutionary heritage continues to influence our actions. Archaeology gives us a sense of scale when speaking of societal trends and is increasingly meaningful for indigenous peoples seeking to reclaim their past.

The primary focus of the course is on modern cultures. To attempt to interpret other cultures, we must first understand language—not just the dictionary meanings of words (even if there were dictionaries of these languages) but the subtleties of communication. Sociolinguistics shows how dialect differences convey a great deal of cultural meaning; in English, for example, even women and men have distinct patterns of speaking that often lead to misunderstanding. Through such examples we will study the ways that language molds the very way we perceive and think about the world. This leads us to examine how mental models and pervasive metaphors (such as "time is money") shape our culture and how religion and magic fit into cultural schemes.

Having started at the level of language and thought—that is to say, with the individual—we move to how the individual fits into society through rites of passage and kinship relations. We focus particularly on the differences between matrilineal and patrilineal societies. This leads us to a discussion of marriage patterns (monogamous and polygamous) and the role of romantic love in societies that practice arranged marriages.

We then turn to an overview of cultures at different levels of social complexity, from bands and tribes to chiefdoms and states. We look to the subsistence strategies of gathering-and-hunting bands and horticulturist rainforest dwellers. We find that economic relations in these cultures are firmly embedded in social relations and that reciprocity and redistribution are the norm under certain circumstances. These societies also have different types of political organization, and we look at the problems of leadership in small-scale societies. We examine violence and warfare, as well as ways of keeping the peace.

Modern native cultures cannot be seen as isolated entities. Since the glory days of Western expansion, these cultures have come into increasing contact with the outside world. We look to some of the deadly misunderstandings that accompanied early European contact. We then turn to the expansion of capitalist economies. We find that the rational choice models of traditional economics do not hold up under cross-cultural comparison, and we review the attempts of economists and anthropologists to come to terms with cultural differences.

The course concludes with a discussion of how globalization has affected native peoples around the world in surprising ways, focusing particularly on the Maya of Guatemala and Mexico, where I have conducted my long-term ethnographic fieldwork. We examine the rise of global economies and how native ways of life have changed as a result. We also look to the resurgence of ethnic groups—and the potentials and pitfalls of a world increasingly divided along ethnic lines.

The Field of Inquiry
Lecture One
The Study of Humanity

Scope: From the Greek *anthropos* and *logos*, anthropology is, quite literally, the study of humankind. And anthropologists take this broad mandate seriously. Other fields give us valuable insights into particular areas (for example, economics, history, or biology), but anthropology's genius is in looking at the interconnections among these spheres, bringing to bear the widest range of knowledge to understand the complexities and contradictions of the human condition.

In attempting a holistic perspective, anthropology spans the divide between science and humanity. Although we develop hypotheses and strive for scientific rigor in collecting data, the signature method of cultural anthropology (participant observation) is fundamentally subjective. Participant observation is going "there" (wherever "there" may be) and studying "them" (whomever "they" may be), living our lives as the natives live, if just for a year or two, so that we can contextualize the hard facts (from survey figures to caloric intake) with a subjective understanding of what their lives are like.

Outline

I. Cultural anthropology studies the range of human diversity found in the world and uses these data to address fundamental questions about human nature.

  A. Culture is learned.

  B. Despite how we often speak about them, cultures are not homogenous.

  C. The one great rule of culture is that it is always changing.

II. Anthropology is the study of humankind.

  A. Anthropology is one of the few academic disciplines that transcends the boundary between the sciences and the humanities.

      1. From the Greek, *anthropos* means "humanity" and *logos* means "writing about" or "the study of." Anthropologists employ the tools of scientific research (testable hypotheses, random sampling, and so on) but also strive for more subjective understanding of the people we study.

      2. Max Weber distinguishes between *Verstehen* ("understanding") and *Erklärung* ("explanation"); anthropologists seek both *Verstehen* and *Erklärung*.

  B. Rather than looking at just one aspect of the human condition, anthropology adopts a holistic approach.

      1. Economics, political science, psychology—these are all valuable disciplines. But alone, they each give us just part of the picture.

      2. Named for a famous Japanese film, the Rashomon effect describes the phenomenon of different people perceiving the same event in different ways.

      3. Anthropology looks at the interrelations between, for example, religion and economics, arguing that the human condition must be understood from a holistic perspective.

III. The discipline of anthropology is divided into four main subfields.

  A. Biological anthropology looks at human evolution and modern biological variation.

  B. Archaeology is the study of ancient civilizations and peoples, attempting to reconstruct past culture based on material remains.

  C. Linguistics is the study of language and the many ways that humans communicate.

  D. Cultural anthropology—called *social anthropology* in England—is the study of modern human traditions, customs, and worldviews.

IV. Despite its wide range of study, anthropology is united around a general perspective on humanity.

  A. Anthropologists affirm that it is fundamentally important to study the range of human diversity, both past and present, in order to situate ourselves in the world.

  B. By encouraging us to suspend our natural ethnocentrism, anthropology also provides an important way of understanding our own culture.

C. It is useful when talking about other cultures to distinguish between *emic* and *etic* perspectives. *Emic* is the view from within a culture; *etic* is the presumably more objective view of an outsider.

Readings:

Thomas Barfield, *The Dictionary of Anthropology.*

Gary Ferraro, *Classic Readings in Cultural Anthropology.*

Emily Schultz and Robert Lavenda, *Cultural Anthropology.*

Internet Resources:

http://anthro.palomar.edu/tutorials/cultural.htm. Cultural Anthropology Tutorials. Dr. Dennis O'Neil, Palomar College.

Questions to Consider:

1. What is the difference between "objective" and "subjective" forms of understanding? How does anthropology attempt to reconcile the two?

2. How can different perspectives of the same event or phenomenon result in radically different memories—and what does this tell us about the limits of objectivity?

3. Can studying other cultures inspire creative thinking about our own society?

Lecture One—Transcript
The Study of Humanity

On Maundy Thursday, the Thursday before Easter in 1994, I was living in Tecpan Guatemala with my wife Maraika, who was pregnant with our first child. I was doing my doctoral dissertation fieldwork in cultural anthropology, which brought us to this predominantly Kaqchikel Maya town in the highlands of Guatemala. On this day we'd woken up early, as usual – one wakes up with the roosters in Tecpan – and fixed breakfast on our propane stove in the little two-room former schoolhouse where we lived. As we were washing dishes at the garden spigot that morning, one of our neighbors came by to give us a plate of sweet rolls.

We invited her in and served her coffee and served her some of the rolls, as is the custom in Tecpan, but we were somewhat surprised by this gift out of the blue, and then, not soon afterwards, the daughter of some other friends in town stopped by with another plate of the same sort of rolls, so we invited her in and began to quiz her on why the sudden gift of the sweet rolls. She explained everybody gave them to their neighbors and friends on Maundy Thursday. She just wasn't sure why; it's just what everyone did. After she left, we rushed to the bakery around the corner and bought the last few rolls and cookies that they had left. Back at home we scrambled to divide up our paltry offerings between all the many people who had opened their homes and their lives to us over the last months, trying to work out the intricate political calculus that has to go into such gifts, and a steady stream of friends dropped by the house delivering their *pan dulces*.

Trying to make too few rolls fit on too many plates, I got aggravated, aggravated first that I, the cultural anthropologist in town, had not known about this obviously important ritual, and then aggravated that my day's plans would be totally ruined as we would have to go around and deliver our embarrassingly small offerings to our friends, and then aggravated a bit by the senselessness of it all. We would be giving out gifts of about equivalent value to people who had earlier that day given us such gifts, and we ended up recycling lots of the rolls, and I suspect everybody else in town was doing the same thing that day. As we made our rounds, however, my aggravation gave way to delight, delight at getting to visit with our friends over coffee, delight at being able to symbolically reaffirm the bonds of friendship that were so important to us.

As I wrote up my field notes that night, I became embarrassed by my earlier aggravation. It wasn't very culturally sensitive of an anthropologist to be aggravated by such cultural customs, and as I wrote of the important role of such exchanges in maintaining community and culture in Tecpan, the way in which seemingly quirky or meaningless customs make sense, not only make sense but appear indispensable when they're understood in their full cultural context, and I marveled at how the exceedingly intricate and elusive social fabric of Tecpan was publicly revealed and fortified that day in the exchange of sweet rolls.

So in this course, we'll be looking at cultures around the world and attempting to explain why they do the things that often seem to us to be odd, or exotic, or even sometimes repulsive. Our goal is going to be twofold: first, to expose you to other cultures and other ways of doing things, to give you an overview of the extent of human diversity and cultural diversity in the world. This may range from the quirky – why do we have traffic lights in the United States that go green, yellow, red? Why don't we have traffic lights that go red, yellow, and green? Why do we call our mother's sister's son cousin? It's just the way it is, but in many societies around the world, mother's sister's children would be called by a different kinship name than father's sister's children, for example, both of which we call cousins. It's going to range from quirky elements such as this to more profound elements. What does it mean to be a man, or what does it mean to be a woman? What's the meaning of death? Is rationality a human universal? And what do we as humans share and what makes us different? What can this tell us about ourselves as human beings and about human nature?

Anthropology, like philosophy, touches on these fundamental questions of being, but anthropology does so in a very grounded way, relying not on hypothetical situations, or on musings, but rather on the data of fieldwork, our observations about what people actually do, what people think, how they act in the world. In addressing these larger issues, the second aim of this class is to turn the anthropological lens on our own culture, our own ways of doing things, making anthropology, in the words of the anthropologist Alfred Krober, a mirror for humanity.

By studying other cultures and other customs, other belief systems, I hope to make you question some of your own assumptions about what is natural, what's human nature, what just is, and it's my belief that in doing so we can provoke new and creative perspectives on our own lives. I think that the study of other cultures is inherently interesting. Of course, I'm partisan, I'm a cultural anthropologist, but it has something valuable to offer all of us as members of our own societies. It's a privilege for me to be able to share with you my passion for anthropology, and I trust that you will find it worthwhile as well.

When you hear the word anthropology, what probably comes to mind is an Indiana Jones-like figure, dressed in khakis and a pith helmet, chopping his way through the jungle in search of hidden treasures and temples; or perhaps you think of scientists studying human evolution, piecing together early hominid skeletons such as Lucy or digging them up in East Africa; or maybe you think of anthropologists as going to study faraway locations, to study exotic peoples. In fact, we do all of these things. I'm a cultural anthropologist—I study living peoples, living cultures—although I work alongside archaeologists, biological anthropologists, and linguists. Cultural anthropology, as the name implies, is the study of modern cultures. Through cultural anthropology, we intend to explain variation and document alternative ways of life.

The word culture comes to us from the Latin root, the same root as cultivate and agriculture, and this sense of cultivate gives rise to its usage as a synonym for high culture. We often think of culture as being the opera, ballet, art, the sorts of things that cultivated people can appreciate. But culture also has this more democratic modern usage, recognizing that everyone has culture and that we all have different sorts of culture. Multiculturalism has become a catchphrase of the day. I'm going to save a more detailed discussion of the culture concept for a later lecture; but since we're going to be using the term so frequently, it deserves defining it now.

We can define culture as the learned behaviors, the ways of looking at the world, worldviews that are shared by a variably defined group of people, a culture group. Culture encompasses symbols and beliefs as well as behavior and things. It's important to remember that the distribution of any one trait within a group is variable; cultures are not internally homogenous. Think of our own culture, think of how diverse U.S. society is, and yet there are discernible overall patterns. We can speak of various levels of culture: national culture, regional culture, various sorts of subcultures based around music or sports or sexual identity or other interests. I'm a member of an academic culture, I'm a member of my campus culture, I'm a member of my neighborhood culture, of Southern culture, of U.S. culture. We each belong to a multitude of different kinds of identity groups and ever more so in this age of globalization.

In this sense, we all juggle multiple identities that we can call on, identities that we improvise on in particular contexts, and this is really the art of living socially. It's too easy to think of culture as simply being this strict category. There's always a lot of eternal diversity within cultures. We allow this for our own culture, and, as we're going to see in this class, we have to allow for other cultures as well. Not all Mayan people are alike, not all Germans are alike, not all Kayapo people are alike, and we're going to focus on some of this diversity in the class. It also bears emphasizing at this point that culture is something that we improvise on. It's models that we hold in our minds, but we're not cultural automatons. We improvise on the cultural schemes that we get through socialization.

There are few cultural universals; there are very few cultural universals in the world. Every culture recognizes different genders; that's a cultural universal. Every culture has language, every culture interestingly enough plays games, but these cultural universals are so broad as to tell us very little about what makes us human. Every culture has a moral code, for example, but what that moral code is varies significantly from society to society. The one great rule of culture is that it's always changing. Indeed, some would argue that it's misleading to speak of culture as a thing, to use it as a noun. In many ways, it's better conceived of as an ongoing process, something, as I've said before, that we're constantly improvising. The anthropologist Arjun Appadurai argues that the term should only be used in its adjectival form—cultural elements, cultural beliefs, cultural practices—and in doing so avoids any implication of stasis or boundedness. Culture's not a thing; it's a process, it's a dynamic process that is changing all the time.

To back up a bit, what is anthropology? We've defined culture. But what is anthropology? if we're going to be studying cultural anthropology. Anthropology comes from Greek roots, and it's most basically defined as the study of humanity. *Anthropos* is the Greek root for man, really mankind or humanity. There was another Greek root for the gender male *Anga* but *anthropos* is man, humanity. *Ology* implies science, the study of, coming from the Greek word logos, for word. Thus we can define anthropology as the science of man or, rather, the science of humanity. But interestingly enough, *logos* can also be translated not as just the study of or the science of but also as discourse. In fact, *logos*, with implications of logic and scientific rigor, was not distinguished from *mythos* until the work of Pythagoras and the other scholars in the 6th century B.C. Before that, the discourse of logos referred to myth as well as science, and even to gossip as well.

This leads us to an alternate meaningful definition of anthropology, the bearer of tales, or the bearer of scandals or the bearer of gossip, which is what we as cultural anthropologists really do. We bring back stories from the field, stories of other people's lives, stories and legends that they tell, and we bring back and we represent—and I use represents here in a dual meaning—we represent these elements to our audience here in the States, and we use them as representatives of larger social truths. We bring stories back and we represent these stores to our audiences here and we hopefully use them to illustrate larger truths about social processes and about the human condition. Clifford Geertz, an anthropologist who works at the Institute for Advanced Study in Princeton, in a very influential 1973 book titled *The Interpretation of Cultures*, gives us a very useful definition of culture. He says, "Believing with Max Weber (a famous German sociologist), believing with Max Weber that man is an animal, suspended in webs of significance he himself has spun, I take culture to be those webs and the analysis of it, therefore, not to be an experimental science in search of law but an interpretive one in search of meanings."

These alternate definitions—Is anthropology a science? Is it the science of humanity or is it an interpretive endeavor, the bearer of tales? Is it a discourse-based discipline?—these alternate definitions reflect a growing division within anthropology between scientists and humanists. Some anthropology departments have even split up. Most famously, Stanford has two separate departments: a department of anthropological sciences and a department of cultural anthropology. Despite this divide, what we as anthropologists really do best is travel these divisions. We anthropologists argue that no one perspective has a monopoly on the truth and thus we should avail ourselves of all the analytic resources available, be they science or not, or discourse on humanities.

In practice, anthropologists are generally a little of both, a little bit scientist, a little bit humanist. We certainly gather data; we're much concerned with the reliability of the data that we collect. We develop hypotheses and theories, we test these based on fieldwork and data collection, and yet at the same time we mold these data into stories, representing our findings in a way that's meaningful for our contemporary audiences. The German sociologist Max Weber made a useful distinction between *verstenen*, understanding, more subjective comprehension, and *erklarung*, clarification, explanation, the nuts and bolts of how something works. Based on this distinction what anthropologists try and do really is to capture both *verstenen,* the subjective sense of the experience, and *erklarung,* the scientific explanation for why things are the way they are.

Anthropology, in contrast to the other theologies—biology, sociology, ecology, psychology—anthropology looks at not one aspect of the human condition but at the interconnectedness of all aspects of humanness. Economists study the economic life of humans, psychologists study the psychology, sociologists the social aspect, and these are all very important disciplines and they have a lot to teach us. Indeed, we as anthropologists frequently poach the insights of biology, of economics and psychology, as we will see in the course of these series of lectures. But anthropology is a very ecumenical discipline and this is really what attracted me to it in the first place. Anthropology sees that what gets lost in such particular perspectives, such disciplinary perspectives, is the interconnectedness of it all, of life, of the human condition.

One aspect of human behavior is influenced by and influences other spheres. We know this instinctively in a way. Politics is tied to religion, economics is tied to psychology, biology is tied to social organization, and this is all tied together with the glue of culture. Again, this is something that we intuitively recognize, I think. One's religion affects the way in which one votes, for example. Politics affects religion; religion affects politics. I was reading not long ago actually that church attendance is a better indicator of party affiliation in the United States than income is. But, anyway, this is something that we as academics can easily forget, the interrelatedness of it all, as we work away in our increasingly narrow perspectives and specializations. Thus a basic tenet of anthropology is its holistic approach, looking at the whole of the human condition and not just one aspect.

In some ways this is akin to Gestalt psychology, gestalt analysis, the school of psychology that interprets phenomena as organized wholes rather than as aggregates of distinct parts, maintaining that the whole is greater than the sum of its parts. Most phenomena, material and social, are simply too complex to be fully understood by looking at just one variable, from being approached from just one angle.

There's an effect we call in anthropology the Rashomon effect, and this comes from, is named for, the classic 1950 Japanese film that looks at a rape outside the city gates of a Japanese city from four different and four contradictory points of view: from the point of view of the victim; from the point of view of a policeman; from the point of view of an observer; from the point of view of the perpetrator—the same objective event, but it gets interpreted in very different ways. In anthropology we say nobody has a hold on the truth. It's good for outside observers and anthropologists to come in and have one perspective, also to record the perspective of cultural insiders, and by combining multiple perspectives, by looking at the same phenomenon from different angles, we get a much richer, a much more complex, a much deeper understanding of the phenomena we're trying to describe.

Using the broadest definition, anthropology is the study of humanity, the study of people, and under this definition we're all practicing anthropologists, not just those of us who have Ph.D.s in the field. We're all practicing anthropologists; we all constantly analyze the world around us. We try and divine the motivations of others and act accordingly. It's our very nature to try and understand the social world around us and thus to be anthropologists. When friends ask how much I work, I tell them I'm working all the time; I'm working right now, studying you, studying human behavior, human interaction. Sometimes studying anthropology can be a burden. It can make one hyperaware of social situations, too aware for one's own good, if that is indeed possible. We're going to give a lecture later on in the series about gift-giving, and I often have students come up to me and say "You know, that lecture you gave on gift giving, it's made me think about giving gifts way too much ever since then," and it can really paralyze people in some ways to know too much about why we do what we do.

Interdisciplinarity is very much in vogue in the academy these days, partly as a reaction to the hyperspecialization of academic fields. Anthropology was interdisciplinary long before it was cool. This is the very basis of the discipline, to look at human behavior and the interconnections of different aspects of human behavior, and why should we be constrained by disciplinary boundaries, which are themselves just historical artifacts of the time when knowledge seemed much more containable. American anthropology is generally divided into four subfields, and these are: biological anthropology, which looks at human behavior and modern biological variation; archaeology, the study of ancient civilizations and peoples, attempting to reconstruct past cultures based on material remains; linguistics, the study of language and the many ways humans communicate, both verbally and nonverbally; and, finally, cultural anthropology, which is often called social anthropology in England and at Harvard, which is the study of modern human traditions, customs, and worldviews.

The structure of this course follows an expanding concentric circle to examine human culture. In the first part of the course, we're going to begin by looking at what makes us human, the role of culture and biology in human behavior, the influence of language on thought and thus culture. We see, for example, how men's speech differs from women's speech in modern U.S. society. We look at the cultural misunderstandings that can ensue from dialectical differences, and we look at how certain cultural metaphors such as "time is money" can mold our views of the world. In the second part of the class, we move out from the individual's relationship with culture to look at the basic social forms that hold communities and societies together. We're going to look at the role of rites of passage as marking stages in people's lives. We're going to look at how kinship ties and religion can bind people together. We'll learn about the Trobriand Islanders of Melanesia, a matrilineal society where descent is traced through female lines and yet where formal positions of power are held by men. We're going to study the Fulbe of northern Cameroon and their unique blending of Islam and indigenous traditions of magic and sorcery.

In the third section of the class, we're going to turn to cultural patterns of societies at different levels of complexity, and we're going to follow a typology of bands, tribes, chiefdoms, and states. We're going to examine, for example, the Dobe Ju/'hoansi of Botswana and Namibia, nomadic gatherers and hunters who have no chiefs or permanent political leaders and who have very little conception of private property. We're going to see how family ties and reciprocal bonds hold society together in such circumstances. We then contrast this with the political structure of groups such as the Yanamamu, who find themselves in frequent conflict and at war with neighboring groups. The Yanamamu exemplify some of the more exotic customs that we're going to examine in this class, but keep in mind, exotic from our perspective. Exotic is always relative; customs are very rarely exotic if ever for the people who are practicing them. But the Yanomamo, they practice cannibalism. They have shamans who ingest hallucinogenic snuff to contact the spirit world. Their headmen often have several wives.

Modern native cultures cannot be seen as isolated entities. Since the glory days of Western expansion, they've come into increasing contact with the outside world, so we're going to look at some of the deadly misunderstandings that accompanied early European contact and try and explain the death of Captain Cook at the hand of Hawaiians in 1779. We're going to turn to the expansion of capitalist economies and look at rational choice models of traditional economics and how these don't hold up in many ways under cross-cultural comparison. We're going to review the attempts of economists and anthropologists to come to terms with cultural differences, and we're going to look at contemporary U.S. culture and the bases of our own economic system, and the symbols and identities that have become highly marketable commodities in this age of late capitalism.

We're going to conclude the course by looking at how globalization has affected native peoples around the world in surprising ways, including the erosion of traditional life ways and the simultaneous resurgence of ethnic groups. Here we're going to focus particularly on the Maya in Guatemala and Mexico, where I've conducted most of my own long-term ethnographic fieldwork. My early work focused on the Mayan cultural activists in Guatemala and their fight for civil rights. My more recent work looks at how Mayan peoples fit into the global modern economy. You might be surprised, for example, to learn that a fair percentage of the broccoli in this country is grown by small holding Mayan farmers in the Guatemalan highlands; and as we're going to see in a later lecture, our vegetable consumption in the U.S. has hidden impacts on native people, such as the Maya, in faraway locations.

There's a pronounced romantic tradition in anthropology; I think it's the allure of the foreign and the exotic that pulls us toward the discipline in the first place, but in the process of doing fieldwork we anthropologists move beyond such shallow romanticization to give a more intimate, a richer, a more complex understanding of the people that we study. In studying such societies, you'll be asked to suspend your natural ethnocentrism. Ethnocentrism is the belief that your culture's way of doing things is the only or the best way of doing things. This can be difficult. We're going to discuss customs that you may find odd or even repulsive: cannibalism, ritualized homosexuality, domestic violence. But before we can pronounce moral judgment, we must fully understand the context in which these customs operate.

Often, what appearss to us to be exotic or even bizarre is seen to make perfect sense within the cultural context in which we find it. Here we can distinguish between emic and etic views of the world. An emic perspective is a cultural insider's view of how things are; an etic perspective is an outsider's view, and what we're doing in anthropology is combine an outsider's perspective, an etic perspective on culture, with an insider's view, an emic perspective on culture, and in combining those the idea is that we can get at a richer understanding of human behavior.

In the beginning of this lecture, I mentioned that my wife was pregnant with our son while we were living in Tecpan in 1994. We went back to Germany, where my wife is from, for the birth, but during the pregnancy in Tecpan we employed the services of Anjelina, a woman widely considered to be the best midwife in Tecpan. Anjelina's mother was a midwife, as was her mother's mother. She suspects the tradition goes back even farther, although she can't say for sure. Anjelina is a trained nurse as well as a traditionalist midwife, and she's able to perform ritual sweat bath therapies which involve herbal massages and prayers to Mayan and Catholic gods and offerings, as well as refer us to the regional hospital for ultrasounds if she thinks we need it.

We became very close to Anjelina and her family during our stay, and I've always respected the way that she's able to manage these diverse and sometimes contradictory cultural identities. Anjelina herself was pregnant at the time, and she delivered her girl a few months after my son was born. Estefani, her young girl, is a precocious, somewhat spoiled, child, the youngest of four sisters. In addition to midwifery, Anjelina sells hand woven blouses and skirts, the colorful dress that you probably associate with Mayan peoples, and she often dresses her daughter Estefani exceptionally well.

I was surprised to find out during a recent visit to Tecpan a few years ago that Estefani was very much infatuated with Pikachu and Pokemon and all of these other Japanese animated characters. I found it ironic that this young Kaqchikel speaking, traditional dress wearing girl was taken with the not quite latest thing in global pop culture. In fact, I used a photo of Estefani holding a Pikachu balloon while decked out in her finest traditional dress on the cover of a recent book, but I've come to realize in looking at this photo over and over again that the irony that I see in Estefani's fascination with Pikachu is my irony; and it's not Estefani's and it's not her parents'. Estefani and her parents see nothing ironic about being Maya and being modern at the same time. They're just trying to live their lives as best as they can given the circumstances, and, as we'll see in the lectures to come, native peoples around the world find themselves in similar circumstances. In this course, we're going to go beyond these ironies to discover the more profound lessons we have to learn from the Maya, from the Trobriand Islanders, from the Fulbe, from the Dobe Ju/'hoansi and from other indigenous peoples.

Lecture Two
The Four Fields of Anthropology

Scope: Anthropology comprises four broad subfields: biological anthropology, archaeology, linguistics, and cultural anthropology. This course focuses on cultural diversity and human commonalities around the world, but we cannot study culture in isolation. Thus, in this lecture, we look to biological anthropology and the study of early humans to discover what makes our remarkable species unique—from big brains and language to opposable thumbs and bipedalism. In a similar vein, we turn to archaeology for lessons from the past about the rise and fall of civilizations, trying to understand the present in terms of the distant past. Much of what we know about other cultures comes to us through interviews; thus, an understanding of language and linguistics allows us to interpret what we learn in the field.

Today, biological anthropologists, archaeologists, and linguists are turning their talents to a number of unconventional uses. Forensic anthropologists, for example, work with the FBI to reconstruct crime scenes and determine causes of death in badly decomposed remains. Archaeologists have excavated garbage dumps to help large cities better understand where waste comes from (with unexpected results). Linguists, working with archaeologists and others, have created signs to mark nuclear waste dumps that are designed to be readable in 10,000 years.

Outline

I. Biological anthropology studies the physical adaptations of humans to their environment; we look to biological anthropology to define what it means to be human.

   A. *Homo sapiens* first arose some 200,000 years ago in the savannas of east Africa.

   B. A small number of very important features make modern humans biologically unique.
      1. Humans possess opposable thumbs, which allows for tool use, and walk bidepally, which frees the hands for other tasks.

    2. Humans have large brains, which, in turn, allows for the development of both language and culture.

    3. Humans practice a "K" strategy of reproduction, meaning we have very few offspring but care for them intensely.

    4. Culture has allowed humans to opt out of many of the environmental pressures of natural selection.

C. *Race* is a loaded term and one that biological anthropologists generally avoid.

    1. Genetic variation is greater within human races than between them, although interracial differences are especially evident in skin color, facial proportions, and similar characteristics.

    2. Thus, race is not very useful as a biological category, although it remains an important social category.

D. Biological anthropology has branched out in recent years to include not only the study of early human evolution and human variation but also the burgeoning field of forensic anthropology.

II. Archaeology is the study of ancient cultures through their material remains.

A. Archaeology can teach us lessons from the past about the rise and fall of civilizations and the histories that go unrecorded in the history books.

B. Archaeologists employ a number of methods.

    1. The most basic is "dirt archaeology"—digging up the remains of ancient societies. Archaeologists are often hindered by the scarcity of remains.

    2. Archaeologists have turned to new technologies, including satellite imagery, mass spectrometry, and isotope isolation analyses.

C. In addition to traditional archaeology, some researchers have used their methods to study uncommon subjects, such as the archaeology of modern U.S. garbage dumps.

III. Linguistics is the study of human language.

A. Anthropological linguists are concerned with understanding how people actually speak, or descriptive linguistics. In contrast, prescriptive linguistics seeks to set standards for how people *should* speak.

    B. Sociolinguistics is the study of language use and social meanings and holds the most importance for cultural anthropology.

    C. Linguists have begun to pursue a number of unusual applications for their research, including artificial intelligence, marketing, and monument design.

IV. Cultural anthropology examines social structures (legal, economic, and civil systems), as well as the more ephemeral cultural glue that holds them together.

    A. Culture provides a template for behavior rather than strictly prescribing actions.

    B. Culture is shared but is not perfectly distributed among any given population.

    C. In recent years, cultural anthropologists have turned their attentions toward their own cultures, and a number now work in marketing and design, among other nontraditional venues.

Readings:

Bill Bass and Jon Jefferson, *Death's Acre: Inside the Legendary Forensic Lab—the Body Farm—Where the Dead Do Tell Tales.*

Michael Brown, *The Search for Eve.*

Brian Fagan, *People of the Earth: An Introduction to World Prehistory.*

William Rathje, *Rubbish! The Archaeology of Garbage.*

Internet Resources:

http://anthro.palomar.edu/tutorials/physical.htm. Physical Anthropology Tutorials. Dr. Dennis O'Neil, Palomar College.

Questions to Consider:

1. What makes humans biologically unique? What could have been the evolutionary pressures that resulted in bipedalism and big brains?

2. What is race—biologically and culturally? Why is it such an important social category?

3. What can the study of ancient societies teach us about our own culture?

Lecture Two—Transcript
The Four Fields of Anthropology

Anthropology has the grand goal of studying all of humanity; anything related to the human condition is fair game for anthropologists to study, and this is an incredibly liberating scope and an incredibly intimidating mandate. Of course, human behavior is too complex to study using a unified overarching paradigm, such as we find in physics or chemistry or biology, and, as a result, anthropology is a very diverse field. We break down the discipline into four main subfields, and those are: biological anthropology; archaeology; linguistics; and cultural anthropology. Each of these subfields has its own set of subfields and is increasingly specialized; yet the benefit of working under the umbrella of anthropology is that we have the intellectual freedom to cross over these boundaries. In the lecture today, we'll review these four subfields, focusing on how they link together to help us understand and define modern human cultures.

What makes us human? If humanity is our subject, then what is it that defines it? To answer this foundational question, we have to turn to biological anthropology. Actually, when I was in school, this was called physical anthropology, but today so many anthropologists are using genetic research that we've redefined it as biological anthropology. Biological anthropology is concerned with the evolution of the human species, with the behavior of nonhuman primates, and with biological variation between human populations. Let me say a couple of words about evolution. It's a common misconception, first of all, that Darwin invented evolution. Evolution was an idea very much in the air at the time in the mid-19th century, linked with notions of the inevitability of progress. This was, after all, the age of industrialization, and dramatic social, political, and technological changes were occurring in the world.

In fact, as we all know, Darwin only published his results when it looked like Alfred Wallace was going to trump his findings, and so it was in 1859 that Darwin published *On the Origin of Species by Means of Natural Selection, or the Preservation of Favorite Races in the Struggle for Existence.* Darwin didn't invent evolution, but he gave us the mechanism for how evolution works, and that is natural selection. Darwin's notion of natural selection or the struggle for existence states that under natural competition, favorable traits will allow certain individuals to be more successful, and this means to have more offspring and thus pass these favorable traits on in greater frequencies to the next generation. Over time, and this can be hundreds of years or thousands of years, maybe even tens of thousands of years, if these traits offer enough reproductive benefits, they may become the norm for a population.

As a sideline, I would mention here that Stephen J. Gould has made his career critiquing Darwin's gradual evolution, and Gould says that actually what we find is punctuated equilibrium, periods of rapid evolutionary change followed by periods of stability and then punctuated once again with rapid evolutionary change. This seems to suit the facts of human evolution better than Darwin's theory in some ways. But Darwin's theory of natural selection gives us the classic definition for evolution: descent with modification enacted through natural selection. Darwin didn't know what caused the variation; we now know that it's caused by genetic mutations and recombination, but he gave us the mechanism through which it works.

The evolutionary history of humans is relatively brief in the big scheme of things. The earth is over 5 billion years old, and modern humans only came along about 200,000 years ago. The hominid line, and this is humanlike apes, of which humans are the only extant species, the hominid line probably broke off about 5 million years ago, and the earliest best examples we have are of the Australopithecines such as Lucy, famous Lucy, which was found in 1974 by Donald Johansson in Ethiopia. Lucy and the Australopithecines evolved into Homo habilus, the first humans to use tools, or the first hominids to use tools, about 2.5 million years ago, which evolved into Homo erectus about 1.7 million years ago and finally Homo sapiens around 200,000 years ago, a drop in the bucket in the big evolutionary scheme of things.

What sets us apart biologically as human beings are the combination of three key traits: opposable thumbs; bipedalism, that we walk on two legs; and having these huge big brains. Alone, these don't distinguish us from our closest living primate relatives. All primates, for example, have opposable thumbs. I was at the zoo recently and I looked at the gorillas, and the gorillas have these incredibly opposed toes as well, big toes so that they can use their feet as they would their hands. Opposable thumbs, the benefit of them is that it allows for more precise tool use, and tool use has been seen as being a distinctly human trait, although some recent studies of chimp population show that chimps can sometimes use tools as well.

For example, they've been observed in the wild going out, and they'll break off a branch of a tree, take off all of the leaves, and then carry that branch around for a period of time, and then when they run across a termite mound or an ant hill they'll stick the branch down in there and let the termites or ants crawl up the branch and then pull it out and eat it like a lollipop or a Popsicle. They also, chimpanzees, will sometimes pick leaves and chew them and make them into a little bundle and then soak up water in the crevices of trees and then squeeze it into their mouths. Granted, these aren't the most sophisticated tools in the world, but crucially they indicate foresight, breaking off a branch of a tree and carrying it around for a while and then sticking it in a termite mound. They're tools; it's tool usage, taking an item from nature, modifying it for a different purpose, and then using it later.

Opposable thumbs, even opposable thumbs that use tools, don't distinguish us from chimpanzees. But combined with bipedalism, walking on two legs, this really sets hominids and the hominid branch apart from the rest of our primate relatives. It's still something of a mystery why there was a switch to bipedalism because it seems there are all sorts of drawbacks to walking on two legs. We have severe lower back problems, we have knee problems, we have ankle problems, but it did free up our hands for tool use and for transportation. But the tool use and the bipedalism really come together when brains start getting larger, and this was late. This was very late in human evolution, long after bipedalism appeared. Lucy and the other Australopithecines, they were bipedal, they had opposable thumbs, they probably used tools, but they had brains the size of chimpanzees.

It's not until we get into Homo sapiens that we get these ungainly large brains, but it was the increase in brain size that allowed us to develop language and thus to develop culture, but it brought problems as well. Big-brained babies are hard to give birth to, and, in fact, the human female's pelvic size and shape are a compromise between having as large of a birth canal opening as possible and still being able to walk upright. And as large as human babies' brains are at birth, they don't stop there. Humans have this sustained period of postnatal brain growth and development. This is why nutrition and intellectual stimulation are so crucial in the first years of life.

Biologists distinguish between different types of reproductive strategies, and there's a continuum their ranges from R—that stands for the rate of reproduction—to K. K stands for carrying capacity (K, carrying capacity, go figure) but it's a continuum. R-selected species have lots of offspring, and they don't invest a lot of time in them, but they offset the higher mortality rate for their offspring by high absolute numbers, and here we can think of all the insects, mice, rats, roaches; even cats and dogs are more R selected, have more offspring than humans do. K-selected species, on the other hand, have fewer offspring and invest very heavily in the offspring they do have, making sure that they survive to reach reproductive age themselves. Having helpless infants with these big brains may well have led—and humans are the most K-selected species of all, and having helpless infants with these big brains may have well led to pair-bonding between parents to care for their children and thus the early foundations of society as a whole.

Big brains allow us the capacity for language and thus the capacity for culture, and big brains and language and culture changes everything. It changes the very rules of the evolutionary game for humans. We can change our environment rather than be changed by it. Look at cities like Phoenix or Tucson, these huge cities in the middle of the desert with manicured lawns and even golf courses outside. It's a remarkable feat of human engineering that we can live in such environments. The National Science Foundation maintains a research station in the Arctic Circle. We can live anywhere as human beings now, but we remain biological beings, and, given this, our ultimate mandate is to go forth and multiply, to reproduce ourselves. But here again, culture has been able to short-circuit the pleasure mechanism that allows us to reproduce ourselves; with birth control, for example, we can have the gratification without the reproductive consequences.

Let me say a word or two here about race. We're all Homo sapiens; this is the first and most important thing. We're all Homo sapiens, and at the genetic level racial categorizations are all but meaningless. There's greater genetic variation within races than between races. Granted, the variation that does exist produces very visible features—skin color, the shape of the face, the shape of the eyes, the shape of the nose, and so forth—and we often use these physical traits as a shorthand for cultural patterns. Race is an important social category but not a very important biological category.

What do anthropologists do, biological anthropologists? They study human evolution, and probably the most famous images we have of biological anthropologists are paleoanthropologists such as Richard Leakey and his family digging up fossils in the deserts of east Africa. Physical anthropologists also work as primatologists, showing how our close relatives might shed light on human evolution. Researchers, such as Jane Goodall working with chimps or Dian Fosse with gorillas, conduct almost cultural studies of these primate populations, and, if you've seen any of the films in this genre, you realize just how human gorillas and chimps can be (or perhaps just how gorilla and chimp-like humans can be). But physical anthropologists are also turning their attention to new areas of research, and foremost among these, the fastest growing field in anthropology, is probably forensic anthropology, using the techniques developed to study ancient human skeletal remains to solve modern crimes.

Police departments, the FBI, will call in physical anthropologists to help sex and date skeletons that they found—for example, reconstruct victims' facial and body appearances. Most famously, the anthropologist Bill Bass, who works at the University of Tennessee, runs what is called the Body Farm, and this was made famous by a Patricia Cornwell novel of the same name. There, he and his colleagues, his graduate students and colleagues place donated human corpses in different sorts of contexts. They'll put them under water, they'll bury them three feet deep, they'll bury them six feet deep, they'll put them in a tin shed, or in the trunk of a car, and then they document the decomposition of the human bodies, the levels of gases, the amino acid breakdowns, the life cycle of maggots that grow in human remains, and these data can then be used to help police departments determine the time of death, post-mortem circumstances, and so forth.

Let me turn to archaeology. Archaeology, we're all familiar with archaeology; archaeology looks at the material remains of past cultures, attempting to understand those cultures through their artifacts. This is no small task, trying to reconstruct a civilization basically based on their garbage, on their trash, and this requires a lot of imagination. Archaeologists are able to document the processes of plant and animal domestication, of urbanization, of the rise and fall of civilizations. They ask the big picture questions. What caused the fall of Rome? Why did Mayan civilization collapse? Was it warfare? Was it environmental degradation? Was it climatic change? To think that we have nothing to learn from ancient cultures is just hubris; just as statesman and diplomats these days still study the Peloponnesian wars, it's good for us to learn the lessons of ancient civilizations that flourished and then failed.

Archaeologists employ a number of different methods; the most basic is dirt archaeology, literally going up and digging up the remains of ancient civilizations. In recent years, technological advances have really changed the nature of archaeology. We can use satellite images to identify new sites; we use mass spectrometry to allow us to source obsidian and clay and reconstruct trade routes. Working with biological anthropologists, archaeologists are using isotope isolation analysis to uncover the diets of ancient populations from their skeletal remains. This is all remarkable stuff, a whole new world of information opened up by these technological changes.

But, as archaeologists are gaining a sharper image of the past, they're also increasingly engaging modern indigenous populations. My colleague Arthur

Demarest, who works in the Maya area, is a great example of this. He made his name discovering ancient Mayan cities; he's been called the real Indiana Jones, and right now he's working at the ancient Mayan city-state of Conquin. As part of the project, he started involving the local communities of Mayan Indians who live in the area, and this started simply, first giving soccer uniforms to the local team, donating a mill, or helping them build a well. But this has gradually evolved into a more holistic plan for the development of the area, and this is an area of extreme poverty, so the archaeologists are working to help set up health clinics, community pharmacies, even promote eco-tourism in the area.

Demarest and these archaeologists got involved because this is just the right thing to do. People were literally dying of hunger outside of their archaeological camp; they had to do something, but it turns out it's good archaeology as well. It makes these local Mayan populations feel vested in the archaeological site; they feel like it's theirs in some meaningful way, and so they protect it from looters, and they see the value in archaeology, especially since it promotes tourism, and it even rekindles a sense of ethnic pride.

Another interesting thing that archaeologists have been doing lately, and this is also another Mayan archaeologist, William Rathje at the University of Arizona. He runs what's called the most unconventional archaeology project in the world, and it's called the Garbage Project, and it's been going on since 1973. Rathje began in Tucson, where he did archaeological methods, laying out a grid, recording the stratography, digging trenches, all of the things that we associate with archaeologists; he did this in the garbage dump in Tucson, and what he found was surprising, especially given the prevailing wisdom of the burgeoning environmental movement at the time. The bad guys, if you'll remember, in the early mid-70s were fast food packaging and disposable diapers, and it turned out, based on Rathje's archaeology, that these don't take up very much space in the dumps. Fast food packaging only accounted for about 0.5% in weight and 0.3% in volume, diapers only 1% in weight and 1.4% in volume.

What was it? There was something that provided clear stratographic layers for Rathje that could mark every year, year in and year out. What it was, was paper products, newspapers, but more than that telephone books, a clear stratographic layer for every year of yellow and white pages. Rathje has gone on to do similar sorts of work in other cities around the world— New Orleans, Milwaukee, Mexico City, even Sydney, Australia—and he's expanded out the scope of his work, not only looking at environmental implications of garbage dumps but looking at diets. For example, it turns out that people, when they self-report what they're eating, often idealize their diet. If you go back and look at their garbage, you see all the Twinkie wrappers in the vegetarian household's garbage and so forth, so we see what's really going on rather than what people say is going on.

Linguistics looks at the different forms of communication, variation among human languages, and how thoughts are developed within the mind. Let me make a clear distinction here; most anthropological linguists are descriptive linguists, and we contrast this with prescriptive linguists. Descriptive linguists try and describe how people actually speak. They very often work with undocumented languages, so they're writing dictionaries and writing grammars. Prescriptive linguistics, and this is probably what you've had the most association with—grammar school teachers, college professors, William Safire's column in the Sunday *New York Times*—prescriptive linguists try and tell us how we should speak, and there's a big distinction here, how we do speak and how we should speak.

It leads to all sorts of political machinations that we probably don't even think about. Dictionaries, for example, who would think that there's a politics of dictionaries? These are just objective documents recording the words in a particular language. But in English dictionaries, there's a wide range of ideological variation. Webster's, for example, is much more willing to accept new words, to include "ain't" or include new technological words, whereas the American Heritage Dictionary is much more conservative, the American Heritage Dictionary leaning toward prescription, Webster's leaning toward description.

The great rule of language is that languages are always changing. In this light, language purity movements are fighting a losing battle. They might slow the pace of change. Take France, for example, very rigid in trying to promote a pure French, it can slow the rate of change, but it can never completely stop it. On the other hand, languages can also be resuscitated from the edge of extinction, and here we can count Welsh, Hebrew. Hebrew was dead for almost 2,000 years, a virtually dead language only spoken by scribes and scholars, and now 3.6 million people speak Hebrew today, the national language of Israel, of course.

We should also keep in mind in making this distinction between prescriptive linguists and descriptive linguists the arbitrariness of grammatical rules. The most famous example, probably, is don't end a sentence with a preposition. This is beaten into us in grammar school and college—don't end a sentence with a preposition—but we can all think of perfectly good sentences that we can end in prepositions. "That's what I was thinking of." "That's where he was going to." In fact, Winston Churchill one time, he spotted a copy editor's remarks in his memoirs where a preposition had been eliminated, and he sent back a missive to this copy editor saying, "This is the sort of English up with which I shall not put." Anthropological linguists work at describing the grammar of languages in a descriptive and not a prescriptive fashion. Prescription often is just an idiosyncrasy that's been codified, that's taken on this status that everybody has to speak in this certain proper fashion, and prepositions at the end of the sentences is one of the best examples.

And linguists, what do linguists do? They describe languages, but also they work in academics and, beyond that, they've long found careers with the CIA, with the military, with the State Department, for example, working as code breakers. A lot of the code breakers of World War II either were linguists or they went on to become linguists, and more recently they branched out into the commercial sector, working for private companies, testing slogans, testing new product names, working with advertising agencies, working as business consultants. The most interesting thing, I think, that linguists have done in recent years, however, concerns the waste isolation pilot project, and this is a project in the U.S. government.

They're creating a place near the Nevada-California border where we can store our highest grade plutonium waste from nuclear weapons production. They want to keep this in a place that's going to be safe for 10,000 years, the half-life of this plutonium, and they're putting it in salt mines, which are very good at soaking up the radioactivity. But they also want signage. They want signs that can be read in 10,000 years warning people of what's there. But what language are we going to speak in 10,000 years? English hasn't been around that long. I mean, just think back to Chaucerian English; we can only understand every other word, words here and there, and that was only 650 years ago. Indo-European, the common language of both Sanskrit and English, is only 4,000 years old. Writing is only 5,000 years old, so how do you create signs that are going to be able to communicate in 10,000 years that there's deadly plutonium at the site?

The linguists working on this commission have developed a couple of different strategies. One is to use pictographs, images, and most famously they used Edvard Munch's *The Scream*, that image, that impassioned, that horrifying image of a person screaming on a bridge, to communicate this idea. They also used a modern-day Rosetta stone, so they include warnings in a variety of languages, including the six official U.N. languages and indigenous languages such as Navajo, with the idea that in 10,000 years in the future, nobody's going to speak English, nobody's going to speak Chinese, nobody's going to speak Russian or German, but by having a warning in all of those different languages they can work out what the warning is. They can break that code.

Finally, let me turn to cultural anthropology. What is culture? Very broadly, culture is everything that people collectively do, think, make, and say. It's an integrated body of beliefs, behavior, technology, ideas shared by a group of people. This is a fine definition, a pretty standard definition, but let me add a couple of important caveats. First of all, culture provides a template for behavior, much more so than strictly prescribing actions. We're not mere cultural automatons, rigidly enacting cultural patterns that have been passed down to us from generations ago. We're creating, we do new things, and it's culture that provides the template for this creation, for this improvisation.

Culture is a way of looking at and acting in the world, and culture significantly overlaps within a given group of individuals, a culture group, but it's also important to keep in mind that culture is never perfectly distributed within a group. We don't all hold to all of the elements of our own culture, but there's enough of significant overlap that allows us to communicate and to create in-group and out-group sorts of allegiances. It's integrated culture; culture is integrated, but it's loosely integrated. Finally, people are generally not aware of their culture; what goes without saying comes without saying. Pierre Bourdieu, a sociologist from France, said that culture is silent about itself as a tradition. It seems normal, our culture seems normal, natural, the only way of doing things. It's what we take for granted.

The study of social anthropology, and this is what is studied in Britain—it's also what the department at Harvard is named—social anthropology implies studying formal legal, economic, and civil structures. Sociology, political science, economics, and social anthropology all work at this level. But culture is more dispositions, it's more ephemeral, it's harder to grasp. It's the presuppositions that we as members of a particular society hold. Of course, the two are intimately connected, but I prefer the moniker "cultural" because it gets at what we have to offer much better.

Like linguists, a number of cultural anthropologists have found employment outside of academia in recent years, particularly in helping large corporations with business consultants and with marketing. General Motors, for example, has employed anthropologists to do shop floor studies, studies of shop floor culture. The United Nations and the World Bank employ anthropologists to help them make their development projects more culturally sensitive. One cultural anthropologist, Clotaire Rapaille, who runs a consultancy called Archetypes International, has helped develop cars—the PT cruiser for Chrysler—and has also advised on advertising for a variety of Ford companies.

One of the most interesting things he did concerns the advertisements, television advertisements of a French importer of French cheeses, importing French cheeses into the United States. And they used as a commercial for their Brie cheese a film, television ad, that had been produced in France and they just used a voice-overlay in English for the States. In the commercial, a woman was picking up unwrapped cheese and squeezing it—you could see her fingerprints on the top of the cheese. She was smelling it, and she was just reveling in this cheesiness of it all, but the television ad wasn't playing in the United States, and they brought in Clotaire Rapaille, this cultural anthropologist, and he said of course it doesn't. The French archetype of cheese is that it's something alive. They relish in the fact that it is living, cultures in cheese. In the United States, our cultural archetype is that cheese is dead, it's sterile. We wrap it tightly in cellophane wrap, and we want to have it not be alive—so some of the interesting things that cultural anthropologists are doing these days.

To conclude, in order to manage the wholism that anthropology strives for, we break down the discipline into these four subfields: biological, archaeological, linguistic, and cultural. At the same time, the greatest strength of the discipline is in bridging these boundaries. For our purposes in this course, physical anthropology can tell us not only about our common evolutionary heritage but about contemporary cultures as well. Take the Maya of Guatemala, with whom I work. It's impossible to understand modern Mayan culture without understanding the civil war that wreaked havoc in Guatemala in the late 1970s and early 1980s, but most of these massacres in Mayan communities were not documented, and the bodies were buried in clandestine graves. Teams of forensic anthropologists are now recording the atrocities of this unwritten history, validating the stories told by survivors.

Likewise, archaeology not only reconstructs the ancient past but also influences the self-perception of groups and even motivates them to redefine their modern cultural forms. Again I mention Arthur Demarest and his work in Conquin in Guatemala in modern Mayan populations. And as we'll explore further in later lectures, linguistics looks not only at abstract language structure but how language is used to form groups and even mold cultural categories. With this background in the four subfields, we move on in the next lectures to discuss concepts of culture in more detail.

Concepts of Culture
Lecture Three
Culture and Relativity

Scope: The modern anthropological concept of culture has been widely adopted across academic disciplines and in popular discourse. Nineteenth-century anthropologists conceived of culture as singular: Synonymous with civilization, it was seen as something that people possessed to greater and lesser extents. Often, such views were developed as part of evolutionary schemes, the most memorable being Lewis Henry Morgan's "savages, barbarians, and civilization" typology of human societies. By the turn of the 20th century, Franz Boas, a German Jewish immigrant to the United States, was challenging such evolutionary perspectives and developing a pluralistic notion of culture. Boas argued that cultures emerge from historically particular circumstances, not from a universal evolutionary trajectory. Modern definitions stress the malleability and fluidity of culture, although anthropologists have come to see the limits of Boas's cultural relativity.

Outline

I. The modern discipline of anthropology was born of a 19th-century fascination with science and evolution.

    A. Evolution was very much an idea in the air in 19th-century European intellectual circles.

        1. Charles Darwin gave us the most scientifically plausible mechanism for how evolution works in his theory of natural selection.

        2. The phrase "survival of the fittest" was coined not by Darwin but by Sir Herbert Spencer in a line of thought that has come to be known as "social Darwinism."

    B. Edward B. Tylor (1832–1917) wrote some of the discipline's founding texts and held Oxford University's first position in anthropology (which came to be known as "Mr. Tylor's science").

        1. Tylor gave the most enduring definition of culture: "that complex whole which includes knowledge, belief, art, law, morals, customs and any other capabilities and habits acquired by man as a member of society."

    2. Tylor's grand scheme ranked societies along a continuum of progress and unilineal evolution; he was also interested in documenting cultural "survivals," those odd elements left over from times past.

  C. In the United States, it was Lewis Henry Morgan (1818–1881) who pioneered anthropology.

    1. Morgan, a semi-retired lawyer, became interested in a Seneca group that lived not far from his home in Rochester, New York.

    2. After second-hand study of cultures around the world, Morgan devised a scheme of unilineal cultural evolution that progressed from savages to barbarians to civilization.

II. Franz Boas (1858–1942) founded modern American anthropology— earning it academic legitimacy and providing its enduring principle of cultural relativity.

  A. Boas's theoretical contributions must be understood in terms of his personal history—as the son of middle-class German Jewish parents and as an immigrant to the United States.

    1. Boas pursued studies in geography and physics, writing his Ph.D. dissertation on the "psycho-physics" of the color of sea water.

    2. After his compulsory military service, Boas pursued his boyhood dream of making an expedition to the Arctic. There, he lived with the Inuit and was deeply moved by their kindness and humanity; his writings on the Baffin Island people began his career in anthropology.

    3. After immigrating to the United States, Boas began to conduct fieldwork among the Kwakiutl people of the northwest coast. He saw this as a form of "salvage ethnography," capturing customs before they died out.

  B. Boas fundamentally changed conceptions of "culture."

    1. His position must be understood in part as a reaction to the evolutionists.

    2. He stressed the historical particularism of each group.

    3. He dismantled pseudo-scientific claims about differences between the races.

C. Boas's most enduring contribution has been the perspective of cultural relativity, which holds that observers must suspend their ethnocentrism to understand cultures on their own terms.

    1. The seed of this idea was planted with Boas's study of the color of sea water, in which he noted the culturally relative way the color spectrum is broken up.

    2. This cultural relativity should also apply to values and moral judgments; anthropologists must suspend judgment of other cultures to understand those cultures.

III. Cultural relativity in many ways defines American anthropology and its contribution to society.

    A. The relativistic concept of culture is no longer confined to anthropology—it has been borrowed by other disciplines and entered popular discourse.

    B. As much as we may romanticize cultural relativity and sensitivity, such perspectives are not without their own moral pitfalls.

        1. Boas himself had to rethink cultural relativity in light of the Holocaust.

        2. Where do we draw the line? The case of female circumcision in parts of West Africa offers some suggestions.

Readings:

Ruth Benedict, *Patterns of Culture.*

Franz Boas, *Race, Language, and Culture.*

Clifford Geertz, *The Interpretation of Cultures.*

Questions to Consider:

1. Is it useful to conceive of *culture* in terms of evolution and progress? What does it mean to be a more advanced culture?

2. How has the Boasian perspective influenced definitions of culture?

3. What are the limits of cultural relativity?

Lecture Three—Transcript
Culture and Relativity

I think most anthropologists feel somewhat proprietorial toward the concept of culture, but we also have to take great pride in the fact that it's been widely adopted across academic disciplines and in popular discourse as well. But what is culture exactly? In this lecture, we're going to look at the concept of culture and how it's changed since the 19th century and pioneers such as Edward Tylor and Lewis Henry Morgan. They and other cultural anthropologists considered culture to be singular, synonymous with civilization, and then Franz Boas, the father of American anthropology, turned attention to the multiplicity of cultures and argued for cultural relativity, not judging one's culture's customs by the moral standards of a different culture. The notion of cultural relativity underlies most modern definitions of culture, yet as we'll see in the conclusion to this lecture, cultural relativity has its limits.

As a formal discipline, anthropology only began about 100 years ago, and in the mid-19th century evolution was an idea very much in the air at the time as we mentioned in the last lecture. Darwin and Wallace, Marx, whose scheme was fundamentally evolutionary as well, and less remembered but just as important in his day was Herbert Spencer. Spencer, who was born in 1820 and died in 1903, was an English social philosopher and an early advocate of the theory of evolution. Indeed, he was the one who coined the phrase "survival of the fittest," which is often attributed to Darwin. Spencer's work attempted to combine biology, sociology, ethics, politics, combine all the fields of knowledge into a unified theory organized around the principle of evolution, and this was his basic theory, that things evolve from being less complex to more complex, from being homogenous to being more heterogeneous.

Spencer and his followers attempted to apply natural selection to human societies, and this is a theory that's come to be known as social Darwinism. The social Darwinists argued that human society was like nature in being a competitive arena with limited resources in which individuals fight to survive. Spencer used this to justify laissez-faire capitalism in England and the English class system; he was a staunch Tory. He believed that welfare programs acted against the struggle for survival. They prolonged human suffering by buffering people against the forces of nature. He believed that humans were perfecting themselves and that without government intervention suffering would eventually be eliminated in the world. Certainly our social lives—take workplace politics for example— certainly some aspects of our social lives look like a competitive arena of natural selection, but it's social and not biological, and this is what Spencer crucially missed, was that culture opts us out of evolutionary processes, that culture holds us to a higher moral standard than mere biological imperative.

Like the idea of evolution, the concept of culture was very much in the air in the mid-19th century as well. We could point to a number of scholars who were dancing around the culture concept at the time—Alexander von Humboldt, for example, in Germany—but here we're going to focus on three men who did more than anyone else to establish anthropology as a formal discipline, and they are: Sir Edward B. Tylor, an erstwhile English businessman who became the country's first professor of anthropology; Lewis Henry Morgan, a Rochester, New York, lawyer and parlor intellectual; and finally Franz Boas, a German-Jewish scholar and an emigrant to the United States.

Edward Tylor had become interested in the study of other cultures during a trip to Mexico. He was largely self-taught, but he went on to write the first general textbook in anthropology in 1881, and in 1884 Oxford University created its first readership in anthropology for him, and it was known, the discipline of the time was known as Mr. Tylor's science. He was often called upon in this context to defend the establishment of a whole new discipline. "There are so many subjects to study," people would ask. "why have another academic discipline?" He responded that it's like a backpack. A backpack adds more weight but it allows us to carry everything else. He said that anthropology serves the same function in the academy. It's an additional discipline but brings everything else together and allows us to carry this weight more effectively.

In his book *Primitive Culture*, and this is a title that we would be loath to use these days, but it was published in 1878, he famously defined culture as "that complex whole which includes knowledge, belief, art, law, morals, customs, and any other capabilities and habits acquired by man as a member of society." There are a couple of crucial points here. First of all, Tylor allowed that culture is learned. We're not born with it, it's acquired, and he allowed that culture is shared as a member of society, but let me go back and read the beginning of this quote: "Culture, or civilization, is that complex whole which includes knowledge, belief, art, law morals, customs, and any other capabilities and habits acquired by man as a member of society."

One thing that we see wrong with this definition today is its stress on the singular civilization, or culture, and Tylor believed that all human civilizations followed a single line of evolutionary development, unilineal evolution, and he believed that societies were progressing. Everything was progressing, everything was getting better, but this is unilineal evolution, where everybody is moving in the same direction. All societies are on a scale of evolution, but they're stuck at different levels. Tylor focused on survivals, ancient traits that are still practiced today by primitive peoples due to the weight of tradition, and he focused on survivals because he thought it gave him a window into the past of his own civilization, the past of all of humanity, since he believed that at one time the Europeans were savages as well. In its own way, this is a very progressive sentiment at least for its day. Primitives are real people too; they're just at an earlier stage of cultural development, a cultural infancy or a cultural adolescence, if you will. He believed in the psychic unity of all mankind, that everybody everywhere has the same basic mental capacities, so that he argued that people are all essentially rational and that they learn from their experiences.

Around the time Tylor was writing in England, Lewis Henry Morgan, another armchair anthropologist, as we call them, was pressing forward on the same front in the United States. Morgan was born in 1818 and died in 1881, and he was a wealthy Rochester, New York, lawyer. He had made his money in railroads and then decided to semi-retire and pursue more gentlemanly pursuits. He was a parlor intellectual, and ever since he was a boy he had been fascinated by the Native Americans who lived in New York, and he actually at one point went out and did some fieldwork among the Iroquois and lawyer work as well. He helped the Iroquois fight the U.S. government taking some land away under duress and then he helped to fight this and get their lands back.

While he was working with the Iroquois, he discovered that they viewed their relatives very differently than he did and, being a lawyer, he was sensitive to issues of descent and of kinship and inheritance. The Iroquois are a matrilineal society; they trace descent through female lines. And another interesting thing he found was that they call the children of same-sex siblings by a different name than they call the children of opposite-sex siblings. This is to say that they had two different terms for cousins. They would call one's mother's brother's children cousins, and they would call one's mother's sister's children brother or sister, just as if they were full siblings. He was fascinated by these differences in kinship, he was fascinated by the legal implications, and so he started sending out questionnaires to whites around the world—missionaries, government officials, colonial officials—and asking them about the native peoples, the kinship customs, the technologies and so forth of the native peoples with whom they worked.

He gathered up all of this data, and he published his magnum opus in 1877 called *Ancient Society*. In this, he put forth a model of evolution that had three stages: savagery, barbarism, and civilization, and he believed that all societies progressed through these three stages. Everybody started out as savages, some eventually moved to become barbarians, and, of course, the rest—civilization was Western European civilization and American civilization. There were some key traits that he associated with each of these stages. For example, savages practiced promiscuous sex, barbarians had multiple spouses, multiple wives, and in civilization we had reached the pinnacle of monogamy. Likewise, savages had fire, barbarians had the bow and arrow, and civilization (at the time anyway) had the steam engine, again the pinnacle of technological development.

Like Tylor, Morgan saw societies progressing through a unilinear evolutionary scheme. All groups had or will progress through the stages of savagery, barbarism, and eventually become civilized. While today this perspective seems highly ethnocentric, at the time it was a fairly radical proposition. Savages and barbarians are just as much people as civilized individuals are; they're just at a different stage of development. Morgan was a staunch champion of private property in the state, and these were both hallmarks of Morgan's highest stage of human development, civilization, but Morgan was also truly an evolutionist, and he saw that civilization doesn't mark the end of evolutionary change, and in ancient society, he concluded by noting that "a mere property career is not the final destiny of mankind if progress is to be the law of the future, as it has been of the past."

We have Tylor and we have Morgan, these 19th-century evolutionists, but the edifice built up by these two men was to be torn down by the work of one quite remarkable man, Franz Boas, widely considered to be the father of modern American anthropology. Boas was born in 1858; he died in 1941; he was born in Minden in Germany, Minden, Westphalia, in 1858, two years after Freud was born, interestingly enough. His family was of the prosperous liberal and well-educated German middle class. As a child, he was somewhat sickly. And as is the German custom of that day and even today, his parents would take him to the seashore for cures, and it was during these trips as a young child to the seashore that he decided that one day he would cross the North Sea and go explore the Arctic Circle, a wonderful dream for a small child, but Boas was more intent than most children and their dreams. He would starve himself; he would go on semi-fasts, not eating very much or not eating at all some days to prepare his body for the rigors of such a journey.

In his university studies, and first he studied at Heidelberg and then he went on to Bonn and finally studied at the University of Kiel, Boas applied himself to both geography and physics. In his 1881 doctoral dissertation, it was in physics from the University of Kiel, and it was on the color of seawater. And he initially started out—he was very much concerned with the objective measures of changes in the color of sea water, light intensities, the polarization of light when it's reflected against the water, the absorption of light in the water. But as he was doing this research, he discovered that people perceived these colors differently. Where one person might see green, another might see blue or bluish-green or greenish-blue, and he came to see that there is this subjective quality to perception of colors. This was the kernel of the line of thought that would eventually lead to his definition of culture. Here he's working really at the intersection of hard science and subjective understanding, and it gets us back to what anthropology does best, traveling this divide, trying to be a science, but also trying to offer more humanistic understanding as well.

In 1883, Boas has gone through his state service in Germany, and, fulfilling a childhood dream, he convinces the German Arctic Commission to send him off to the North Pole, or not quite the North Pole but actually to Baffin Island, which is today in the far northwest of Canada, but it's within the Arctic Circle. He was to stay there for a year, and he was going to map Baffin Island and also study the relationship between man and his environment. What better place to study the relationship of man in the environment than such an extreme environmental place. He goes to Baffin Island; he starts living with the Eskimo. Let me mention here that today we call the Eskimo, Inuit. Like the names of many ethnic groups around the world, Eskimo was actually a pejorative. It's a word from a neighboring group, an Algonquin group, and it means dog eater or eater of raw meat. It's not what these people call themselves; they call themselves the Inuit, which means real people.

Anyway, he goes and works among the Inuit, lives and works among the Inuit, and his trip was in many ways a disaster. He arrived late, the winter was exceptionally bad, the hunting was bad, the dogs were dying. He describes these trips where the men would go out and spend 24 to 36 hours wandering around in this really deathly cold. Nonetheless, he was able to survey most of

Cumberland Sound and Davis Strait, these sections of Baffin Island, and he did so with the aid of the Inuit. They were able—and he was quite amazed by this—they were able to draw incredibly detailed maps of the coastline, which Boas then used as a basis for drawing his own maps, and he was very much amazed by their sophisticated comprehension of geography.

During his stay, he immersed himself in Inuit culture, living just as they did, and he was very much struck by their basic humanity and generosity. He wrote to his fiancée at the time, "I often ask myself what advantages our good society possesses over those of savages, and I find the more I see of their customs that we have no right to look down upon them. Where among our people could you find such true hospitality?" This experience really sharpened Boas's idea of the basic equality of all peoples, and it wasn't necessarily based on logical reasoning, but on emotion. The kindness and sensitivity these Inuit people had shown him, combined with the behind-the-scenes look that he got of Inuit culture, led him to develop the discipline of anthropology in many ways. "It was with feelings of sorrow and regret," wrote Boas. "that I parted from my Arctic friends. I had seen that they enjoyed life as we do, that nature is also beautiful to them, that feelings of friendship also root in the Eskimo heart, and that the Eskimo was a man just as we are. His feelings, his virtues, and his shortcomings are based on human nature, like ours."

After his work on Baffin Island, Boas returned to Germany, and then fleeing anti- Semitism—of course anti-Semitism was nothing new to Germany; it didn't arise with the Third Reich—he emigrated to the United States, and in the United States he founded anthropology programs at the American Museum of Natural History in New York City and at Columbia University and single-handedly produced a generation of students who went out and founded anthropology programs across the country, establishing the discipline. While in the States, while working at the American Museum of Natural History, he initiated an expedition to the northwest coast of North America to study the northwest coast Indians, and the northwest coast goes from British Columbia up through Alaska.

He worked in particular with a group known as the Kwakiutl. The Kwakiutl are best known for their masks and the totem poles. If you've ever been to the Field Museum in Chicago or the Museum of Natural History in New York City, you can see some of Boas's collections from the Kwakiutl, and he went to the Kwakiutl and he had this notion that he had to do salvage ethnography. The whites are starting to encroach. I have to go in there, Boas thought, and save all of their stories, save all of their legends, record their language, record the grammar and dictionaries, take physical measurements even, and collect all of these artifacts, totem poles and masks and so forth.

This really gets at the heart of Boas's method. Boas stressed that anthropology and our understandings of culture have to be inductive. We don't start out with theory, like Tylor and Morgan had, and then try and prove or disprove it. He says we have to go and live with the people that we're studying, soak all of this information from daily life up and develop theories out of that. Boas argued that cultures are guided by what he called an unreflected logic and that the job of anthropologists is to go in and record this unreflected logic. Boas argued forcefully against the 19th-century evolutionists. He was a German-Jewish immigrant; he had a vested interest in arguing against racial determinism. He argued that humans are born with certain capacities: the capacity to learn a language; the capacity to learn a culture. But what language, what culture, doesn't matter, or rather it's a matter of chance where one is born, the chance circumstances of birth.

One line of thought that Boas is associated with is called today historical particularism, and this was his argument against unilinear evolution. Morgan and Tylor had said that all societies fall along this unilinear chain of development. Boas said no, each culture has its own history, each culture has its own past. Different cultures aren't set upon a unilinear scheme of evolution, but rather there are multiple lines of evolution and development, and to understand the culture we have to look at these bases, their particular circumstances and development.

This came to play most vividly in a dispute he had over mask displays at the American Museum of Natural History, and actually the Smithsonian as well. The normal practice of the day was to group masks together based on how they looked: Let's put all the bird masks in one section; let's put all the fantastical god masks in another section. And Boas said no, based on this principle of historical particularism, we have to put the masks in their cultural context. A mask made by the Kwakiutl is not the same as a bird mask made by the Trobriand Islanders or a bird mask made by the Maya. They all have very different meanings in their own culture, and so he argued that rather than group things together by their aesthetic appearance we have to put them together based on their particular cultural histories. Boas was also an early and an ardent opponent of scientific racism; and think back to the day in the late 19th and early 20th centuries, this was still very much the norm.

In an 1894 address to the American Association for the Advancement of Science, a very controversial speech, he systematically refuted all of the scientific claims for Negro inferiority. Their position in society, he argued, reflects the discrimination against them. Their plight is not the cause of racism—it's the product of racism—and he argues, "We might rather wonder how so much has been accomplished in so short a period of time against such heavy odds." Likewise, he very much argued against discrimination against immigrants, and in 1907 he began a massive study that looked at 18,000 immigrants and their children, immigrants from southern Europe and from eastern Europe, and in measuring their skulls (these were physical anthropology tests), in measuring their skulls, he found that in the first generation the skulls of immigrants approached the size of native-born Americans; and so it wasn't their biology which kept them this way, it was the circumstances in which they lived, their nutrition, and once they were living in an American environment, eating an American diet, their children physically became more like American children.

He used these lines of thought to build up a theory which is known today as cultural relativism. Remember his early work with the color of seawater, that different people perceive of the color of seawater in different ways. Color, as it occurs in nature, the color spectrum of course is a continuum. It documents different wavelength frequencies of light; there are no distinct colors such as green or red given in nature. Our language leads us to break up the spectrum into these neat categories, red, green, blue, and so forth, and languages differ in how they break up the color spectrum. There are some languages in the world that only have two colors, dark and light. Many languages around the world conflate green and blue, a color that linguists often call grue.

He used this idea of people perceiving the world differently to develop the notion of cultural relativity, and this is a central idea in modern cultural anthropology, and it is that a culture has to be evaluated in terms of its own values, not according to the values of another culture, and that these values are relative. One person's terms and categories cannot be transposed to another. There's no culture that's better or worse than another; they're just each products of the unique history. This was very much opposed again to the 19th-century evolutionists, and it was the idea, I think, that most of us probably take for granted these days: Don't judge until you understand the culture. Sometimes this is easy. The Eskimo kiss by rubbing their noses; the Belgians put mayonnaise rather than ketchup on their French fries.

Sometimes cultural differences like this, especially the quirky ones, are easy for us to digest.

But very often, the issues are much stickier. My colleague Tom Gregor, for example, works with the Mehinaku in the Amazonian rain forest, and a culturally sanctioned punishment for young girls and for women who have entered into adulterous relationships is gang rape. And one time he reports that he was in the field and a young woman was accused of having sex with another young man, and the men in the village were preparing to rape this woman. In circumstances like this, and fortunately in that circumstance, the tensions diffused and nothing happened, but he had to make this choice. This is the tradition of another culture. I'm a cultural anthropologist, I need to be sensitive to this, but where do we draw that line? Where is it OK to step in and say, "No, that's over the boundary, and we have to take action"?

We could take Nazi Germany as well, and this is where Boas really had to modify his own views of cultural relativity. An extreme cultural relativistic point of view would say "Nazi Germany, the ideology of National Socialism, this is the product of German culture; we have to take it as that. We can't judge it based on our own sentiments." But of course we do judge such things, and Boas himself backed off from his extreme cultural relativism in the early days of World War II. But in a broader, more practical sense, cultural relativity means temporarily suspending judgment of other people's customs and practices until we can understand those customs and practices on their own terms. The debate these days about cultural relativity, one debate these days, focuses on the practice of female circumcision, and this is the removal of the clitoris, surgical removal of the clitoris.

Female circumcision was practiced in the United States and Europe through the 1800s as a medical treatment for masturbation, and it's still practiced today in large parts of Africa, particularly Muslim areas of Africa. In Somalia, for example, girls are circumcised when they're between the ages of six and 12, somewhere in there. The operation is performed without anesthetics in not sterile conditions. The girl is normally restrained by an older woman, circumcised with a razor blade, but after this the girl is no longer a girl, she's a woman, and the staunchest advocates for this, even in Somalian society, are the women themselves, arguing that women have to go through this process to not be girls anymore but to become true women, and it also offers the additional benefit of being able to visually prove virginity at the time of a wedding. Most Westerners find this custom of female circumcision repulsive, and the World Health Organization has even condemned female genital mutilation, but it continues to be widely practiced, and again it's even advocated by the women themselves. Not all Somalian women are proponents of female circumcision, but a fair number are, and this is one of those ironic circumstances where human rights is at odds with cultural diversity.

We've come a long way in terms of our understanding of culture from the work of Spencer and Tylor and Morgan and their evolutionary scheme of things. Boas's concept of cultural relativity is widely held not only in the academy but throughout society. We often speak of multiculturalism, cultural sensitivity, and so on. This is part of our vocabulary today, and yet now more than ever we're faced with the difficult moral questions and this question of the limits of cultural relativity. Where do we draw the line? At what point must ethical obligations trump respect for cultural differences and force us to take action? We could all probably agree that genocide is beyond the pale, but what about female circumcision? Is a woman's right to have her body intact more important than the right to respect the traditions of other cultures? What about when women's rights come into conflict with cultural rights? These are issues that we're having to grapple with these days.

In the next lecture, we'll look at the work of two cultural anthropologists who have really pressed the envelope in this issue of cultural relativity and strongly advocated for an extreme position of cultural relativity and changed the discipline of anthropology in doing so.

Lecture Four

Fieldwork and the Anthropological Method

Scope: Anthropologists are drawn to the exotic otherness of distant locales, and no other place has held more romantic fascination for Western observers than the Pacific Islands. Two early anthropological pioneers, Bronislaw Malinowski and Margaret Mead, are particularly associated with Pacific studies. In 1915, Malinowski traveled to the Trobriand Islands off the coast of northern New Guinea, where he would live for two years. Documenting the Trobrianders' matrilineal kinship system, Malinowski challenged the universality of Freud's Oedipal theories, showing that tensions between father and son were nonexistent in Trobriand society. Margaret Mead, a student of Franz Boas, traveled to Samoa at the tender age of 23, to prove theories of cultural relativity. Like Malinowski, she found a much more sexually liberated culture with fewer conflicts between adolescents and their parents than was the case in the West. Mead's data have since been challenged, but recent research on the meaning of sex on Samoa partially vindicates her view.

Outline

I. Cultural anthropology's primary methodological tool is participant observation—actually going and living with the people being studied to gain a more intimate understanding of their daily lives.

   A. Extended fieldwork is a hallmark of modern cultural anthropology.

   B. The process is often referred to as "doing ethnography," which is documenting the lifeways of another culture in a sensitive fashion. Doing ethnography primarily involves participant observation and other forms of social science data collection.

   C. Cultural anthropologists write their results in *ethnographies*, representations of other cultures.

II. The greatest early champion of anthropological fieldwork was Bronislaw Malinowski (1884–1942).

A. Born in what is today Poland, Malinowski studied at the University of Cracow, where he received his Ph.D. with the highest honors of the Austrian Empire.

    1. Malinowski went on to study in Germany and, finally, at the London School of Economics in its burgeoning anthropology department.

    2. At the outbreak of World War I in 1914, Malinowski was on his way to study a small group off the coast of New Guinea. As an enemy national in allied territory (via Australia), Malinowski was not allowed to travel back to Europe.

    3. Making a virtue of this necessity, Malinowski became the biggest proponent of conducting long-term fieldwork and participant observation.

B. Malinowski ended up spending two years living among the Trobriand Islands off the east coast of New Guinea.

    1. Malinowski was struck by the matrilineal kinship system of the Trobrianders and the jockeying among chiefs for power.

    2. Malinowski was a prolific writer, and his oeuvre covers everything from marriage and sexuality to trade and subsistence goods.

    3. Malinowski shows why Trobrianders use magic in building long-distance canoes—to symbolically tame forces outside of their control—but not in building other sorts of canoes.

C. Malinowski's view of culture was, like Boas's, fundamentally relativistic.

    1. He viewed cultures as integrated wholes, the parts of which all served a particular function.

    2. He disproved that native peoples were somehow irrational, showing that within their cultural contexts, natives act perfectly rationally.

    3. He argued against the universalizing of Freudian theories of the Oedipus complex, showing that the tensions between father and son did not hold true in the Trobriands.

III. Margaret Mead (1901–1978), a student of Franz Boas, conducted fieldwork in the Pacific islands not long after Malinowski. She went on to become the public face of anthropology in the last half of the century.

A. A student of Franz Boas, Mead was driven by Boasian ideals.
   1. Like Boas, she saw the field as a laboratory to test social theories.
   2. Like Malinowski, she sought to disprove universal psychological theories. In their place, she proposed a Boasian relativity.

B. In 1925, at age 23, Mead headed off to do fieldwork in Samoa. Her work would later be published in the best-selling *Coming of Age in Samoa*.
   1. Mead was attracted to the romantic view of Polynesia in the popular imagination.
   2. She spent a lot of time with adolescent girls and young women.
   3. She wrote about Samoans' adolescent sexual freedom.
   4. She used these data to argue against the Freudian notion of a conflict-ridden adolescence and contrasted the Samoans positively with contemporary U.S. culture.

C. Mead's data were later attacked by Derek Freeman, an anthropologist who studied in Samoa in the 1940s.

IV. Modern definitions of culture tend to stress its dynamic, ever-changing nature.
   A. We generally conceive of culture as learned and shared, but it is shared to varying degrees.
   B. Culture is not so much a "thing" as a process, a text being written.
   C. Clifford Geertz sees culture as a text to be interpreted; Michael Herzfeld views cultural anthropology as the study of "common sense."

Readings:

Bronislaw Malinowski, *Argonauts of the Western Pacific*.

Margaret Mead, *Coming of Age in Samoa*.

Michael Young, *Malinowski's Kiriwina*.

Questions to Consider:

1. What sorts of data can participant observation yield that other methodologies miss?

2. Why might the Pacific Islands hold such a fascination for Victorian-era Europeans?

3. Do Margaret Mead's critics negate her social observations, or do they still hold true?

Lecture Four—Transcript
Fieldwork and the Anthropological Method

We anthropologists distinguish ourselves from most of the other social sciences based on our emphasis on fieldwork: going there, wherever there may be, to study them, whoever they may be. We build our theoretical models not out of ivory tower ruminations but from observed experience. As an anthropologist, I'm very much concerned with observable behavior, what people do rather than what they should do. Political scientists and sociologists and economists develop abstract models of human behavior, very interesting abstract models that tell us a lot about human behavior, but anthropology has a lot to offer in building up theory from fieldwork, from data that we gather on the ground. In the lecture today, we focus on the ethnographic fieldwork of two anthropological pioneers, Bronislaw Malinowski and Margaret Mead, both of whom were drawn to life in the Pacific. Malinowski worked in the Trobriand Islands, Mead worked in Samoa, and their writing set the early standard for 20th-century ethnographic fieldwork.

What is ethnography? Cultural anthropologists do ethnography. The term comes to us from the Greek *ethnos*, which means race or people or ethnicity, and *graph*, writing or representation of. Thus, ethnography is writing about other peoples, but ethnography, the way in which cultural anthropologists use it, refers to both a process, doing ethnography, and a product, the ethnography, a book that we wind up with. In terms of the process, it involves participant observation, going and living in the place being studied for an extended period of time, and learning the culture as a child, learning the culture from the inside out. We gather data; we have a number of methods for data gathering. We do formal and informal interviews, we map out fields, we conduct surveys, we do time allocation studies, we look at the caloric intake of families, and so forth, but we also try and get a more subjective understanding, walking in the shoes of the people who we're studying. That's the process of doing ethnography.

The act of writing ethnography, we come back, digest all of this information that we've gathered and write it up, using the minutiae of everyday life that we've gathered in the field to interrogate larger issues, theories, stereotypes, public policy even, whatever it may be. In this, as Boas pointed out, anthropology is fundamentally inductive rather than eductive, building up theory from all of this data that we find in the field. Morgan did some fieldwork with the Iroquois, as we have mentioned. Boas saw the importance of fieldwork and instilled this in his students, but it was Bronislaw Malinowski who became the most vocal proponent of long-term modern fieldwork.

Malinowski was born in 1884; he died in 1942; he was born in Krakow, what is today Poland but at the time was part of the Austrian empire; his parents were minor Polish nobility, his father an expert in Polish folk dialects. At school, Malinowski studied physics and math with an additional emphasis on philosophy, and note here that, like Boas, there's a blurring of the boundary between what were considered to be hard sciences and the softer humanities. He received his Ph.D. in 1908; dissertation was on the principle of economic thought, and it was conferred with the highest honors of the Austrian empire, *Sub auspiciis Imperatoris*. He went on to Leipzig to study folk psychology and continued moving westward and moving toward the discipline of anthropology, eventually winding up in London, studying under an early anthropologist, Edward Westermark, in this burgeoning new field at the London School of Economics.

In 1914, he got a fellowship to go and study the peoples of an island Malus, off the coast of New Guinea, and when he was traveling there, he was traveling, first to Australia, and this was going to be his home base during his fieldwork, but as he was traveling en route, World War I broke out. This is in 1914, World War I, 1914-1918, and he found himself an enemy alien in Allied territory. He had been born in Krakow, he was an Austrian citizen, and so the Australian authorities were very kind, given the circumstances, once he reached there. They allowed him to travel around Australia, travel around in New Guinea, which was part of Australia, even helped fund some of his exploration and research, but they wouldn't allow him to go back home, wouldn't allow him to go back to Europe. He was stuck, and what was meant to be a relatively brief trip turned into a several years' stay.

His fieldwork, he began by exploring some of the islands off the coast of what is today Papua New Guinea, and you'll remember that New Guinea is divided into two parts today. The western part is part of Indonesia; the eastern part is Papua New Guinea. And in 1915 he goes to the Trobriand Islands, which are located off the coast of New Guinea, off the southeast coast of New Guinea. He stayed there for a year, from 1915 to 1916. He returned briefly to Australia for a respite, and then went back to the Trobriand Islands from 1917 to 1918. Thus he spent two years in total on the Trobriand Islands, and he became the most vocal proponent of what would become anthropology's signature method, participant observation, but really he was making a virtue out of a necessity. He couldn't go back to

England even if he wanted to; he couldn't go back to Krakow even if he wanted to. He had to stay in the Trobriand Islands, but having been forced to do that, he saw the value in long-term fieldwork, long-term participant observation, and he compelled the discipline out of its armchair.

He learned the local language, he lived in the local communities, and he generally took part in everyday life. Allow me to read a quote from one of his books where he describes his early fieldwork experience: "Imagine yourself suddenly set down, surrounded by all your gear, alone on a tropical beach, close to a native village, while the launcher dinghy which had brought you sails away out of sight. Since you take up your abode in the compound of some neighboring white man, trader, or missionary, you have nothing to do but to start at once on your ethnographic work. Imagine further that you're a beginner without previous experience, with nothing to guide you and no one to help you, for the white man is temporarily absent or else unable to waste any of his time. This exactly describes my first initiation into fieldwork on the south coast of New Guinea. I well remember the long visits I paid to the villages in those first weeks, the feelings of hopelessness and despair after many obstinate but futile attempts had entirely failed to bring me into real touch with the natives or supply me with any material. I had periods of despondency, when I buried myself in the reading of novels, as a man might take to drink in a fit of tropical depression and boredom."

The culture he found in the Trobriands, he was eventually able to break into Trobriand society and to commune with the Trobrianders as much as he could, and the culture that he found there was radically different than anything he'd ever encountered. The Trobriand Islands are a group; there are four main islands, numerous small ones off the coast of New Guinea. The main island where Malinowski worked is called Kiriwina. The Trobrianders are a matrilineal society. Descent and kinship are traced through women, not men, and you'll recall that it was the matrilineality of the Iroquois that had piqued Lewis Henry Morgan's interest in anthropology as well. The Trobrianders were also a classic chiefdom, a ranked chiefdom. Certain families were ranked higher than others; there were chiefly families, there were noble families, and there were commoners, and there were various levels of chiefs as well.

He found a society that was in some ways infatuated with the yam. Yams were the staple crop of Trobriand society, but they were also the symbolic part of Trobriand society. Yams formed much of the wealth of Trobriand males. He found a system where there were intricate trade networks connecting these islands with one another and trade not only in subsistence goods but in symbolic items as well. We're going to have a chance to come back to Trobriand culture later in this course, and it's a fascinating place and Malinowski was very much taken by it, and living there for as long as he did allowed him to go beyond just the most striking exotic customs, just the most unusual things, to look at what he called the imponderabilia of everyday life.

Malinowski wrote widely on a wide variety of topics. He wrote about Trobriand gardening, he wrote about Trobriand magic, he wrote about trade, he wrote about sex, and he did more than almost anyone else to popularize anthropology, especially in England. To give you an idea, these are some of the titles of his books published in the 1920s and '30s: *Crime and Custom in a Savage Society*; *Myth in Primitive Psychology*; *The Sexual Life of Savages*; *Coral Gardens and their Magic*, wonderful titles, wonderful catchy titles, but also all very fine-grained ethnographic analyses, the sort of work that we still read today in anthropology because of its vivid and comprehensive descriptions of Trobriand life.

I will mention here in passing that his diary was published posthumously. Now his daughter, in fact, wrote the preface and edited parts of the diary, and it turns out, based on this, and it was supposed to be a very private diary, but it turns out that he was also bad-tempered, he was contemptuous of the natives at times, he was a bit of a misogynist, he had very explicit sexual fantasies, but, as the quote I read a moment ago said, he was on the verge of going crazy at times, literally isolated, the only person who spoke his own language, no one much to interact with. And in his vindication, I should note that he always publicly argued very vigorously against racial prejudices, and, in fact, one of his students—after he got back to England, he started teaching at the London School of Economics—and one of his students was Kenyata, the future independence leader of Kenya, and many of his students stressed how much he valued cultural diversity and fought against entrenched racial prejudices of the time. So, like Boas, Malinowski came to the conclusion that societies or cultures are integrated and that one must study them as integrated wholes.

Also, like Boas, Malinowski stressed the native perspective on things, an emic perspective, a perspective from inside the culture, and he was very much concerned with cultural context. He said that if somebody understands why a native person, a Trobriander, does a certain custom that we might find odd, if you understand it within the cultural context, there's a logic to what they're doing. We might not understand that logic, but they do, and they're just as logical, just as reasonable as ourselves, but they have a different set of resources and knowledge to work with. Malinowski showed that there was always a logic if we understood the full cultural context. He's reported to have once run into a cannibal in New Guinea and it's said that the cannibal asked him, "What were the Europeans doing with all of these bodies that were being killed during World War I? How did the Europeans eat all of that flesh?" Malinowski said, "You know, well, we don't eat the bodies," and the cannibal replied, "That's crazy, that's barbaric. Why would you kill without any real object?" So, like Boas, Malinowski was very much concerned with cultural relativity

He also, in terms of theory, he promoted a theory called, which we call today anyway, functionalism, and this is the idea that every custom in a society serves some sort of function, and we could divide these up into three main types. There are basic functions, shelter, food, sex, and so forth. There are integrated functions, customs that keep the society integrated as a whole. And there are psychological functions, and a couple of examples of the psychological functions: He noted, for example, that the Trobrianders are very proficient gardeners. They can grow these huge yams, and yet they religiously follow certain rites, certain magical rites, when they're doing their planting. He said, "Why would they do that? They're such wonderful gardeners. Why do they have to resort to magic in their gardening?" He concluded that it was because they were trying to control those variables outside of their control, the weather, things that they could not possibly control; they took recourse to magic to try and bring those into their own control.

The same thing holds true for canoes. He noted that the canoes that the Trobriand islanders built for traveling in the inlets and bays around the islands, they were nothing special, that people would just build them and there were no special rites or rituals that went along with it. But for their long-distance voyaging commutes, there was an elaborate ritual process that had to go into building the canoes, and the reason why, Malinowski argued, was to relieve their anxiety over these uncertain conditions of weather and the sea that they had no control over at all. So he said that lots of magical customs, they serve to relieve people's anxieties about the future, to, in his words, "to ritualize man's optimism." Likewise with the family, he said that the family served a function in society, and that function was to satisfy certain basic human needs, to domesticate sex, to cope with caring for a child and training a child, and to serve as the locus for the primary emotional attachments and social ties of individuals. Malinowski's contribution was, much like Boas's, stressing cultural relativity in the study of other cultures. The natives, they're not primitives, they're not savages, they just have a different set of values and perhaps a different logical structure than we do.

So as Malinowski was shaking things up in England in the 1920s with these racy titles of his books, Margaret Mead, who was a student of Boas's, was doing the same thing in the United States. Mead was younger than Malinowski; she was also more self-consciously provocative than Malinowski, and she was getting Americans to think about their own and other cultures in new ways. Mead was born in 1901; she died in 1978, a proper middle-class Midwestern Episcopalian girl. In 1920, she goes to New York City, she transfers to Barnard College, which is associated with Columbia University, and she starts hanging out in the wonderfully vibrant counterculture of New York City in the 1920s, in Greenwich Village, the questioning of gender roles, the fight for women's rights, the questioning of sexual norms and so forth, and in her senior year in college she takes a class from Franz Boas, and she's hooked. She says, "This is what I have to do. Anthropology is what I've been looking for."

She goes on and she writes her M.A. thesis under Boas, looking at the correlation of IQ tests, or looking at IQ test results of immigrant children, particularly Italian immigrants in the States, and this was building on Boas's earlier work where he had looked at head size, skull shapes and sizes of immigrant children, and what Mead found was that there was a close correlation of the native language of the household and how well children did on IQ tests. At the time, a number of people were arguing that the immigrants are getting stupider every year as they come over, and we're doing these IQ tests as they get off the boat to show that they're getting dumber. What Mead showed was that wasn't the case at all. The better someone spoke English, the better they did on an IQ test, and so the longer children of immigrants had been in the States, the better they did on these IQ tests. They weren't naturally mentally inferior, just different, something we would take for granted today, but at the time, in the 1920s, it was rather revolutionary.

In 1925, she sets off for Samoa. She wants to go and do fieldwork in this most exotic of locations, Samoa. She's 23 years old, she's five feet, two and a half inches tall, 98 pounds., and this really gutsy young woman—and this was no small journey in those days. A train trip across the country, she stopped in Santa Fe and dropped off a friend, went to the west coast, got on a ship and set sail for Pago Pago, and this was where she was going to do her work—it was the capital of American Samoa at the time—but once she gets there, she decides it's been too corrupted by American missionaries and American colonial officials, and so she changes course for the island of Tau, and she goes there because "It was the most primitive and unspoiled area of Samoa." There was this pull; I've got to go to the place that's been least corrupted by Western civilization to record their culture for future generations.

She saw the field as a laboratory to test various hypotheses, and primarily she went into the field to test the hypothesis that a troubled adolescence was universal and necessary, and this is something that Freud at least implied, and a number of Freudians were expanding, that adolescent conflict between children and their parents is inherent the world over. But Mead sets out to prove Boasian cultural relativity, and this is something that went very well with her gender politics as well. She was fighting for women's rights, and she saw that these were cultural constructions, the way in which women and men were conceived, and she believed that this was also the case of children and parents. She was conducting a type of salvage ethnography; she wanted to go in and save these customs before they died away, before the decline brought about by the influence of whites and missionaries and colonists.

Working on Samoa, she learned the language. We're not sure how well, but she learned the language and she worked mostly with adolescent girls, 60 girls in particular. She got most of her information from 25 girls, and these were teenagers and early twenties, and most of her data came from just two individuals, two key informants, and she strived for a subjective understanding of what life was like on Samoa. She recorded lots of gossip, lots of stories and so forth, and she came back and she wrote a book in 1928 called *Coming of Age in Samoa*, which became a nationwide bestseller. In this book, what she described was that adolescence in Samoa was largely smooth. It was free of the conflict that we find in American society, and she tied this to the freer norms of sexuality on Samoa.

She said that young children, girls and boys, are encouraged to experiment sexually. Very often, older men will initiate younger women into the pleasures of sex. She writes of the adolescents going off and romping, having sex underneath the palm trees, the custom of young adolescent boys sneaking out of their houses at night, after everyone has fallen asleep, and sneaking into their lovers' house and sleeping with their lover and then waking up before anyone else the next morning and leaving. She writes that sex was the pastime par excellence for the Samoans.

She admitted that there were differences. Samoan society was a chiefdom, like the Trobriand Islanders. There were different rankings of families, and the chiefly families had certain obligations, and, among these, chiefly families would choose one of their daughters to become a ceremonial virgin. It was called a *taupu*, and these girls were expected to maintain their virginity until there was a defloration ceremony at marriage, and it brought a lot of honor on the chiefs' families to have a taupu in the house. But, given this exception among chiefly families, she said that with this major intergenerational conflict, control over sexuality, parents trying to control the children's sexuality, that there were really no adolescent tensions on Samoa.

She writes, "Growing up can be free, easy, and uncomplicated. Romantic love as it occurs in our civilization, inflexibly bound up with our ideas of monogamy, exclusiveness, jealousy, and undeviating fidelity, does not occur in Samoa." This was proof of Papa Franz, as she called Boas, of Papa Franz's theories of relativity over these Freudian notions of the universal elements of human culture. After the publication of *Coming of Age in Samoa* in 1928, she becomes really a national star up until her death in 1978, playing to a growing liberal sensibility in the United States, a growing interest and willingness to talk about sex. She had a column in *Redbook*, she was on the *Merv Griffin Show*, she was the public face of anthropology for at least a generation, if not a couple of generations.

Another anthropologist, Derek Freeman, had worked in Samoa after Mead; he worked there in the '40s, so some 20 years later, and after Mead's death, in 1983, Freeman published a book which debunked a lot of what Mead had argued for Samoa. He says that in fact virginity was highly valued among Samoans; yes, by the elites, yes, by the chiefs, but that this had trickled down to the commoners as well. He notes that Samoa has a relatively low rate of pregnancy. If everybody's going off and having sex underneath the palms, why isn't there a higher pregnancy rate? He says that Mead romantically confused rape with consensual sex, that these night crawlers, these young adolescents who had left their homes to crawl into the homes of their girlfriends, this wasn't romantic lovers meeting illicitly, this was rape, and he argues that the girls of Samoa intentionally tricked Mead, that there is a cultural valuation of teasing other people and tricking other people, and that her informants played to what she was wanting to hear and told her these fantastic stories about their sex lives.

Whatever the case, and there's been a wealth of data produced over the last years supporting Mead and attracting for Mead, and we're not really sure what went on, but Mead's notions of cultural relativity and bringing it to the fore of U.S. society and really putting it in people's faces shook up American popular culture and our notions of what is acceptable, and of cultural relativity. And this relativity, put forth by Boas, put forth by

Malinowski, put forth by Mead, underwrites our modern understanding of culture, not only in anthropology but in popular culture as well and popular usage as well.

Let me add a couple of things to this cultural relativity. First of all, that culture is dynamic; it's a constantly changing process, a creative dynamic process. It's like a text being written, like jazz or improvisation. We play off of themes, we develop our own riffs, and in this light it's interesting to listen to a quote by Clifford Geertz in his book *The Interpretation of Cultures*: "The culture of a people is an ensemble of texts, themselves ensembles, which the anthropologist strains to read over the shoulders to whom they properly belong." I love this image of the anthropologist straining to read over the shoulder of an informant, this text of culture that's constantly being written. Culture's not a thing; it's not a list of traits but an ongoing creation. Just as we ourselves are not cultural automatons, acting out preordained roles, neither are the Sherpa, neither are the Bedouins, neither are the Trobrianders, neither are the Samoans.

A lot of times we give ourselves more cultural leeway they we do these other ethnic groups. Of course we're creative, of course our culture is constantly being changed, but we tend to view other ethnic groups as being more static in some way. Michael Herzfeld defines anthropology as the study, the comparative study of common sense, the things we take for granted, just the way the world is, and that's what we do as anthropologists in many ways. We study other common senses; we juxtapose those with our own way of doing things to shake up our conceptions of the world, and this is what Malinowski and Mead did so well. Geertz, going back to Clifford Geertz, his book, *The Interpretation of Cultures*, Geertz also defines ethnography for us, and let me read this "Doing ethnography is establishing rapport, selecting informants, transcribing text, taking genealogies, mapping fields, keeping a diary and so on, but it's not these things, techniques or received procedures, that define the enterprise. What defines it is the type of intellectual effort it is, an elaborate venture in thick description." Thick description, thick description in Geertz's words, is looking for the multiplicity of possible meanings in any given situation.

The example he uses is, let's say a person closes one eye and opens it again rapidly. What goes on there? It could be a twitch; the person might have a neurological disorder that makes him twitch. Perhaps it's a wink. Is their information trying to be communicated? Maybe it's somebody parodying another person who has a twitch, so maybe it's someone parodying another person's winks, so there can be multiple winks upon winks upon winks, if you will, and this is the problem of anthropology, and what anthropologists strive to do is to uncover these complexities, to divine the difference between a wink and a twitch or a sincere wink communicating information or a parody wink.

Whatever the faults of fieldwork, and Malinowski's legacy is tainted by his diary, as we'll see later in the course, it seems like he missed a number of female aspects to Trobriand society. Mead's study has been contested by Freeman and others, but, whatever the faults of their fieldwork, we still read both Malinowski and Mead today for their evocative and deep descriptions of native life in the Trobriand Islands and on Samoa.

Lecture Five
Nature, Nurture, and Human Behavior

Scope: Questions of nature versus nurture have intrigued thinkers throughout the ages. How much of who we are is determined by biology, and how much is learned culture? The relatively recent field of sociobiology (or evolutionary psychology) addresses these questions by looking for evolutionary origins for social behavior. Biologists have traditionally defined evolutionary "fitness" in terms of individuals—how long they live and how many offspring they produce. Sociobiologists shift the focus from individuals to genes. Stemming from studies of ants, bees, and other social insects, sociobiology sees individuals as simply containers for genes. This, in turn, allows them to show an evolutionary basis for altruism and nepotism.

Sociologists also study "attractiveness" from an evolutionary perspective. They argue that evolutionary pressures act differently on men than on women, producing different conceptions of what is considered attractive (most simply, that men value physical beauty and youthful appearance while women are more concerned with character and social status). Recent cross-cultural studies of conceptions of beauty, however, call into question the universality of sociological claims.

Outline

I. To what extent is human behavior determined by nature and to what extent through nurture? This question has long plagued philosophers and social thinkers, and it gets to the heart of anthropology.

   A. John Locke famously weighed in on the side of nurture with his *tabula rasa* idea of human development. Most cultural anthropologists today emphasize cultural development over biological determinism.

   B. The case for biological determinism in human nature has a dubious past, associated with eugenics and racism. Shedding this taint, the field of sociobiology (or evolutionary psychology) has emerged to uncover genetic bases for human behavior.

II. Sociobiology builds on Darwin's theory of natural selection and advances in our understanding of genetics to redefine what is meant by evolutionary "fitness."

    A. The synthetic approach to evolution combined Darwinian selection with Mendelian genetics and the discovery of DNA's structure.

    B. Sociobiology emerged in the mid-1970s, offering a new synthesis.

        1. E. O. Wilson, on the basis of his work with social insects, put forth a comprehensive theory of the evolutionary bases of cooperation.

        2. Richard Dawkins captured the core idea of sociobiology with his phrase "the selfish gene."

        3. Sociobiologists point out that *Homo sapiens* evolved in a particular environment (the environment of evolutionary adaptation, or EEA), roughly corresponding to the Pleistocene period from 1.8 million to about 11,000 years ago. Early in the development of *Homo sapiens*, culture came to trump environmental pressures on evolution. Thus, our basic biological adaptation is to a Pleistocene environment.

    C. Sociobiologists base much of their theory on a reconceptualization of "fitness."

        1. Fitness is generally considered to be an individual's direct success in reproducing.

        2. Sociologists argue that we should look at humans as containers of genes—it is not so important if the individual survives or dies or reproduces, but how many of his or her genes get passed down to the next generation.

        3. As genes are shared among related individuals, sociologists argue for the concept of "inclusive fitness," which takes into account the survival not only of individuals but of the genes they carry.

        4. Thus, it sometimes makes evolutionary sense for individuals to sacrifice themselves for their relatives.

III. Sociobiologists have contributed to our understanding of altruism and reciprocity, reproductive strategies between the sexes, and the biological basis of attractiveness.

    A. Dawkins's selfish genes ironically result in sociability. Altruism and reciprocity—the glue of social relations—actually provide a selective advantage to the genes of a person.

B. Sociobiologists have posited fundamentally different pressures at work on men and women in their reproductive strategies.

    1. Humans pursue what is termed a *K strategy* of reproduction—having very few offspring but investing greatly in their care. This is made necessary by the long period of helplessness that characterizes human offspring.

    2. Using an economic metaphor, sociologists argue that sperm is in plentiful supply while eggs are in short supply. This results in men and women having different goals and strategies.

    3. This line of thought argues that men are looking for youth, fidelity, and health in women, while women look for material success and commitment in men.

C. Sociobiologists also study the biology of sexual attractiveness.

    1. They argue that men prefer younger women to maximize childbearing potential, as well as a certain waist-to-hip ration that indicates childbearing potential.

    2. Nonetheless, a number of these traits seem to be specific to U.S. culture, calling into question the universal applicability of the theory.

Readings:

Richard Dawkins, *The Selfish Gene.*

Desmond Morris, *The Naked Ape.*

E. O. Wilson, *On Human Nature.*

Robin Wright, *The Moral Animal.*

Questions to Consider:

1. To what extent is our behavior predetermined by our genes?

2. Do men and women have fundamentally different goals for marriage and mating?

3. Can "subjective" attractiveness be based in genetic predispositions?

Lecture Five—Transcript
Nature, Nurture, and Human Behavior

In this lecture, we turn to the eternal question of nature versus nurture. Now this is a phrasing that comes to us from Prospero's description of Caliban in *The Tempest*, which says, "A devil, a devil born, on whose nature nurture can never stick." So what part of who we are as individuals is determined by birth and how do such innate predispositions affect culture? Mainstream anthropology comes down firmly on the nurture side of this debate. Since the times of Boas, we've argued against scientific racism; we've argued that culture can be determinate in who we grow up to be.

At the same time, we must acknowledge that we're biological beings, that we live within the bodies that were given, although perhaps less so in these days of plastic surgery, and there's certainly give and take between biology and cultural constraints and possibilities, and it's at this nexus between biology and culture that sociobiologists, also called evolutionary psychologists, look for common elements, common elements across cultures and trying to look back and see which of these common elements might have a genetic basis, might have some sort of evolutionary cause. In this lecture we're going to look at what sociobiologists have to tell us about altruism and nepotism, attractiveness and mating strategies. The question is how much of who we are is determined at birth. In contemporary terms, this would mean how much of who we are is genetically given, and these questions really hit at the heart of anthropology.

On the one hand, we as anthropologists argue that all humans are fundamentally alike, at least biologically. We're all Homo sapiens, we're all members of the same species, and further subspecies differentiation is virtually meaningless at the genetic level, and yet, in addition to setting the commonalities of humans, this fundamental similarity of humans, we anthropologists also study the many differences between human populations, what makes us different, the different marriage patterns, different kinship patterns, different sorts of religious beliefs, political organization, and so forth, so this idea of what is natural and what is given to us by culture gets at the heart of anthropology. For predecessors to this, we can look back to Herbert Spencer and the social Darwinists of the 19th century, who argued that who we are is determined at birth. We could look at John Locke and his idea of the *tabula rasa*, that children are born a blank slate on which everything that we learn in life is written after we're born. Who we become as adults is based on what we learn as children.

Before we get deeper into a discussion of sociobiology, I want to talk a little bit about the politics of this discipline, or the sub-discipline. Actually, there are sociobiologists who are anthropologists, there are sociobiologists who are psychologists, there are sociobiologists who are biologists as well, and a number of them these days prefer the term evolutionary psychologist to distance themselves from the negative implications that sociobiology has taken on over the years. Now I think that there is a resistance to sociobiological explanations, in part because we like to see ourselves as unique, as humans. We don't like to see ourselves as animals; we like to see ourselves set apart, and so looking for biological explanations for our behavior offends our sensibilities in some way. But it's also a fact that looking for any sort of explanation for human behavior is tainted by histories of racism, the histories of eugenics, the Nazi ideologies of trying to create a superhuman race, these Ubermensch, by breeding what they thought were particularly good-looking human beings, so looking at the biological bases of behavior has this taint of eugenics as well.

There's also the taint of racism in looking for biological bases for behavior. Take IQ tests, for example; there are vast differences in cultural responses to IQ tests, and we've found that IQ tests are extremely culturally dependent. If you were brought up in a Western culture, which values this linear logical way of thinking, you'd probably do quite well on standardized tests such as the IQ test. People from other cultures around the world, who don't share our same linearity of logic, do very poorly on IQ tests, and this doesn't mean that they're stupid, it doesn't mean they don't have the same sort of mental capacities that we have, they just see the world in a different way, and thus it's a way that's not measured very well by IQ tests. We can look at correlations between IQ and race and a number of books in recent years have done this, *The Bell Curve* most famously, but what does this really tell us?

It really tells us more about the different cultures of the people rather than biological differences between them, rather than differences in what their minds can think. And it's telling us more—at least in the United States, where most of these studies have been done—about economic status. It turns out that economic status is a much better indicator of IQ test results than is race. It just so happens that in the U.S. race is highly correlated with economic status, and so it's easy to confuse these variables in the cause and effect here. This is just to give you an idea of some of the reasons why sociobiology has been viewed by some as a suspect discipline, as potentially a racist discipline. From my own point of view, I think we cannot ignore plausible sociobiological explanations for human behavior and we have to keep an open mind in this. Sociobiology itself is not racist; people can use sociobiological findings toward racist ends, but, as a methodology itself, it's not racist.

We've mentioned before that Darwin gave us the mechanism for human evolution, which is natural selection, natural forces acting on individuals to favor certain variants, but he didn't tell us where this variation was coming from. Darwin observed variation, but he didn't say where it was coming from. Gregor Mendel was on to the reasoning behind this, this 19th-century Moravian monk who was doing his experiments with different colored and shaped peas. His work went ignored for about 70 years, and it wasn't rediscovered until the early 1920s in a line of research that ultimately led to Watson and Crick discovering the double helix structure of DNA in 1953, and all of the changes that that has brought about.

Along with a rise in our understanding of the field of genetics, we've also developed a new approach to evolution which is called the synthetic approach, and the synthetic approach basically just combines genetics, Mendelian genetics with Darwin's theory of natural selection, explaining variation, what is the source of variation, which we know today comes from random genetic mutation and from recombination, and this provides the variation upon which natural selection acts, so it is in the new synthesis, biologists have argued, that it is the genotype rather than the phenotype, our external physical appearance which is important in evolution, and this leads us to an important modern definition for evolution: changes in gene frequencies within a population over time. We used to say that evolution was just biological change within a population over time, but now we can be more specific. We can say that it's changes in gene frequencies, and this becomes crucially important as we turn to sociobiology.

The sociobiological revolution really happened in the mid-1970s, and it started with a famous biologist named E.O. Wilson, and in 1975 he published a work called *Sociobiology: The New Synthesis*, and he was obviously playing here very self-consciously on the synthetic approach, and he was offering the new synthesis. Other people writing around the same time introduced the same ideas into the field. Richard Dawkins in particular in 1976 published a book called *The Selfish Gene*, and the ideas of sociobiology have probably been most popularized by Desmond Morris, the British scholar who gives us the sexed-up version of sociobiology. He had published a book in 1968 called *The Naked Ape*, and after all of this vocabulary of sociobiology entered the field in the mid-1970s, he became one of its most vocal and most prominent proponents. He has a number of television documentaries that are out, for example.

Now going back to E.O. Wilson, in 1975 he published *Sociobiology: The New Synthesis*, and he was a specialist in social insects, ants in particular, and he was fascinated by the behavior of ants. Why do we observe all of this sacrificial behavior on the part of worker ants? Why do they spend all of their time provisioning the queen when they could be out looking for mates themselves? Why aren't they investing all of this time and energy in reproducing themselves, in improving their own rate of reproduction? What explains this altruism, Wilson was asking, that we find among social insects? And his answer was that the workers shared their genes with the queen, and so, if they help the queen reproduce, they're actually helping reproduce their own gene pool. Now this changed the way we looked at things, not looking at an individual and the individual's reproductive success but the influence of the reproductive success of their entire gene pool.

Richard Dawkins is the one who made this most clear, and he said that individuals are just containers for genes and that we're containers for selfish genes. He says we have to stop looking at ourselves as individuals to understand human nature. What we want is not necessarily just to have a bunch of children ourselves but to pass our genes on into the next generation, and so if we help somebody who shares our genes, then we're actually helping ourselves. We're helping push our genes on into the next generation, so if we help a brother or we help a sister or we help a cousin, any of our close relatives, we're really helping ourselves. We share our genes in known proportions with our relatives: You share half of your genes with a parent; you share half of your genes with a full sibling; you share a quarter of your genes with an aunt or uncle; you share an eighth of your genes with a first cousin.

What Dawkins and Wilson were arguing, and this is the sociobiological position, that if we look at ourselves and we try and pass our genes on to the next generation, we're helping our relatives, we will help our relatives, the relatives that have a proportion of the same genes that we do. Thus it makes evolutionary sense. Let's take a hypothetical situation. You could rush into a burning house, and you would sacrifice yourself in order to save other people. A sociobiologist would say that it would be worthwhile, it would make sense for you to run into the house, if you could save three siblings or if you could save five of your aunts or uncles or if you could save nine of your cousins, because collectively that group of people would have more genes, more of your own genes than you do as an individual.

Sociobiologists say that there are certain human behaviors that are universal, that these are deep-seated propensities that have evolved way back when in what they call the environment of evolutionary adaptation, the EEA, the environment of evolutionary adaptation. Conveniently, this environment of evolutionary adaptation is more or less coequal with the Pleistocene, and that's about 1.8 million years ago to about 11,000 years ago. Human evolution, modern humans emerged about 100,000 or 200,000 years ago, so it really ends there, but for convenience's sake we can say that the environment of evolutionary adaptation is coequal with the Pleistocene. Evolutionary biologists, sociobiologists, argue that humans evolved in East Africa way back when and that we are stuck with these bodies that were adapted to the East African savanna and the East African grasslands and that the pressures that acted on us then, in these early days of evolution, continue to live on in our bodies today. Now, of course, we've developed these big brains, we have culture, we have language, we have all of these mechanisms that we can reduce the pressures of natural selection acting on us, but the sociobiologists point out we're still stuck in these bodies that are best adapted to Pleistocene East Africa, and to a degree this is certainly true.

We're predisposed to stock up on fatty foods, for example, and proteins, to eat as much sugar as we can get at any given time. This would be very adaptive again living in the Pleistocene savannas of East Africa; you have to pig out when you can because you don't know where your next meal is coming from. But in contemporary society, this predisposition has become a health problem. The newspapers are full of descriptions of the problem of obesity in modern American culture and the economic repercussions that come from this, so we have this absurdity really that's developed of diet industries, which for most of the world is crazy. Half of the world's population today lives on less than $2.00 a day; they think that paying someone to tell you to eat less and exercise more is simply absurd, but we do it, we have to do it, because we have these Pleistocene bodies stuck in this incredibly wealthy society, this affluent society where we can gorge ourselves, where we can indulge our pleasures as we see fit.

So what is fitness? What is genetic fitness? What is evolutionary fitness? We can talk about two types of fitness. The first is direct fitness, and this is really the old view of evolutionary fitness, how many children an individual has, how many of these children live to be of reproductive age and have children of their own. Indirect fitness is something that the sociobiologists began emphasizing, and indirect fitness refers to helping not only yourself, not only the number of children that an individual has, but what percentage of an individual's genes get passed on into the next generation. And by looking at indirect fitness, it leads us to what sociobiologists term kin selection, that we're much more likely to help out our close relatives than other people because they share our same genes. The sociobiologists say that we should think about inclusive fitness in addition to direct fitness, and inclusive fitness again includes not only yourself and your children but other close relatives as well.

There's a recent book by Adam Bellow called *In Defense of Nepotism*, and Adam Bellow is the son of the great contemporary American literary figure Saul Bellow, and in this book Adam Bellow argues that nepotism is really a good thing for American society, that it tempers some of the excesses of blind meritocracy. He says it's natural for humans to be nepotistic, and here he calls on sociobiological data that says that kin selection makes a lot of sense, and he argues that it's a good thing for the economy and for American society today in that it provides some sort of long-range view. Of course, beyond the obvious irony here of Adam Bellow writing a defense of nepotism, it also seems ironic and at odds with American meritocracy, this idea that you get what you want, you become who you are in American society through your own merits and your own work.

But sociobiology was and is revolutionary because it addresses not only competition, which Darwinian theory was very good at, but it addresses cooperation as well. Why do people cooperate with each other? Is there some sort of biological basis for this? It makes sense to sacrifice yourself for your family if you can, because more of your genes can get passed down into the next generation, so the sociobiologists argue that what appears to be true altruism, what appears to be true self-sacrifice, is really self-interested behavior because we're containers for these selfish genes. Why might somebody do something sacrificial or altruistic to non-relatives? Why might a soldier, for example, throw himself on a hand grenade to save the other members of his platoon, to whom he's not related at all?

A sociobiologist would probably argue that we have this deep-seated propensity to help out our relatives, but culturally we extend who our relatives are to non-relatives at times. You may know somebody as a child that you called an aunt or an uncle, who was really just a close friend of the family, this sort of fictive kin, and among soldiers and platoons, very often they treat each other like brothers. There was that Stephen Ambrose book, *A Band of Brothers*; soldiers working together day in and day out treat themselves like siblings in some way, and so sociobiologists would argue that a soldier would be willing to throw himself on a hand grenade to save the other members of his platoon because in his mind he's thinking of them as if they were brothers of his, as if he were saving his own blood relatives and thus his own genes.

Some of the most controversial work in sociobiology has looked at the difference between men and women, the psychological and biological differences between men and women. I need to insert here another disclaimer: a number of these studies were done like psychological studies. Professors will take groups of their students in a classroom and conduct a study and then extrapolate out from those results to the rest of humanity, and so sometimes the results of these studies ring true to college-educated people in the States, for example, where they don't hold true in other cultures around the world, so we have to keep that in mind when we're talking about sociobiology.

Sociobiologists remind us that humans are an extremely K-selected species. You'll remember that there's this continuum of reproductive strategies from K to R; R-reproductive species have lots of offspring and don't invest a lot in any one of their offspring; K-selected species like humans have very few offspring and invest a lot of time and energy in the offspring that they have, and we, as humans, we give birth to these incredibly helpless infants. We have to invest a lot in our children. I was reading the other day that if humans were born at the same level of development that gorilla infants are born at, the gestation period would be 21 months long. Can you imagine a pregnancy 21 months long, giving birth to a one-year-old baby? It would be physically impossible, but that's the difference between our development. We're such a K-selected species.

Sociobiologists approach human sexual attraction and mating from an economic and evolutionary perspective. They argue that women have a window of opportunity during which they can become pregnant, and that ranges from menarche, their first menstruation, which can be in some societies as late as 17 or 18 years old—in our own society the age of first menstruation has been going down from 13 or 14 to these days about 12 years old or even younger in some cases—so the window of opportunity for pregnancies ranges from first menstruation to menopause, which happens sometime in a woman's late 40s. This varies a lot, but sometime in the late 40s. After a woman gives birth, there's a period of natural infertility.

There's some evidence here to suggest this is related to lactation; producing mother's milk releases hormones in the body that act as a natural form of birth control. So giving birth to a child, you have a nine-month gestation period, you have a period of natural infertility after birth, so it's a one- to two-year year commitment on the part of a woman to have a child, and she can only have children during this window of opportunity, from first menstruation to menopause, and even having children in the late 30s becomes biologically problematic very risky for women. You have this period of 20 to 30 years in which women can have children, and raising those children is incredibly costly, not only in our own society, where we have to pay for clothes and CDs and video games and college tuition and so forth, but even in less developed societies, if you will, it's incredibly costly to have children.

In economic terms, women have access to an incredibly valuable commodity. A woman's eggs are extremely valuable; her pregnancies are extremely valuable, and they're risky. A woman can die during childbirth. In contrast, the cost of male reproductivity approaches zero. I hate to tell you men, but the cost of sperm, the value of sperm, is virtually zero. Men produce an unlimited amount of sperm in their lifetime, and so their reproductive costs approach zero. So the sociobiologists say we've got competing intentions going on here between men and women. The women are trying to guard those pregnancies and make sure that the children are going to be cared for, that they grow up and flourish, and men can be more careless about how they spread their seed.

The sociobiologists argue that there's a point of diminishing returns here, and for women that point is reached very early. If a woman has sex with ten men and this results in one pregnancy, the other nine men, the other nine besides the one who impregnated her, are irrelevant; they're unimportant. Men, however, don't have this point of diminishing returns; a man can impregnate a virtually unlimited number of women, assuming that he has access to receptive females, so men don't have this problem of decreasing returns. Some sociobiologists—not surprisingly men here—some sociobiologists have argued that men have a genetic propensity to infidelity, an infidelity gene, if you will, and they point out that humans are not a naturally monogamous species.

Of course it's not all up to men; men don't have the only say in this. Sociobiologists would argue that men should have as much opportunistic sex as they can, that this makes mathematical sense for their reproductivity. But men have to have access to women in order to reproduce, and women thus have a very important say in who they will choose to reproduce with, and thus the women can select for certain types of males. Sociobiologists argue that females look for men who are going to be good providers, who have access to resources, money, or the possibility to make money in the future. They're good with kids, men who are going to be willing to invest in their common offspring, make sure their kids are going to grow up and grow up right, and so women want this sort of dependability, sociobiologists argue, in a man, a commitment, a willingness to invest in children.

I was taking German classes this summer, and the teacher would throw up these slides on a screen of groups of men and women, and she would ask us to describe the people, who would we like to go out and have a cup of coffee with, for example, and we were supposed to use our adjectives here. "I would go out with the tall one or the short one" or whatever it may be, and the class is about halfway divided between men and women, and she would show pictures of groups of women to the men, and they would say things like, "I think I would like to go out and have coffee with the blond one, with the tall one or the cute one. I really like blond girls," or "I really like tall girls," or "I really like slender girls," and so forth. She would show pictures of groups of men to the women students in the class, and the women had problems with this. They would say, "Well, I don't really know who I would like to have coffee with," but then when she pressed them, they would use adjectives, but different sorts of adjectives, personality adjectives. "Well, that guy in the tweed suit looks like he would be nice. The guy in the beard looks like he would be sympathetic. That's who I would like to go and have coffee with."

We have very different criteria at work here, the men looking at external physical appearance and the women trying to get at internal personality traits, people who would be good providers for their offspring. Sociobiologists say that there are a number of things that we look for when choosing a mate, a number of things that lead us to see certain people as being attractive, and that these are biologically programmed; so the sociobiologists argue that men look for youth—that's going to indicate a longer period of potential fertility—they look for youth and fertility, and that women look for stability, access to resources, and this is often correlated with age, with being older, and so the stereotype is that men look for younger women and that women look for older men.

Sociobiologists say that we find a number of physical features naturally inherently attractive, naturally beautiful—facial symmetry for example— and there have been studies where they will take a picture of a person's face and they will digitally manipulate it. They'll cut it down the middle, and they'll create a mirror image, so we have a perfectly symmetrical face, and in studies of individuals, people almost inevitably choose the perfectly symmetrical face as more beautiful. Now why might that be? Why might we see facial symmetry as being beautiful? Sociobiologists argue that it's because it's a sign of genetic healthiness; it's an indicator that this person is genetically healthy and can have healthy offspring as well. Other symbols of such genetic healthiness that sociobiologists point to include full lips, few skin blemishes, a waist-to-hip ratio for women of 0.7, and this means having a big bust and narrow waist and then back out to have large hips, good childbearing hips. That ratio, women prefer men with a 0.9 waist-to-hip ratio, which is like an inverted triangle.

A lot of these sociobiological explanations hold true for American college students at least, maybe for large portions of American society, but we can find counterexamples in various cultures around the world. We studied attractiveness, for example, among Andean populations in Peru and Bolivia and they don't find the hourglass figure that's supposed to be inherently attractive to human males, Andean men don't find this attractive at all. They prefers short, squat, sort of square-figured women, and one could argue that this is adaptive for the environment that they live in, this harsh, high-altitude environment with extremely cold temperatures, so sturdier women perhaps are better adapted, but it derides the sociobiological explanation that this is a universal human propensity. Think back in our own culture, in Western culture, think back to the pictures of Rubens or Titian, or any of these other painters who painted these voluptuous women who today we would consider to be slightly overweight at best.

Sociobiologists argue that women are trying to get men to commit. It's in men's best interest to commit very often because they'll have a sure thing. They can make sure it makes economic, biological, economic, evolutionary sense to have a single partner, to be in a monogamous relationship, to ensure that the children are going to be raised well and to survive and reach reproductive age themselves. However, sociobiologists also argue that men have this infidelity gene, this metaphorical infidelity gene that encourages them not only to have the sure thing at home but to seek out opportunistic sex as well. What the sociobiologists ignore in all of this is the power of culture, the power of culture in changing the way in which people live and work.

Take celibate priests, for example. Sociobiologists have a really hard time explaining why we have celibate priests, and there's been a lot of news lately about priests who are not celibate, and yet the vast majority of them remain celibate. How does a sociobiologist account for that? What reproductive sense does that make? They can't, and so what the sociobiologists, I think they have a lot to offer us in terms of basic propensities that are built into the human condition, perhaps evolving in this environment of evolutionary adaptation, but they miss that culture trumps biology very often.

Language, Thought, and Culture
Lecture Six
Languages, Dialects, and Social Categories

Scope: Language is an element of existence that makes us human: The fact that we have language, that we can communicate with each other, gives rise to culture and sets us apart from other animals. It is unclear when language first arose among our ancestors (perhaps as early as 300,000 or as recently as 100,000 years ago), but writing came along only about 6,000 years ago. All humans have a language, but languages vary greatly around the world. It seems that mental maps of a language's particular sounds are laid down early in life and are incredibly resilient; the older one becomes, the harder it is to master the phonology and grammar of another tongue. Linguists study how people communicate; this involves not just syntax and grammar, but also body language and facial expressions. The linguist Charles Hockett proposes a list of features that make human language unique. These include the ability to say totally new things and to talk about events not in the present. However, recent work with apes has shown that many capabilities we have thought were uniquely human are shared among higher primates.

Language certainly tells us a lot about the speaker, not just the words spoken but how they are said. Dialects, for example, are important markers of one's social origins, and a number of studies have shown that speaking a particular dialect calls into play a whole host of stereotypes and preconceptions.

Outline

I. Humans are both united and divided by language.

    A. Although spoken language has been around for at least 100,000 years, written languages are relatively recent.

    B. Languages vary greatly in their particulars, but there are a few important common elements.

        1. All languages have a grammar (whether it is written or not) and are wholly functioning systems.

    2. Languages are constantly changing.

II. Technical linguistics looks at the structures of languages.

    A. Spoken language is based on sounds, or *phonemes*.

    B. Written languages imperfectly represent phonemes.

        1. In logographic writing systems, symbols are used to represent units of meanings (and, sometimes, whole words).

        2. *Syllabic* and *alphabetic* systems combine a smaller number of symbols ("letters") to represent the sounds of words.

    C. Phonemes are combined to create *morphemes* (the minimal units of meaning in a language); morphemes combine to create words; and words combine in a way prescribed by syntax and grammar.

        1. All languages have a grammar.

        2. Noam Chomsky has suggested that there is an innate capacity for the mind to produce grammar.

    D. Linguists have also discovered that a great deal of what we communicate occurs nonverbally.

        1. As much as 80 percent of the meaning conveyed in a conversation may come from body language (*kinesics*).

        2. *Proxemics* is the study of the physical distance between speakers, showing how notions of personal space vary between cultures.

III. The ability to produce language is a hallmark feature of the human condition, giving rise to the unique cognitive and cultural capabilities of the species.

    A. Most scientists agree that language is uniquely human, but there has been great disagreement on what exactly this means. The linguist Charles Hocket proposed a number of features that, combined, make language human.

        1. Language is an *open system*, as opposed to the closed call systems of other animals. This is to say that human language is infinitely variable, not confined to a few predetermined signals.

        2. Human language exhibits *displacement*, the ability to talk about the past, the future, and things not immediately present.

        3. The words used by human languages are arbitrary representations. This builds on Ferdinand de Saussure's observation that a sign (such as a word) is composed of a *signifier* (the combination of sounds that make up a word) and the *signified* (the actual object, idea, or person referred to).

   B. Studies with apes have shown that with intensive training, apes can be taught rudimentary language skills.

      1. The most famous "talking apes" are Washoe the chimp and Koko the gorilla. Both learned a variant of American Sign Language.

      2. Washoe and Koko have proven that apes can use language productively; that they can discuss distant events (displacement); and that they can even lie (prevarication having been thought to be uniquely human).

      3. Nonetheless, apes never reach beyond a two- to three-year level of language mastery, even after years of training.

IV. The language one speaks, and the way one speaks it, carries a good deal of information about one's background and social class.

   A. The linguist Max Weinreich famously defined a language as a dialect with a navy, meaning that language distinctions are politically loaded and often privilege dominant cultures.

      1. A *dialect* is commonly defined as a mutually intelligible variety of a language, but often, it is difficult to know where exactly to draw the line.

      2. As languages are not easily mastered, and dialects hard to eschew, the way one speaks acts as a good indicator of identity and class.

   B. Different dialects carry different prestige values and are often used in the exercise of power.

      1. In Spanish, French, German, and many languages, one uses two sets of pronouns, one familiar and the other more formal. Such pronouns require speakers to constantly acknowledge social distance in communication.

      2. William Labov has studied the pronunciation of a final *r* following a vowel between social classes in New York City.

      3. Speakers who have mastered two dialects often switch back and forth, depending on social context.

      4. Controversies exist over how much a dialect should be valued, such as with black vernacular English (Ebonics) in the United States.

Readings:

Edward T. Hall, *The Silent Language*.

Steven Pinker, *The Language Instinct*.

Internet Resources:

http://www.koko.org/. The Gorilla Foundation.

Questions to Consider:

1. How does human language differ from animal call systems?
2. What does the use of a particular dialect tell us about the speaker?
3. What are the politics of dialect and language distinctions?

Lecture Six—Transcript
Languages, Dialects, and Social Categories

Language is something that makes us human. We have language so we can communicate with each other, and not just facts, but ideas, hopes, dreams, emotions, theories. It's what allows culture; language allows culture. Most of what we know about culture, indeed most of what we know at all, comes to us through language, so in this lecture we're going to look at just exactly what language is and what it is not, what are its components. We'll talk about the sounds of language, alphabets, grammars, what sets it apart from other forms of animal communication and what do we have to learn from chimps and apes who have learned variants of language. We're going to conclude today by looking at dialects as markers of identity and how one speaks can tell a lot about who one is.

We don't know when language first arose among our ancestors. The physical remains that would tell us about this are mostly soft tissue, like vocal chords, and they don't last very long in the archaeological record, but at some point our larynx falls, creating our Adam's apple and allowing us to produce the vast range of sounds that we need to speak. There are dangers in this as well. When the larynx falls, it also allows us to choke on our own food, so there had to be some huge evolutionary benefit to allowing our larynx to fall, and that evolutionary benefit is spoken language. This first occurred maybe 300,000 years ago, maybe 100,000 years ago. We're not really sure because the tissues don't remain in the archaeological record. Writing, this is important to note, writing only comes along about 6,000 years ago. Most languages in the world were not written and are not written.

We do know that if language is not learned early on, it cannot be fully mastered, so we have this biological capacity to produce language. But if we don't learn a language early in life, we'll probably never learn it, and we can see this in the very few cases we have documented of feral children. In 17th-, 18th-, 19th-century Europe, there would occasionally be these children found that were raised in the wild by wolves or whatever it may be, and they never fully mastered language, so if they didn't learn it from a very early age they could never master it in later life.

Language is a system of communication. It is one of the great rules of languages that, like culture, it's always changing. Languages are always changing. There are about 6,000 languages spoken in the world today, although they're dying out fast, actually. There may be as few as half of that in 100 years' time, by some estimates. Following European contact in the new world, for example, the number of native languages fell by half, and very quickly. Languages are always changing. Languages are also all fundamentally equal. If a speaker of any language has something that they want to say, they can communicate that idea, so languages are all fundamentally equal in that way as well.

Some languages have a larger vocabulary than others in certain domains. Technology in English, for example, we have this huge vocabulary of technological words that some other languages don't have, but when those languages need to refer to that computer or to that software, or whatever it may be, they come up with a word. In Kaqchikel Maya, the language in which I worked, for example, until not long ago there was one word, *ch'ich*, for all metal things—it could be a typewriter; it could be a bus. If it was metal it was called *ch'ich*, but today, as more Maya are becoming educated, as more Maya are participating in the modern economy, they have elaborate vocabularies, not only for cars and typewriters but for computers and software, so when there's a need for someone to say something, when there's a need for language to communicate an idea, that language can always be flexible enough to meet it.

Anthropological linguists work mostly with undescribed languages, undocumented languages, and a lot of what they do is writing dictionaries, writing grammars, recording these languages for posterity. In describing languages—technical linguistics, we can call it—we can break this down into several different components, the most fundamental of which are sounds, different sounds and languages. I would like to introduce two vocabulary terms here, *phonemics* and *phonetics*. Phonemics refers to the sounds that a native speaker hears. Phonetics refers to the more objective qualities of the sound waves. You remember early on, we made this distinction between emic and etic, emic being the view from within the culture, and this comes from phonemic, and phonetic gives rise to etic, the more objective, the more scientific, the outside view.

Just as we learn to divide up the color spectrum into meaningful segments—red, yellow, green, blue and so forth—we also learn to break up the sound spectrum into meaningful segments as well, A, E, I, O, and U, and these are culturally specific. There are very few cultural universals in terms of language; all languages, for example, distinguish between vowels and consonants. But beyond that, there's a huge range of variation, and not every language recognizes the same sounds. In Japanese, for example, they don't recognize the difference phonemically, from within the culture, between Rs and Ls, something that sounds very distinct to an English speaker, but for a Japanese speaker it doesn't sound very distinct. In Spanish, we find the same thing with V and B; they don't really hear this distinction, and so it's very hard when they learn English that makes a clear distinction between V and B. In my own dialect—I'm from the south; I grew up in Alabama—in my own dialect of English, we refer to this as a pen [pronounced pin], the same word that we would use for the sewing instrument, a pin. We sew with a pin, and I write with a pen. In many dialects of English, there would be a clear phonetic distinction between those two sounds.

There are also tonal languages, and in tonal languages the inflection changes the meaning of a word, and the most famous example comes from Chinese, which is a tonal language, where the word which is transcribed in English *ma*—we would pronounce as ma—can mean four different things. You can say ma, which is mother; you can say ma, which is linen; you could say ma, which is horse; or you could say ma, which is scold. Depending on how just this one-syllable word is inflected, it changes the difference, and lots of students of Chinese, English speakers learning Chinese, have said things like, "My horse and my father and my brothers and sisters, we all live together in one happy family." These tonal differences are very hard for native English speakers, for example, to learn; if you don't learn these sound differences early on in life, they're very hard to pick up later on.

Another interesting phonetic structure we find in sub-Saharan languages called click languages, and here there are a number of sounds, clicking sounds. For example, you have [click click], you have [click click], sounds like this that are difficult. English speakers can make these sounds, but it's very difficult to put them in a word. Try and put these sounds in the middle of a word, and our tongues just can't seem to wrap around it. So if you don't hear the sounds of a language before the age of six, maybe seven, maybe eight, and maybe as late as 12 years old, you can never fully internalize the phonetic maps of these other languages.

Most languages, as I said, are unwritten. Written languages are really the exception rather than the rule, although we associate writing with language these days, but in terms of written languages there are three main types, and these are logographic, meaning that one sign stands for a word or an idea; syllabic, a sign stands for a syllable; or alphabetic, like our own system. In logographic systems, the problem is, you have to have an immense number of characters to represent all of the words in the language. Let's take Chinese again as an example. Chinese is commonly called a logographic language, although actually it's a combination of logographic and phonetic elements. Chinese has 1,300 logographic components; it's an incredible barrier for people trying to learn this language. The benefit to this is that speakers of Cantonese and Mandarin though can look at the same symbol and pronounce it in their own language, so it's not as closely tied to the sound patterns.

Syllabic languages first arose with the Phoenicians. Mayan hieroglyphs are syllabic, for example, and they represent a vowel-consonant combination, with one sign, and English famously is alphabetical. It's alphabetic, only 26 characters; we have 26 characters in our alphabet to represent the whole range of words and sounds that we can make, so alphabetic systems are much more flexible and much more streamlined in this manner, although there's always a slippage between the alphabetic sign, not always but there can be, slippage between the alphabetic sign and the sounds that it produces. My five-year-old daughter, for example, thinks that *car* is spelled with a K, and we learn over time when to pronounce a C as a K and when to pronounce it as an S sound. We learn all of these variants, but it's not necessarily given in the alphabetic character itself.

Linguists study phonetic differences and phonemic differences between languages. They study how these phonemes are combined to create morphemes, and morphemes are the minimal units of meaning, usually a word, but it doesn't have to be a word. Bike is a morpheme, but if we add an S to that, bikes, it becomes a two-morpheme word, so linguists look at how phonemes are combined to create morphemes, how morphemes are combined to create words, and how words are combined through the rules of syntax and grammar. Grammar is basically the rules of the language, how you put words together to make meaningful sentences. All languages have a grammar; not all languages have a *Little Brown Handbook*, not all languages have a *Chicago Manual of Style*, not all languages have a written grammar, but all languages have a grammar.

These grammars differ rather dramatically. If you've ever tried to learn German or Chinese, you'll appreciate the vast differences in grammars in different languages, but functionally they're equal, and this gets back to a point that we made earlier in the lecture, that any language can communicate any idea, so functionally grammars all serve the same purpose, creating common rules that everybody can understand in order to facilitate communication. The linguist Noam Chomsky has argued that humans are not only born with a capacity for language but really what he calls a black box in the brain which produces grammar, and he says that there is some sort of proto-grammar that's innate in human brains. Is grammar innate? I'm not sure. Do humans have an innate capacity for language? Most certainly. The language that humans learn, however, is precisely that: it's what they learn; it's not given at birth in any way.

So linguists study phonetics, they study grammar. Linguists also study semantics, the meanings of words, not just the dictionary meanings but the subtle shades of meanings that particular words can carry. For language to work, there has to be some fundamental agreement about what words mean. Right? This is the whole purpose of communication; we all agree what certain words mean. But a lot of times there's slippage here as well. Take, for example, have you ever had the experience of using a word perhaps frequently and then discovering that you don't really know what it means? You may have read it in a newspaper, you read it in a book, you intuited the meaning of the word from the context, and then it turns out later that that's not really the word, but it suited you very well to use it in your own particular idiosyncratic way, so these sort of things happen all the time.

We have phonetics, we have grammar, we have semantics, the meanings of words, but linguists have also been turning recently to the study of body language, and they point out that a lot of what we communicate actually happens nonverbally. In some studies, they estimate that as much as 80 percent of the information communicated happens nonverbally, and this can happen in a variety of ways through body language, which we call kinesics, body language. Do you speak to someone with your arms folded or do you speak to someone with your arms open? What sorts of subtle signs are you giving to the people that you're communicating with? One interesting thing that I read not long ago is that if you raise your eyebrows, and we subconsciously do this when we meet somebody, or when you see somebody that you like a lot, you unconsciously raise your eyebrows, and so we can use these things to manipulate social situations as well. Next time you meet somebody, raise your eyebrows and see if the interaction happens any differently.

So body language, a lot is communicated by body language, a lot is communicated by proxemics, how we stand in relation to the person that we're communicating with. In the U.S., we have a fairly big comfort bubble. We need to have two or four feet between us and a person that we're having a casual conversation with. In other cultures around the world, that comfort bubble is much smaller, and if you've ever traveled, if you've traveled in Latin America, for example, you may feel uncomfortable when everybody comes up and puts their arms around you and touches you in a way that we would consider to be very intimate, but for them it's just a natural way of showing their friendship and their appreciation. This can result in a sort of ballet in certain situations.

There was a study done of different banks in New York City, and this graduate student went to a really WASP bank, a really white bank, where all of the clientele were white, and then she went to a bank in an Italian neighborhood in New York City, and what she would do is she would stand in the teller line and she would get gradually closer to the person in front of her, and when she was at this WASP bank, she would basically end up chasing these patrons around the bank. As she got closer, they would move away, and she would get closer and they would move away still, and then when she went to the bank in the Italian neighborhood, she could practically be hugging the person in front of her and they wouldn't move, so there was this very different cultural sense of space and what's appropriate.

We can apply this to all sorts of things, office design, how our office is designed, what is the height of the chair of the person behind the desk and the person in front of the desk, for example. In my office at my university, I have a chair that's very, very low that students sit in, and I sit in a normal chair, and this creates this very subtle power differential between us. So there are all sort of ways in which proxemics can facilitate, often in subtle ways, but facilitate communication and communicate lots of ideas. So that's the basic overview of what linguists do.

But I'd like to talk to you specifically about language and what language is. We generally consider language to be uniquely human. This is something that only humans have, is language, but what is then language? The linguist Charles Hockett tried to come up with a list of features that define language as uniquely human. He came up with a total of about 13, although I'm only going to go over a few here today. Hockett argues that language is one—it's an open system; it's not a closed system. Chimpanzee communication is what we call a call system; they can only say a limited number of things. Bees can communicate, but they can only say a limited number of things. In human language, we can say an infinite number of things. It's an open system; it's productive. We routinely make up entirely new constructions. Think of some of the great literary figures in the world: James Joyce. Reading *Ulysses*, this is so difficult because he's really using the productivity of language, putting words together in a totally new way, or

Allen Ginsberg's *Howl*. We can all think of literary pioneers in this way. Language is an open system; it's not a closed system.

The second feature is displacement. Human language can talk about things that are not in the here and now. We can talk about the past; we can make up fictions; we can talk about our hopes and dreams for tomorrow and the future. Animal closed systems can't do this. And it's a fundamental feature of human languages. We can teach a dog to bark on a certain command, but we can't teach that dog to bark tomorrow if it's raining, for example, so there's a fundamental limitation in closed systems and other forms of communication in terms of displacement. Third, we have arbitrariness, that language is arbitrary. The symbol and sound combination that we use, that we link together in language, is arbitrary. You can call this furry, four-legged creature a dog; you can call it a hound in Germany; you could call it a perro in Spanish. All of these are perfectly good words and we just agree that we're going to use those words to refer to this object, but there's an arbitrary relationship there.

There's not a natural relationship between the words that we use and what is denoted by those. This is something that was actually given to us by Ferdinand de Saussure, the father of scientific linguistics, of modern linguistics, and he said that we can divide signs up into two components. In a sign, you have the signifier, and that could be a symbol, it could be a word, it can be a written word, it can be a spoken word, and then you have the signified, and the signified is the thing that is being referred to, and Saussure, one of his important contributions was to make this distinction, that there's an arbitrary relationship between the signifier, the word that we use, and the signified, the object that we're referring to. Can you think of any exceptions? When I ask my students, most of the time they say, "Well, what about onomatopoetic words? What about animal sounds?" Even here, if you studied foreign languages, you'll know that even here foreign languages have different sounds for different animals. In Spanish, for example, a rooster says *kikirikí*, whereas in English it says *cockle-doodle-doo*, so even onomatopoetic words share this quality of arbitrariness.

Studies with apes have shown that with intensive training apes, chimpanzees, and gorillas can be taught rudimentary language skills, and here I'd like to mention two in particular. The first is Washoe, and this was a chimp who was trained first at the University of Nevada and then moved to the University of Oklahoma, and work was done with Washoe in the 1960s. She was taught a modified version of American Sign Language. They worked with her for about four years, and, all in all, she learned 150 different signs and could communicate basic ideas, so we have Washoe, the chimp, and Koko. Koko, the gorilla, now lives in a foundation in California. Koko was born in 1971. She was first in the San Francisco Zoo and then she was taken for research at this private foundation, and researchers have worked with Koko for over 25 years, also teaching her a modified version of American Sign Language, and she now has a vocabulary of over 1,000 words.

I bring this up at this point because work with these apes has made us question some of Hockett's list of what is distinctly human about language. Let's take productivity, first of all, that we can produce totally new linguistic phrases to encompass new ideas. We find this among these apes. Washoe, for example, when she first saw a fur coat, called it a hair coat. This seems pretty basic, a hair coat, but she took two words that she knew previously from other contexts and put them together to describe something that she'd never seen before. She was being productive in her language use. The first time she saw a candy bar she called it a sweet banana, again using two words that she had known before and putting them together in a different way. We've also seen productivity with Koko, the gorilla. The first time, Koko was out on a field trip one day and saw a duck for the first time and signed to his trainer "water bird," and the trainers just went crazy because, again, a sign of productive speech.

Let's take displacement. Koko's erstwhile mate, companion, recently died, was Michael, another gorilla that was captured in the wild as an infant. It was captured while it was an infant in Vienna, and eventually mated to this foundation in California, and at one point Koko taught Michael a lot of signs. The trainers also taught Michael a lot of signs, and at one point he described seeing his mother being killed, and it's assumed that his mother was killed by poachers and that as an infant he was taken away and sold, but this describes displacement. He was able to talk about something not in the here and now, something way back when, displacement.

So Hockett and others started adding to this list of features that make language uniquely human. Language has to be uniquely human, so let's add to this list of features, and one thing they added was prevarication, lying. Only in human language can you lie, but actually we've seen evidence of this as well. Koko, unbeknownst to her, was filmed all the time, 24 hours a day, a little video camera in the corner of her, you can't really call it a cage—she really lives in a room—and one night she broke her feeding bowl, and the next morning her trainer comes in and says, "What happened to the bowl?" and she signs back, "The other trainer did it," and she didn't realize that she was being filmed, but she lied. She lied because she was embarrassed about what had happened.

We've also seen in the wild—we have evidence of lying among chimpanzees in the wild. Chimpanzees have been seen to find a slaughtered animal, let's say an antelope that a lion has killed, eaten part of and then left, and sometimes chimpanzees will call out a warning signal to the rest of their troop, saying, "Watch out, there's a lion in the area." Everybody leaves, all the other chimps leave. This chimp comes down, gorges on the antelope meat and then presumably comes back to the troop later and says, "Yeah, that lion just left. I don't know what happened to him." We find lying, we find displacement, we find productivity, all of these among apes who have learned variants of American Sign Language. Nonetheless, Koko, Washoe, the other apes who have been studied this way, they never get beyond the vocabulary of a three- or four- or maybe a five-year-old human. They never reach beyond a few hundred words. Koko is the most, with a thousand-word vocabulary today, so it's still very limited, but they do share some of these characteristics with human languages.

There are 6,000 languages spoken in the world today. The most widely spoken are Mandarin Chinese, Hindu, English, and Spanish. English is by far the most widely spoken language if we include second-language speakers as well for whom English is a second language. In some places, especially where there are dramatic ecological geographic barriers to communication between communities, we find high densities of different languages. For example, in Highland New Guinea, there are hundreds, perhaps as many as 900 different languages spoken in this little area of Highland New Guinea because the geography is so grand. One community couldn't communicate very effectively with the community on the other side of the hill, and so over time they develop distinctive variants. In Guatemala, where I work with the Maya, there are 21 separate Mayan languages spoken, not dialects, languages, 21 languages spoken, and this is in a country smaller than the size of the state of Tennessee.

But what is a language and what is a dialect? Languages, if one speaks a different language, it implies mutual unintelligibility. You cannot understand what the other person is saying. In contrast, a dialect implies mutual intelligibility. It's a variant of the language, but we can still understand what is being said, and the variations can be phonemic, they can be grammatical, they can be in terms of vocabulary intonation, body language. We can have all sorts of dialectical variations. Language is not mutually intelligible from others, but there are a lot of gradations here.

Swedish and Norwegian, for example, are considered to be separate languages, and yet among good-willed speakers they can understand each other, but there's this whole history of political conflict between the two countries that leads them to establish themselves or promote themselves as being two separate languages.

Spanish and Portuguese, a bit greater distance there, but again among good-willed speakers. I'm a pretty good speaker of Spanish, and I can follow a basic Portuguese conversation, and so where is that line then between a separate language and a dialect? We often speak of the Chinese language, but of course there are many Chinese languages, Mandarin and Cantonese, for example, and it's a very powerful political statement to talk about the Chinese language, grouping all of these heterogeneous groups together as a single entity. The linguist Max Wienreich famously defined a language as a dialect with a navy. A language is a dialect with a navy, and what he was getting at here is that language distinctions are really very often political distinctions as well. It's not based on science.

There is a science to this to distinguish between a dialect and a language, and the way in which we do this is judging the percentage of cognates, and cognate words, or words that have the same root or can be recognized as being the same cognates—hound in English and hound in Germany for example—so we can look at the percentage of cognates between two languages or two dialects and we can create a cutoff point. For example, if these two variants have less than 70 percent shared cognates, they're separate languages, or we could say 80 percent, or we could say 90 percent. But at some point we can draw a line and say this is a separate language and not just a dialectical variation. But where do we draw the line? It seems very scientific to use percentages like that, but where do we draw that line? It ultimately becomes arbitrary. Is 70 percent a common vocabulary? Is that a different language, 80 percent? 90 percent? Who knows?

Languages and dialects can serve as very powerful identity markers. Languages are not easily learned; they're not easily shirked off—we don't lose a language very easily—so they can serve as powerful symbols of a person's cultural heritage, and we use them this way. In English, take English English, British English, a public school dialect versus a commoner dialect. This tells a lot about a person; the way in which the person speaks tells a lot about that person. In English, we refer to Standard English as SAE, American English, Standard American English, this non-descript, Midwestern dialect of standard American English, and this is the most highly valued form of English in the United States. A number of studies have been done showing that people have prejudices against those with strong Southern accents, strong Northeastern accents. Any sort of strong accent invokes a number of stereotypes about the person who is speaking.

One interesting study was done by the linguist William Labov, who went around to different department stores in New York City looking at whether the final "r" in a word was pronounced, if people would pronounce the final "r" in "floor," for example, and he found that at Saks Fifth Avenue, all of the shoppers and all of the storekeepers would pronounce this final "r," and he said that this was a sign of a certain socio-economic status, a high status. He found at Klein's, a much lower-priced department store in New York City, that hardly anybody pronounced this "r," again an indicator of socio-economic status. We could talk about black vernacular English, also encompassing lots of stereotypes about how people speak and about who they are.

We've looked at a great diversity of language. Even if Noam Chomsky argues that there's a common foundational grammar, there's a great diversity of languages spoken in the world, but we communicate not only with words but with body language as well. Not only what we say but how we say it, our language, our dialect, tells a lot about our social identity and about our politics in cases as well. While the capacity for language may be innate, its realization is always a unique, creative, productive process.

Lecture Seven
Language and Thought

Scope: Can you think of something that you cannot put into words? To what extent is thought determined by language? The linguist Benjamin Lee Whorf argues that linguistic structures actually determine the way we look at the world. He asserts that the way Hopi grammar treats verb tenses, for example, results in what whites perceive as a lackadaisical attitude toward time. In a similar vein, scholars have shown how American men and women speak subtly different varieties of English (resulting in much miscommunication) and how common metaphors in American English (such as "time is money") shape the way we think about the world around us.

The way we talk to one another—our discourse strategies—shapes and reflects our social relationships. In this light, discourse analysis uncovers the often hidden power structures encoded in everyday speech.

Outline

I. The Sapir-Whorf hypothesis posits that language structures the way we look at the world.

   A. Benjamin Lee Whorf (1897–1941), a part-time linguist and fire insurance investigator, conducted influential work to examine how language structures influence thought.

       1. In a wonderful piece titled "Blazing Icicles," he shows how semantic misunderstandings led to a number of easily preventable fires.

       2. He also proposed that Hopi conceptions of time (not as linear and rigid as ours) have led to their characterization as "lazy Indians," unable to keep to a schedule.

   B. Whorf studied linguistics under Edward Sapir and took his inspiration from Sapir's writings about language.

       1. The line of thought he developed has come to be known as the *Sapir-Whorf hypothesis*, and it has two main variants.

    2. The strong version of the Sapir-Whorf hypothesis (or the linguistic determinism approach) posits that linguistic structures (vocabulary and grammar) determine the way one can think.

    3. The weak version (or linguistic relativity) holds simply that linguistic categories and structures influence thought (and are, in turn, influenced by it).

    4. The context in which languages arise necessitates certain vocabulary differences—Inuit have many words for *snow*; the Bedouins many words for *sand.*

    5. In Mayan languages, certain numerical classifiers are grammatically required, which may influence worldview.

II. Research on metaphors and discourse strategies shows the real-world implications of language use.

    A. Recent research by linguist Deborah Tannen has found a number of gender-specific forms of speech.

        1. Women tend to speak more indirectly, asking rather than commanding and hedging many of their assertions.

        2. Such indirect speech is associated with women but often employed by men as well.

        3. Flight recorder data from a 1982 Air Florida crash shows how indirect speech may have devastating effects.

    B. George Lakoff and Mark Johnson argue, in *Metaphors We Live By*, that certain core metaphors in American English structure the way we think about the world.

        1. One key metaphor is "time is money," in which time is treated as a valuable commodity, an object that can be spent, wasted, saved, invested, and so on.

        2. "Argument is war" is another salient metaphor that shapes the way we argue and think about argument.

III. Discourse analysis examines real speech as used in particular contexts. We all use—often unknowingly—a number of discourse strategies and shortcuts.

    A. But language is not simply enacting scripts—we use language actively and creatively. In this light, it is useful to look for broad strategies that individuals employ in their interactions.

B. Presuppositions are a powerful rhetorical tool and may be used to mark in-group versus out-group (with a private joke, for example) or establish social distance.

    1. To save face, we often employ varieties of pre-invitations—subtly checking to see if an invitation would be accepted before proffering it (e.g., "What are you doing Saturday night?").

    2. Examining turn-taking in a conversation can reveal a lot about the power dynamics between the individuals.

Readings:

George Lakoff and Mark Johnson, *Metaphors We Live By*.

Deborah Tannen, *You Just Don't Understand: Women and Men in Conversation*.

Benjamin Whorf, *Language, Thought, and Reality*.

Questions to Consider:

1. How do men and women speak differently? Is this a serious barrier to communication?

2. How can the categories given by our language mold the way we think about things?

3. How much of our daily speech is scripted and how much is improvised?

Lecture Seven—Transcript
Language and Thought

As we said last time, the language and dialect we speak can tell others a lot about who we are, and this is a symbolic quality, independent of what's being said. In fact, it might overshadow what's being said in certain contexts, but language, of course, also serves as a vehicle for communication, and so in this lecture we're going to look at the relationship between languages, how we communicate, and thought, what we want to communicate. Can you think of something that you cannot say? Can you think of something that you can't put into words? If so, the responses that I normally give are that it's an emotion, "I'm so mad I can't speak," "I'm so in love with you that words escape me," or perhaps it's a visual or an auditory impression, a painting or a piece of music that touches you in ways that are impossible to fully articulate.

But given these exceptions, to a large extent, our language does mediate our thought. We don't simply express ourselves through language; we also think through language in many ways. Language gives us the categories, the vocabularies, the verb structure and so on that frame not only how we talk but how we perceive the world. We see green where other cultures might see blue because of the linguistic category that we've constructed called green. In this lecture, we examine the ways in which language influences thought. We're going to look specifically at the Sapir-Whorf hypothesis and the ways we construct ourselves and present themselves linguistically, such as in men's and women's speech, and the role of metaphors in the way in which we look at the world.

I'd like to begin by discussing the work of Benjamin Lee Whorf. He was born in 1897; he died in 1941. He got his degree from the Massachusetts Institute of Technology, a B.S. in chemical engineering in 1918. After graduation, he went to work for the Hartford Fire Insurance Company as a trainee and fire prevention engineer, and after graduation he kept up with his interest in linguistics, so he studied on his own. He studied Hebrew; he studied Nahuatl, the language of the Aztecs. He studied Maya; he even traveled to southern Mexico to look at Mayan cliffs. And he took a few classes from Edward Sapir at Yale, and Sapir was a student of Boas's. Whorf remained with the Hartford Fire Insurance Company for the rest of his short life, developing a national reputation as an expert in industrial fire prevention.

He authored several articles on fire prevention, including one titled "Blazing Icicles," and this offered a linguistic interpretation of fire prevention; it's probably the most readable fire prevention report ever written. He looked at a couple of case studies in particular. At one, there was a warehouse that had burned down in a fire, and so he goes and investigates, and he finds out that what they would do is, they used in their production process, they used gas, and they would take empty containers and put them on the loading dock, and they were labeled as empty gas containers. On the same loading dock is where the workers would come out and take their breaks, and one day a worker was out taking a break, smoking a cigarette, and flipped his cigarette into these empty gas containers, which promptly blew up of course and burned down the building.

Now what Whorf said was that the seeds of this disaster lay in the semantics of empty. Empty means both without its usual contents and null and void or inert. Here these gas containers were without their usual contents. They weren't filled up with liquid gas, but they were all the more dangerous because of that, because an empty gas can is actually full of gas vapors, which are more flammable than the liquid gas was in the first place, and so it was a linguistic, a semantic slip, that allowed for this disaster to take place. He looked at a couple of other instances like this, instances of inflammable, labels saying inflammable being confused, because it's a very confusing word. Inflammable means flammable; it throws us off because this in- prefix usually means a negation, inconsistent, incoherent, so why inflammable? He showed that it led to a number of fire disasters.

Spun limestone, he gave another example of a factory that used spun limestone that people would treat very carelessly because it was stone, it's limestone, but actually this particular product, spun limestone, when it's heated up produces acetone, which is very volatile, can catch fire very easily, and so he was looking in "Blazing Icicles" at these cases where linguistic misunderstandings led to fire disasters. The categories employed by a language, he argued, determined the way in which people looked at the world. The words these workers were using influenced their behavior and led to these disasters. This line of thought that he developed has come to be known as the Sapir-Whorf hypothesis. It's probably more accurate to call it the Whorfian hypothesis; he took a sentence from a book written by Edward Sapir and expanded on that and made this whole theoretical structure.

The Sapir-Whorf hypothesis, or the Whorfian hypothesis, if you will, says that the structure of a language determines cognition. The way we think about the world, and thus culture, is given to us by the structures of our language. The Sapir-Whorf hypothesis has two main variants. We can talk about the strong version and the weak version. The strong version of the Sapir-Whorf hypothesis, also called linguistic determinism, posits that linguistic structures, vocabulary and grammar, determine the way in which one can think. The strong version, linguistic structures determine the way in which one can think. Probably the best example of this comes to us from literature, in George Orwell's novel *1984* and the language Newspeak, which was developed to enforce the ideology of the society that Orwell described in *1984*. Let me read just a short passage here because it illustrates so nicely the strong version of the Sapir-Whorf hypothesis.

"The purpose of Newspeak was not only to provide a medium of expression for the world view and mental habits proper to the devotees of Insoc, but to make all other modes of thought impossible. A thought diverging from the principles of Insoc should be literally unthinkable, at least so far as thought is dependent on words." Its vocabulary was so constructed as to give exact and often very subtle expression to every meaning that a party member could properly wish to express while excluding all other means, language determining thought in this case, the strong version of the Sapir-Whorf hypothesis. The weak version of the Sapir-Whorf hypothesis, which is much more palatable and is also called linguistic relativity, holds simply that there is a relationship between language and thought, that language influences the way in which we think and that the way in which we think influences language. This weak version is the most accepted version; it still doesn't resolve this chicken and egg question, however, of what comes first, thought or words.

Now Whorf used a couple of different lines of evidence to support his hypothesis, and the first came from vocabulary. He famously noted that Eskimos have more words for types of snow than English speakers do, and he deduced that therefore Eskimos must perceive of snow differently. This is an example that has come to take on apocryphal proportions in anthropology. Sometimes you'll read in introductory textbooks that there are 100 different Eskimo words for snow, this word that we only have a single word for in English. We can trace this back, however, to the work of Franz Boas, and in 1911 he published *The Handbook of North American Indians* and he noted that Eskimos have four different words for snow, where English just had one.

The Eskimo have *aput*, means on the ground; *gana*, falling snow; *piqsirpoq*, drifting snow; or *qimuqsuq* for a snowdrift. In English, we can make these decisions, but we need a phrase to make a distinction, where Eskimo just have the one word, so Whorf latches onto this idea that he read in Boas's booked and then takes off with it, and he publishes an article in 1940 called "Science and Linguistics," and let me quote from him here. He writes, "We have the same word for falling snow, snow on the ground, snow packed hard like ice, slushy snow, wind-driven flying snow, whatever the situation may be. To an Eskimo, this all-inclusive word would be almost unthinkable. He would say that falling snow, slushy snow, and so on are sensuously and operationally different, different things to contend with. He uses different words for them and for other kinds of snow."

You'll notice here that he's taken Boas's observation that there are four Eskimo words for snow and sort of made it a little bit more nebulous, so it sounds like there are more than four words for snow. There's been a lot of controversy in anthropological linguistics about this. Exactly how many Eskimo words for snow are there? It turns out that the Eskimo have certain prefixes and suffixes that can make words look like different words when they're actually just variants of the same word. One linguist that I read not long ago estimates that, in fact, there are probably about 12 to15 words in the Inuit language for snow, and in fact this isn't so different from English. Think of English words for snow: avalanche; blizzard; a dusting; a flurry; frost; hail; hard-packed snow. We have a fairly extensive vocabulary as well, although it varies. It varies on how much you need to use that vocabulary. Skiers have a very extensive vocabulary for snow. English speakers living in Miami probably have a minimal vocabulary for snow, so it depends on the need to use those words. It doesn't mean that English speakers don't perceive of different types of snow, but Eskimo speakers have more of a reason, a need, to use these fine gradations.

We can use this line of reasoning, this vocabulary line of reasoning, to talk about other words as well. In Brazilian Portuguese, for example, there's a word, *saudade*, and it means—it's hard to translate into English—it means a longing, a sort of nostalgia, but it's like a pleasurable feeling tinged with regret or with pain. We don't have a good word for this in English, and not having a good word for it, and it being a very salient and often- used word in Brazilian Portuguese, tells us that there's something going on here. There's something about Brazil and about Brazilians that we can learn because of their emphasis on this word. It doesn't mean that English speakers don't feel the same sort of emotion, but that it is more salient for Portuguese speakers.

Or take the German word *Schadenfreude*; it's the secret delight that one takes in the misfortunes of a friend. Say you have a friend who has a very healthy ego, and some small misfortune—they don't get the raise that they were looking for; they don't get the contract that they were looking for—and you might take a little secret delight in the back of your mind. "I'm glad nothing really bad happened to him, but he needed to be put in his place." Schadenfreude, we've probably all experienced this at one time or another. We don't have a good English word for it; we borrow the German word. It doesn't mean that we don't experience this emotion, but it's not as salient in our own language. There are differences in vocabulary; whether these determine different ways of looking at the world is very much open to question, but they do indicate important differences between cultures.

Whorf's more radical claim concerned grammar. He argued, based on somewhat questionable translations of Hopi, the North American Indian language of Arizona, Whorf argued that they don't have the tense system; they don't have past, present, and future tenses that he assumed to be a sort of natural way of things, or at least the way in which English is organized, so whereas in English we see it is quite natural to say "I saw the girl, I see the girl, I will see the girl," in Hopi those sorts of distinctions aren't made, at least not in the same way. Whorf also argued that the Hopi don't break time up into units the way in which English speakers do. What he used this for, to argue for, and a really neat thing, that the image of a lazy Indian that the Anglos in Arizona and the southwest held about the Hopi was really based on different grammatical structures of verb tenses, and it wasn't that Indians were lazy; they just conceived of time in a different way.

Subsequent research has shown that Whorf actually misunderstood Hopi Indians in fundamental ways. They don't have the same sort of past, present, future tenses that we have in English; instead, they have what are known as validity markers, and so in Hopi, rather than putting a verb tense, you will say whether something is mythic, whether something is known to be true, or whether something is conjectural. These don't make the same distinctions that our verb tenses make in English, but they can get at the same sort of idea. It's a similar kind of categorization. Future events, for example, are always conjectural. Events in the past, which one doesn't know for sure happened, are conjectural as well, so there's a little bit of play there, but more or less you can get the idea of past, present, and future.

Whorf himself observed, "The Hopi language is capable of counting for and correctly describing all observable phenomenon in the universe." Yes, and this has precisely been the critique of Whorf. Yes, Hopi can describe all observable phenomena in the universe; so can every other language. Therefore, how much can language dictate what we think? But that's the critique of Whorf, and I'm going to come back to more critiques in just a moment, but let me give you one more example, and this comes from Yucatec Maya, and I take this example from the worker Victoria Bricker. In Yucatec Maya, there's an obligatory grammatical category called numerical classifiers. This means that every time you mention a number of some object—one, two, three, 500, 1,000, whatever it may be—any time you number an object, you have to use this descriptive classifier with it.

To give you an idea of what these are, at one point there were a couple of hundred of these. Today used in everyday Yucatec speech, there are a couple of dozen, and they're things like elongated, handful of, a chunk of, torn piece, a slice, a slab, a bite. Any time you talk about a plural, or even a singular, if you number an object, you have to use one of these modifiers with it. Therefore, when a Yucatec speaker talks about three bananas, for example, he or she cannot simply say three bananas, as you would in English. It always has to be modified: three elongated bananas, or three chunks of banana, or three torn pieces of banana. It always has to be modified by one of these numerical classifiers. I would think that Yucatec speakers therefore not only talk about bananas differently, they see them differently. English speakers can see these differences as well, but we don't have to invoke them every time we talk about bananas, but Yucatec speakers do, and so certainly this leads to a different way of perceiving the world.

The linguist Steven Pinker has summarized very effectively a number of arguments against the Sapir-Whorf hypothesis. He notes that first, supposed limitations on expressions in various languages are almost inevitably based on faulty linguistics, such as Whorf's misunderstanding of Hopi. The Hopi do in fact have words for time; the Hopi can in fact talk about time in different ways. Second, that thought is possible without language. We talked about emotions a moment ago, or things that you may see or hear that impact you enough in a non-linguistic or a pre-linguistic way. Babies can think, certainly they can, but they don't have language yet, so thought is possible without language. Finally, language is an inadequate medium for communicating thought. Language always contains ambiguity; what I try and say—I try and be as clear as possible in giving these lectures, for example, but there's always going to be a bit of ambiguity, and what you perceive is going to be different slightly at some points, maybe radically at other points, but it's going to be different than what I intend to say.

While it's difficult to say to what extent language influences thought, there's certainly some sort of relationship here. It's probably not determinate—language doesn't determine thought—but there's a back-and-forth between language and thought, and in this respect it's interesting to look at the recent work done on gender and language. Here I refer particularly to the work of Deborah Tannen, the linguist Deborah Tannen, who's looked at men's speech and women's speech in the United States. She makes a distinction between two types of discourse strategies. One is called rapport, and she associates this more with women, and the other she calls report talk.

In rapport, there's much more of a back-and-forth going on between the two interlocutors, so for example a woman will back-channel (this is a term we use in linguistics) back-channel a lot. When she's conversing with someone, she will give little indicators that she's following along with the arguments and the conversation. It could be nodding the head, it could be saying "Right, uh-huh, yeah," things like this to remain engaged in this back-and-forth of rapport talk, which Tannen associates more with women.

If this doesn't occur, a woman will often use confirmation requests, will ask for her interlocutor to do this, so if somebody's not back-channeling and nodding their head and saying "Right, uh-huh, yeah," then a woman will ask for these by saying. "Right? Huh? What do you think?" or using a final rise in intonation. This is particularly prevalent in teenage girls. "We went to the movies," and it's a statement, it's supposed to be a declarative statement, but it sounds like a question because you rise in intonation. It's asking the person that you're telling the story to, "Give me some help; give me a sign that you're still alive. Nod your head; say yes," and Tannen argues that this is more important for women than it is for men. She argues that men have much more of a direct way of speaking, and this is report talk.

This ties in to another distinction that she makes between men's and women's speech, that women tend to speak more indirectly and men tend to speak more directly. We can see this, and there's a continuum here of directness and indirectness. Tannen says let's take commands, for example. A very direct command would be "Take the garbage out," and then we could move toward more indirect speech: "Take the garbage out, please." "Could you take the garbage out?" "Would you take the garbage out?" Then we can move to the other extreme, a very indirect speech: "The garbage can's full," so not saying what you really want to communicate, "Please take the garbage can out," but just noting this and allowing the other person, "What's today?" "Today's Tuesday." "When does the garbage man come?" something like that, a very indirect way of communicating these ideas.

Tannen also notes that indirect speech includes lots of hedges, and these are qualifications, "I think," "That's what I think," or perhaps things like this to sort of hedge what we're saying, to make it a little bit less direct. She associates this with men's and women's speech, and she's made her career showing how men and women miscommunicate very often in relationships, but it's not that easily divisible. Lots of men have indirect speech patterns. I'm from the south of the United States, and we have more indirect speech than people from the northeast or people from the west, for example. There are lots of women who speak very directly, so we can't correlate this exactly with gender, but there does seem to be some overlap. It also occurs that subordinates tend to talk to their superiors in indirect speech, and superiors talk to their subordinates using direct speech.

This can lead to some problems, and there was research done by a linguist named Charlotte Linde, and she's at the Institute for Research and Learning in Palo Alto, California, and what she's done is analyze the black box recording from airplane crashes. One in particular I'd like to go over today. This occurred on January 13, 1982; it was an Air Florida crash, left from Washington National (today Reagan National), left from Washington National Airport, took off. Just a few seconds after takeoff it crashes into the Potomac. It was in the middle of a winter storm, the Potomac was icy, and 74 out of the 79 people on board died. It turns out later the reason, the cause for the crash, was that ice had formed on the wings. The plane had waited too long after being de-iced. Then it took off, and the rudders and flaps couldn't move, and it crashed into the Potomac.

What Charlotte Linde has done is look at the black box recordings from this flight, and let me read you a little bit of the transcript, and take note of the indirect speech that the copilot is using to communicate his concerns to the pilots.

Copilot: Look at how the hot ice is just hanging there, on this back there. You see that?

Pause. No response. Pause.

Copilot: See all those icicles on the back there and everything?

Captain: Yeah.

Copilot: Boy, this is a losing battle here, trying to de-ice those things. It gives you a false sense of security; that's all it does.

Pause. No response from the pilot. Then they're given clearance for takeoff.

Copilot: Let's check those tops again since we've been sitting here a while.

Captain: I think we're good to go here in a minute.

Copilot: That doesn't seem right, does it? That's not right.

Captain: Yes, it is; there's 80.

Copilot: No, I don't think that's right; maybe it is.

Captain: 120.

Copilot: I don't know.

And then they take off; 37 seconds later, they've crashed, and they haven't communicated anymore. The copilot knew what was going to happen or he suspected what was going to happen, and if he had communicated more directly, rather than using these indirect forms of speech, if he had told the captain, "Hey, I'm not taking off. I'm getting off of this plane because this is dangerous," this could have been averted. It's interesting the way in which indirect speech and direct speech can be used to communicate and miscommunicate with each other.

More sophisticated interpretations of linguistic determinism have recently been produced by scholars such as George Lakoff and Mark Johnson, and they wrote a wonderful little book—it was published in 1980—*Metaphors We Live By*. They argue that there are certain central metaphors in the English language and that these metaphors condition the way in which we think about and thus act in the world. My favorite example that they give is that time is money. In American English they say there's an overarching metaphor that time is money, or that time is a valuable commodity. Based on this overarching metaphor, we create a whole substructure of metaphors: "You're wasting my time." "This gadget's going to save you a lot of time." "How do you spend your time?" "I'm investing a lot of time in doing this project." "I have to budget my time." "Living on borrowed time"—we can go on and on and on.

There are tons of metaphors that tie into this idea that time is a valuable commodity. It's like money: we can spend it, we can save it, we can waste it, we can invest it, and, as a result, we act as if time were a commodity. We use this metaphor as a basis for acting in the world. Another example they give is that argument is war, and again we can give a couple of examples here. You win or lose arguments. Your claims are indefensible, you attack weak points in a person's argument, you can demolish an argument, you can shoot down particular facts, and so forth. We act as if argument is war in some fundamental way. Using such metaphors allows us to invoke powerful presuppositions in our conversation. It allows us these shortcuts when we're communicating with one another because we all understand the metaphorical base of this.

When you presuppose something—this is a very powerful linguistic device—when you presuppose something, you're able to start talking about it like the people that you're talking with know exactly what you're discussing. The most famous example of a presupposition is the joke where a politician is asked, "Have you stopped beating your wife?" That presupposes—I mean, the politician can't—what do you answer? "Yes, I've stopped beating my wife; I used to beat my wife and I've stopped," or you answer "No, no, I haven't stopped beating my wife; I still am." It's very hard to combat that presupposition that's encoded in that first sentence there. Presuppositions are a powerful linguistic tool, but the trick with presuppositions, and this is especially true for me as a lecturer, but for everybody in your everyday conversations the trick is not to presuppose too much or too little.

If I presuppose too much, I could easily right now start talking in the rarefied language of anthropology and social theory, and I could speak over your heads. It doesn't mean that I'm smarter than you; it just means that I command the specialized vocabulary that you haven't studied, so I could presuppose too much and try and wow you now with my knowledge and speak over your head and try and intimidate you in some way. On the other hand, the other danger is presupposing too little and coming off as pedantic, explaining every little thing, and if I did that as a professor you would get bored very quickly. It's the same thing in everyday conversations. We have to figure out what we can presuppose with the person that we're talking with, and we use these as very powerful social tools. A group of your friends, you have little jokes among yourselves; you can presuppose all sorts of knowledge that creates a sense that we are a group and that excludes other people from that group as well, so presuppositions are very powerful political tools to mark social groups, in-group and out-group.

Here, I'd like to briefly review what we've covered so far; we've covered quite a bit of ground today. The Sapir-Whorf hypothesis and its two varieties, strong and weak. The strong version is unprovable; Steven Pinker points out that what we think doesn't always correspond to particular words, as with emotions, for example. He also reminds us of the linguistic fact that every language can communicate any idea that it needs to. The weak version of the Sapir-Whorf hypothesis is much more palatable;

certainly language does influence thought, just as thought influences language. It gives us the salient categories with which we can think. You could take Mayan speakers—think about bananas in a particular way. We think about time in a particular way, given our linguistic structures. In the next lecture, we're going to build upon these observations to look at how we construct mental models of how the world operates.

Lecture Eight
Constructing Emotions and Identities

Scope: In going about our daily lives, we build mental models of the world around us, some highly individual, others more conventional. We are bombarded with so much information in the course of our daily lives that we need the shortcuts provided by mental models (for example, "high price equals high quality") to survive. Mental models, even when they contradict scientific findings, are incredibly resilient, as seen in American folk beliefs about catching a cold from the weather and understanding how a thermostat works.

Often mental models are linguistically based, like scripts that we can enact in greetings and other routinized social settings. But mental models go beyond language to affect us physically. This is best seen in a variety of culturally specific mental illnesses found around the world, from "Arctic hysteria" to the Latin American "evil eye." The anthropologist Nancy Scheper-Hughes has shown how schizophrenia and maternal bonding—seemingly innate phenomena—are differently conceived across cultures. Even something as seemingly natural as gender varies significantly across cultures.

Outline

I. Building on such linguistic research, a new subfield of cognitive anthropology has emerged.

    A. Cognitive models are mental models of how the material and social world works. These may be idiosyncratic or widely shared.

        1. A number of key cognitive models are often set down early in life, through both formal and informal learning.

        2. At the same time, cognitive models are always dynamic and malleable, being formulated and adjusted to meet new circumstances and reconcile new information.

    B. Idiosyncratic (or personal) models develop through one's particular life history.

         1. These include mental prototypes (of a car, dog, or house) and even the definitions of words.

         2. Most individuals have idiosyncratic cognitive maps of the areas in which they live.

  C. We term cognitive models that are widely shared *cultural models*. Indeed, a useful definition of *culture* is that it is composed of overlapping cognitive models.

         1. Although certain models may be widely shared in a culture, there is never a perfect distribution.

         2. Notions of the American Dream are a cultural model.

II. Cognitive models also affect us physically, in the way that we conceive of illness and the ways we express emotion.

  A. There are a number of documented culturally specific diseases, including Arctic hysteria, nervios, and the evil eye. Some of these are psychosomatic, but others are clearly biological ailments.

  B. In the United States, for example, we can see the impact of changing cultural notions of illness: the expansion of addiction theories, the explosion of diagnoses for attention deficit syndrome, and the recognition of post-traumatic stress syndrome.

  C. Anthropologist Nancy Scheper-Hughes studied schizophrenia in Western Ireland in the mid-1970s. At the time, schizophrenia was associated with post-menopausal women in the United States, but in Ireland, it was almost entirely confined to young celibate men.

         1. Scheper-Hughes worked in the pseudonymous village of Ballybran. The region suffered the effects of massive male migration to larger cities and abroad.

         2. As a result, many households became effectively matrilineal—held together by the mother. Scheper-Hughes argues that such social structure, combined with rigid Catholic teachings on the sinfulness of sexual pleasure, made it difficult for the young men who did not migrate to develop healthy heterosexual relations.

         3. Scheper-Hughes employed Thematic Apperception Tests (TATs) with both schizophrenic and "normal" males. Where the former saw sexual themes, the latter constructed elaborate stories with innocent plots.

      4. Rates of schizophrenia decrease with the distance of migration from one's home village, but rates of alcoholism increase proportionately.

  D. Scheper-Hughes went on to conduct ethnographic fieldwork in an impoverished shantytown community in northeastern Brazil, the Alto do Cruzeiro. There, she looked at the way mother-love is expressed.

      1. The Alto do Cruzeiro suffers from extreme poverty and a high infant mortality rate.

      2. Scheper-Hughes showed that mothers in the Alto are very distant with their infants and show little emotion when one dies.

      3. She argues that this is not just an outward stance, but a reflection of the mother's true feelings. She argues that "mother-love" is basically a Western ideology that we have assumed is universal.

III. Just as illnesses and emotions are socially constructed, so, too, is gender, although here, there are more biological constraints.

  A. *Sex* refers to the biological categories of male and female. *Gender* refers to the social categories associated with the sexes (femininity and masculinity).

      1. All cultures recognize these two genders, although they assign different meanings to them.

      2. In some cultures, third genders are recognized, such as with the Berdache of the North American Plains Indians.

  B. In Samoa, the fa'fa'fine are a recognized third gender.

      1. Fa'fa'fines are boys who choose to dress and act like girls and are raised by their families as girls.

      2. Often misunderstood by Westerners as "gay" or "transvestites," the fa'fa'fines see themselves as fitting in an entirely different category.

  C. Research has also shown that the widespread belief in erroneous cultural models can have real-world effects. This is seen in U.S. perceptions of how thermostats function.

Readings:

Nancy Scheper-Hughes, *Death without Weeping.*

————, *Saints, Scholars and Schizophrenics.*

Bradd Shore, *Culture in Mind.*

Questions to Consider:

1. Is mother-love an innate emotion or something learned?
2. Why might different cultures show dramatically different rates of mental illnesses, such as schizophrenia?
3. What are some idiosyncratic mental models you hold? How do these compare to broader cultural models?

Lecture Eight—Transcript
Constructing Emotions and Identities

In the last lecture, we discussed possible ways that language can shape and influence our views of the world, central metaphors for example, but today we're going to turn to cognition and cognitive models. Cognition is the way in which we think; it's the process of thinking; it's the interplay of the mind and how it perceives and interprets the world. Cognitive models then are models of thought, mental models about how the world works, and we're all constantly building up cognitive models, mental models about the world around us and the way in which it works.

In many ways, these are similar to scientific models. We develop hypotheses, we test those, seeing how people in the real world react to our hypotheses, and then we modify those hypotheses. Cognitive models can be more or less idiosyncratic; we can have very particular personal cognitive models about the world around us, or we can have more widely shared or conventional cognitive models, and the more overlapping the cognitive models are between individuals, this is the area that we talk about which is culture. In this lecture, we're going to look at cultural models, cognitive models of illness, of emotions, and of gender, but first I want to begin by talking a little bit about personal cognitive models, idiosyncratic cognitive models, models that are unique to you as an individual based on your own unique life experiences.

Let me start off by doing a sort of psychological experiment. I'll say a word, and picture the first thing that comes into your mind; just note the first image that comes into your mind. Car, what do you imagine when I say car? We probably imagine something fairly similar; it probably has four wheels, it has doors, it has windshields, and so forth, and yet beyond that, the particular sort of car we pictured in our mind's eye probably varies significantly. It could be your car. It could be the car that you would like to have. It might be the car that your parents had when you were a kid. For me, I picture a 1970s Ford LTD or something like a kid would draw, very boxy, four doors, four wheels, and so forth, so we can still talk, we can use the word car, we have this mental prototype of what a car is, but the variation between us is fairly significant as well.

The best example of personal or idiosyncratic mental models is probably maps. What could be more objective than maps, you might think, but we all hold very different mental maps of the world around us. Let's say, if we all lived in the same city we would have very different mental maps of the city. I would know my area of town very well and have a very detailed map, and that detail would probably gradually diminish the farther out I went from my own little section of town. You likewise would have your own areas of town that you would have more detail on, and this would diminish the farther out you went. If we were giving directions to someone how to get from Place A to Place B, you and I would probably use different landmarks. Some would be the same, but we would also have different landmarks and even different routes that we would take. Routes that we would take to work would vary, routes that we would take to the airport.

In the last couple of months, I've taken three trips, taken three taxi rides from my home to the airport, and each time the taxi driver took a different route to the airport. At first, the first time this happened, I was a little bit nervous. I was in the back of the taxi, and I was thinking, Is this guy taking me to some road somewhere out in the middle of nowhere to rob me or kill me. But actually he had thought of a very clever way to go, given rush hour traffic, a route to the airport that I had never thought of it. I took three taxicab rides to the airport in the last month, three different routes, and all different from the normal route that I would take. We have these idiosyncratic models, these mental models, maps of the world, but also maps of the social world, models of the social world.

We also have cultural models, models that are more shared among individuals, broadly shared among members of the same culture, and these shared mental models are really the basis of culture. It's what we talk about when we talk about culture, shared views of looking at the world. A lot of cultural models we use in everyday life are simply handy shortcuts. Take going to buy something, for example. Let's say you're going to buy a bottle of wine. You could spend weeks or months or really even years learning about wine, and you could pick out just the right red to go with that steak. I need a strong Merlot to go with the taste of this steak, or I need a really good Gewurztraminer to offset the spiciness of the hot Thai food we're going to be eating tonight, so we can develop your cognitive models, the cultural models of the wine world.

You could invest the time and develop those very highly, or you could take a shortcut. You could go to the store, and if there's no clerk around to help you, you could say "Well, I want to get a $15 bottle of wine, so I'm going to look through the reds and I'm going to find something in my price range." We use this shortcut, the price, as an indicator of quality. I want to buy a $15 bottle of wine for dinner tonight, or I want to buy a $20 bottle of wine, or I want to buy a $50 bottle of wine, and we're using the shortcut that says that higher price equals higher quality. But, in fact, in lots of blind wine tasting tests, higher price doesn't always equal higher quality. You can get a very good $20 bottle of wine and a very bad $50 or $60 bottle of wine, but we use this as a handy little shortcut. We're bombarded with so much information in our daily lives we have to use these shortcuts to get by. We can't investigate every aspect of every product that we buy, for example, and so we just assume that what's more expensive is better.

That's one example of a cultural model, but let me give you another, a broader or more widely shared notion of a cultural model, and that is of the American Dream. This notion, this Horatio Alger story, if you work hard you'll get ahead and you can move up in the world. We can all pull ourselves up by the bootstraps in the United States. This is a very powerful cultural model for people in the United States and also for other people around the world, particularly immigrants who come to the United States, but look at the facts here.

A recent study showed that 19 percent of Americans believe they are among the top one percent of earners in this country, 19 percent believe they're among the top one percent of earners. Another 20 percent say that one day they will be; one day they're going to be in the top one percent of earners, so 39 percent of Americans think that they're one day going to be among the richest one percent of Americans, and the average median annual income of the richest one percent is $1.5 million a year. It's not going to happen, but having this model, having this cultural model that it's possible, really affects the way in which they feel patriotic, the way in which they feel tied to their country, the way in which they vote, the way in which they act in the world. One point of that is that our cultural models don't have to correspond to material reality. They're just as powerful even if they're not backed up by what's going on in the world around us.

Just as we model the physical world around us in cultural and in idiosyncratic ways, so too we model our own bodies, and here we can talk about body perceptions, the disconnect often between our perceptions of our bodies and the way our bodies actually are. I'm a professor; I work in the universities. There is literally an epidemic these days of eating disorders, particularly among young college-age women, anorexia, bulimia, and very often this results from having a mental image of how their body is that doesn't correspond with what their body actually looks like.

We could also mention powerful cultural models concerning illness, and there are a number of culturally specific illnesses around the world. In Guatemala, where I work, for example, we can talk about one illness called *susto*, or fright, and it's when the soul gets frightened and leaves the body. Let's say you're walking down the road and a snake runs across the road. You could get so frightened that part of your soul leaves your body, and this makes you physically ill. It physically debilitates you; you can lose your appetite, you might become tired, you have a disregard for your personal appearances. It sounds a lot like what we would call depression, clinical depression, but there it's *susto*, and it's treated not by medicines, not by a medical doctor, but by a shaman, who can call the soul back in and reseat it in the body once again.

There are a number of other culturally specific illnesses to the Maya in Guatemala. There's a condition called *nervios*, having nerves. There's a condition of *ojo*, the bad eye; if someone looks at you or looks at one of your children with envy or with greed, again it can steal part of your soul and physically debilitate you, physically make one sick. We would call these psychosomatic illnesses, but for the Maya, with whom I work, these are real illnesses. They are really sick; it's the real deal. This isn't something purely or just only psychological. This is the real cause of their illnesses, and so there are these cultural models of what causes illness surround the world.

Let me just mention a couple of others. The Inuit have a condition called Arctic hysteria; this is only found among the Inuit. At certain points, they will just go crazy. They'll run out of their igloos, they'll rip their clothes off, they'll roll around in the snow; sometimes they'll jump in the water, and sometimes they'll die. Is it cabin fever? Is it deficiency of a particular vitamin? Perhaps, but it's only found among the Inuit, and the Inuit have developed this cultural model to explain it and to understand it, and to work it into their own cultural system. There are other examples: *windingo psychosis*, we find among the Chippewa and the Ojibwa of the northern Great Lakes region, and this is a paranoid belief that others are turning into cannibals and that one might be turning into a cannibal oneself. There's *koro*, which we find in China, the irrational belief that one's genitals are retreating into one's body.

But the best way to illustrate this notion of cultural models of illness is to look at our own society. Take, for example, addiction in the United States. This is a cultural category which has changed radically over the last 20 years or so. For the better or for the worse, I'm not sure, but we've changed the way in which we perceive addiction. We now see it as a real illness. The fact hasn't changed; an alcoholic, a coke addict, any of these people, the physical reality of it is still the same, but the way in which we talk about addiction now, it's not a moral problem. It's a physical problem. It's an illness; it's a real illness that can be treated by medical doctors. Attention deficit hyperactivity disorder, also, similarly, it's a condition unheard of 20 years ago, and now it's estimated that somewhere between four and 12 percent of school-age children suffer from attention deficit hyperactivity disorder, and there's a large percentage—four percent of all children's prescriptions in the United States these days are for Ritalin to treat this disorder that wasn't recognized 20 years ago.

This isn't to say that these aren't real illnesses; it's not to say that our expansion of what we consider to be addictive, not only alcohol and drugs anymore but also gambling and sex and all of these other things, it's not to say that these aren't real illnesses. It's not to say that attention deficit hyperactivity disorder didn't exist 50 years ago, but it existed in a different way. If we didn't recognize it, if we didn't build up a cultural model to culturally sanction this, then it wasn't real in the same way that it's real today. Identifying them makes them more real in a cultural sense, and we can elaborate these cultural models and how these help us form our relationship with reality. We have these culturally specific illnesses round the world.

I want to go into some more detail about a couple of more culturally specific models, both outlined by one anthropologist. Her name is Nancy Scheper-Hughes; she works at the University of California at Berkeley, a very prominent anthropologist. Nancy Scheper-Hughes, she's working in the mid-1970s in Western Ireland. She goes to this small village in Western Ireland which she uses a pseudonym for, she calls Ballybran, and what she finds there is what we would consider to be a particularly dysfunctional system, dysfunctional in all sorts of ways. It's a very poor part of Ireland. There's a lot of out migration. Males are leaving their home villages and going to work in London or immigrating to the States, leaving their home villages. Children, particularly the sons, are also leaving; the older sons leave and the younger sons are left behind, so as a result you have families that are really matriarchal in many ways. You have a woman and her children. The older sons as they get older will leave, and the daughters and the younger children will stay at home.

This creates this virtual matriarchy in Northern Ireland and Western Ireland, and as a result there's a very tight bond between brothers and sisters, the brothers that stay behind, the younger brothers that stay behind, and their sisters, and Nancy Scheper-Hughes argues, and quite controversially, I will add, that the combination of the Catholic doctrine about sex that's practiced in this part of Western Ireland, that sex is a dirty thing, it's a nasty thing, it's something that's only for reproduction, it's something that we really shouldn't talk about, and this is an area of Ireland where they have a really strict Catholicism, combine this view of sex with the demographic fact that most of the males are migrating out, and you have these households being run by women, a few males in the household, but as a result of these two factors, the youngest boys who stay behind have a really hard time overcoming their Oedipal complex, incestuous feelings toward their mother and toward their sisters.

She also finds, and these are quite remarkable figures here, she finds, and this was a survey that she did in 1971, that 20 percent of the men in Western Ireland at this time were in a mental hospital, 20 percent of the male population were in a mental hospital. Remember, this is mostly the younger children, the younger male children that stayed behind; the others have migrated out. Of those, 89 percent were celibate—89 percent had never had sex—and half were diagnosed with schizophrenia, so you have 20 percent of the men in a mental institution: 89 percent of those are celibate and half of those are diagnosed with schizophrenia. At the time—this has changed a bit in the States since then—but at the time, schizophrenia in the United States was associated with middle-aged married women, very much a middle-aged married woman's disease, but in Ireland it was these bachelor men, the celibate bachelor men, and why is this?

Scheper-Hughes said it's because they have a hard time overcoming, handling their sexuality, overcoming their heritage and handling their sexuality in a productive way. They've been raised in this household, in a society that's ostensibly patriarchal, led by a man, but in this case the elder men have left and it's run by a woman, and so they never really overcome their psychosexual feelings toward their mothers and toward their sisters either, and it's very hard for them to establish a healthy relationship with other women. As a sideline here, it's interesting to note that with the distance of migration away from Western Ireland, the rates of schizophrenia went down. The farther men left, the farther away they went when they left, the lower the rates of schizophrenia, but there was a proportional increase in the rates of alcoholism the farther away men left.

I'm trying to tie this into cultural models, and to do this, one of the techniques that Nancy Scheper-Hughes used was to show her subjects TATs, Thematic Apperception Tests. It's a test used by psychologists; it's sort of like a Rorschach test, except it's a real image. They're charcoal drawings, and you can see real people—it's not abstract—so you show these images to a person and ask them to describe what's going on in the picture. In one picture in particular, there was an image of a woman, a bare-breasted woman, lying in bed with the covers pulled up to right underneath her breasts, and a man standing beside the bed, turning away, sort of with his arm over his face a little bit, as if he were ashamed just a bit.

She shows this to the men in Ballybran, this town in which she's working, and asks them to describe what was going on. Healthy men, the normal men, the non-schizophrenic men that she interviewed, would give stories such as, "There was a boating accident, and his sister fell into the water, and her clothes were wet, and so he's brought her back home and undressed her and put her into bed, and now he's turning away." The schizophrenic man would say, "They've just had sex, and now the man is embarrassed. He's feeling bad about this; he's feeling guilty, and that's the reason that he's turning way." Some very different interpretations of the same images, and I'll mention here that when I show these images to my undergraduate students, sex is inevitably one of the primary themes. Either I'm dealing with a lot of schizophrenics or what we consider to be schizophrenia varies dramatically from culture to culture.

Nancy Scheper-Hughes went on to write her next big book, another very important work in anthropology, about Brazil, where she had worked earlier in the 1960s as a Peace Corps volunteer before she went to graduate school. She goes back to northeastern Brazil after she's worked in Ireland, a little town that she calls, using a pseudonym, Bom Jesus, and really she worked in the shantytown on the edge of this Brazilian city, and the shantytown was called Alto do Cruzeiro. This is a big sugar cane region; the Amazon jungle in this area has been cut down. If you look at satellite photographs, the National Geographic satellite photographs, this is the splotch of brown in the middle of all of this Amazon region because it's all been cut down to grow sugar cane.

It's an extremely poor part of Brazil, poverty in the way they can we can hardly even imagine, poverty of people going hungry, dying of hunger, literally dying of hunger, and experiencing the delirium that goes with dying of hunger and when your body starts eating itself from the inside out. You may have gone hungry for a day, or you may have felt hungry one day, but it's hard for us to relate with this kind of hunger. We've never felt this kind of hunger, not eating for days at a time. In the Alto do Cruzeiro, in the shantytown on the edges of this Brazilian city, most of the people work in sugar plantations. Some of the women work as domestic help.

109

It's very harsh conditions. There's a very high death rate, poverty and hunger are extremely high, and the infant mortality rate is astronomical. The average woman in this community has 9.5 pregnancies in her lifetime and 3.5 child deaths, so the average woman has 3.5 of her children die. Most of these occur before six months of age and virtually all of them before one year old. In addition, they have an average of 1.5 stillbirths, so the average woman in the shantytown, the Alto do Cruzeiro in Brazil, the average woman gets pregnant 9.5 times, and a total of five of those, over half, results in the death of the baby, either through a stillbirth or through an infant death. Nancy-Scheper Hughes sees this, and she notices that the women aren't mourning over their dead infants. They go to the grave, they bury their babies, but they don't cry, and in fact she titled her book on the subject *Death Without Weeping*.

She asked herself: What's going on here? Why are these mothers not crying when their babies die? She says we have this idea in the West that we consider to be totally natural, that women bond with their children. It's like a woman gives birth, and we expect the violins to go up in the background and this instant bonding. The baby is put in the mother's arms and there's this instant metaphysical bonding between mothers and their children, this moment of epiphany, and, in fact, and there's been some recent research done on this showing that a lot of post-birth depression results from women not experiencing this instant bonding, and that all women don't experience this feeling, and a lot of women feel guilty if they don't because we've built it up to be such a romantic ideal in our culture that everybody needs to experience this same sort of bonding, that it's supposed to be natural; it's the natural scheme of things.

But here, the women don't cry when their babies die, and why is that? Nancy Scheper-Hughes says, because the conditions are so harsh, they don't want to put any emotional attachment into these children until they're over a year old, until they know that they're going to survive and that they're going to live and this relationship can really flourish. And so what Nancy Scheper-Hughes argues is that this notion of mother-love is really, in her words, a bourgeois myth. It's a myth developed in the West that romanticizes a natural bond between mothers and their children that doesn't have to exist, that doesn't exist in this area of northeastern Brazil, where the women don't cry when their children die.

This research has created quite a stir in the academy. A lot of people think that there is a natural bond. Sociobiologists, for example, would argue that we have evolved an evolutionary propensity for women to become attached to their children, and Nancy Scheper-Hughes says no, this is a cultural model. It's a cultural model that's especially insidious because we take it to be the natural scheme of things. But, she says, in Alto do Cruzeiro, where they have these lifeboat ethics, where you know people are going to die, the chances are greater than 50 percent that any child a woman has is going to die, why invest all that time and attention in that child? We have these cultural models of illness around the world, sometimes radically different models about the relationship between mothers and children and the nature of mother-love.

I would also like to mention in the lecture today about cultural models of another thing we take to be quite natural, which is gender. Of course, there are women and men in the world. Men act one way, women act another, and this is just the natural scheme of things. But, in fact, there's quite a bit of variation in the way in which men and women are expected to act in different cultures. Every culture around the world recognizes two genders, a masculine gender and a feminine gender, and here let me make a distinction. We use gender to refer to the social categories associated with masculinity and femininity, and we use sex more precisely to describe biologically male and females.

Every culture around the world recognizes at least two genders, but some cultures recognize a third gender. Take, for example, the berdache, these so-called two-spirit people of the Pueblo Indians, the Zuni and the Navajo. These were men, biologically men, but they lived as women. They dressed as women did, they did women's work, and it turns out that they were very highly valued because women were seen as potentially polluting, and so on hunting trips and in important rituals shamans didn't want to take women along because they could corrupt the hunt because they're just a little bit polluting, so they could take along these berdache, these men-women who could do all of the cooking, who could do all of the taking care of the clothes and so forth on the hunting trips, and yet wouldn't corrupt the nature of the hunt or this contact with the spirit world in certain rituals.

On Samoa, remember Samoa, where Margaret Mead studied and romanticized the sexual life of the people of Samoa, on Samoa there's a group of people call fa'fa'fines. *Fa'fa'fine* means in the manner of a woman, and these fa'fa'fine, they are males who wear women's dress, who do women's work, and they're fairly highly valued among Samoan families because they can do both things that men can do and things that women can do. But these fa'fa'fines, when you talk to them, they say that they're really uncomfortable with foreigners who try and categorize them in a specific way. If they go, if these Samoan fa'fa'fines, when they go to Australia on vacation, they say, "All the Australians think that we're transvestites or we're gays, and we're not. We're a different sort of thing. We're a third gender; we're neither male nor female. We don't fit into this Western binary opposition."

These are some pretty radical differences: mother-love, conceptions of mother-love in different cultures; conceptions of gender in different cultures. And I would like to end here on somewhat of a lighter note, another example of cultural models, and one that comes from our own culture. Let me ask you something. Let's say that it's extremely cold outside and you go back to your home and the heat has been turned off, and you go inside and it's freezing cold. You've just been out in the cold, and you really want to get your house warmed up quickly. What do you do? You go over to the thermostat, and let's say that your ideal temperature would be 78°. What do you set the thermostat on? Lots of people that I ask this question to in my classes, and lots of people in the States as a whole, would say "I would go in, and first I would turn it up to 90° and get it really nice and warm, and then I would go back and turn it to 78°."

This is a very particular cultural model of the way in which a thermostat and heating works. It's a valve model; we're picturing the thermostat like the valve on a faucet that we can open it up wider and more hot air will come out. In fact, the way in which heating works, it's this binary operation. The heating elements either come on or they turn off, and it's not this gradation. The air isn't hotter or colder. The fan can blow; you can put the fan on low or you can put the fan on high, so the fan can blow at different speeds, but actually the operation of the heating system is binary, off or on. Having a cultural model, though, that it's like a valve, has real-world implications. If we go in, the house is freezing cold, we turn the thermostat on 90° and then we forget it. We go out and we run an errand or something, we come back and the house is burning up, and we've wasted all of this electricity that we didn't need to do because if you had set the thermostat on 78° in the first place it would have gotten to that temperature just as quickly as if you had set it on 90°.

Mental models are the way in which we look at the world; these can be more or less idiosyncratic. The less idiosyncratic or the more conventional they are, this is what creates what we call culture. Today we looked at cultural models of disease, of emotion, of mother-love, of gender, and to the ways in which cultural models can influence our own behavior: when we go shopping, equating high price with quality, for example, or the way in which we use thermostats in our homes or apartments. In the next lecture, what we're going to do is apply the scheme of cultural models to the Fulbe of northern Cameroon.

Lecture Nine
Magic, Religion, and Codes of Conduct

Scope: Anthropologists, when discussing spirituality (a belief in souls), often distinguish between *magic* and *religion*. Magical beliefs hold that humans can control natural and supernatural forces; that is, magical rites, if conducted properly, should have a desired practical result (such as making the rain come). Religion, in contrast, rests on the belief that humans are subjects of a higher power; rather than controlling the spiritual world, they must do its bidding and seek their desires through prayer and supplication. In practice, the distinction between religion and magic often breaks down.

In this lecture, we look to the Fulbe of northern Cameroon, a nominally Muslim culture with a rich tradition of magical beliefs. The Fulbe world is inhabited by cannibal witches, but it is the Islamic Mullam who has the power to cure their soul-eating illness. We see also how women are treated in this patriarchal system and the unexpected ways in which they are able to assert their power.

Outline

I. All cultures have spiritual beliefs, although these vary greatly from society to society.

   A. Edward Tylor, in his 1871 book *Primitive Cultures*, observed that a belief in souls ("animism") is found in all cultures.

   B. The distinction between magic and religion goes back to another early anthropologist, James Frazer, who wrote an encyclopedic survey of the world's religions in *The Golden Bough* (1922).

      1. In his formulation, magic is directed toward immediate problems. It seeks to force supernatural powers to do one's will in a sort of "primitive science."

      2. Accusations of sorcery and witchcraft serve important social functions.

   C. Religion is conceived as more conciliatory toward the supernatural, involving prayer and supplication to a higher power.

Religion is usually highly organized and revolves around group activities.

II. The Fulbe of Domaayo in northern Cameroon illustrate how difficult it often is to distinguish between magic and religion.

    A. The Fulbe are an ethnic group that lives across West Africa.

        1. There are some 8 to 10 million Fulbe peoples, who are also known as the Fulani. They all speak varieties of the language Fulfulde.

        2. The Fulbe are mostly Muslim, and they trace their origins to the *jihads* that expanded Islam to this part of Africa in the early 19th century.

        3. The Fulbe have a chiefdom system of traditional organization, but today, they all live under modern nation-states.

    B. Domaayo is a small Fulbe town in northern Cameroon that has been studied by anthropologist Helen Regis.

        1. Cameroon—first a German, then a French colony—gained its independence in 1960.

        2. Domaayo (population about 1,000) is located far to the north, far from the capital and much of the country's political and economic life.

    C. *Pulaaku* is the Fulbe code of conduct. It mandates stoicism, the withholding of emotion, and a clear deference to elders.

    D. The Fulbe are farmers, but they see themselves more as cattle herders.

        1. Farmers mostly grow millet, which, served as porridge, is the staple of the local diet.

        2. But the Fulbe were historically cattle herders—and most still are although not in Domaayo. Fulbe culture tends to equate farmers with pagans because most farmers they come into contact with are not Muslim.

        3. Thus, for the Fulbe, the difference between farmers and herders is an important symbolic distinction, and given that they are not pagans, they must be herders.

        4. This provides evidence for Claude Lévi-Strauss's idea that humans tend to organize the world through binary oppositions, the most crucial of which is culture and nature.

    E. The Fulbe are a patrilineal society.
1. Men may have more than one wife, but all wives have to be cared for in good fashion. Men are required to supply their wives with annual gifts of cloth.
2. Women are seen as potentially dangerous, and there is a fairly rigid segregation of the sexes. Men do not interact much with their wives.
3. Divorce is not uncommon and may be initiated by either the husband or the wife. The average woman will be married 2.6 times in her lifetime.

III. Although Fulbe society is nominally Muslim, its members also maintain a dynamic indigenous tradition of magical beliefs.

    A. Virtually everyone in Domaayo self-identifies as Muslim, although some are recognized as being more pious than others.
1. *Mallum* is a term of respect bestowed upon a man who has read the whole Koran. Mallums serve as Koranic teachers and village elders. They also play important roles in native religious rituals and beliefs.
2. Boys and girls are expected to attend Koranic schools, where they learn to read and write and memorize scripture. Girls, however, drop out by the time they are 12 or 13, while boys continue with their studies.
3. It is too easy to lump together all of the Muslim world into a single culture area. The Fulbe practice just one of countless varieties of Islam practiced around the world.
4. Indeed, the Fulbe are generally devout, especially in following the customs of daily prayers and celebrating holy days.

    B. The Fulbe do not restrict their spiritual beliefs to Islamic traditions. They also see the world as inhabited by malevolent spirits that must be averted with magic. Children are especially vulnerable to spiritual illnesses.
1. Looking at a child with an envious eye can actually cause deadly physical illness for the child. Therefore, adults treat their children with what seems to foreigners as a distant nonchalance.
2. Children are also given protective amulets to wear; these may contain magical talismans and written verses from the Koran.

3. A pregnant woman should avoid looking at a lizard or her child might have a wasting disease. If a pregnant woman looks at an antelope, however, the child may take on the long, graceful features that the Fulbe see as an ideal of beauty.

C. The scariest creature in the Fulbe pantheon of demons is the cannibal witch.
   1. Cannibal witches eat the intestines and souls of their victims, who in turn, become cannibal witches.
   2. The Fulbe prize meat, which they feel they do not get enough of. It is also said that human flesh is the best in the world. Thus, the image of the cannibal witch, while it is feared, is also understood.
   3. Too much desire (which goes against the code of *pulaaku*) is dangerous. The desire for meat brings one dangerously close to being a cannibal witch.

D. Women have a wide range of their own medicinal magic, including birth-control potions. They are especially vulnerable to the river spirits, because they often go alone to fetch water. Attacks from river spirits must be treated by a Mallum, or a woman could die.

Readings:

Claude Lévi-Strauss, *The Raw and the Cooked.*

Helen Regis, *The Fulbe of Northern Cameroon.*

Questions to Consider:

1. What social functions do witchcraft beliefs and accusations serve in other cultures?

2. How do the Fulbe reconcile their Muslim faith with their magic practices?

3. How do stories of river spirits convey Fulbe perceptions of white people?

Lecture Nine—Transcript
Magic, Religion, and Codes of Conduct

In the last lecture, we talked about cognitive models, mental models of how the world works, and really this is in many ways our reality, the reality that we live in. These models may be highly idiosyncratic, our personal quirks, the uniqueness of our personality, or they can be more widely shared: the proper distance to stand from someone; what to do when the national anthem plays, and so forth, and to the extent to which these are shared, they constitute what we call culture. In this lecture, what I would like to do is apply our understanding of cultural models to a particular case, and that is the Fulbe of northern Cameroon, and, in particular, I'm going to talk about three aspects of Fulbe culture. The first is their code of conduct, which is called *pulaaku*. The second is their self-identity as Muslim herders, even though they're farmers. Third is the relationship between religion and magic. They're an Islamic culture although they still have a rich tradition of indigenous magical beliefs.

There's been a long concern in anthropology with religion and magic and with various forms of spirituality. Edward Tylor, the man who gave us that classic definition of culture, noted that every culture around the world has a conception of some sort of soul, of some sort of spirituality. He believed that in primitive culture, the belief in the soul emerged from dreams, from trying to come up with an explanation for dreams. It seemed to these people that a part of their body had to leave and go somewhere else, and so they assumed that there was a part of their body which wasn't physical, a soul. Tylor argued that this belief in souls eventually evolved—he called it animism, a belief in souls—and that this eventually evolved into polytheism and finally into monotheism, which he took as a hallmark of civilization. Tylor gave us the idea of animism, a belief in souls, and this is found in all cultures around the world. Our own culture generally conceives of souls as being uniquely human, but in many cultures souls can be found in animals, in plants, in rocks, and the inanimate world as well.

We have Tylor. Another important early scholar on the anthropology of religion was James Frazer, and in 1922 he published a book, *The Golden Bough*. At first, it was a two-volume series, and he expanded it over the years into 13 volumes. It was an encyclopedic coverage of religious practices around the world, and it's a classic text in anthropology and in religious studies to this day. In this book, Frazer made a crucial distinction that we still hold today between magic and religion, and he argued that magic is a type of primitive science. It's a belief that we can control the world around us, the spiritual world, the supernatural world, and that if we do certain rituals, if you do certain rituals, just like in a scientific experiment, if you follow the plan exactly, a predetermined outcome will occur. If we follow all of the rules of the rain dance ritual, for example, and we don't bring along any menstruating women, if we don't have sex for a week before we conduct the ritual and we do the rain dance properly, the rain has to come. It's a belief that humans can control the supernatural world and their natural environment.

That's magic, and he contrasted this with religion, and religion sees humans as being more at the mercy of a higher power. This is a sort of spirituality associated with a conciliatory view toward a higher power, a larger power, recognizing that we're at the mercy of something greater than ourselves. In Frazer's scheme, prayer is crucial to religion because prayer is requesting something from a supernatural being. It's not demanding something, it's not making something happen, but it's supplicating, asking for a favor from the greater powers that be. Now religion generally is also more highly organized, more large-scale, often has a written tradition to distinguish it from magic.

Taking this into account, the difference between religion and magic, I would like to turn now to the Fulbe of northern Cameroon. The Fulbe, they're an ethnic group. There are about 8 to 10 million Fulbe living in western Africa, and they range all the way from Senegal, far in the west, all the way over to Chad, Sudan, and Cameroon. They speak varieties of the Fulbe language. Most of them are cattle herders, which is a very common economic pattern in western Africa. Most of them are Muslims; they trace their history back to jihads in the 19th century, which was moving Islam westward. They were traditionally organized into chiefdoms, although today all Fulbe live within the boundaries of modern nation-states.

The anthropologist Helen Regis has worked among the Fulbe in a community in northern Cameroon, a community that she calls Domaayo. This is a pseudonym, but it's a community in northern Cameroon, a small village of about 1,000 people. There's a little mosque, a small government health center, a local school, but in many respects Domaayo is far removed from national Cameroonian life. National life in Cameroon is oriented around the port cities and the capital, and Domaayo way to the north is far removed from the workings of national life.

Ostensibly, Domaayo is ruled by the laws of Cameroon, but actually, in fact, in daily life it's governed more by a moral code called pulaaku. Pulaaku is a moral code that really stresses stoicism. One should always refrain from displaying emotions; one shouldn't show anger or grief or love. Even physical pain should be endured silently. In terms of this moral code, pulaaku, men are especially expected to adhere to it closely, and there's even some competition between men of who can embody the most pulaaku. For example, the staple diet among the Fulbe is millet porridge, and they'll serve this in a bowl along with a little sauce for spice. They'll serve this in a common bowl, and everybody will dip out of it with their hands and eat from their hand. If a man dips into a scalding hot bowl of millet porridge, he's not supposed to show any pain or any emotion and take it up, put it into his mouth and eat it like nothing has happened, and then pass it on to the next unsuspecting man sitting next to him.

Women also are expected to adhere to pulaaku, although they're given a little bit more leeway. Under the rules of pulaaku, anger should always be muted, grief should always be muted, no powerful emotion should be shown. Regis writes about child deaths, the number of child deaths that have occurred in Domaayo while she's been there, and this is a fairly poor region of West Africa and so child deaths are not unheard of. She notes that the women in Domaayo, when their children die, refrain from crying at their child's death. You'll recall Nancy Scheper-Hughes, working in the northeast of Brazil, also noted that poor Brazilian women didn't cry when their children died. *Death Without Weeping* was the name of the Nancy Scheper-Hughes book.

In contrast to Scheper-Hughes, Regis argues that the women in Domaayo do feel grief when their children die, but it's muted. It's muted because it's filtered through this cultural model of pulaaku. Being too much in love with one's wife is similarly seen as being a bad thing, a violation of pulaaku; it's akin to a mental illness because there's a passion there, a passion that one expresses, a passion that can be debilitating to the individual. Excessive laughter, happiness, all of these emotions have to be muted under the code of pulaaku. It doesn't mean that the Fulbe don't experience happiness, that they don't experience love or grief or pain or any of these emotions; they just express it in a very different way.

Now pulaaku is also closely tied to notions of respect and modesty. One should always have respect for elders in this society, and yet one can never be too modest, the Fulbe say. And so in pulaaku, we have this cultural concept, this cultural model, tied to relations of respect and modesty, and it's a cultural model that people talk about openly. Many cultural models, perhaps most cultural models, are less implicit in cultures. They go without saying and they come without saying. But the pulaaku moral code is debated very often among the Fulbe trying to figure out exactly where to draw these lines about what is acceptable behavior and what isn't.

One thing about cultural models is they don't have to conform to what we would consider to be the objective reality, the objective world, truth. Take cultural models that we mentioned last time of the thermostat. Many people in the country hold a valve model of how a thermostat works. This isn't objectively true, it's not scientifically true, and yet it is their reality, and they act on that reality, so it becomes real in some meaningful way. We as human beings, with these huge brains that we've been given by evolution, we have an incredible capacity for cognitive dissonance, holding contradictory beliefs at the same time. For example, let's take the Fulbe and their image of themselves as compared to reality.

The Fulbe of Domaayo are farmers. They raise millet; you'll remember that millet porridge is the staple of the Fulbe diet, millet porridge mixed with a little bit of sauce. Millet in many ways is at the heart of the Fulbe economy and at the heart of the Fulbe symbolic life. But these Fulbe don't see themselves as farmers; they see themselves as herders, as cattle herders. Most of the other Fulbe people in western Africa are cattle herders, and they come from this tradition of being cattle herders, so even though the villagers of Domaayo are farmers themselves, they don't like to be associated with farmers. This doesn't mean that they're delusional; they do have some cattle. They wouldn't say that we don't farm at all, but their self-image of themselves as a group is of being Muslim herders.

They contrast this with their neighbors, their pagan neighbors whom they call the Mundang, and they view the Mundang as being almost subhuman. They're not Muslim, so they're pagan; they're farmers, and the Fulbe of Domaayo want to distance themselves as much as possible from the Mundang. We're Muslim, we're civilized, we're the real people, and these Mundang are pagan farmers. They don't believe in the teachings of Islam, they're not like us, they're subhuman, they're more of nature than of culture, so this interesting disconnect between the Fulbe cultural model of themselves and the reality of their subsistence points to the fluidity of identity.

What does it mean to be Fulbe? In a sense, it means to be a cattle herder because most Fulbe are cattle herders, and this is the origin of Fulbe culture; yet the Domaayo have found themselves in a situation where they have to be or they want to be farmers and yet still consider themselves to be Fulbe, so they have this paradoxical association between herding and farming. This brings to mind a distinction made by the famous French anthropologist Claude Levi-Strauss, and he says that human beings tend to think in dichotomies, that mental models ultimately boil down to binary oppositions. For the Fulbe, they consider themselves to be real humans in contrast to the Mundang, who they consider to be pagans and almost subhumans, so this idea of us against them, the believers against the pagans, the herders versus the farmers, the Fulbe and the Mundang.

Levi-Strauss's most impressive work is a series of books that he published starting in the mid-1960s up through the early 1970s called *Mythologiques*, and the first was *The Raw and the Cooked*, the second was *From Honey to Ashes*, the third was *On the Origin of Table Manners*, and the fourth was *The Naked Man*. What Levi-Strauss did in the series of books was he took 813 myths, and he started with the Bororo, who live in the Amazonian rain forest, and he moved up through each of these books up through South America, up through Central America, all the way up the northwest coast of North America up to the Inuit speakers, and he traced their mythologies and he said that all of the mythologies of both continents, this whole hemisphere, boil down to one basic dichotomy, a dichotomy that can be extrapolated out to other realms, and that dichotomy is the distinction between nature and culture.

He says that it's almost human nature to distinguish between nature and culture. Nature is chaotic, it's unruly, and culture is ordered and civilized, so we have nature is to culture as chaos is to order, as pagans are to believers, for example. Culture is civilization; it's who we are. We can control what we do within our culture; outside of our culture area, in the wilds of nature, we cannot control the forces that go on there, so nature is to culture as chaos is to order. It's also, as Levi-Strauss pointed out, as raw is to cooked. Raw food starts out in nature, it's picked, it's brought into the cultural realm physically by cooking it, and it becomes a cultured product. Cooked food is more cultured; we take it out of nature and we make it culture. That was the myth that he started out with among the Beroro, that raw concerned the origin of cooking food.

He moves up through these four volumes and these 813 myths up to the Inuit, and he finds the central metaphor, the central dichotomy in Inuit mythology, is naked and clothed. They're living way up north. I mean, clothing is obviously very important to us, but clothing is also something that makes us human, that sets us off from nature. We wear clothes, we have some sense of modesty, so we're not the animals of nature. Nature is to culture as animal is to human, and Levi-Strauss went on to argue as women are to men. In many cultures around the world, women are considered to be more natural, more chaotic, not as civilized as men.

There's this notion that women are a little more dangerous because they're more in touch with this natural side of things, and we see this among the Fulbe. Fulbe men, it's a nominally patriarchal society but Fulbe men have a real fear of women, so perhaps there's something to Levi-Strauss's idea, some sort of binary basis in our minds for these kinds of cultural models. Or perhaps we could take an analogy from quantum physics. Rather than saying that things are binary in quantum physics, what we've traditionally seen as being binary, either off or on, one or zero, they can be both at the same time, off and on, one and zero, just as the Fulbe can simultaneously be farmers and herders in a meaningful way.

Men and women in Fulbe society, Fulbe women go and live with their husbands' families, and as a result they're always outsiders. They leave their own family, and they go and live with their husband's family. If their husband dies, if they get divorced, they have to depend on their children to help care for them because they have left their natal family behind when they get married. Fulbe society tends towards patriarchy, or male dominance. The male ideology is patriarchal; they want to keep women subordinated, keep them in their place. It's not extreme, but they're definitely patriarchal. Fulbe men may have more than one wife, but a man has to care for each of his wives in a proper fashion, a fashion fitting their rank in society. If they don't care for their wives, that's grounds for divorce, and divorce is not unheard of. This is an Islamic society, but nonetheless women can initiate divorce, and in fact the average Fulbe woman has over two husbands, over 2.5 husbands in her lifetime.

When they get married, men have to compensate their wife's family. They're taking her away, they're taking this reproductive resource away from the wife's family and bringing it into their family, so they have to pay, and what they pay is what we call in anthropology bride price, the price that a husband pays for his wife. In Fulbe society, this payment occurs through cloth. Fulbe women use bolts of cloth—they're about 6 yards long—that they use to make skirts and blouses from, so this cloth is very important in Fulbe society. The best cloths, a man who pays a high price for his wife will give wax cloths, and these are made using a batik method, where wax is put onto the cloth and then it's dyed and it comes out with these incredibly intricate patterns; so the best cloths are these wax cloths, and they're generally imported—they're not made locally. They come from Nigeria, but more often from Java and from the Netherlands, so a powerful man, a man who wants to keep his status in society, who wants to marry a good woman, a good woman from a good lineage, will have to supply lots of these wax cloths to her and to her family in order to secure her hand in marriage.

Less desirable are print cloths that are made to mimic the look of wax cloths, and these are made in Cameroon and other African countries, and today, actually, a great number of them are made in Asia, so if a man doesn't have a lot of money, he doesn't have a lot of resources, he can't pay a high bride price, then he will give these print cloths. There's always this economic component to the negotiation of marriage. The woman's family is trying to get the best payment they can for the woman; the man is trying to give as little as he can, and this occurs not only at the moment of marriage but throughout their marriage, throughout their time together. Every year, the man has to give his wife gifts of cloth, preferably wax cloth, but in a rough situation he can give print cloths as well.

And so men see the women as dangerous, and, as a result, there's a strict segregation of the sexes in Fulbe society. A man has to get married; it's seen as an imperative of a Fulbe man. He can't make his own millet; that would be humiliating. A man has to have a wife at home who can care for his children and do all of the things that a man has to have done for him. But men don't interact with their wives very much, and they prefer that their wives not go out in the street very often, either, so there's a segregation between the sexes, partly due to the fact that women are seen as polluting, and if men have too much contact with women, then they can get polluted as well and get debilitated.

Fulbe is a Muslim culture, at least nominally a Muslim culture. Virtually everyone in the town of Domaayo is Muslim, and they're devout Muslims in their own way. There are local Koranic teachers called Mallums, and a Mallum is a person who has read the whole Koran from front to back, and these are spiritual guides in Domaayo society. They also serve as magical healers, something we'll come back to in just a moment. Girls normally go to the Koranic school as well as boys. The girls will only go until about age 12 or 14, at which point they get married and they drop out school. The boys will continue on with their Koranic education.

Let me make a point here about Islam, it's misleading to talk about Islam as if it were a unified, singular, monolithic religion. It's impossible to say that Christians believe X. We have such a wide variety of Christianity: the

Greek Orthodox church, the Roman Catholic church, the Church of God, the Church of Christ, Methodist, Episcopalians, it goes on and on, so think of all of these varieties of Christianity. It's hard to say what Christians believe, and the same holds true of Islam. Islam is also a religion of great diversity, and the Islam of these Mallums of Domaayo is very far removed from the Islam of Osama bin Laden or the Taliban in Afghanistan, for example. The Fulbe, like people across Africa, like people across the Middle East and central Asia as well, have adopted Islam, but it's combined, it's fundamentally mixed and melded with traditional religious practices, what Frazer would have called magic. The people of Domaayo are very devout Muslims. On the one hand, they practice daily prayers, they fast during Ramadan, and they see no contradiction in doing all of this and at the same time using amulets, for example, to protect their children against spirits and demons and souls that live in the Fulbe area.

The Fulbe world is inhabited by these spirits that are potentially detrimental, and the Fulbe believe that children are especially vulnerable to spirit attack, and the younger they are, the more susceptible they are to attack by spirits and demons. They believe, the Fulbe believe that it's very dangerous to be too loving toward a child, and as a result Fulbe mothers and Fulbe fathers, Fulbe adults, take what we would consider to be a very nonchalant attitude, if not negligent attitude, toward their children. They don't run over immediately when they're crying to cuddle them and kiss them and make them feel better. They don't do a lot of things that we would consider to be natural signs of loving a child because they believe if you lavish too much attention on a child it's going to hurt that child, it's going to steal part of their spirit, and others who pay too much attention to your children are hurting that child as well.

If a neighbor woman looks at your child very lovingly, it's really a love of envy there and a love of greed, and that greed can physically hurt the child and result in physical debilitation, so one of the worst things that you can do in Fulbe society is what would seem quite natural to an American. If you walked into a Fulbe household and you saw a child, and you went over and patted its head and pinched its cheek and said, "This is just the cutest kid I've ever seen in my life," this would be an awful insult and an awful danger to the child by paying too much attention to it. What the parents do to protect their children is they put amulets around their necks, and it's interesting here that the most powerful amulets are those that contain passages of the Koran, written down on a piece of paper, rolled up and then put into the amulet, and the word of the Koran has special preventative powers in keeping these souls from being stolen. And here we see a mix of what Frazer would have called magic and religion—Islam, certainly a religion; these beliefs about demons and spirits, certainly magic—so we see this intimate mixing of these two sorts of beliefs.

Women are important medical practitioners in Fulbe society. Women keep a little medicine chest—a lot of this involves fertility. Often in the medicine chest there will be a bit of an umbilical cord from a child, and if a woman is infertile they will conduct rituals with this umbilical cord to make her fertile once again. Women also control a body of knowledge concerning herbal potions that can be used as birth control, for example, or day-after potions, if you will, so women serve this important medical function, this religious medical function in Fulbe society.

In terms of spiritually caused illnesses, the worst fate that can befall a Fulbe person is an attack by a cannibal witch. The cannibal witches come and they eat one's insides. They eat one's intestines, and they also steal part of one's soul. In stories about this, they tell of a bird that will fly out of the anus of a cannibal witch, and it carries a torch of fire with it, and it goes and attacks people, steals their intestines, steals part of their soul, and goes back and takes it to the cannibal witch, who can pig out on this human flesh. Why is this such a fear for Fulbe people? Let's remember that the Fulbe of Domaayo are farmers, but they see themselves as herders. They used to be part of this herding tradition and they highly value meat, although they don't have a lot of access to meat these days, so the beliefs about cannibal witches are tied up in this valuation of meat.

One man that this anthropologist Helen Regis interviewed talked about, "Oh, wouldn't it be great to be a cannibal witch? You could eat a plateful of intestines every day," and then he quickly corrected himself and said, "But I would never do that; I would never go that route," but it shows that there's this fear of cannibal witches because of this fear of their own passion, of wanting to eat meat, and of the ultimate rejection in some ways of the norms of pulaaku. If you gave in to eating human flesh, which the Fulbe say is the tastiest flesh of all, if you gave in to this base desire, you would really be rejecting all of the code of pulaaku. We have desire, we have envy, we have witchcraft, all wrapped up into one, and to be treated from an attack by a cannibal witch one has to go to the Mallum, the spiritual leader, the Koranic spiritual leader, who's going to protect you from this cannibal witch attack.

Less debilitating but more common than cannibal witch attacks are attacks by river spirits, and women are especially susceptible to this because Domaayo is located on the side of a river, and they will go down every day and collect water and bring it back up, and these river spirits can steal part of their soul. It's interesting that the Fulbe have a lot of lore about river spirits, and some of it ties in with tales about white engineers, French and English engineers who've come to Cameroon and started building roads as part of the development program in these remote regions of Cameroon. Regis quotes a story that was told to her by a man that she heard from several other people as well, about the relationship of these river spirits to the engineers who were building bridges over the rivers. Let me quote this; this is a Fulbe man:

"I hear it said that there are some whites who build bridges; then the spirits destroy them during the night. They bring out the engineers, the whites who know how to catch spirits. They say they capture the spirit—they say they catch it—and the spirit says, 'I leave you be." They then release him, and they can go on with their construction. I learn that the spirits had captured a white man in Chad, not in Cameroon, strategically a distance away in Chad. Until now, the man is there. If they come with their binoculars, they see him captured. He's alive; he's in the water. Africans can see him too, but the whites have gadgets. They have binoculars they can look with, and they see him. The Africans don't have these tools. It's far, a thousand meters or so, a lot of water."

This is a wonderful story; it's a commentary on neo-colonial relations between whites and the Fulbes, and it also recognizes the power of the outside world, the power of these engineers, with their binoculars, with their technology, and also the power of the native spiritual world as well. It seems to be a morality tale, but paradoxically the morality is somewhat ambiguous here, and I think this reflects a fundamental ambiguity of many native peoples around the world, trying to work out their place in an increasingly globalized world.

Life Stages and the Family
Lecture Ten
Rites of Passage

Scope: Most cultures around the world mark significant stages in the life cycle with rituals and celebrations. The most important of these rites of passage is when girls and boys become women and men. Such coming-of-age ceremonies are marked by a separation from the group, a transitional period in which normal social strictures are suspended, and a reintegration into the community as adults.

For Fulbe boys, the initiation ceremony occurs when they are between 7 and 12 years old. During a several-week-long "circumcision camp," boys are taken from their mothers, made to eat food considered unclean by Muslim practice to the point of vomiting, and physically pushed to the point of exhaustion—all the while being socialized in the stoic Fulbe code of manly behavior. Once they are circumcised, they reenter their communities as adult men.

A similar ceremony is performed by the Sambia of New Guinea, a culture marked by strong divisions between men and women. Among the Sambia, initiated boys will go to live in a communal men's house until they get married and have their first child; women, during their menstrual period, must stay in a menstrual hut outside the village. The Sambia believe that boys are born without semen and, thus, without manhood. During their initiation, boys are required to engage in ritualized homosexual behaviors in order to build up their manhood. We will see how these rituals relate back to Sambian origin myths and Freudian theories of development.

Outline

I. Every culture around the world recognizes important stages in the life cycle.

    A. Arnold van Genep in his pioneering *Rites of Passage* (1909) proposed a sequence for rite-of-passage ceremonies that holds well for many cultures.

    B. First, there is a separation of initiates from their families and the group.

        1. During the ceremonial transition period, normal rules are often turned upside down. Victor Turner calls this a period of *liminality.* and notes that it produces a sense of bonding (or *communitas*) between the initiates.

        2. Finally, the initiates are reintegrated into the society.

II. Male rites of passage among the Fulbe illustrate van Genep's model.

    A. Fulbe boys must be made into men through an initiation ceremony that culminates in their circumcision.

        1. During this ritual, they are instilled with the stoic principles of *pulaaku.*

        2. Before their initiation, boys have not had much contact with their fathers.

    B. The circumcision camp takes place when there is an adequate number of boys from about 7 to about 12 years old.

        1. The boys are separated from the village and taken to a makeshift camp on the far side of the river.

        2. The camp lasts only a few weeks but produces lifetime bonding among the boys and serves as an important symbolic break with the world of women.

    C. During the circumcision camp, the boys enter a stage of liminality where the normal rules that govern everyday life do not apply.

        1. They are made to eat road kill and other unclean foods. They are also made to eat excessively, to the point that they vomit.

        2. The boys endure physical hardships and punishments and are, finally, circumcised.

    D. The coming-in ceremony for the boys' return is an unusually festive time for the normally reserved Fulbe.

        1. A huge feast is thrown.

        2. The boys are paraded around as if they were sex objects, and the girls eye them with lust—behaviors that would ordinarily be severely punished.

III. The Fulbe mark four important phases in a woman's life.

    A. First is the status of "virgin," which lasts from birth until marriage. A virgin is not yet fully a woman.

B. After marriage, sometime between the ages of 12 and 14, a girl takes on the status of a married woman and is then considered to be a real woman.

C. After a divorce, a woman enters a liminal period and is known as a "free woman" until she marries again. Free women are seen as potentially dangerous because they have no man to control their sexuality.

D. After menopause, "old women" become more assertive and enjoy many more freedoms. They are no longer feared by men for their sexuality.

IV. The Sambia of Papua, New Guinea, also practice a dramatic coming-of-age ceremony for males.

   A. The Sambia, like the Fulbe, are a patrilineal society with a clear segregation between the sexes.

   1. Sambian communities have men's houses on the edge of the village. Women are not allowed to enter these houses.

   2. There are also menstrual huts located outside the village, where women must go during their periods.

   3. Houses are clearly divided between the men's side and the women's side, and there are even separate male and female paths through the villages.

   B. Boys are raised by their mothers until about age 7. They are seen as being potentially polluted and debilitated by such close contact with women and, thus, must be made into men through a series of rituals that will last until their first child is born, usually in their early 20s.

   1. Boys are not believed to be born with a supply of semen, which is closely linked to male virility. They are, thus, initiated by ingesting semen from older boys.

   2. This initiation reenacts the Sambian myth of Numboolyu and Chemchi, the two original beings, and provides an unusual resolution to the Oedipus complex.

   3. After the ritualized homosexual phase of initiation, adolescents are expected to marry women.

   C. The prolonged Sambian initiation process makes men suspicious and fearful of women. They often have difficulty moving from the men's hut and adjusting to living with their wives.

Readings:

Thomas Gregor, *Anxious Pleasures*.

Gilbert Herdt, *The Sambia*.

Victor Turner, *The Ritual Process*.

Questions to Consider:

1. What rights of passage are important in our own culture? What functions do these serve?

2. How do the conditions of Fulbe initiation forge bonds between the boys?

3. Why are severe male initiation rites associated with antagonistic relations between the sexes?

Lecture Ten—Transcript
Rites of Passage

Rites of passage are found in cultures around the world. They mark significant events in the life stage of an individual. In our own culture, we have birthdays, anniversaries, bar mitzvahs, bat mitzvahs, in some parts of the country debutante balls, various sorts of ceremonies that mark different life stages. But, in other cultures, these rites of passage often play a much more central role than they do in our own society. In this lecture, we're going to review theories of rites of passage and look to two case studies. First, returning to the Fulbe, we're going to look at male circumcision camps that change boys into men, and then we're going to turn to the Sambia of Highland Papua New Guinea and their most unusual rites of passage that mark the same transition.

The typology that we have for understanding rites of passage comes to us from the anthropologist Arnold van Genep, who published a book in 1909 titled *Rites of Passage*, and he noted that there are three main stages to rites of passage. The first is separation from a group. You take the individual who's going to go through this process out of the normal social group, take them away from the group; then you have a period of transition, and this period of transition might last a few minutes, a few days, a few weeks, even a number of years in extreme cases. You have a period of separation, a period of transition, and then reintegration back into the group, taking on this new stage of life, a boy becoming a man, a girl becoming a woman. The anthropologist Victor Turner published a landmark work in 1969 titled *The Ritual Process: Structure and Anti-structure*. In this book, basically what he did was theorize van Genep's middle stage, this stage of transition, and he gave it the term liminality.

In Turner's words, liminality is an ambiguous state of being; it's betwixt and between normal states or normal conditions. It mediates between inner desires and social controls. Turner, when he was writing about liminality, saw it present in all sorts of rituals, and he stressed that it's an inverse state, a situation of anti-structure, where normal social norms are reversed. The normal rules of social life don't apply during a liminal period; the world is literally turned upside down. What's normally forbidden is allowed; what you would normally do is forbidden during a period of liminality. For Turner, liminality symbolically represents a period of regression, away from culture and this ordered aspect of life and toward nature and the untamed chaos of nature. He said that it's a very important ritual for people to undergo because it allows them to get in touch with their natural sides and then reemerge and reaffirm the social order of things.

We can apply the concept of liminality not only to rites of passage but all sorts of other things. University students, for example, in the States are in this period of liminality. They're no longer children, they're not living at home with their parents, and yet they're not fully adults either. They're probably still relying on their parents for financial support. So we have these certain periods of liminality. Some scholars have argued that a problem in contemporary U.S. society is we don't have clearly marked rites of passage. It's not clear when a boy becomes a man or when a girl becomes a woman. We have all of these little steps along the way. At 16, an adolescent can get a driver's license; at 18, they can vote; at 21, they can buy alcohol, but there's never this one defining moment that says, "Yesterday you were a boy and today you're a man," or "Yesterday you were a girl and today you're a woman."

Turner and others have applied his concept of liminality to carnival celebrations, for example, carnival celebrations around the world, these moments when the normal social structure is turned upside down. It's a period of liminality. Where public drunkenness would normally be looked down upon, it's OK; where public nudity would be prohibited, it's allowed, the normal social order of things being turned upside down. Turner said that during carnival celebrations, for example, it serves this powerful collective psychological safety valve; it allows people to shed the shackles of the social order and to get back in touch with the untamed chaos of nature, and then on Ash Wednesday, after Mardi Gras, after carnival is over, then they can reintegrate and reaffirm the social order of things.

Turner also argued in talking about liminality that periods of liminality can induce what he termed *communitas*. Communitas is this feeling of tight solidarity, of group unity that's facilitated by collective liminality, so he said that when a group, especially when a group goes through a rite of passage and they have this period of liminality, it bonds the group together. Here we can think of hazing rituals in fraternities and sororities at universities, in the military. Various sorts of hazing rituals serve to bond groups together because the group undergoes a common hardship, this period where the normal order of things is turned upside down, and it creates solid bonds that can very often last a lifetime.

Getting back to the Fulbe initiation ceremonies and rites of passage, boys are the focus of the Fulbe initiation ceremony. When boys are growing up in Fulbe society, their fathers are very distant. They're taken care of by their mothers, they spend most of their time at home with their mothers, and their fathers are off with their male friends. A strong bond thus naturally emerges between boys and their mothers. But, keep in mind, this is a patriarchal society; this is a society where men are suspicious of women, where men see women as being potentially polluting, debilitating to the male, and so boys have to be taken away from women and this world of women and made into men somehow. It's a little bit dangerous for them to spend all of their time with their mothers and in the company of women.

The Fulbe men, they see women as potentially polluting; they're especially scared of menstrual blood. Menstruating women are not allowed to enter a mosque, for example, and so all of this pollution can rub off on the boys and this has to be cleansed away during the ritual process, the rite of passage. In Fulbe ideology, women and young children are also seen as being a bit pagan. Recall in the last lecture we talked about Levi-Strauss's dichotomy of nature and culture, and nature is to culture as chaos is to order, as naked is to clothed, as women are to men, and so forth; so women and children are seen to embody this unrestrained chaos of nature in some ways that men, who are seen as being more cultured, more civilized, are not, so they have to take the boys out of this women's world, cleanse them of any pollution they might have undergone, and make them into men.

What they do is they have a circumcision camp, as Regis calls it. It's an odd verbal image for me, a circumcision camp; when I think of camp, I think of Boy Scout camp or something, and this is very different, letters being written home, I would imagine, from the circumcision camp. Anyway, when there are enough boys in a village between the ages of seven and 12 years old, when there's a critical mass to form a cohort, these boys will be gathered up and taken out of the village to a camp set up on the far side of the river. The boys are separated from their families, literally taken out of their mother's arms sometimes, and housed in this camp across the river. The camp will last for several weeks, and in the camp the boys are forced to do all sorts of things that they would never do in everyday life. They enter this period of liminality; they've been separated from society and their mothers, and they enter this period of liminality.

During the camp, the boys will eat unclean animals, and they'll even eat roadkill, and as you're all aware, the Muslim tradition has very clear guidelines about what sorts of meats can be eaten. The boys are fed polluted meats, the meats that they're taught not to eat in Koranic school, and not just fed a little bit but they're fed so much that they get sick, and they throw up, and they vomit, and they're fed too much millet and they get sick. And so during this camp the normal rules are turned upside down. What they normally couldn't eat, they would eat. Where they would normally show restraint in pulaaku in not eating too much, they're forced to consume more than they normally would. So you have this situation where boys are separated from their mothers, they're breaking with the world of women, and put together in the circumcision camp, which creates a real sense of communitas between these boys, a sense of togetherness. They go through all the same hardships; they form a bond, and a bond that will last through the rest of their lives

The Fulbe circumcision camp basically follows the scheme put forth by van Genep: separation from the village, followed by a period of transition, what Turner would have called liminality; and then reintegration. The circumcision itself, in one way the focal point of the camp, the boys are being taken there to be circumcised, but in another sense it's an anti-climactic part of this process. The boys are taken apart one by one, and the foreskin of their penis is cut off, using sometimes a razor blade, sometimes a knife, sometimes a pair of scissors. It will be wrapped up with an herbal package and allowed to heal. It's not unlike in some ways female genital mutilation in other parts of Africa. Some symbolic anthropologists argue that cutting off the foreskin removes the female-looking part of the male genitalia, just as female circumcision removes the erectile tissue from the female anatomy, and so it's not only symbolically making them into men and women, it's physically making them into men and women, taking those parts of the anatomy that look like the other gender and permanently inscribing the symbolic statement on their body.

After they've undergone circumcision, they have a number of days to heal, and then there's reintegration back into Fulbe society. In this reintegration, after they've undergone the ceremony, there's a huge feast in the village that's thrown to welcome these boys, now men, back into society, and the boys are paraded around, almost as if they were brides or some sort of West African Chippendales, and the women are allowed to ogle and look at them with lust in their eyes. This is a carryover of this period of liminality. Normally women aren't supposed to show any sort of overt sexuality; it's dangerous. But in this coming-in ceremony, they're allowed to go around and ogle the boys who are being paraded around as new young men. And so there's an overt sexuality in this reintegration ceremony that would normally be opposed to everything in Fulbe society. But once they're reintegrated into society, their interaction with women ends. They will still though get married—marriage is very important for the Fulbe—but they won't spend a lot of time with their wives. They don't spend a lot of time with their mothers or sisters either.

Women in Fulbe society go to Koranic school, as do the men. The boys generally attend Koranic school until their late teens or early 20s, so they've gone through the circumcision camp between the time they're seven and 12 years old. They attend a Koranic school with their Mallum, learning to memorize the Koran and repeating the Koran verbatim, and boys will do this until their late teens or early 20s, and then they're allowed this period of license, where they can go out, and sometimes they leave their community, go to a big city, maybe drink alcohol, maybe experiment sexually. They're allowed this period of freedom, and then they are expected to come back to Islam, to come back to being devout Muslims in their late 30s and 40s and go on studying the Koran. That's basically the life cycle of a boy changing into a man in Fulbe society.

Here I'd like to mention the stages that women go through, that girls becoming women go through as well. In Fulbe life, the women have four distinct stages of life, four distinct life phases that they will hold. The first is that of a virgin, a young girl up until the age that she gets married, and girls get married between 12 and 14 years old. They often marry a much older man, and these virgins are seen as being pure, as being unformed, still a girl, not a woman yet, not as dangerous as a woman would be. Then after marriage, after she's been deflowered by her husband, she's no longer a girl, she's a woman, and she's betrothed. She might have a bit of say in who she marries, but not a whole lot; her family's really going to decide this for her. A 12-, 13-, 14-year-old girl really doesn't know who to marry anyway, one could argue. The marriage is presumptively, at the beginning anyway, for a lifetime; yet most women in Fulbe society get divorced. The average woman has 2.6 husbands in Fulbe society, and women can initiate these divorces. If the husband doesn't give enough cloth at the annual exchanges, doesn't give enough good cloth, only gives print cloth and not wax cloth, these are perfectly acceptable grounds for a woman to divorce her husband.

When a woman gets divorced, she enters into the third stage of her life, and that is the status of a free woman. Free women, they're women who have been divorced and in between marriages; they're probably going to get married again, and they're considered to be very dangerous beings by the Fulbe men. They're more subject to their passions than men are. Men are considered to be more disciplined in regards to sexuality, and this really turns upside down our own Western cultural model of men and women. We would assume that men have this unrestrained sexuality and that women are more reserved. Among the Fulbe, it's women who would be nymphomaniacs if they didn't have a man, if they didn't have a husband to keep them in their place, so men are scared of these free women, these divorced women. They have no husband to control them, and sometimes they have affairs. They will have affairs with younger men or with married men sometimes.

Eventually they'll get married again. As I've said, they get married two to three times generally during their lifetime. So you have the stage of virginity, and then a girl-woman is married, and then after she gets divorced she can be a free woman; and then finally after menopause, when they can no longer have children, they become asexual in a way. They're seen as not being as tied to the passions of nature as they once were, not as potentially dangerous as they once were, but seen as being wise, as someone who's lived through all of the travails that a woman, a mother, a wife has to live through. Very often they return to studying the Koran at this stage. They stopped, you'll remember, when they got married at 12 or 13 or 14 years old, they stopped going to Koranic school, but after they become these old women, they can go back to the Koran, and often they're seen as elders. People will go to them for advice, and people sometimes feel able to talk to them in a way that they couldn't talk to elder men.

Continuing this discussion of rites of passage, I'd like to turn to a group known as the Sambia, who live in Papua New Guinea, the Highlands of New Guinea. New Guinea, you'll remember, is off the coast of Australia. The Highlands are a very ragged territory, high elevations, seven or eight or nine thousand feet high, dramatic peaks and valleys, so you have lots of little groups that are geographically separated and don't have a lot of contact with one another, and, as a result, there are literally hundreds of languages, not just dialects, but hundreds of languages spoken in New Guinea, and the Sambia speak an Anga language. The Sambia are made famous by a number of studies conducted by the anthropologist Gilbert Herdt. He started going there in the late 1960s and early 1970s, and he's kept going back year after year, even to this day.

The Sambia is a pseudonymous name; the name of the group is well known among people who live in the area, but Herdt wanted to protect their privacy and to protect them from the curious tourists because of their unusual rituals, which we will talk about in just a moment. The Sambian, they live in Highland New Guinea. It's a tropical climate; they get about 150 inches of rainfall every year. The seasons, they have two seasons, rainy and dry. It's a region where there are these hundreds of groups divided by rough geography, divided by language, and you get lots of warfare and conflict between the different groups. In Sambian society, you also find a strong division between the spheres of men and women. They're not Muslim, so this isn't an Islamic division—it's not based on Islamic scripture—but men and women are even more segregated in Sambian society than they are in Fulbe society.

In a Sambian village, you have the village proper, and then on the outside of the village, there'll be a men's house—a clubhouse, we could call it—and this is where the men go and live when they start their initiation ceremony, and they'll actually live there from the time they're seven years old until their early 20s, sometimes their mid-20s. They'll live in this men's hut, live communally only with other men, until their first child is born. You have a village—on the outside is a men's hut. Inside the village, there's a central plaza area and circular houses around it, and inside these houses, these huts, will live a nuclear family, a man, his wife, and their children, but even inside the hut there's literally lines very often in the middle of the hut, and women cannot enter the man's side of the hut, so the women's side in the hut is when you first go in the door. A man would walk in, step over the woman's side of the hut, and enter his own side of the area.

So you have the men's clubhouses, the village proper, and then outside the village as well you'll have a menstrual hut and this is where women who are menstruating have to go during their periods. They leave the village, they leave their family, and they go out and they stay in this menstrual hut during their period. There's a strict segregation of men and women in the Sambian villages, and concerning these menstrual huts, there's been conflicting reports about whether they're—at first they were seen as a very bad thing for women. What an awful way of subjugating women; these men are forcing women to leave their homes when they're having their period and go out and live in these menstrual huts. Some recent revisionist research has suggested, however, that the women don't mind this at all. A woman's daily life in Sambian society is not easy: waking up at four in the morning; starting a fire; cooking food for the family; when breakfast is over starting to cook lunch. It's a very grueling lifestyle, and this is a chance for women to get together outside of the watchful eye of men and spend some leisurely time. And so is the segregation of women into a menstrual hut, is this an ugly side of patriarchy or is it a way in which women can live their lives a little better? The evidence is conflicting on this.

But getting back to the segregation of the sexes in Sambian villages, there are even separate paths through the village for men and women. Men walk on one path and women walk on another. I bring this up just to reinforce how divided men and women are in Sambian society. Men in Sambian society are expected to embody a quality that they call *jerungdu*, and this means fierceness. Historically, there have been a lot of battles between these groups in Highland New Guinea, and they value warriors. The men need to become warriors, and so they want to instill them with this sense of jerundu or fiercety, fierceness. And they do this through the initiation process.

Initiation for Sambian boys starts around the age of seven years old, about the same time that it starts for Fulbe boys, but for the Sambian boys initiation is not completed until their mid-20s, until the birth of their first child, and so it's this really long period of initiation, and throughout this whole period they will live in the men's house, live away from the women. During initiation, the boys are taken out of the village in a ceremony, again not unlike the Fulbe ceremony, where they're ripped out of their mother's arms. The mothers very often are screaming, "Don't take my child away. Don't take my son away," and the older men and the older boys come and they take these boys away. The boys don't know what's going to happen, so they're incredibly scared, and you take them out to a temporary camp set up outside of the village.

When the boys are in this camp, they're put through incredible hardships. They're made to dance for hours and hours on end. They're made to take long hikes. They're not given enough to eat. They're really pushed to the edge of consciousness, not unlike the way in which certain religious sects brainwash their converts, really pushing them to the edge of consciousness so that the mind opens up and is willing to accept all of these new things and internalize these new ways of looking at the world. Among the Sambia, unlike in Fulbe initiation, the initiation process is supposed to be very secret. The women in society aren't supposed to know what goes on; there are these huge secrets. Gilbert Herdt, the anthropologist who has worked there, calls them screaming secrets because the women actually know what goes on, but they can't talk about it. They have to act like they don't know what's going on, so the boys are taken out of their homes, away from their mothers, and they're put in these camps where they learn the secrets of manhood.

In these initiation camps, they learn how to play flutes, and with these flutes, and these are secret flutes—the women aren't supposed to see these flutes—with these flutes, the boys, they're made to play the flutes, they're hit on the head with the flutes, and then the flutes are used as a prelude for teaching them the basis of Sambian initiation, and this really has to be one of the most unusual rituals ever observed by anthropologists in the world, and it is ritualized homosexuality between the older boys and men and these younger boys. To understand a Sambian initiation here, we have to go over a bit of Sambian ethnobiology. The Sambian believes that men are not born with a supply of semen and that they don't produce it themselves. Instead, the men are born with an empty organ called a *tingu*, and the semen has to somehow get built up in the body, and the semen is the source of *jerungdu*, of fierceness.

It's crucially important for boys to develop, healthy physically and psychologically and socially, that they undergo this process, that they undergo this insemination, and so the young boys are forced—they're taught—to perform fellatio, oral sex, on the older boys, and they do this because they really believe that the young boys don't have any semen, and so they have to ingest this from the older boys so that they can grow up and become a strong man. The Sambia will tell you, "Of course it works. Look, we take these prepubescent boys, and they undergo this process, and in a couple of years their genitals start growing, they start getting pubic hair, so it obviously works."

The justification for this ritual goes back to the origin myth in Sambian society, which boys don't learn until the very last stage of initiation, when they're in their mid-20s, after their first child has been born. The Sambian initiation myth says that in the beginning, there were two individuals, Numboolyu and Chemchi, and these were basically asexual beings. They both had incipient genitalia of both sexes, but it wasn't very highly developed. Over time, what happened was Chemchi began performing fellatio on Numboolyu, and Numboolyu became a man and Chemchi grew larger breasts and became a woman. Over time, and the Sambia believe that a woman can become impregnated either through intercourse or through oral sex as well by ingesting semen, they believe that Chemchi got pregnant, and then Numboolyu, when she came to term, cut an opening in her which became the vagina, and she gave birth to a child, so we have this first couple, Numboolyu and Chemchi, the Sambian Adam and Eve, although they're definitely eating from a different apple tree than our Adam and Eve ate from.

They have a son, and they have another son a few years later, and when the older son starts going through puberty he comes to his father and he says, "I have these feelings. I have an erection. I don't know what to do with it. Why can't I have sex with Chemchi, my mother, your wife?" Numboolyu, the father, says "No way, that's totally out of the question," so we have this classic Oedipal conflict reflected in the Sambian mythology, a boy wanting to have sex with the mother, the father not allowing that to happen, the father prohibiting that. But the Sambia have come up with this unique solution to the Oedipal conflict, and that is, the father Numboolyu told the older boy to have his younger brother perform oral sex on him so that it would both serve as a sexual outlet for the older boy and build up the seminal fluids in this organ, the *tingu* of the younger boy.

Throughout their lifetime, males have to be very careful about not wasting their semen. They have to be very possessive toward their semen, and women are seen as being semen-hungry, so men have to be careful around women, about having sex with women. They don't want to have sex too often because the women are going to soak up all of your semen, and if this life source is depleted, a man can die; so after the Sambia have sex, they will actually go out and lick the sap of this particular tree to help them rebuild their semen supply.

When they're away during this camp, at the beginning of initiation, they learn to perform these homosexual activities. Gilbert Herdt, who's worked with them, calls it ritualized homosexuality, and it's important to point out that most of the boys don't want to do this; they're forced to do this. It's something that they are embarrassed about, they don't want to talk with the women about, and very often they don't even want to talk to anthropologists about this process at all. The elders are forcing them to do it, and through the initiation process they haven't been fed much, they've been dancing all night, they've been taken on these long hikes, they're really pushed to the edge of consciousness, and they're very susceptible to internalizing these new ideas. This goes on for a period of time. Once boys enter into puberty, they become the active partner in this relationship of oral sex with younger boys. They will eventually get married in their late teens or early 20s, and they go through a period of bisexuality, where they're still living in the men's house where these ritualized homosexual acts are performed, and they start having sex with their wives as well. We have this transition, this fairly unique transition of homosexuality, bisexuality, and then men are expected to become fully heterosexual after the birth of their first child.

This is an unusual ritual, but it's not out of the question. There are other groups in Papua New Guinea who practice similar sexual practices. There are groups in Amazonia, although they don't have this ritualized homosexual aspect, they do have menstrual huts; they have secret men's cults and so forth. While this is an extreme example, the same general sort of pattern of antagonism between the sexes holds in a number of different cultures. These rites of passage, marking a transition from childhood to adulthood—and in most cultures this is a defining feature of becoming an adult, is getting married and having a family, and this is going to be the topic of our next lecture.

Lecture Eleven
Family, Marriage, and Incest

Scope: All cultures practice some form of marriage, if we define marriage rather broadly. Arrangement marriages are the norm around the world, with romantic love seen as a weak basis for a lifetime partnership. The most casual form of marriage comes from the Nayar of India, where women have a number of "visiting" husbands," yet even here males are required to publicly recognize their relationships and claim paternity for their children. Many cultures favor cousin marriages—making children marry outside of the immediate family, but not too far outside that family relations get diluted. Nonetheless, even among cultures with such marriage rules, in practice we find a degree of flexibility in choosing a spouse.

In a majority of cultures, men may have more than one wife, although usually it is a small percentage of males who can afford to support multiple wives. About 15% of cultures practice monogamy, or serial monogamy, as is the case in the West. The rarest form of marriage (found in only six cultures) is polyandry, where a woman has more than one husband. Polyandrous marriages are generally found in extreme environments (for example, on the Himalayan highlands of Nepal), where it is advantageous to limit population growth.

While romantic love is often not seen as a valid basis for marriage, it is found in virtually all cultures. All cultures also enforce a prohibition on incest—the fundamental restrictions on whom one may marry. We find that the range of what are considered incestuous relations varies significantly.

Outline

I. In less complex societies, kinship serves as the basis for economic, political, and other social roles.

    A. There are two primary types of kinship relations, *consanguines* (blood relatives) and *affines* (in-laws). These are biological and legal relations, but their significance is culturally constructed.

B. Descent is the intergenerational relationship between consanguines. Descent groups serve important social functions but vary in size and composition.

    1. *Lineages* are groups of consanguines who can trace their relationships back to a known common ancestor.

    2. *Clans* are groups of lineages that claim common descent from a mythical ancestor.

II. There are three main forms of descent groups: patrilineal, matrilineal, and cognatic. These determine paths of inheritance, as well as social roles in society.

    A. About 40 percent of all societies practice patrilineal descent, in which relations are traced through male lines.

        1. Patrilineal descent is associated with patriarchal societies. Even where the ideology of male dominance is muted, however, women in patrilineal systems often live their lives as outsiders.

        2. In a patrilineal system, one simply does not feel related to one's mother and her family as one does with the father's side of the family. Sisters are members of their father's patrilineage, but their children belong to their husband's patrilineage.

    B. Matrilineal systems are much rarer, found in only about 15 percent of all societies.

    C. The most common form of descent is cognatic descent, in which relationships are traced through both male and female lines. About 45 percent of all societies practice cognatic descent.

        1. Cognatic descent is associated with mobility and is, generally, a much more flexible system. It is practiced in most modern Western cultures, as well as in smaller-scale societies around the world.

        2. The Dobe Ju/'hoansi, a nomadic band–level society in the Kalahari region of southern Africa, practice cognatic descent, which helps them maintain large networks of kin to call on in times of need.

III. Monogamy is relatively rare cross-culturally. Most cultures allow men to have multiple wives, and a very few permit multiple husbands.

    A. About 82 percent of societies allow polygyny, the marriage of one man to multiple women.

        1. Having multiple wives is a sign of wealth and prestige.

        2. There are also clear political and economic benefits to having more than one wife.

        3. Trobriand chiefs strategically marry a number of wives from different lineages in order to increase their political networks.

    B. There have only been about five reported cases of societies that are polyandrous, with women having more than one husband.

        1. Polyandry appears to emerge in harsh physical circumstances with extremely limited resources and a need for low population growth.

        2. Tibetans in Nepal practice fraternal polyandry, in which brothers will marry a single wife. This prevents family lands from being broken up.

IV. Marriage, in some form or another, is found in all cultures.

    A. Evolutionarily, human beings are predisposed to pair-bonding. Given the incredible helplessness of human infants, it has, until recently, been a biological imperative to have two caregivers.

    B. Most Americans marry for love, although this is the exception rather than the rule around the world.

        1. Some historians and social scientists believe that the notion of romantic love is a Western ideology first developed by 12th-century French troubadours.

        2. A survey I conducted of 166 cultures found some form of romantic love in all of them. Perhaps, then, some have speculated, there may be a biological predisposition to falling in love.

    C. Although pair-bonding may be universal, the precise form of marriage varies greatly. The most extreme example comes from the Nayar of southern India, who practice two types of marriage.

        1. When girls reach their early teenage years there, they participate in *tali-rite marriages*. The couple will cohabitate for only a few days or weeks, and the marriage may or may not be consummated. Few obligations follow this initial ceremonial period.

    2. Women then enter into multiple *sandbadham marriages*. These are fairly casual unions; the couples do not live together, and a woman may maintain any number of these relationships at one time. Despite this openness, when a child is born, it is crucial that a man claim paternity.

V. Even though romantic love appears to be a cultural universal, arranged marriages are by far the norm in societies around the world.

VI. Just as marriage is found in all cultures, so too are restrictions on whom one can marry. Incest taboos may appear as a sort of natural law, but their precise formulation varies from culture to culture.

    A. In the Judeo-Christian tradition, incest rules go back to prohibitions spelled out in Leviticus. These were greatly expanded by the Catholic Church in the 12th century.

    B. Incest taboos may have a biological basis in that they avoid the ill effects of recessive genetic traits, although inbreeding would also have weeded out such traits over the long term.

    C. Edward Westermark argued that familiarity breeds contempt and, thus, that children raised together would lose sexual passion for one another. Several studies seem to bear out his hypothesis.

        1. On *kibutzim* in Israel where children were raised together, virtually no members of the same cohort married one another.

        2. Very poor Chinese families sometimes practice infant betrothal with their daughters in what are called *sim-pua marriages*; the future husband and wife grow up together in the same manner as siblings. These marriages have low fertility rates and high divorce rates.

Readings:

Helen Fisher, *Anatomy of Love: A Natural History of Mating.*

Melvyn C. Goldstein, "When Brothers Share a Wife," *Natural History*, March 1987, pp. 39–48.

Jack Goody, *The Development of the Family and Marriage in Europe.*

Yolanda Murphy and Robert Murphy, *Women of the Forest.*

Arthur Wolf, *Sexual Attraction and Childhood Association.*

Questions to Consider:

1. What evolutionary pressure would promote pair-bonding?
2. Is incest a natural aversion or is it learned?
3. Why is polygyny so common and polyandry so rare around the world?

Lecture Eleven—Transcript
Family, Marriage, and Incest

Today I'd like to talk about marriage and the family, both of these as the nucleus of social relationships. Kinship, which is the culturally recognized relationships based on blood and on marriage, has long been a staple of anthropology, something we've been concerned with. Your own kinship system probably seems natural to you. We were raised from earliest age to learn our kinship terms. Your father's brother is of course your uncle; your mother's sister is of course your aunt. But in many societies around the world, your father's brother would be called father; your mother's sister might be called mother; you might have a number of relatives that you would call brother and sister that aren't what we would consider to be your biological brothers and sisters.

We generally take kinship terms to be the equivalent of biological relationships, and kinship terms do try and represent biological relationships, but it's important to keep in mind that the anthropological concept of kinship is concerned with these cultural models of relatedness, and they overlap with biological relationships, but they're distinct in certain ways. It's a model, it's a scheme, it's a cultural model, as we've talked about in previous lectures. In this lecture, we're going to review different sorts of kinship structures, lineages and clans; matrilineal, patrilineal, and cognatic societies; and then we're going to turn to marriage, romantic love, and the universal prohibition against incest.

I would like for you to keep in mind during this lecture that the rules of kinship, like any role of culture, like any rule of language in fact, they're always flexible, they're always changing. We're improvising, based on these rules, and changing them, based on the situations in which we find ourselves, so as we talk about them, these rules may seem hard and fast. In practice, they're very often much more flexible. We have two main types of kinship that we distinguish in anthropology, consanguineal kin and affinal kin. Consanguineal comes from consanguines, and the Latin root for blood, sanguine, and it refers to blood relatives. Affinal kin, what we would call our in-laws, refers to relatives by marriage rather than by blood. We also have fictive kin, godparents, for example, or family friends who we might call aunt or uncle or even brother or sister that don't have any sort of biological relationship.

Consanguines are called descent groups, and descent groups have lots of important functions in societies that don't have formal legal structures, formal economic systems. Descent groups can regulate marriage; they often serve as economic units holding land in common, for example. They even serve religious functions, as certain rituals will be passed down from generation to generation in a descent group. There are two main types of descent groups. The first is clans, and the second is lineages, and the big difference between these is that clans trace their common origin back to a mythical ancestor and lineages trace their origin back to a known ancestor, so they both believe that they're descended from a common ancestor, but in lineages you know who that person is, and in a clan it's very often a mythical figure. Clans are very often made up of groups of lineages; they're larger than lineages.

There are several types of descent groups. The first we can talk about is patrilineal descent groups. In patrilineal societies, and they make up about 40 percent of societies around the world, everyone is related through the males. Descent is traced only through male lines; the chain of descent always stops with the female, so in a patrilineal society you're not really related to your mother and your mother's side of the family in the same way that you're related to your father and your father's side of the family. This seems odd to us because we see ourselves as being related equally to both sides of our family, but not in patrilineal societies, and relatives are conceived in different ways as well. Mother's brother, whom we would call an uncle, mother's brother, an uncle, is a very different sort of relative in a patrilineal society than your father's brother, also whom we would call uncle. So we have patrilineal descent groups.

We also have matrilineal descent groups, which, as the name implies, descent is traced through female lines. There's a much smaller percentage of societies in the world that are matrilineal, only about 15 percent, so it's fairly rare, and here descent always stops with the male. For example, a man's children are not members of his own matrilineage; they're not members of his family in this cultural model. They're members of their mother's family. In matrilineal societies, ironically, it's not women who really run things. If women ran a society, we would call that a matriarchy. Where descent is traced through female lines, we call this matrilineality, and we have 15 percent of those societies are matrilineal, but in none of these do women hold the formal positions of power, so they're not matriarchies. Men still are the chiefs; they hold the formal positions of authority and power in these societies. There's no recorded case of a matriarchy in the ethnographic record.

So I have patrilineal societies, matrilineal societies, and finally cognatic societies, and this is the system that our own culture uses. We're neither matrilineal nor patrilineal; we trace our relationships through both the mother's side of the family and the father's side of the family. Generally, you have the possibility in our own society, in a cognatic society, of feeling equally related to your mother's side and your father's side of the family. Cognatic descent is found in about 45 percent of the world's cultures, and it's the most flexible system. It's obviously a lot more flexible than matrilineality or patrilineality and it's often associated with mobility, and so, strangely enough, it unites gathering and hunting groups, nomadic groups who need a very flexible kinship system, and industrial and post-industrial societies like our own. We'll come back to these in this lecture and in later lectures, but right now I want to move on to marriage for a moment.

Why do people get married? It seems obvious to us. You get married because you fall in love; you find your one true-life partner, fall madly in love and get married, and hopefully live happily ever after. But for most of the people in the world, marrying for love, marrying for these romantic notions that we hold so dear as Westerners, is not seen as a valid reason. Love is seen as a youthful folly in many cultures, something fickle, whereas marriage is the ultimate contract, a lifetime bond between individuals, and not only between individuals but between families as well. In many cultures around the world, love is not seen as a good reason for getting married, and when marriage is occurring at such an early age—you'll remember that among the Fulbe, girls get married when they're 12, 13, or 14 years old— maybe they're not capable of choosing their best partner.

This seems odd to us. Who would know better than I who I should marry? But if you're 12, 13 or even 14, 15, 16, 17 years old, how do you know who your best spouse is going to be for the rest of your life? These kids have no idea. Their hormones are raging wildly, they have these crazy romantic notions in their head, so the parents think that they should choose who their children's spouses should be. It's not just a question of personal choice. The idea of monogamy is not the norm in marriage customs around the world.

A number of historians and anthropologists believe that romantic love is a Western invention. This is actually probably the standard view in history and in anthropology as well, that romantic love arose in the 11th and 12th century France, in the courtly culture where there were all of these troubadours and the immensely wealthy courts of the time, all these people just hanging around the court with all of this leisure time, and so the men and the women, to divert themselves, came up with this idea of romantic love, and men started falling in love with women and writing love poetry and so forth, and the women started falling in love with men. The vocabulary of romantic love really entered in the popular discourse at this time.

I did some research about 10 years ago with my co-author, Bill Jankowiak, looking for evidence of romantic love in cultures around the world, and we took a sample of 168 cultures and we read everything we could find about these cultures, looking for evidence of romantic love. It's hard to find, because in most cultures they practice arranged marriage, so people aren't marrying for romantic love, so we had to look for things like suicides of unrequited love and elopements or love poetry, and in the study we found evidence of romantic love in 90 percent of the societies that we looked at, 90 percent, and in the other 10 percent it was very often probably a case of ethnographers overlooking or not including the data that we needed to make a determination.

So a number of sociobiologists picked up on this finding to argue that perhaps romantic love evolved early on in hominid evolution to facilitate pair-bonding and perhaps there is some biological basis for feelings of romantic love, the function that would be to create a pair bond, to facilitate raising of children, and some studies have shown in recent years that when people are in love there are elevated levels of dopamine and other hormones, and so there are actually physical chemical changes that occur in the brain when one falls in love. An interesting thing is, researchers at first thought that they would find the brain waves of people in love would look like obsessive-compulsives, people suffering from obsessive-compulsive disorder, and what they actually found is, when they do these brain scans, PET scans and MRIs and so forth, that the brain patterns of people in love, deeply in love, look more like coke addicts than they do like obsessive-compulsives, and so perhaps there's this addictive quality to love as well that evolved to help us form pair-bonds.

Monogamy is the exception in cultures around the world rather than the rule. Most cultures allow some form of polygamy, of multiple spouses. Let me make a clarification here about the terminology that we're using. Polygamy is the overarching term, and it means having more than one spouse, a man having more than one wife or a woman having more than one husband. In anthropology, we use two more precise terms: polygyny, which refers to a man having more than one wife; and polyandry, which is when a woman has more than one husband. Both polygyny and polyandry are forms of polygamy. Polygyny is very common around the world; about 82 percent of the world's societies allow men to have more than one wife. But, on the other hand, polyandry is extremely rare. We only know six or seven cases, less than one percent of the cultures that have been sampled in the world practice polyandry. It's extremely rare, and it seems to be most closely associated with extreme environmental conditions.

The best known example is of the ethnic Tibetans living in Nepal, a very rough environment, 12,000 feet above sea level. Most of the families are poor and have very little cultivatable land, and they practice a very specific form of polyandry in which brothers share a single wife, and this is called fraternal polyandry, when brothers share a single wife. Why might this be? They live in this harsh environment, not a ton of land to go around, and fraternal polyandry keeps land together. These men are marrying the same woman, so they can all farm the same land. They compose a single household, and, too, it reduces the rate of reproduction. Women are limited in the number of children that they can have in their lifetime, and if one woman has several husbands, the absolute rate of reproduction will be very low.

Marriage is generally considered to be a human universal; people in all cultures bond with members of the opposite sex, but there are a few exceptions, and actually the exception that might prove the rule in this case is a group called the Nayar, and we find them in southwest India. They're the example that's often held up to show that marriage is not universal, but even among the Nayar we find bonding between men and women, something that looks a lot like marriage and is very important to their culture. The Nayar are matrilineal; they're a matrilineal society. The core of the household is a brother and sister, or brothers and sisters, and they will live together and have their lands and their houses in common. Traditionally, the Nayar have been a very warlike society. The men are warriors. They would go off for long periods of time and fight and then come back periodically to their own households.

Among the Nayar, we find two forms of what we can call marriage. The first is called a tali-rite, and this is basically a rite of passage, a puberty rite, a coming-of-age ceremony for girls, much more so for girls than boys. When a girl is somewhere between the ages of seven and 12, very often prepubescent, before she's begun her menstrual cycle, she will marry a man who lives in the same village and who's been selected by her parents, but this man should be from another matrilineage. They will cohabitate for a few days. The man has the right to have sex with this wife, but they don't always do it. Especially if the girl is very young, the man will not have sex with his wife, but once the girl has gone through this cohabitation, whether she's had sex or not, before she goes through it she's a girl and when she comes out she's a full woman, she's a real woman in Nayar society, and in fact is called by the term that they use for women, the honorific term for women. This marriage, this tali-rite marriage, might only last for three, four, or five days, but it's an important part of making girls into women.

Afterwards, when a girl gets older, she's going to have very little to do with this first husband, this tali-rite husband. There are a few points in the life cycle where they have to get back together, and the husband will give certain ritual gifts to his wife, but for the most part this is a three- to five-day marriage, if you will, and then it ends there. But afterward, when the girl gets older, she can enter into another form of marriage, which we call sandbadham marriages, and these are marriage based on mutual consent. They're not arranged marriages, and they also have this serial quality. Sandbadham husbands are also called visiting husbands, and what they'll do is, after dinner—and you'll remember that men are living with their sisters in their family household—a man will leave his home after dinner, go to his sandbadham wife, put his spear in front of the doorway to let other people know that he's there. He'll spend the night with his wife and then leave the next morning and go back to his sister's house, where he'll eat and have breakfast.

A woman can have various sandbadham marriages at one time, up to 20, for example, and most women have two, three, four or five—up to 10, 20 is very unusual—but they can have multiple sandbadham marriages at the same time. In some ways, these are very casual relationships, and they can be terminated without any legal recourse, and people don't seem to really get upset. They can be ended by mutual consent in that way. The visiting husbands, sandbadham husbands, will give things to their wives, some cooking oil, maybe a little bit of money, not too much, but a little bit to help them get by in their everyday lives. The women don't depend on their husbands for their survival, but it's a nice little extra bit that he gives them.

The crucial thing occurs when a woman gets pregnant. Every child has to have a father in Nayar society. Paternity has to be acknowledged, but if a woman has eight sandbadham husbands, for example, how does she know who the father is? We can always be sure of maternity, but we can never (at least in the days before DNA testing), we could never be absolutely sure of paternity, and what happens is one of the husbands has to step up to the plate and claim to be the father of this child. Often a lot of negotiation goes on between the woman and her sandbadham husbands, getting them to claim paternity in this case. Marriage among the Nayar is not exclusive. The couples don't cohabitate; it's a very different form of marriage than our own form. However, it's very important. This form of marriage, both the tali-rite and the sandbadham, are very important in Nayar society, and it's important to validate paternity, to show who the father of a child is, and this is a common thread in marriage and cultures throughout the world, claiming paternity.

I'd like to move on at this point and talk just a bit about incest. Incest is based around rules of exogamy. Exogamy is marrying outside of a particular group, and endogamy, endogamy is marrying within a particular group. One of the universal taboos found in cultures around the world is a prohibition against incest, against having sexual relationships or marrying some category of kin. You have to marry outside of a given group; you have to marry exogamously. But the rub is, what that category of kin is changes and varies significantly from society to society. In our own culture, whom one can marry varies from state to state. First-cousin marriage is prohibited in most states, I believe all states, and in some states second-cousin marriage is prohibited as well, although not that long ago there were a lot of first- and second-cousin marriages, even in our own culture.

Interestingly, we generally take a revulsion about incest to be natural. It's disgusting; why would anybody want to do that? It's just one of those perversities of everyday life. But, as I said, the range of what we consider to be incestuous has changed over time. The universal prohibition against incest is just with one's siblings, one's parents and one's children, so just the basic nuclear family, what we would consider to be the nuclear family. This is the universal prohibition against incest; no culture in the world allows marriage or sexual relationships within this group. I have to admit, there are couple of very rare exceptions, Hawaiian nobility, Egyptian kings and queens, this idea that where royalty is descended from the gods and the bloodline has to be kept pure, they allow brother and sister to marry occasionally, but these are very rare cases, and for the most part every culture in the world prohibits sexual relations between brothers and sisters and parents and children.

But the range of incestuous relatives is culturally defined. Is first-cousin marriage incestuous? Most people would agree. What about second-cousin marriage? Most people would still agree, but where do we draw the line? At what point does incest start? In the Western tradition, our prohibitions against incest come from the Judeo-Christian tradition, come from the Bible, in particular Chapter 18 in Leviticus, verse 6, and in parts of Chapter

20 of Leviticus as well, where we find a number of prohibitions listed. For example, do not dishonor your father by having sexual relations with your mother. She is your mother; do not have relations with her. Do not have sexual relations with your sister and so forth, but this isn't a very wide range of relatives that are prohibited. One is not supposed to have sexual relations with parents, with aunts or uncles, with grandchildren and so forth, but it's a very narrow range of what is explicitly prohibited in Leviticus.

But beyond that, the Catholic Church started expanding out what was considered to be incestuous, and in A.D. 385, Pope Theodeus I prohibited first-cousin marriage. This wasn't prohibited in the Bible, it wasn't found in the scripture, but the Pope decided that that was a little bit too close and prohibited it, and then gradually the Catholic Church expanded out the range of what was considered to be incestuous so that by A.D. 1059, Pope Nicholas II prohibited marriage to the seventh degree. That means you couldn't marry—you would have your father, your grandfather, your great-grandfather, great-great-grandfather, great-great-great-grandfather, great-great-great-great-grandfather, great-great-great-great-great-grandfather, and any of their descendants would be prohibited from marriage. If you're living in rural France in the 11th century, you can't marry anybody; nobody in your village would be eligible to be married.

But of course there was an exception. You could buy a dispensation from the church; you could buy the right to marry your second cousin or your third cousin or even your first cousin, so one intent, whether it was intentional or not, of the Catholic Church's expansion of the incest prohibition was an increase in the sales of dispensations, of licenses to break canonical law. The range of what was considered to be incestuous was gradually shrunk back in the Catholic tradition. In 1215, it was reduced to four degrees. In 1537, it was reduced to two degrees. It was reduced for South American Indians first and then later for descendants of Africans. In 1917, it was reduced to two degrees, and finally it was reduced to two degrees for everyone in the world.

But some sort of prohibition against incest is found in all cultures, and why might this be? The obvious answer that comes to mind is inbreeding. We don't marry our relatives because of the dangers of having recessive genes come to the fore. There's one study that has found that the children of very close incestuous relationships are eight times more likely to be born with birth defects. This is true, but it doesn't help us understand why there are different cultural conceptions of what is incest, why the group that is considered incestuous varies from culture to culture. Is marrying your second cousin incest? What if your second cousin was adopted? Would that be incest? Most people would still consider it to be incest, but it's adopted, so there's not a biological relationship there, so incest is cultural; it's a social prohibition. Inbreeding is a partial answer, but it's an incomplete explanation for fully explaining incest taboos.

The scholar Edward Westermark offered another explanation, and he coined the phrase "familiarity breeds contempt," and this is from his 1891 work *The History of the Human Marriage*. What he means here is if you're raised with someone day in and day out, like a brother or sister, even if they're not your biological brother or sister, it's a turnoff. It's not romantic; sexual relationships won't flourish because growing up together mutes that kind of lust and sexuality. In the last decades, a few studies have been done that give support to the idea that familiarity breeds contempt, and the most famous were done in kibbutzim in Israel, kibbutzim, the communal communities in Israel that were started in the 1950s, and there were studies done in the 1960s and 1970s looking at marriage patterns and looking at sexual relationships between people who were raised on very traditional kibbutzim.

On these rigid kibbutzim, children would be raised in dormitories away from their parents. They would visit their parents every day, but they would be raised as a cohort away from their parents, so they were raised with this peer group, intimately seeing each other every day, boys and girls, men and women as they grow up. One study looked at 125 couples that had been raised since birth on the same kibbutz, and none of them got married to each other, none of them, and you'd say, "Who would you find for a potential mate?" The obvious example would be someone that you were living with day in and day out. This would be an obvious pool of potential marriage partners, but none of the people in the study married one another, and there have been other studies that show that there are very few sexual relations as well among youths on kibbutzim.

The other example I want to mention that moves toward proving this hypothesis that familiarity breeds contempt was done by the anthropologist Arthur Wolf. He worked with the Chinese exile community living in Taiwan, and he noticed that there was a prevalence of a certain type of marriage called the sim-pua marriage. The sim-pua marriage is infant betrothal. It's normally done by very poor families who can't afford to raise their child, especially a daughter, and so they betroth their daughter at a very early age, sometimes as early as six or seven months, sometimes as old as three or four years, but betrothing them to their future husband at a very early age. The girl then goes and lives with her future husband's family and is raised like a sister. They very often sleep in the same bed, they bathe together, they eat together; it's just like she becomes a daughter in this family, until she comes of age, and then she's expected to marry who she's been living with as a brother and live the rest of her life in marriage that way.

Arthur Wolf looked at these marriages to see how successful they were. He found that the fertility rate was 30 percent lower than other sorts of marriage, so something's going on here. The fertility rate was 30 percent lower. He started interviewing people who were in sim-pua marriages, and he found out that these marriages were incredibly tumultuous. The husbands were more likely to cheat on their wives; there were more avid consumers of prostitutes and pornography; there was lots of familial strife, domestic abuse, and a high rate of divorce. Wolf concludes that it's because familiarity breeds contempt; these children were raised with one another since infants, just as if they were brother and sister, and then when it came the moment to initiate the marriage, to have sexual relationships, both sides, the boys and the girls, very often refused. There are accounts of mothers having to use a broom and force the children into the bridal chamber to consummate this marriage.

Does incest have a biological basis? Probably, potentially. Are there also important cultural, psychological factors going on here as well? Most certainly. Does marriage have an evolutionary cause? Perhaps. To facilitate pair-bonding, it makes a lot of sense, but, as we've seen, marriage is conceived of very differently in cultures around the world. We have arranged marriages, we have these multiple spouses, we have these infant betrothals of the sim-pua marriage. Even our kinship terms, which seem so natural to us, are cultural constructions. Yes, they're based on biological relationships, but we extend that out to step siblings and adopted siblings and so forth, and so we see here the importance of culture. In the next lecture, we're going to apply these concepts of kinship and culture to the Trobriand Islanders.

Lecture Twelve
Multiple Spouses and Matrilineality

Scope: Matrilineal and patrilineal societies often distinguish between different types of "uncles," "aunts," and "cousins." For example, we call our mother's sister "aunt" while many matrilineal societies would refer to her as "mother." Likewise, cousins are distinguished as "cross" (children of opposite sex siblings) or "parallel" (children of same-sex siblings, and thus members of the same lineage).

In this lecture we return to the Trobriand Islands to look at how matrilineality affects social, political, and economic relationships. We find that among the Trobrianders, the brother-sister bond far eclipses the husband-wife tie, and that a boy will inherit his position in society from his maternal uncle (his mother's brother) rather than his biological father. This leads to conflict not between father and son (as Freud would hypothesize) but between nephew (sister's son) and uncle (mother's brother), leading Malinowski to proclaim that the so-called Oedipus complex was not about sex but about resisting authority.

As in all matrilineal societies, men hold the formal positions of power, and the Trobrianders have a highly stratified social order based on one's matrilineage and clan membership. Children are expected to practice clan exogamy, and a young woman's ideal marriage partner would be her mother's brother's son—although in practice it seems that young people have a great deal of flexibility in choosing their husbands and wives. At funeral ceremonies, elaborate networks of kin come together to publicly display their ties and obligations to one another.

Outline

I. The Trobriand Islanders were studied by Bronislaw Malinowski and Annette Weiner.

   A. The Trobriand Islanders have a matrilineal kinship system and a political structure led by hereditary chiefs.

       1.   Trobriand chiefs are always men; they inherit their positions, however, not from their fathers but from their mothers' brothers (that is, their matrilineal relatives).

       2.   Fathers provide important symbols of paternity to their children.

       3.   Brother-sister ties are much stronger than husband-wife ties.

   B.   Trobriand origin myths tell of four pairs of brothers and sisters who came up from the underworld to start modern society.

       1.   Trobrianders have four major clans that are descended from these original ancestors: the Pigs, the Dogs, the Crocodiles, and the Iguanas.

       2.   These clans are ranked in a hierarchy of prestige. Each is made up of a number of lineages, which themselves are ranked.

II. Every person is born a member of his or her mother's clan and will have to marry outside of that clan.

   A.   Across cultures, love is often seen as a fragile basis on which to build a lifetime partnership. In this light, parents feel best suited to pick out marriage partners for their children.

   B.   One often preferred marriage partner is one's cross-cousin.

       1.   *Cross-cousins* are children of opposite-sex siblings (for example, one's mother's brother's children). *Parallel cousins* are children of same-sex siblings (for example, one's mother's sister's children).

       2.   Among the Trobriand Islanders, a young man's father's sister's daughter (a cross-cousin) is the preferred marriage partner, although, in fact, men often end up marrying someone else.

   C.   For future chiefs and lineage leaders, married couples prefer to live in the husband's mother's brother's hamlet.

   D.   Malinowski argued that Trobriand boys have tense relationships with their mothers' brothers, not with their fathers, arguing that Freud's Oedipus complex was more about power than sex.

III. Trobriand kinship ties are especially important during the rituals conducted at funerals.

A. The Trobrianders believe that a dead person's soul travels to the primordial island over the horizon, where it is reborn and travels back to impregnate a woman of the same clan.

B. The Trobrianders believe that no death is accidental, and, thus, a dead person's spouse's kin must demonstrate their innocence and sorrow at the loss by organizing and performing the funeral rituals.

C. In turn, the deceased's matrilineal kin compensate his wife's kin with payments of woven skirts, yams, and banana-leaf bundles.

Readings:

Bronislaw Malinowski, *The Sexual Lives of Savages.*

Annette Weiner, *The Trobriand Islanders.*

Questions to Consider:

1. How does Trobriand matrilineality refute Freud's Oedipus complex?

2. Why is it preferred in some societies to marry one's cousin?

Lecture Twelve—Transcript
Multiple Spouses and Matrilineality

In this lecture, we return to the Trobriand Islands, a chain of islands 150 miles off the coast of New Guinea that were made famous by Bronislaw Malinowski; you remember he worked there in the early 20th century, Malinowski, one of the earliest founders of anthropology and one of the big advocates of doing long-term fieldwork. Malinowski was there from 1914 to 1917, and the Trobriand Islands, based largely on his work, have become a classic case study in anthropology, and rightly so, given the richness of their cultural patterns. Indeed, on the Trobriand Islands we find ample illustrations of a number of topics that we've talked about in this class so far: the role of language; the importance of cultural models and magic and religion; and the crucial role played by kinship.

We have not just the work of Bronislaw Malinowski but also the anthropologist Annette Weiner, who worked in the Trobriand Islands in 1971 and 1972 and actually made a number of short trips back in the 1970s and 1980s. Weiner, as a woman, is able to provide us with a different perspective on Trobriand society. Malinowski had more access to the men—he spent more time with the men. There may have been a bit of sexist bias built into his work, understandable, given the age in which he worked, but Weiner had unique access to the female society in the Trobrianders, which really complements what Malinowski had to say.

The Trobriands are flat coral reefs, covered in very rich soils. The subsistence bases of the Trobriand Islanders are growing yams, taro, tobacco, and other crops, as well as fishing. Both Malinowski and Weiner worked on the largest and most important island in the Trobriand chain, which is the island of Kiriwina. Kiriwina has a population of about 12,000 and that's divided among more or less 60 villages, so a fairly dense population, about 200 people per village. Each of the villages on the Trobriand Islands are composed of groupings of houses, hamlets, and each village will have six, seven, or eight of these hamlets in a village. The hamlets are composed of houses, and the Trobrianders have these log houses that are built off the ground with very steeply arched thatch roofs, and in front of the houses are yam huts or yam houses, and these are often more elaborate than the main house.

Yams, and we're going to talk about yams in the Trobriand Islands later in the course, but yams are not only important staple items of the Trobriand diet but really important symbolic items in Trobriand cosmology. They symbolize a man's wealth. The chief's house, for example, will have a huge yam hut out front that will be filled with yams to show the world his wealth. Trobrianders speak variants of the language Kilivila; they also very often speak a neo-Melanesian pigeon language, and, interestingly enough, they have different languages for gardening. They have a different language for garden magic, and this is a language that has different words, different pronunciation, even a different rhythm to their speak. But what we know most, what we remember most about the Trobriand Islanders, is the fact that they are a matrilineal society; descent is traced through female lines, and, as we mentioned last time, in a matrilineal society children feel related to their mother and their mother's brother and their mother's sister as well in a way that they don't feel related to their father, much less their father's brother or their father's sister.

The Trobriand Islanders are a chiefdom. They have chiefs; chiefdomship is hereditary. They have lineages and clans, and these are ranked, some are ranked higher than others, but women are not the chiefs, only men, and men will inherit their position not from their fathers but from their mother's brother, their matrilineal male relative on the matrilineal side. A young man will inherit his position in society from his mother's brother. Likewise, a father will not pass on his position in society to his own biological son but rather to his sister's son. In Trobriand society, there's a great deference paid to chiefs. One is not supposed to make eye contact with chiefs, commoners always sit lower than chiefs, and there's this rigidity of contact between chiefs and commoners.

A number of things are passed down matrilineal in Trobriand society. Magic spells, for example, are passed down from men to their sisters' children, their sisters' sons. Each of the hamlets in a Trobriand village is a matrilineage, although not in practice. Not everyone who should live in a hamlet does—it depends on their particular circumstances—but everyone would maintain close contact to their home hamlet. Ancestral names are given by the mother's side of the family. It's a matrilineal society; they're named by the mother's side of the family but fathers also give names to their children, and this is significant. A father will ask his sister to give him a name to bestow upon his biological child, and this is the name that's most commonly used in everyday life, comes from the biological father.

Fathers also in Trobriand society give their children certain crucial adornments to wear, especially shell necklaces, these cowry shell necklaces. It makes the child look nice and also acknowledges paternity, and it also reflects on the social standing of the father. If he can afford to give his child really nice adornments to wear, it reflects well on him. As Annette Weiner pointed out, Malinowski got it a bit wrong when he described the relationship between fathers and their sons, and their children. Malinowski said that fathers and sons don't have anything to do with each other; they're like strangers. But Weiner says that actually fathers play a very important role. They give these adornments, they give these names; it's just not as important as mother's brother.

The key relationship in a matrilineal society is not between a husband and a wife; it is between brothers and sisters. This forms really the core of matrilineal society. A brother is related to his sister in a way in which he's not related to his own wife, a way that he's not related to his own children. His own children are not going to be members of his matrilineage, not going to be members of his family, but his sister's children will be members of his family. This very often leads to a joking relationship. This seems paradoxical to us, but fathers often have a joking relationship with their children, whereas what we would call uncle, mother's brother, has this strict authoritarian relationship, so fathers have more of what we would call in English an avuncular relationship, an unclety relationship with their children.

Let me mention here the origin myth that Trobrianders tell. The Trobrianders believe that in the beginning of all time, the primordial times, there was a society underground. There were Trobriand villagers, there were yam fields, there were chiefs. Everything that exists in Trobriand society today existed underground in this mythical world, and in the beginning of time brother and sister pairs came up through a hole from the underworld up onto the current earth. When they came up, they came up in pairs, and the first pair came up, and then the second pair came up, and then another pair, and all in all four brother-sister pairs came up from the underworld, and each of these was associated with a particular animal. There were the pigs, the dogs, the iguanas, and the crocodiles, so in Trobriand society today you have four clans, four people who trace their relationships back to a mythical ancestor, these mythical brother-and-sister pairs who came up from the underworld, and all Trobrianders are a member of one of these four clans.

They're named the pigs, the dogs, the iguanas, and the crocodiles, and these clans are ranked. The pigs came up first, then the dogs, and then the iguanas, and then the crocodiles, and everyone is born as a member of one of these clans in Trobriand society today. In the Trobriands, everybody has to marry outside of their clan, but one doesn't want to marry too far down. These clans are ranked: the pigs are first, the dogs are second, the iguanas are third, and the crocodiles are ranked last. Everybody has to marry outside of their own clan, but they don't want to marry too far down, so a pig wouldn't want to marry an iguana. A pig would want to marry someone from a dog clan, and so there's clan exogamy, but you don't want to marry too far down.

In many societies around the world—I want to talk about Trobriand marriage, but let me preface it with the general note—in many societies around the world, the preferred marriage partner is one's cross-cousin. In anthropology, we have two different terms for cousins, cross-cousins and parallel cousins. Cross-cousins are children of opposite sex siblings. This means that your mother's brother's children would be your cross-cousins, and your father's sister's children would be your cross-cousins. Parallel cousins, on the other hand, are children of same sex sibling, and so your mother's sister's children would be your parallel cousins and your father's brother's children would be parallel cousins. In many societies around the world, including the Trobrianders, these are two very different types of relatives. They're not all cousins, cross-cousins and parallel cousins. Many societies consider parallel cousins to be like brothers and sisters, and very often they'll use the term brother and sister to refer to parallel cousins, and in a number of cultures, like the Trobrianders, the preferred marriage partner is one's cross-cousin.

In the Trobrianders, there are four clans, and each person must marry outside of the clan; to marry inside of the clan is considered to be incestuous. Malinowski reported that the preferred marriage partner for men is the father's sister's daughter, cross-cousin; father's sister's daughter would be the preferred marriage partner for a man. This is neat because the father's sister's daughter is always going to be a member of a different lineage and clan. Remember that the children, your father is a member of a different matrilineage. The father's sister would be a member of that same matrilineage, and father's sister's children would be a member of that matrilineage, so it's marrying outside of one's lineage and outside of one's clan, but not marrying too far way. There are already relationships between those families, and so it's marrying outside of one's clan, but keeping the two clans held together, their interests being intertwined.

Malinowski said that children have to marry their father's sister's daughter, sons do, boys do. Weiner said actually that's not the case. That's the preferred form of marriage, this is what people would like to do in an ideal world, but in fact people very often—you know, your father's sister might not have gotten married; your father might not have a sister, the children might not be the right age; you might not like your cross-cousins. A multitude of factors could come into play here, and so people very often don't marry their father's sister's daughter; sons don't marry their father's sister's daughter, so there's some flexibility at play here.

Yams, as I've mentioned, are at the heart of Trobriand culture. It's a staple of the diet, but it's also the symbol of wealth and prosperity. In terms of marriage it's significant, because in the early days of marriage, for the first year of marriage, a couple will live together and the husband's mother will cook their food, will cook their yams, and bring it to their house, and this is like a probationary period for the marriage. And if the marriage lasts a year, the wife will set up a hearth in their own home and start cooking the yams, and when she cooks the first meal of the yams for her husband, this means that the marriage is going to last, it's going to solidify.

Trobriand men can marry several different women; they have a polygynous society, and this is very useful for Trobriand men because if they have aspirations of a noble lineage, of a chiefly lineage, if they have aspirations to build up their political power, by marrying different women they can make kinship alliances with various families. Economically, it's helpful to men to have more than one wife because there are more people in the household, more women in the household to help tend the gardens, to produce children, to help take care of the children and so forth, so polygyny is really a sign of wealth. It's a public symbol of being a powerful person. But the Trobriand husbands, just like Fulbe husbands, they can have more than one wife, but they have to support all of those wives in appropriate fashion.

Weiner paints a Margaret Mead-like picture of Trobriand life in which there's a lot of sexual experimentation going on among adolescents. The parents aren't very controlling. Couples go off into the forest and have trysts in the jungle, and there are all these little signs that adolescents will use to show that they're having relationships with someone else. A woman will bite off her lover's eyelashes, for example—I guess this is the equivalent of a hickey in our own culture. Over time, this period of experimentation often flowers into romantic love. That young girl and boy will go off with each other repeatedly, and eventually they may fall in love and get married. If they're not cross-cousins, the parents may allow it anyway because they want to indulge their children, and so romantic love comes into play as much as arranged marriage. There's also a very rich tradition of love magic in Trobriand society.

I want to talk a little bit about what happens after marriage in the familial relationships in a matrilineal society. A chief in Trobriand society is going to inherit his position from his mother's brother. Men get their position in life from their mother's brother, so it's inheritance through the female lines, but it's men who occupy these positions. How do ranks get established in the family? One gets chosen. The best analogy is English nobility. They would still have a basically high rank if they're from a chiefly family, but then there's a lot of negotiation, a lot of jockeying for power for people who can move up these ranks. You have to be born into a noble lineage, but then you can move up.

What's interesting about Trobriand society is that it's matrilineal, and it has what we call avunculocal residence, from avuncular, uncle, and local, so, ideally, a woman when she marries a Trobriand man goes to live with him, and they will both live with the husband's mother's brother, his uncle, avuncular residence, so a couple will go live with the husband's mother's brother. Again, this is an ideal rule, but in practice it doesn't always happen. If the boy is scheduled to inherit a position, a chiefly rank from his mother's brother, they always go and live with the mother's brother. In fact, there's a lot of play going on here where people can live elsewhere. Generally, boys who were destined to become their chiefs will go at age seven, eight, or nine years old. They'll move out from their father's household and go and move in with their mother's brother.

This leads to an unusual situation concerning the Oedipus complex in the Trobriand Islands. Property and status are inherited from a mother's brother in Trobriand society. Men exert control over their sister's sons like a father would. In a nutshell, as you're all familiar, just to remind you, the Oedipus complex argues that young boys, their first sexual attraction is toward their mothers, but they realize that mothers are the sexual property of their fathers, and so there's a conflict that goes on between boys and their fathers over sexual access to the mother. Malinowski, writing against Freud, said that in Trobriand society, the conflict that we find is not between fathers and their biological sons but between boys and their mother's brother, and so Malinowski said Freud got it wrong. Yes, there are these tensions between fathers and sons in Western society, but it's not about sex—it's about authority—and the authority figure is going to be resisted, and in Trobriand society, the father figure, the authority figure, is the mother's brother, and so that is who is resisted.

The Trobrianders have elaborate ceremonies that go on after the death of an individual. These are called *lisaladabu*, which literally means releasing emotional energy, and it's releasing the emotional energy which surrounds death. Women are considered to be the custodians of this emotional energy, and it's their responsibility to discharge it. In the death rituals, in the mortuary rituals, funeral rituals of the Trobriand Islanders, they divide up relatives of the dead person, and I'm going to speak about it today as if it were a man, the dead man, into two groups. There are the owners and the workers. The owners are the dead man's matriclan, the dead man's real family, his matriclan. The workers are the dead man's wife's family, the dead man's wife's matriclan, and the dead man's father's matriclan, so it's relatives. The affinal relatives are the workers, and the consanguineal, the blood relatives, the matrilineally related relatives, are the owners.

I'm going to come back to this in just a moment, but let me mention here that no death in Trobriand society is accidental, no death is accidental. There are no deaths by natural causes; they don't have a cultural model of dying from natural causes. It all comes from sorcery. There's always magic and sorcery involved. People don't die of disease; the disease concept of illness and death really doesn't exist. If you don't like somebody, if you're envious of somebody, if you have hard feelings, you can actually kill that person. This comes into play into this distinction between owners and workers at the death ceremony. The workers have to show that they didn't want the dead person killed. They're not of the dead man's family—they're his affinal kin; they're his in-laws, if you will—and since they're members of another competing lineage, they're automatically suspect of the death of an individual.

Did you not like this person? Did you think that they were taking resources from your lineage? The workers have to show the owners, the members of the dead man's matrilineage, that they're innocent of this death, and that they're truly sorry that the dead man died. The workers bring gifts: they'll bring stone axes; they'll bring betel nuts, this nut that Trobriand Islanders chew that's a mild stimulant, widely chewed in the South Pacific. They'll bring small gifts to give to the owners, and with these gifts they're saying "We didn't want this person to die; we're as sorry as you are that this person died. We didn't do the sorcery. We didn't make this person die," and they go through all of these ritualized wailings at certain times of the day. They'll scream as a group to indicate how sorry they are for the death that has occurred.

On the other hand, the members of the dead man's matrilineage, the owners of the body are not allowed to touch the body. They're only allowed to participate in certain ways in the funeral rituals; they're not allowed to have anything to do with the preparation of the body itself. They can't dress the dead man, they can't paint the person, all of the things that would go in for getting a body ready for burial. The owners can't get involved because that would pollute them, and so the workers have to do all of the work in the funeral ceremony. They have to get the body ready and go through all of the physical preparations that actually involves touching the body.

Some months after the burial and the funeral ceremony, there is a series of gift exchanges that occur, and what happens is the owners distribute gifts to the workers to compensate them, so let's go over what happens here. A man dies, the owners, his matrilineage, can't touch the body and they suspect his other kin, his wife's matrilineages and his father's matrilineage, of committing sorcery. Those kin, the workers, have to prove that they haven't done anything, and so they do all of the work, all of the preparation, and give gifts to the owners to show how sorry they are for this death, and then some months after the funeral ceremony the owners of the body will then give gifts back to the workers. They've accepted their explanation that they weren't involved in the death, so they give gifts back, and a lot of this involves women's wealth, which on the Trobriand Islands yams are men's wealth, and women's wealth are grass skirts made out of banana leaf bundles, very beautiful dyed grass skirts, and the women owners will give these to the workers to compensate them for all that they did. There's also some exchange of men's wealth, yams and so forth, but it's really the women's wealth that goes on in these final exchanges.

These mortuary ceremonies are very closely tied with the Trobriand notions of spirituality. They believe that every person has a spirit, and this is called *baloma*. A person's spirit, what we would call the soul, at death the soul doesn't die, but it goes off to a mythical island that they call Tuma. When a person dies, the soul, the spirit, *baloma*, goes off to Tuma, and there it gets old again and goes through a whole life cycle on this mythical island of Tuma, and when the spirit gets old and dies, it comes back to the Trobriand Islands, enters a woman's body and gets reborn as a fetus and as a member of the same matrilineage of the person who died, so from death is rebirth of the matrilineage. It's a cycle they keeps going on and on and is reborn again and again, so they literally see death as being crucial to the rebirth of their culture, not just a spiritual rebirth, but actual rebirth.

Famously, Malinowski said that the Trobrianders believe that a woman, that they didn't have a clear biological notion of procreation, and that the Trobrianders believe that a woman got pregnant by wading into the water and when she waded into the water, these spirits, these baloma would enter her body, and she would become pregnant. Malinowski pointed out that they noted that sex was required, but this was sex to build up seminal fluids in the woman's body, to form the bones and the brain and so forth. Weiner points out that these days lots of Trobrianders share our biological notion of where babies come from, but they continue to practice this idea of what Malinowski euphemistically called copulatory vigilance, and it means that having sex one time isn't enough for the fetus to grow, that a couple must have sex repeatedly in order to build up semen in the woman's body to form the brain and the bones and the other crucial parts of the body, and these are cultural models of biology, cultural models that we talked about last time that don't have to correspond exactly with what we will call the object of truth.

All of this ties into kinship, because when a person dies that person's spirit is also a future member of their lineage. You have all these rituals around you. With the burial ceremony, there are the workers who have to do the work, the owners who own the body and cannot work, and the workers have to show that they were not responsible for the death of the body and that they didn't want this to happen, and this is all made necessary because no death is accidental. All death is caused by sorcery; not even death by old age is considered to be accidental.

We have the Trobrianders, and they illustrate a number of points that we've made in this class. They illustrate the role of cultural models, cultural models of folk biology, the way in which people get pregnant, for example, cultural models of death, that the spirits cause death. The Trobriand Islanders also illustrate the role of kinship in a matrilineal society, this complex relationship of a child to his or her father, not what we would consider to be a natural relationship of a child to their father, but for the Trobrianders very natural, and the relationship of children to their mother's brother, who is the authority figure in this society, and this makes sense because a man's sister's children are going to be the ones who are going to carry on his lineage. They're going to be the ones who reflect on him when they grow up, so it's very important that he be the authority figure in their lives, and so children have a joking relationship with their biological fathers, and they have this authority, this more of a parent-child, what we consider to be a parent-child relationship with their mother's brother.

The Trobrianders illustrate our earlier discussions of cultural models. They illustrate our discussions of magic, their practice of love magic, of garden magic, their fear of illness and death through sorcery, and while Weiner critiqued Malinowski for underplaying the role of women in Trobriand society, together their work really gives us an incredibly rich picture of this fascinating place, and we will have an opportunity to come back and discuss the Trobrianders in later lectures.

Bands, Tribes, and Chiefdoms
Lecture Thirteen
Gatherers and Hunters

Scope: Anthropologists often categorize human societies in terms of social complexity, from bands and tribes to chiefdoms and states. Today, about a quarter million people live in band-level societies, subsisting mainly from gathering wild plants and hunting. Yet, in the great scheme of human history, this was the most common form of social organization.

Bands of the Dobe Ju/'hoansi of the southern Kalahari Desert in Africa are one of the most studied groups in history. Despite the sense imparted by the popular label of *hunters and gatherers*, anthropologists have shown that the Dobe get about 70 percent of their food from gathering roots, nuts, and berries; only about 30 percent of their calories come from hunting. Further, we find that the Dobe place very little value on private property and spend only about 20 hours a week working. Thus, although bands live what may seem an extremely impoverished existence, from another angle, they enjoy greater food security and more leisure time than the affluent societies of the West.

Outline

I. Although the evolutionary schemes of the 19th century have been discredited, there remains something useful in categorizing societies based on their social complexity.

   A. In an influential 1962 work, *Primitive Social Organization: An Evolutionary Perspective*, Elvin Service proposed a typology of societies composed of bands, tribes, chiefdoms, and states.

   B. *Bands* are nomadic food gatherers with no institutionalized political structure.
      1. Bands are normally composed of 25 to 50 related individuals and practice a flexible cognatic form of kinship.
      2. Bands subsist from gathering foods and hunting game. There is very little specialization, private property is not generally recognized, and leadership is situational.

C. *Tribes* are larger than bands, numbering from a few hundred to a few thousand individuals.

    1. The higher population densities of tribes are supported by horticultural production (low-intensity farming).

    2. Tribal-level societies, such as the Yąnomamö, have some status differences, but these are generally fluid; social organization is governed by kinship ties.

    3. Tribes are led by *headmen*, whose position is based on *achieved status*, the recognition of accomplishments, rather than inherited status.

D. *Chiefdoms* are larger than tribes, often with several settlements inhabited by thousands of individuals.

    1. In chiefdoms, such as the Trobriand Islands, status differences are institutionalized and important. Often, lineages are ranked.

    2. The status of chiefs is based on *ascribed authority*, or inherited position.

E. *States* are the largest and most complex form of social organization. States are marked by centralized authority, with a standing army or police to enforce order.

    1. All of the world's remaining bands, tribes, and chiefdoms are today subsumed under state organizations.

    2. Today, we speak of these peoples in terms of ethnic groups.

II. The Dobe Ju/'hoansi are the archetypal band-level society and one of the most well documented groups in the anthropological literature.

A. A "bushman" peoples of the southern Kalahari, the Dobe (also known as the !Kung San) speak a San "click" language.

    1. About 50,000 Dobe individuals are living today in Botswana and Namibia.

    2. Richard Lee and Irven DeVore have led a large-scale ethnographic project there since 1963.

B. The Dobe are a band-level society.

    1. Leadership is situational, although elders are accorded special respect.

    2. The Dobe are nomadic, following seasonal fruits, nuts, roots, and game. Water is always a concern, and each band will have a number of water holes to which it migrates.

    3. Some Dobe men practice polygyny, but Dobe marriages in general are marked by a high divorce rate.

C. We have long termed bands as hunters and gatherers, but research shows that gathering is more important than hunting in terms of caloric intake, if not social prestige.

    1. Dobe women are the primary foragers and provide about 70 percent of the total calories consumed by a band. Mongongo nuts are a Dobe staple.

    2. Although meat provides only about 30 percent of the caloric intake, it is highly valued. Men hunt giraffe, wildebeest, antelope, warthog, and other game.

D. Band-level societies are notable for their fierce egalitarian ethic. There are few status distinctions, and these are limited to age (the opinion of elders is respected) and situational leadership.

    1. When a hunter makes a kill, he must distribute the meat among all in his band. To mute any ego building that might threaten the band's egalitarian ethic, gifts of meat are met with insults about the quantity and quality offered.

    2. Beyond the gender division of labor, there is virtually no specialization in band-level societies.

III. Band-level societies, such as the Dobe, are often portrayed as the most impoverished of societies. However, anthropologist Marshall Sahlins argues that, depending on the criteria used, bands are, in many ways, more affluent than industrial societies.

A. Within bands, there is usually very little sense of private property, and goods are freely borrowed without even asking.

    1. The lack of economic specialization means that almost everyone can make almost every item.

    2. Because bands are nomadic, having many personal possessions is maladaptive.

B. In contrast to industrialized countries, no one in a band-level society goes hungry except in the most extreme circumstances.

C. Sahlins argues that affluence may be achieved in two ways: (1) by wanting a lot and producing a lot or (2) by wanting little and, thus, being satisfied with little. He calls the latter the "Zen road to affluence."

    1. The Dobe work, on average, about 20 hours per week. In 2 hours of Mongongo nut collecting, a woman can harvest enough to feed her family for several days.

2. If affluence is measured in leisure time, then band-level societies are the most affluent in the world.

Readings:

Richard Lee, *The Dobe Ju/'hoansi*.

Marshall Sahlins, *Stone Age Economics*.

Majorie Soshtak, *Nisa: The Life and Words of a !Kung Woman*.

Film:

Jamie Uys, *The Gods Must Be Crazy*.

Questions to Consider:

1. What is affluence? Are the Dobe more affluent than the average American?
2. Why is an egalitarian ethic so important to a band-level society?
3. What holds Dobe bands together in the absence of strong political leadership?

Lecture Thirteen—Transcript
Gatherers and Hunters

Having covered the basics of human culture, the way in which it's expressed through language and cognitive models, how it's codified through social structures and marriage and kinship and so forth, having done all of this in the first 12 lectures of the class, today we're going to turn to the political and economic organization of different societies around the world. We're going to begin with an influential typology that divides societies up into bands, tribes, chiefdoms, and states, and then we're going to focus today primarily on band-level societies and in particular one named the Dobe Ju/'hoansi of southern Africa.

Let's begin by looking at Elvin Service's very influential 1962 book entitled *Primitive Social Organization: An Evolutionary Perspective*. In this work, he proposes a scheme that divides all societies in the world into these four types: bands, tribes, chiefdoms, and states. Before I get into this, let me add a couple of caveats. First of all, this typology has been criticized for being ethnocentric. In some ways it's just updating, critics would say, Louis Henry Morgan's scheme of barbarians, savages, and civilization, and we as anthropologists spend a lot of our time breaking down typologies, showing the great diversity of different cultures in the world. Many would say that anthropology is the discipline of exceptions. We always say, "Yes, but among the people that I work with; yes, but among the Bororo, that's not the case," and so we're very skeptical toward typologies such as this.

Nonetheless, they can be useful, and this typology, like all typologies, it's important to keep in mind, is one of ideal types. No one society perfectly fits into any of these categories, but nonetheless it can be useful in categorizing different levels of social complexity and social organization. A lot of this boils down to size. In a country like the United States, with the population approaching 300 million, we need very formal legal and political and economic structures in order to function, but a nomadic society, with a few hundred members, doesn't need the same sorts of mechanisms.

We're going to talk about bands, tribes, chiefdoms, and states, but keep in mind that this is not an evolutionary typology. Bands are not inevitably moving toward becoming states. As Franz Boas taught us, every society has its own historical trajectory, and all bands or all tribes are not going to eventually becomes states. States have been the most successful form of political organization and the most expansive form of political organization in the world, but it's not the apex of an evolutionary scheme. Size is an important distinction in these categories. Bands are very small, generally between 25 and 50 individuals. Tribes are larger—they generally have hundreds of individuals—chiefdoms larger still with thousands, and states, nation-states, millions, hundreds of millions of people.

They also differ in terms of their economic relations. Band-level societies, generally their economies are based on hunting and gathering, and they're generally nomadic peoples. In tribal-level societies, we find hunting and gathering as well, but they combine this with gardening and with shifting agriculture, so they're a bit more sedentary as well. They might move around every few years, but they'll stay in one place for a few years at a time. With chiefdoms, we find intensive agriculture, and we need intensive agriculture, chiefdoms need intensive agriculture, to sustain the population densities that they have. Finally, in states we find market economies, occupational specialization, market economies and more impersonal relations, more impersonal economic relations.

Finally, in terms of political leadership, they're distinguished from one another. In band-level societies, we find situational authority. A leader will emerge just in a particular context on a hunting trip, for example. The best hunter will emerge as the leader of that hunting trip, but after the hunting trip he'll meld back into society and not retain that position of power. In tribal-level societies, we find headmen, people who have a formal position of power that they will occupy, and yet this is what we call in anthropology achieved status. They have to constantly gain the support of the people that they're leading, and they have to reify this constantly in order to keep their position of power as headmen.

In chiefdoms, we have chiefs, as is obvious given the name, and chiefs are denoted by having ascribed authority, so we have achieved authority in tribes and we have ascribed authority in chiefdoms, and ascribed authority is basically inherited authority. One gains one's political position based on one's lineage, one's position in society, and this is ascribed authority. Finally, in states we have centralized authority, and states can be kingdoms, they can be democracies, they can be dictatorships, but one thing that's distinctive of all states is that they have a standing army or a police force to enforce the social order and the political order.

In anthropology, we tend to avoid these days terms like primitive. We even avoid tribal except when we're using it in this very specific context of a tribal level of social organization. More often today, we talk about small-scale societies or large-scale societies or ethnic groups, and we'll return to ethnic groups in a later lecture. It's important to note that today all bands, all tribes, and all chiefdoms live in nation-states. There's no independent band-level society in the world; they all live within modern nation-states.

To talk about bands for a bit, today about a quarter of a million people, about 250,000 people, are primarily hunters and gatherers living in band-level societies, and this is out of a population of 6 billion in the world, so a very small percentage of the world's population are today band-level peoples. However, they've been the object of an immense amount of anthropological investigation. So why is this? Partly, well, the idea is that for most of human history we all lived in band-level societies, so if we go back and look, or if we go to band-level societies and look at their adaptations today, maybe it can tell us something about our own common heritage. Also, in band-level societies, we find a lot of the basic patterns of human behavior that we find in every society in the world. Men and women pair off—they raise children together. We have an institution that we can call marriage. They share food in the same way that societies around the world do.

Finally, they're rapidly vanishing, and so there's a bit of salvage anthropology involved here. We need to go out and collect this data and save this information before it gets lost for all of humanity. As I've said, hunters and gatherers live in bands of 25-50 people. They're all related to one another by kinship or marriage. The size of a band is limited by the carrying capacity of the environment in which they live, and most of the time actually bands stay below their carrying capacity, and they do this by employing a number of birth control methods, primarily a long postpartum sex taboo. It's taboo to have sex a birth for a period of time, which may be one year or two years or even longer in some societies. In band-level societies, the division of labor is based almost primarily on sex. Women do certain work, men do other work, but there's no occupational specialization. There are no full-time political specialists, no full-time religious specialists.

Today, I'd like to focus the lecture on a band-level society, the Dobe Ju/'hoansi. They live in the Kalahari, on the edges of the Kalahari Desert in southern Africa, across the border of Botswana and Namibia, and for band-level societies like the Dobe, these borders mean very little. They'll cross over the border into Namibia and they'll cross back over into Botswana, and there are no fences, there are no border guards, there's no way to distinguish what is one side or the other. There are only 50,000 Dobe people living in the world today. They're also known as bushmen, the Kalahari bushmen. They were formerly known as the !Kung, but this is a label that they don't use themselves. They call themselves the Dobe Ju/'hoansi, and this means the real people.

Interestingly enough, this is what lots of ethnic groups around the world call themselves. We're just people, we're the real people, and we're the only people that we know. The term !Kung and the term bushmen were given to them by neighboring groups. They speak a San language, and the San language is a click language, as you can tell from the name, the Dobe Ju/'hoansi, so they have a number of very particular click sounds, and these are very hard for English speakers to say. You'll remember in one of the earlier lectures we mentioned that phonetic maps get laid down very early in life, and so it's very difficult for English speakers to learn these dramatically different phonetic patterns.

The Dobe are one of the most studied people in the world. We have more anthropological research done on the Dobe than just about any other group, and this is primarily due to the efforts of a team of people led by Richard Lee and Irven DeVore, who started working with the Dobe in 1963 as part of the Harvard Kalahari Project. They went on to publish a very important volume in 1968 called *Man the Hunter*, which correlated the behavior of groups like the Dobe with ancient human ancestors. I would also mention Richard Lee has gone on to write the Dobe Ju/'hoansi text, which is one of the best-selling texts for introductory anthropology classes in the country. You may also know the Dobe from the film *The Gods Must Be Crazy*. This was a feature film in the 1970s which highlighted the Dobe and their encounter with a Coke bottle that had fallen out of an airplane flying overhead.

Like any band-level society, the Dobe have only situational leadership. Elders are respected in this society, elder men; elder women as well are more highly respected, but for the most part it's highly egalitarian and again situational leadership. An especially good hunter will lead a hunting party. He'll send one group around with a net, and he'll send another group around to push the animals up into the net and allow them to capture them. But then these hunting leaders will meld back into society and be just like everyone else. Their standard of living is like everyone else's. There's no chief, there's no headman, there's no other form of permanent leadership.

The Dobe are nomadic; they move around. They're living on the edges of the Kalahari Desert, and so water is very important, and so they move around according to water holes, where there are water holes. They practice polygyny; a man may have more than one wife, and there's marriage, obviously, if there's polygyny, but divorce is very easy. Marriage is much more casual than we would consider it to be in our own society, and it's not uncommon for a man or woman to have several spouses in their lifetime. In terms of descent, they trace their descent cognatically, and you'll remember that that means that they're not matrilineal and they're not patrilineal. They're more like ourselves in tracing descent both through male lines and female lines. This is very adaptive for a group like the Dobe, who are living on the edge of the Kalahari Desert, fairly harsh environmental conditions, and so cognatic descent gives them a larger web of kin that they can call upon in times of need.

The division of labor, as I said, is based mostly upon sex. The women forage, and they will gather fruits, nuts, berries, seeds, eggs, and so forth, and this provides most of the Dobe's caloric intake. Men hunt, and this is a less important source of calories, but it's a very important social function, hunting, and meat is very highly valued. Sometimes females will hunt small animals, but mostly hunting is confined to men. About 70 percent of caloric intake comes from foraging, comes from gathering, and so it's really a misnomer. We say hunters and gatherers, but that's really a misnomer. We should probably say gatherers and hunters, and it's women who are going out and getting most of this, 70 percent of the caloric intake from foraging, which is mostly done by women. We find this among hunting and gathering groups, or gathering and hunting groups, if you will, around the world.

One of the staples is mongongo nuts. This is a staple of the Dobe diet; they will eat these mongongo nuts raw or they'll roast them. They also collect tubers, water tubers, and various sorts of fruits and nuts. The men hunt giraffes, they hunt wildebeest, they hunt antelope, they hunt warthogs, and they use poison arrows to hunt these. Sometimes they'll shoot a giraffe, but the giraffes are so big they won't go down. The poison isn't powerful enough to kill these animals right away, and so they'll chase these animals for days at a time, sometimes two, three, four, or five days until the giraffe finally falls down and they're able to butcher him and bring the meat back to the camp, so only about 35 percent of calories come from hunting.

There's an egalitarian ethic among hunting and gathering societies and among the Dobe, no status distinctions, a bit of distinction by age. We have the situational leadership, but everybody lives according to the same conditions. As part of this egalitarian ethic, they highly value meat, and when hunters come back from a hunt they divide up the meat and they share it with everyone in the band. But when they do so, the people who receive the meat don't act grateful, and in fact they have a custom called insulting the meat, And so when they get the meat, they say, "This is really scrawny. It's not very fatty. This isn't really going to be enough to fill us up," and this functions to keep the hunters in their place. They highly value meat, this is a good thing, but they don't want the hunters to get a big head, they don't want their ego to become inflated, and so they insult the meat to keep them in their place.

Richard Lee, the anthropologist who's worked with the Dobe for most of his life, tells an interesting story. As he was preparing to leave the field one day—this was in the mid-1960s; it was in December. And he wanted to do something nice for the Dobe who had opened up their lives to him for so long. He goes and finds a cow. He searches for several weeks, looking around among the pastoralist groups who live around the Dobe, and finds just the right cow that he can get. He gets the cow, he buys it, and he brings it back to the Dobe to butcher and he's going to throw a huge feast. But when he brings the cow back into the band, everybody says, "That's the scrawniest cow I've ever seen. This is going to be a horrible feast. It's going to be a disaster. Why did you buy this cow? This is awful."

He felt terrible, but it was this same function of putting him in his place. You're no better than us, so in Dobe society this egalitarianism. There's also very little specialization. Everyone of the same sex does the same sorts of jobs. All the women go out and gather; all the men go out and hunt. There's very little specialization because everybody can do everything. All the men know how to make bows, all the men know how to make arrows, all the women know how to hunt, and so there's very little occupational specialization—no rich and poor, very little accumulation of stuff, of goods.

An interesting thing about the Dobe is the notion of affluence. What is affluence? We generally think that the Dobe would be the least affluent society in the world. They're living on the margins of states, of pastoralism. They're living in this area of harsh ecological conditions, living hand to mouth in some ways. The anthropologist Marshall Sahlins, however, has suggested in a book called *Stone-Age Economics* that actually anthropology has done a poor job of representing band-level societies because they've been viewed through the eyes of Western observers who were raised in a market economy. Sahlins says scarcity is a myth; scarcity is a product of civilization. He says that among primitive peoples like the Dobe, among primitive economies, economy is art. It's not science, and it's fully integrated into society and culture. People trade to make friends more than to accumulate stuff.

Sahlins argues actually that the Dobe and other hunting and gathering societies were the original affluent societies. Why does he argue this? First of all, there's very little sense of private property. This is a mobile group; they will move around following game and following the harvest of nuts and tubers and so forth throughout the year. They set up temporary huts made out of wood and grass that they can break down very easily and just build a new one when they move to their next water hole, where they'll live for a few months. They accumulate very few possessions. Having a lot of possessions would actually be maladaptive in this context. You've got to carry them around with you, and so if you have a lot of stuff, that's maladaptive for the environment.

In addition, since everybody can make everything that's available, there's very little sense of envy. If I really like your spear, I'll go out and make one like yours, so there's very little sense of private property and little attachment to things. In fact, there's fairly free lending and borrowing, and this is something that we'll come back to in a later lecture, but you don't even have to ask if you go and borrow something from someone else in your band. You can just go into their hut and borrow their spear or borrow their arrowheads or borrow their ostrich shell water containers, for example. There's free lending and borrowing, very little sense of private property. This mobility makes the accumulation of goods not very adaptive, and, in Dobe society, nobody goes hungry. This strikes a lot of Western observers as odd. These are gatherers and hunters. Surely they're hungry all the time; they're living from hand-to-mouth. But, in fact, that's not the case. Hunger is very, very rare among the Dobe Ju/'hoansi.

Finally, in terms of work, the Dobe worked about 20 hours a week. This converts to about 2.5 days a week, about half of our normal workweek. The Dobe don't distinguish between work and play in the same way that we do, but, nonetheless, if we just took into account their hunting activities and their gathering activities, they only work about 20 hours a week, half of what we do. What Sahlins says is that if we measure affluence in terms of leisure time rather than in terms of the accumulation of goods, the Dobe are much more affluent than we are. Mongongo nuts, these are the staple of the Dobe diet. A person can go out and collect enough mongongo nuts in two hours to feed themselves for a whole week, and so, in a worst-case scenario, if there's no other food around they can go out, spend a couple of hours collecting these nuts, and live for a whole week off of them.

Sahlins says that people can be affluent in two ways. You can either want a lot of stuff and produce a lot of stuff to satisfy those wants, or you can want very little, and the Dobe want very little. Sahlins says that it's a myth that in traditional societies people's wants are great and that their means are limited. Their only hope is to produce enough to satisfy people's great desires. People's wants in Dobe society can actually be satisfied very easily, and scarcity is not at all common. So hunting and gathering societies enjoyed the original affluent society, a world with few wants and more material goods than necessary to satisfy these wants. Sahlins calls this the Zen road to affluence, wanting very little and thus being able to satisfy these wants without working a whole lot.

He also notes, interestingly enough, that as we move up the ladder of social complexity, and again it's dangerous to think about bands, tribes, chiefdoms, and states as on an evolutionary scale, but if we did take it that way, as we move up this ladder of social complexity, the more evolved, the more complex civilizations get, we have a decrease in leisure time and a decrease in the importance of kinship ties and tight social networks. As societies move from hunting and gathering to becoming industrial societies, the amount of work per capita increases and the amount of leisure time decreases. This contradicts earlier thought, which held that societies develop complex culture because of the leisure time that it affords them. This is just as valid a way of measuring affluence, leisure time. The affluent have much more leisure time than we do. We generally hold, all the recent studies have shown, that the more money you make, generally the less leisure time you have, even in our own society.

Sahlins also points out that hunger increases relatively and absolutely as cultures evolve, as cultures go up this ladder from band to tribe to chiefdom and states. Evidence from the Dobe shows that even in the Kalahari Desert one man's labor can feed four or five people, and this is more efficient than was French farming or U.S. farming in the mid-1940s and 1950s, for example. In modern society, one-third of the population goes to bed hungry at night, one-third of the population. According to World Bank figures, about half of the world's population lives on less than $2 a day, so a third of the world's population goes to bed hungry at night.

This is a condition that is unthinkable for hunters and gatherers. Hunters and gatherers never go to bed hungry at night. They don't store up food. They can't store up food; mongongo nuts don't store well. It's not very adaptive to have to carry around large stores of food. They don't store it up, but when they need food they just go out and get it, and if there's not any food around, they'll move to another watering hole where there is game and there is food, or they can call on these kinship networks to supply them with food as well. If we look at affluence in terms of leisure time, once again the Dobe and other band-level societies come out ahead, and this is the great irony of progress. As we've progressed, or as we've evolved, to use the terminology of the 19th-century thinkers, we've become more technologically advanced, a more complex society. We can produce more commodities and more goods, but we have less leisure time to enjoy them.

This raises questions about the origin of agriculture. Why, if all of our early human ancestors were hunters and gatherers, lived in band-level societies, why make the switch to agriculture? Agriculture first arose about 8,000 years ago in the Fertile Crescent. It arose independently in the new world about 5,000 years ago. But why make the switch? The conventional wisdom has been, of course, all hunters and gatherers would want to become agriculturalists because they can produce more food and presumably have more leisure time. But, in fact, as we've seen, they don't have more leisure time. Some have suggested recently that stories of the Garden of Eden, for example, are collective memories of this past in which food was much more abundant, in which we were all hunters and gatherers.

Now the switch to agriculture allows for higher population densities, and we've generally thought that people would switch to agriculture, they're able to produce more food, they have higher population densities, and as a result more complex forms of political organization and social organization emerge. But, in fact, we've seen from this data that the switch to agriculture involves a decrease in leisure time, and archaeological evidence has also shown that early agricultural populations healthwise were not as healthy as hunters and gatherers are, for example. We can look at bones and we see bone stress as indications of disease that emerged once people began settling down, and diseases were much more common because they were transmitted much easier. When you had larger settlements of people living closely together, they were much more vulnerable to diseases. They were also much more vulnerable to food loss, crop loss. When they're planting the same crop, if there's a disaster, if there's a disease, they can lose the whole crop, but if they're hunting and gathering and moving around, they don't have those same sorts of problems.

Whereas we've traditionally seen the move from hunting and gathering to agriculture as allowing for or necessitating these forms of permanent political leadership and authority, more complex social control, perhaps, in fact, it was the opposite. Since switching to agriculture didn't increase people's standard of living, then maybe it was because of political leadership, political leaders banding people together, keeping them in the same place for long periods of time, becoming sedentary, planting crops and becoming agriculturalists, which would allow for permanent political leadership to emerge, and so we can see this; we can turn the normal evolutionary scheme on its head. It's not population density that requires permanent political leadership, but perhaps the drive for permanent political leadership led to agriculture and so forth.

Sahlins's argument of the Zen road to affluence is really revolutionary. Band-level societies aren't the impoverished people that we once thought they were, and if we look at affluence in terms of other measures, and leisure time is just as valid of a measure as the accumulation of material goods, if we look at it in this sense, the Dobe are better off than we are. So far from being an evolutionary scheme in which bands lead to more complex and better, in some ways, tribes, leading to better chiefdoms, leading to states, that's not the case. In fact, the Dobe, who we would put at the bottom of this evolutionary hierarchy, are better off in many ways than we are in our own society today.

Lecture Fourteen
Headmen and Horticulturists

Scope: The Yąnomamö are a tribal-level society living in the Amazon rainforest in northern Brazil and southern Venezuela. Based on the work of anthropologist Napoleon Chagnon, the Yąnomamö have become famous as "the fierce people." As is characteristic of tribal societies, the Yąnomamö have headmen in their villages, although these figures must lead by example and persuasion rather than exercising the power to command.

The Yąnomamö live in a world filled with malevolent spirits and demons. They divide the cosmos into four layers, and demons from the underworld roam Yąnomamö territory in search of souls to consume. Yąnomamö shamans maintain contact with the spirits of the other layers of the cosmos and are called on to exorcise spirits from afflicted individuals.

Outline

I. The Yąnomamö comprise a classic case study in anthropology.

    A. The Yąnomamö live in the northern region of Amazonia, along the border of Brazil and Venezuela.

        1. The Amazon River competes with the Nile for title of the world's largest river—the Nile is a bit longer, but the Amazon has more volume.

        2. The Amazon rainforest—roughly the drainage basin on the Amazon River—has a rich yet delicate ecosystem. It holds a large percentage of the world's biodiversity, yet its sandy soils are ill suited for large-scale agriculture.

        3. It was long assumed that the Amazon could not support the population densities for large-scale and complex societies to emerge, although recent archaeological evidence suggests that intensive agriculture may have been practiced some 4,000 years ago.

   B. The Yąnomamö live in the basin of the Orinoco River.
- **1.** About 22,000 people live in more than 200 scattered villages. When a village gets too large, it will fission into two smaller villages.
- **2.** Yąnomamö villages are called *shabonos*, large circular structures surrounded by palisades and with a large open-air plaza in the middle.

   C. Napoleon Chagnon began his fieldwork with the Yąnomamö in 1964. He was impressed by the fierceness and enforced egalitarianism of the Yąnomamö.

II. The Yąnomamö are a tribal-level society.

   A. Political leadership is based on achieved status. Headmen have some authority but very little power to make others act.

   B. The Yąnomamö practice slash-and-burn (or *swidden*) horticulture.
- **1.** Their primary crops are plantains, manioc, taro, sweet potato, and tobacco. The Yąnomamö also hunt pigs, monkey, deer, and armadillos.
- **2.** The Yąnomamö shift their fields about every three years. Conventional wisdom argues that this is the result of poor soil quality, but the Yąnomamö themselves say it is because they get tired of weeding.
- **3.** Like the Dobe, the Yąnomamö work much less than people in modern Western societies.

   C. The Yąnomamö are a patrilineal society with often tense relations between the sexes.
- **1.** The ideal marriage partner for the Yąnomamö is one's cross-cousin, although exceptions are often made.
- **2.** Men may have more than one wife, and this is most common for headmen.
- **3.** Males see women as weak and potentially polluting. Domestic violence is common.

III. The Yąnomamö live in a world filled with spirits—mostly malevolent forces with which they must contend.

   A. The Yąnomamö cosmos is divided into four layers.
- **1.** The very top layer is uninhabited today but is where the first beings lived. Below is the sky layer, which contains the Yąnomamö versions of heaven and hell.

  2. The third layer is the present earth. The bottom layer is an underworld filled with cannibalistic spirits.

B. The architecture of the Yąnomamö village *shabono* reflects the meeting of the sky, earth, and underworld layers of the cosmos.

  1. The Yąnomamö make a clear distinction between "things of the village" and "things of the forest."

  2. The spirit demon Titiri lives at the low end of the *shabono*.

C. The Yąnomamö believe humans possess several types of souls.

  1. The "will" soul leaves the body at death, climbing up the hammock rope to the sky layer.

  2. Another soul leaves the body to become a mischievous, if not malevolent, jungle spirit.

  3. The liver soul is vulnerable to being stolen or cannibalized by *hekura* and other spirits. This may result in physical illness and even death.

  4. Finally, humans all have a spirit-double soul (a *nahual*), and the fate of an individual is linked to that of his totemic animal.

D. Yąnomamö shamans serve as mediators between the spirit world and the material world and are called upon to heal spiritual illnesses.

  1. Shamans' power resides with the ability to attract *hekura* spirits (who inhabit their livers) and tame them as much as possible to do their bidding.

  2. *Hekura* are microscopic, unearthly beautiful spirits that come from the underworld.

  3. Shamans inhale a hallucinogenic snuff and smoke massive quantities of tobacco, entering into trance-like states in which they can see and communicate with the spirits hidden to the normal eye.

Readings:

Napoleon Chagnon, *The Yąnomamö*.

Florinda Donner, *Shabono*.

Jacques Lizot, *Tales of the Yanomami*.

Questions to Consider:

1. How do Yąnomamö headmen substitute moral authority for coercive force in their political leadership?

2. How does *shabono* architecture illustrate Yąnomamö cosmology?

3. Are spirit-induced illnesses "real" sicknesses?

Lecture Fourteen—Transcript
Headmen and Horticulturists

Last time we talked about band-level societies and the Dobe in particular as part of Elvin Service's bands, tribes, chiefdoms, and states typology. Today we're going to look at a tribal-level organization, that of the Yąnomamö of the Brazilian and Venezuelan rain forest. We're going to look at their forms of political organization in which headmen lead by example and how this is related to their kinship structure. We're going to also look at Yąnomamö cosmology and their cultural models of the world.

The Yąnomamö live in the South American rain forest, what is generally called Amazonia, but this requires a little bit of explanation. What is Amazonia? Amazonia is a state in Brazil; we also call Amazonia the Amazon River Basin drainage basin, which is an area the size of Western Europe. We also call Amazonia a cultured area, and in the greater cultured area of Amazonia it includes not only the Amazon River, which is one of the world's largest rivers, right up there with the Nile—20 percent of the world's river water is held in the Amazon River, quite amazing—but it includes not only the Amazon River but a number of other river systems as well, the Orinoco, the Rio de la Plata, and the Xingu, among others.

Conventional wisdom has held that no high civilization, no grand civilization ever arose in the rain forest because of the poor ecology of the rain forest environment. This is somewhat paradoxical because we think of the rain forest as being the source of the greatest biological diversity in the world, the richest ecozone that we can think of. But in fact, rain forest ecology is very fragile. Most of the diversity is tied up in the biomass above ground. The soils of the rain forest are actually very sandy and poor, and they leech out nutrients very quickly, and so conventional anthropological wisdom has held that no high civilization ever arose in the rain forest because they just couldn't sustain the population densities, given this fragile ecology. Betty Medgars calls civilizations that arise in the rain forest sand castles that inevitably will dissolve over time. Some recent archaeological research has looked at satellite photography and has discovered what looked like raised fields in the Amazon, and this leads to the possibility that perhaps in fact there was intensive agriculture in the rain forest thousands of years before the Portuguese or the Spanish arrived, but nonetheless a very fragile environment.

Today we're going to talk about the Yąnomamö. The Yąnomamö live in southern Venezuela and northern Brazil. They live in the Orinoco river basin, which drains out through Venezuela into the Atlantic, and there are about 20,000 Yąnomamö people today, and these are divided into about 200 villages. Yąnomamö villages are called *shabonos*, and shabonos may have as few as 40 people, may have as many as 300 people, but generally they're in the 100- 150-person range. These shabonos are built in clearings in the forest. The Yąnomamö will come in and they'll clear out an area of forest. They'll use that wood to build up a round palisade and then they'll build a thatched roof over that. In the center will be an open-air plaza, and so if you look at a Yąnomamö shabono from the air, a bird's-eye view, it looks somewhat like a doughnut. You have the palisade on the outside, the thatched roof coming about 10 to 15 feet in, and then a large open-air plaza in the middle.

Families set up their households in the shabono. They will hang their hammocks in an area, they'll set up a little hearth to cook at, and each family will have its own place in the shabono, but there are no walls between one family's living area and the next, and so all of life in the shabono is for everyone to see. This would be very claustrophobic socially for Americans; it's like living in a glass house. A Yąnomamö person can lie in their hammock and look and see everyone else in their same village, and these would be the same 100 or 150 or 200 people that they've lived with throughout their whole lives, very few secrets in Yąnomamö society, very little privacy.

We know about the Yąnomamö. The Yąnomamö were a famous case study in anthropology, based mostly on the work of an anthropologist named Napoleon Chagnon. Chagnon began studying with the Yąnomamö in 1964; he's been going back there year after year since then, and this has really been a lifelong study of his, to work with the Yąnomamö. His classic text on the Yąnomamö, when it first came out, was titled *The Yąnomamö: The Fierce People*. But in subsequent editions starting in the 1990s, he dropped the subtitle *The Fierce People*, and there was criticism that Chagnon had misportrayed the Yąnomamö, that he was there during a particularly violent time in their history and that his very presence had exacerbated tensions and violence and that he had overplayed the violence in his writing as a result.

We're going to talk about more about this later, but bear in mind that the Yąnomamö are a very aggressive society. They highly value aggressiveness, and, again, to Western observers this seems very odd. It's an in-your-face aggressiveness, and their body language and their spoken language are very aggressive. This is combined with a fierce egalitarianism, not unlike what we found with the Dobe. People are supposed to live in very similar circumstances. The best example of this is, Chagnon, he goes down to the field in the early mid-1960s, a young graduate student, doesn't know what to expect, heading out into the Amazonian rain forest, and so he takes with him lots of food. He takes sardines and peanut butter and crackers. He doesn't know what he's going to eat; he doesn't know how he's going to be received by the Yąnomamö, so he takes this storehouse of food to have just in case.

He is accepted by the Yąnomamö. He winds up at a shabono—the Bisaasi-teri is the name. He sets up camp right outside of the shabono. Whenever he eats, however, whenever he breaks open his store of food, a group of Yąnomamö appear and start demanding that he give them some. He gives them some crackers, gives them some peanut butter and gives them some sardines, but they don't stop there. They demand more and more, and he can never eat in privacy and finds himself sneaking off trying to have a little bit of food for himself, but the Yąnomamö won't let him do it because you're not supposed to have something that nobody else can have. By hoarding food, he's standing in the face of this fierce egalitarianism, so he had problems adapting to Yąnomamö life. It took him a while to integrate himself into Yąnomamö society.

One of the first things he started doing when he was working with the Yąnomamö was collecting kinship data. This is something we as anthropologists do, a standard part of our tool kit. We go down to work with the new group of people and we collect genealogical charts and kinship data to figure out the social structure. This is a problem with the Yąnomamö because the Yąnomamö have a taboo against saying a dead person's name, so if you're trying to reconstruct genealogies, it's very difficult. The Yąnomamö name people very, very obscure names so they can avoid using that name in the future. For example, a child might be named "Toenail of a Sloth," and once that child grew up and died, that name might never be used again, and it will be taboo for his relatives to say. Chagnon, after some cajoling, finally gets people to start talking about their genealogies and their kinship, and he records all of these elaborate kinship charts.

He works on this for about five months, and then one day he sets off from the village where he was living to a neighboring village where the Bisaasi-teri, whom he lived with, had some relatives, so he goes down to visit another shabono to see what life is like there. He meets the headman of this new shabono and he inquires about his wife, whose name he had learned from doing his genealogical charts. But it turns out when he inquired about his wife—he had been told that her name was, well, the translation would be quite obscene in English, but "Smelly Vagina" will do as a translation—so he comes to this headman and says, "So how's your wife, Smelly Vagina, doing today?" He realizes right away, given the reaction of this headman, that he's been fooled, and that five months of fieldwork had gone totally down the drain. The Yąnomamö had been tricking him this whole time, making up names and just tricking him. So he's not fitting in; he's done five months of fieldwork, but it amounts to nothing. But this all changes one day.

And what happens was—let me give you a little bit of background. The Yąnomamö use canoes, but they're handmade canoes and they leak fairly generously. Chagnon got tired of riding around in a canoe and getting his feet wet in the water in the bottom of the canoe. He had hired some Yąnomamö men to cut planks and to put basically a floorboard in the bottom of this canoe. He was very proud of this, he had just had this done, and then he wakes up one morning and missionaries had come down the river and had set up camp on the other side of the river. And whenever the missionaries came, they brought with them trade goods—metal pots and axes and so forth—and the Yąnomamö, when they saw the missionaries set up camp across the river, they were very eager to go across and to get some of these trade goods.

So they rushed down to the river, and everybody wants to get across of the same time and they don't have enough paddles, so they take the floorboards that he had had painstakingly made with the machete for his canoe and they use those as paddles to get across to the other side of the river. Chagnon—the anthropologist of course always shows up a little late for these kinds of events—shows up a little while later and realizes what has happened and he's furious. This is the straw that's going to break the camel's back. "I can't believe that they did this," and so he unties his own canoe, gets a makeshift paddle, paddles across and cuts loose all of their canoes that they had tied up on the other side of the river, and they all float down the stream and he, very satisfied with himself, paddles back across and awaits what's going to happen.

He really doesn't know what's going to happen; the Yąnomamö are fairly fierce, aggressive people. He could be beaten, he could be killed, he could be expelled from the village. He doesn't know what's going to happen. But, as it turns out, after this event he became accepted in the shabono, in the village. The Yąnomamö said, "You're not as weak as we thought you were;

you're actually a real person, just like we are, so we're going to finally accept you into the village." This is his coming-into-the- field story, that one day to the next he was finally accepted. Chagnon worked in a village named Bisaasi-teri. It was actually divided into two parts. There was the upper Bisaasi and she and lower Bisaasi. Teri is a suffix which means place, and so all Yąnomamö shabonos are the Bisaasi-teri or Mahekoto-teri or Patanaowä-teri and so forth. He became good friends with the headman of the village, Kabawa, and integrated itself into daily life.

The Yąnomamö are a tribal-level society in Service's bands, tribes, chiefdoms, and states scheme. As a tribal-level society, they're led by a headman, what we call a headman. This is a position of permanent leadership and it's recognized as such, a permanent leader, but it's based on a cheat status. The Yąnomamö headmen, they have some authority, they have a little bit of power, but they have to constantly reify this power and authority by doing good things for the village as a whole. They have to constantly gain the support of people living in the village so that they can continue to be the headmen. They're not guaranteed this position for life, for example. So the Yąnomamö headmen are consummate hosts. They're the best hosts; they're very good negotiators.

Most Yąnomamö men take great pride in being hunters, being skilled hunters, and gardening is seen as being more of women's work, but for the headman, interestingly enough, they spend more of their time gardening, because whenever there's a feast the Yąnomamö headman has to be the most generous person, has to give more than everybody else, has to prove his generosity and thus reify his position of political power. They don't have the power to order other people to do work, but rather they lead by example. There's a film of the Yąnomamö, and I remember vividly seeing the headman out in the middle of the shabono cleaning up the ground plaza, the dirt plaza, with his machete and calling to everyone else saying, "We need to clean up the shabono. Look at me, I'm out here doing all of this work. You need to come out and help as well." They lead by example and by cajoling others into following along with what they're doing. They have in this headman level of achieved authority in Yąnomamö societies.

In terms of their subsistence patterns, they practice what we call swidden agriculture. This is also known as slash-and-burn agriculture. This is where a group will come in, you cut down the forest, you cut down all of the underbrush, let it dry, burn it, and then you work the ash into the soil and then you plant on that soil so it releases all of the nutrients in the biomass into this fairly poor soil, and this will be good for three, four, maybe five years, and then you move on to another plot, cut down the forest, burn it, work the ashes into the soil and do it all over again, so this is swidden, or slash-and-burn agriculture.

The conventional wisdom, as I mentioned earlier, is that the soils are so poor in the Amazonian region that groups have to move their gardens every few years; about every three years is the norm for the Yąnomamö. Chagnon says that actually the reason they move their gardens every three years is not because the nutrients in the soils get depleted but because they get tired of weeding, and all this thorny underbrush starts growing up after a few years, and he says they could actually farm on the same land for four, five, maybe even six years, but they get tired of this tedious task of weeding and so they move their gardens about every three years. In the gardens, they grow plantains, they grow manioc, they grow taro, they grow tobacco and, interestingly enough for the Yąnomamö, to be poor is to be without tobacco. You call a poor man a man without tobacco.

Women do a lot of the gardening. The men will work in the garden as well, especially in the slash-and-burn phase of it. The women will tend the garden day to day. The women also gather fruits, nuts, and vegetables, wild nuts and vegetables, and honey. Honey is very important in the Yąnomamö diet and is very highly valued. The men, for their part, they hunt. They hunt pigs, they hunt deer, they hunt monkeys, and they make these poison-tipped arrows that they use to hunt with. It's a very powerful, very potent poison they put on the end of the arrows. They'll hunt some armadillos as well, and they do a little bit of fishing. Like the Dobe, like band-level societies, they actually only work a few hours a day, and also like the Dobe most of their subsistence comes from the gardens and comes from gathering. Meat is very highly valued, but, in terms of caloric intake, it only provides a small portion of their daily calories.

The Yąnomamö are interesting for a number of different reasons. One is their kinship pattern. The ideal marriage partner for a Yąnomamö is their cross-cousin. You may remember from earlier lectures there are two types of cousins. There are parallel cousins and cross-cousins. Your parallel cousins are your mother's sister's children, and your father's brother's children. Those are parallel cousins, children of same-sex siblings. Then we have cross-cousins, children of opposite-sex siblings, so your father's sister's children and your mother's brother's children are your cross-cousins. In many societies around the world, including among the Yąnomamö, the preferred marriage partner is the cross-cousin, a boy's father's sister's daughter or his mother's brother's daughter, for example.

Parallel cousins among the Yąnomamö are called brother and sister, and it would be incestuous to marry or to have relations with one's brother or sister. Even if they're not your biological brother and sister, you call them by those same terms, and it would still be incestuous.

What's interesting about the Yąnomamö system is that they prescribe cross-cousin marriage as the ideal pattern, and if this is practiced over generations a young man can marry a woman who is simultaneously his father's sister's daughter and his mother's brother's daughter, both forms of cross-cousin, and so the perfect marriage partner for a Yąnomamö man is this double cross-cousin, we might call them, and if they keep marrying cross-cousins in this fashion, it works out over generations that they can marry that person. In fact, a lot of times this doesn't work out. Like most kinship prescriptions or marriage prescriptions, there might not be a girl of the right age for a young man to marry; they might not like each other. Maybe your father didn't have a sister; maybe your mother didn't have a brother. There are all sorts of contingencies that can come into play, and the Yąnomamö are able to work around this, but, nonetheless, the ideal marriage partner is the cross-cousin.

The Yąnomamö practice polygyny, especially for headmen. Headmen will have more than one wife, sometimes as many as four, five, or six wives, and this provides extra hands to help out in the garden and kinship ties with other families, so the headmen can solidify their position. There's an ideology of male superiority, and, as we'll talk about later, there are separate origins for males and females. But they have very mild rites of passage for young girls. Once they go into menstruation and menarche, they will be isolated for a few days and are not supposed to touch anyone or anything. But for young boys, there's not a clear rite of passage. The Yąnomamö male dress, traditional male dress, consists solely of a string tied around the waist that is linked to the foreskin of the penis and holds the penis up against the body. It seems very immodest to us, but for the Yąnomamö males it's very important to always wear this penis string, and they talk about if they go down to the river and they're caught with their penis string off, it's incredibly embarrassing. You should never be seen without your penis string, but the rite of passage for a young boy is simply getting the penis string. Once he starts wearing a penis string, he becomes no longer a boy, but a man.

The Yąnomamö have a view of the cosmos that divides the world into different layers, and there are four main layers to the world. The very top layer is uninhabited today. Back in primordial times, this is where the ancient ancestors lived, but today no one lives at the very top layer of the world. The next layer down is the sky layer. We can see the bottom of the sky layer, and on top of the sky layer are two main sections. Above the sun is an area that's sort of like a fiery hell, and on the other side is an ideal Yąnomamö village. There are shabonos and hunting grounds and gardens, an idyllic Yąnomamö village, so in the sky layer we have this fiery hell and an ideal Yąnomamö village; so the top layer is uninhabited, the sky layer, the heavens, and below that is the earth, where the Yąnomamö live today, the current earth.

Below the earth is the underworld. The Yąnomamö say that way back when, in primordial times, a piece of the sky layer broke off and came down and hit the earth layer and pushed it down and created the underworld. It pushed down with it a shabono and some people, but it didn't push down any hunting grounds, and so today the underworld is inhabited by spirits who are like the Yąnomamö, but they don't have hunting grounds and so what they have to do, and the spirits are called hekura, these hekura have to come back up to the earth layer to hunt, and they become cannibalistic. They will enter into people's bodies and eat a little bit of their liver, and so people have to be on their guard for these hekura, which can come up from the underworld and eat human beings.

The shabono, interestingly enough, the shabono, the architecture of the shabono ties into this four-tiered layer of the universe. They believe that the shabonos connect the sky layer with the earth layer and the underworld. The roofs of the shabono go up, and at the top of the roof, and so it's said that it meets the sky layer, where the sky layer comes down. At the bottom of the shabono, where the shabono comes down and meets the earth on the outside, some demons live here as well, and some underworld demons. It's a very dangerous place. In fact, they have a story of Titiri, and this is the giant penis demon. He lives at this nexus of the shabono and the forest in the outside world, and at night when people are sleeping, this penis demon will go around and sometimes rape people, rape women as well as men, and can steal part of the soul. This ties into a belief that there's a sharp distinction between things of the village, the shabono, things of civilization, Yąnomamö culture, and everything else that's outside, the wilds of the jungle, the wilds of the forest, the chaos of nature, and that the shabono connects the upper world, the sky layer, the earth layer and the underworld as well.

When a person dies—the Yąnomamö conceive of there being different kinds of souls—and when a person dies, one of the souls, the soul, which we could gloss in English as being the will, the will to live, when a person dies, this part of the soul travels up the hammock strings to the top of the shabono and then goes up into the sky layer, and so it's very much like our heaven, but it's our heaven and hell combined, and when he gets to the sky layer, there's a god, a spirit person up there, not unlike our Saint Peter figure, and he asks the Yąnomamö person, "Have you been a good Yąnomamö? Have you been a good citizen? Have you been generous? Have you treated your family well?" and so forth, and, if he has, he will be sent over to the idyllic Yąnomamö village in the sky, and, if he hasn't, he'll be sent over to the fiery hell, which is the top of what we see as being the sun.

Now the Yąnomamö are very fierce, they're very aggressive, and so Chagnon would ask them, "But aren't you worried about the afterlife? Aren't you worried about having to go to this fiery hell?" The Yąnomamö would always answer him, "No, we're just going to lie. When the sky asks us if we've been good Yąnomamö, we're going to say yes, and we're going to go to the ideal village, so it's really not an issue." The Yąnomamö have different forms of souls. There's this one part of the soul, the will to live, which upon death travels up the hammock strings to the overworld. Another part of the soul is released at cremation, and it lives in the jungle—and remember the jungles are this wild chaotic area— and they become these malevolent spirits in the jungle. You go out and they might throw rocks at you or trip you as you're walking along and do just little tricks like that, bugging people.

Another sort of soul is the liver soul, and they believe that this is actually located in the human liver. This is what these hekura spirits, who come up from the underworld, will eat, these cannibalistic spirits will eat part of the liver soul, and if they do that it's debilitating not only spiritually but physically. A person can literally start wasting away. If that happens, they call upon religious specialists. The Yąnomamö have shamans, these religious specialists, and what they're able to do is connect the upper world, the earth layer, and the underworld. They can act as a conduit for the forces that travel through these three layers. To become a shaman, and this is a very powerful calling, they have to get spirits, hekura spirits, to come and live inside their body, and so they charm these hekura to come and live inside their body, and then they're able to use the force of those hekura to cure other people.

To call upon the hekura, they ingest hallucinogenic snuff, and this is called ebony, and they make this from natural plants that they find in the area. They grind it up and they make the snuff, and the way in which they ingest it is, they have a long hollow tube, and they'll pack it full of snuff, and the person who is going to ingest this will put it to their mouth or their nose, their nose more commonly, and the other person will blow as hard as they can and force all of the snuff up into their nasal passages. I've seen films of this, and green-blue snot runs out of their nose, and they get into this state. They sort of just walk around in a sort of trance, but in this trance they're able to see the spirit world. They're able to see the hekura, and they're able to see if a person is ill from a spiritual illness. They can look inside them and see the spirits that are causing them this harm and call them out or physically pull them out, and so the shamans serve this important and powerful healing function.

I should also mention that the Yąnomamö have a final kind of soul, a fourth kind of soul, which is a spirit double. The anthropological term is a nahual, and this is a very common belief throughout the Americas, that when a person is born, their future is intimately tied with that of an animal. It could be a beaver, it could be an eagle, it could be a jaguar, whatever it might be, and that is the person's spirit double. If anything ever happens to the animal, the same thing would happen to the person. If the animal is killed, the person would die as well. People very often are prohibited, they're not supposed to hunt their own nahual or their own spirit-double.

So in many ways the Yąnomamö are a classic tribal-level society. They have headmen; this is achieved status. The headmen have to be more generous than everybody else to solidify their power and authority. They practice horticulture or gardening, the slash-and-burn or shifting agriculture, moving around their villages every two or three years or so. They live in these shabonos, with 100 or 150 or 200 people, very open-air living, and knowing what everyone else in your village is doing, in your shabono is doing—very few secrets. They live in a world filled with malevolent spirits, and in this way not unlike the Fulbe, whom we mentioned in earlier lectures, who also live in a world filled with malevolent spirits, but the Yąnomamö have these shamans who are able to mediate between humans and the spirit world. The Yąnomamö also have a reputation as an especially violent society, and this is the topic that we're going to turn to in our next lecture.

Lecture Fifteen
Cannibalism and Violence

Scope: After death, Yąnomamö souls travel to the heavens while their bodies are cremated and the ashes eaten by relatives. Such ritualized cannibalism ensures the rejuvenation of Yąnomamö society.

The Yąnomamö have a reputation for being one of the most violent societies known. The most common cause of death for adult males is by far murder, and fierceness is a highly valued cultural trait. Yąnomamö villages are enmeshed in constantly shifting alliances, and raids and warfare between villages are facts of daily life. Yąnomamö men who have killed another man are called *unokais*, a designation of high status in what is basically an egalitarian culture. *Unokais* have more wives and more children than less fierce men, and thus, the pattern of fierceness is widely reproduced through family structure. Some anthropologists argue that Yąnomamö warfare is caused by chronic shortages of protein and resulting fights over hunting grounds. The Yąnomamö themselves say that although they like meat, they like women better and the true reason they go to war is to capture more wives.

Outline

I. Yąnomamö society is violent by almost any measure, and the Yąnomamö place a high value on fierceness (*waiteri*).

   A. Yąnomamö fierceness can be traced back to the mythical origin of their society.

      1. The story of "Moonblood" tells of a primordial village of supernatural humans. After the cremation of one of these beings, the moon stole the ashes waiting to be consumed. The villagers shot the moon, and where the blood puddled arose Yąnomamö society.

      2. The moon blood is associated with *waiteri*. Neighboring peoples are said to have been formed from lesser puddles of moon blood and are, thus, inherently weaker.

B. The Yąnomamö practice a form of cannibalism as part of their funeral rituals.

    1. For the Yąnomamö, death is intimately tied to rebirth. From their dead fields of plantains and manioc comes new growth. And by ingesting ancestors, one may ensure the continuation of the lineage.

    2. The Yąnomamö practice endocannibalism (eating one's own people) as opposed to exocannibalism (eating one's enemy). Nor is theirs a gruesome caricature of cannibalism: They merely mix some of the ground-up ashes of cremated bones in with a gruel and eat it.

    3. Anthropologist Beth Conklin has written on cannibalism among the Wari of Brazil, who eat the roasted flesh of their deceased as a form of compassion.

II. The Yąnomamö are known as an especially violent society.

    A. Yąnomamö violence varies in its intensity and frequency, ranging from hitting a spouse or child to all-out warfare.

        1. Disputes between men arise over women, accusations of theft, stinginess, and other such causes.

        2. Disputes begin with verbal arguments and may escalate into chest-pounding duels, in which fighters take turns beating the other's chest until one backs down.

        3. When such duels escalate further, participants arm themselves with clubs or axes, with the intention of inflicting grievous bodily harm.

        4. When a death does occur, the deceased's relatives are honor-bound to avenge his murder. Such revenge is generally carried out in clandestine raids on the enemy village to kill the murderer or one of his relatives.

        5. When such raids escalate back and forth, all-out war may follow in which one village tries to destroy the *shabono* and fields of its enemy.

    B. With their frequent wars, Yąnomamö villages must maintain an ever-shifting web of alliances with other villages.

        1. Allies can be called on to fight a common enemy that threatens one village.

        2. They also provide an economic safety net in cases of crop failure or fields burned by an enemy.

3. Alliances are established and maintained through periodic reciprocal feasts in which one village hosts another over several days. The balanced reciprocity of the feasting system is a key organizational principle of Yąnomamö society.

III. The question of why the Yąnomamö go to war has been hotly disputed.

    A. A sociobiological perspective highlights the fact that Yąnomamö men who have killed another are accorded special respect.

        1. All killers go through a cleaning ritual and are then given the prestigious status of an *unokais*.

        2. A *unokais* has, on average, 2.5 times more wives and 3 times more children than non-killers.

        3. Thus, killing ensures reproductive success and, it is argued, through a combination of genetic predisposition and family context, violence comes to dominate the society.

    B. Marvin Harris and others have argued that warfare among not only the Yąnomamö but many peoples is based in protein shortages.

        1. Harris and Michael Harner argued that the Aztecs practiced war and exocannibalism to supply protein to their capital city.

        2. Harris argues that the Yąnomamö have chronic protein shortages and that war between villages creates a no-man's land between them that acts as a natural preserve to maintain supplies of game.

    C. Chagnon argues that war is not about protein but another scarce resource: women.

        1. Protein intakes vary from village to village, but the overall average is well above the minimum need. Further, high-protein villages fight as much as low-protein villages.

        2. The Yąnomamö themselves say that they fight mostly over women.

    D. Patrick Tierney and others argue that the Yąnomamö are not as violent as Chagnon suggests and that Chagnon himself incited much of the violence he documented. These accusations bring up difficult ethical conundrums for anthropologists.

Readings:

Beth Conklin, *Consuming Grief.*

Marvin Harris, *Cannibals and Kings: Origins of Culture.*

Patrick Tierney, *Darkness in El Dorado*.

Film:

Timothy Asch, *The Ax Fight*.

Questions to Consider:

1. How does cannibalism fit into the spiritual beliefs of the Yąnomamö and the Wari?

2. What are the ethical implications of Chagnon's fieldwork style? Did he take advantage of the Yąnomamö?

3. Regarding the causes of war, is the more convincing argument for meat or women?

4. Are the Yąnomamö more aggressive than we are, or do they just have different means of channeling disputes?

Lecture Fifteen—Transcript
Cannibalism and Violence

In this lecture, we continue to talk about the Yąnomamö, who live in the rain forest in southern Venezuela and northern Brazil, living in these shabonos of 100 or 200 people in a world filled with spirits and demons. In this lecture, we're going to focus on two hot topics in anthropology, cannibalism and violence, and use the Yąnomamö to illustrate these two themes.

The Yąnomamö, as I've mentioned before, are famous as being a violent society. The first editions of Chagnon's classic book were *The Fierce People, Yąnomamö: The Fierce People*, and this fierceness goes back really to their origin myths. The Yąnomamö say that in the beginning of time there were a people who look a lot like the Yąnomamö, but they were spirit people, they were spirit ancestors, and they lived in shabonos. One day— this is the myth of Moonblood, as it's called—one day the moon came down into this primordial shabono with these spirit ancestors living there and stole the remains, the bodily remains, of the dead ancestor and took him off. For the Yąnomamö men living in the shabono, these spirit ancestors, this was the ultimate insult, stealing our relative, stealing our ancestors, and so they set off to catch the moon and to shoot the moon.

They set off with their bows and arrows and they leave the shabono, and the men are furiously shooting at the moon up in the sky, trying to shoot the moon down. They keep missing, and the arrows fall short and the moon is slowly falling and falling, going down over the horizon, and everybody's running out of arrows. Finally, one young warrior, who hasn't shot yet, sort of slowly pulls out an arrow, pulls back his bow and shoots at the moon and hits it in the stomach, in the belly of the moon, and the moon bleeds on the earth, and where the moon's blood puddled up formed the Yąnomamö. The deepest puddles of blood form the Yąnomamö, and in other areas, where the blood just sprinkled down or where it was diluted with water, formed the other peoples who live around the Yąnomamö, not quite real people, not quite fully humans.

It was this blood, the blood of the moon, that formed the fierceness of the Yąnomamö, and in Yąnomamö society, in the language, fierceness is called *waiteri*, and this is a highly venerated trait, especially for men, an ethos of fierceness, not ever letting anyone take advantage of you, always having your guard up, to not be taken advantage of by others. When the moon's blood spilled on the earth, this created men, created Yąnomamö men. They actually have a separate origin myth for the beginnings of women, and women are said to have come from a fruit, a wabu fruit, which looks something like the female genitalia. The Yąnomamö believe that they are the most fierce people because they are where the moon's blood puddled up.

Interestingly enough, when Chagnon first showed up in Yąnomamö land, they were able to integrate his origins into their own myth of Moonblood, and they said, "Well, this land to the north, this United States that you talk about, the moon's blood must have really piled up there because you obviously come from a powerful society. You flew down in an airplane and you have all of this technology, all of this stuff that you bring with you," so they were able to, and people around the world are able to do this, incorporate new data into their existing cultural models in some way. They also asked Chagnon if his airplane hit the sky layer when he flew down to Venezuela because they believe that the sky layer comes so close to the earth.

I want to talk for a moment about cannibalism, and I use this tale of Moonblood both as an entrée to talk about Yąnomamö violence but cannibalism as well, because there were the bones, there were the remains of an ancestor in one of the shabonos. This is what the moon stole, and this was what the big offense was about. This ties into a Yąnomamö practice of cannibalism. Let me say a few things about cannibalism. First of all, its practice today is extremely rare and extremely ritualized. What we're going to describe as Yąnomamö cannibalism is not your stereotypical cannibalism of eating raw flesh, for example. Cannibalism is practiced in a number of cultures around the world, in New Guinea and some of the Pacific islands and Amazonia, but it's not practiced as widely today as it once was.

It seems that early European explorers overplayed the importance of cannibalism in native societies around the world. There's some visceral reaction to cannibalism that seems especially savage, and so when the European explorers set out and they were trying to portray the people that they encountered as savages, it was natural for them to call them cannibals and to play up this cannibalism. We can all probably conjure up images in our head of the white explorer in a pith helmet and a khaki suit in a pot with the natives standing around rubbing their hands ready to eat him. But this kind of cannibalism is very rare.

Let me distinguish between a couple of types of cannibalism. First of all, there's crisis cannibalism. In extreme situations people will eat human flesh to survive. There was the case of the Paraguayan rugby team whose plane crashed in the Andes. There was the Donner party crossing the Rocky Mountains. In these extreme circumstances, when there's no other food around, people will resort to cannibalism in order to survive, will overcome our natural aversion to it. That's one sort of cannibalism that's known in the modern world.

There's also aggressive cannibalism, which is sometimes called exocannibalism, and this is eating people from another group, normally an enemy group. You go out and you kill your enemy and you eat part of their body, and this is the ultimate insult. You not only defeat them in battle but you eat them as well. We have a number of examples of this from groups around the world, including in modern times in the Congo. There are examples of this sort of cannibalism, this exocannibalism, this aggressive cannibalism as the ultimate insult, and really a way of instilling terror in a population because cannibalism really can terrorize people as well. So we have exocannibalism, eating one's enemy, and this is what we generally think of as being cannibalism.

But the far more common form of cannibalism is endocannibalism, eating one's own people or one's own relatives. Here we find endocannibalism not uncommon in the Amazon region. My colleague at Vanderbilt, Beth Conklin, has worked with a group called the Wari, who live in a Brazilian Amazon, and the Wari believe that cannibalism is really a form of compassion and, in fact, her book is called *Compassionate Cannibalism*. They say the worst thing you can do to a relative of yours who dies is to plant them in the earth and to let the worms and the maggots eat at them and to let their body decay. This is really a fate worse than death, the Wari believe. The thing that you can do to be nice to your dead relatives, to show respect for them, is to cook their flesh and to eat it. In eating their flesh, you're able to regenerate your lineage, your kinship group, physically regenerate it and spiritually as well. A person's soul will live on through the people who have eaten part of their flesh, and so in many societies around the world cannibalism is tied to cultural beliefs about death and rebirth, that ancestors can actually live on in current generations through the process of cannibalism.

This is the sort of cannibalism that the Yąnomamö practice, endocannibalism. The Wari, they will actually butcher up humans and eat large chunks of human flesh. They don't anymore actually, but they used to, and people remember the days when they did this. Among the Yąnomamö, it's a much more sterile form of cannibalism and much more acceptable, not as repulsive to our sensibilities. When a person dies in Yąnomamö society, they burn the body, they take the bones and they crush the bones up into a powder, and then they'll save this powder in a gourd inside the shabono, and this is what the moon came down and stole in the primordial shabono, these ashes of ancestors, and then they'll mix these ashes with a gruel and then drink this ritual, so it's not really as repulsive as many forms of cannibalism that we normally think about, but it's very important in Yąnomamö society to continue the regeneration of their lineage.

Yąnomamö violence, a violent people, a fierce people: When we talk about Yąnomamö violence, we can talk about several different forms of violence. The first would be internal violence, internal to a shabono, and this may arise over disagreements over women, a person being stingy, insults that are thrown from one person to another; and these sorts of internal tensions generally increase the larger the size of the shabono, so the shabono starts off with 100 people, let's say, and over time it grows to150, 200, 250 people, and the tensions grow and grow and grow, and eventually a portion of those people will split off and form a separate shabono. But in these internal disputes, which may be over women, over stinginess, over all these sorts of things, they start off with verbally assaulting one another, and this can escalate into chest-pounding duals. It's not unlike grade school kids, who'll hit each other on the shoulders as hard as they can until the other person says uncle, except these are done with clubs, and they will actually hit their opponents in the chest as hard as they can, and if they hit hard enough, it will force all of the air out of their lungs and make the person pass out, and then their opponents have won.

They start off arguing; if they can't settle their disputes through verbal argument, they'll start with these chest-pounding duels, and if that doesn't settle it, they'll move on to club fights or axe fights. They have these clubs, and they're about 10 or 15 feet long, and they'll hit each other with these long wooden poles, and if it doesn't stop there, if they want to escalate the violence a little bit more, somebody will run and get an axe, and they will fight with these axes. They normally fight with the blunt side out so it doesn't actually kill people—occasionally they'll turn it around—and if they kill someone, that raises the level to a whole new stage of violence. If a death occurs, it has to be avenged, but normally they'll fight with the blunt side out. Again, they'll hit people until someone finally backs down.

There's a famous film by the filmmaker Timothy Asch which looks at one of these axe fights. You have internal disputes within a shabono, and then you have external disputes between shabonos. These may be based on the same sorts of issues, fights over women, raids to steal women from other shabonos, fights over garden lands, and so forth. They start off as raids usually, and they will raid another shabono and steal some women, maybe steal some food, and they go back to their own shabono. This raid will have to be reciprocated by the other shabono, who will then in turn raid them, and they'll go back and forth with these raids, and if it gets bad enough they will escalate this to killing wars, where one shabono will actually invade another, kick them out of their land, kick them out of their shabono, and take over their land.

In this context of violence and warfare, alliances are very important for Yąnomamö shabonos. Villages are constantly fissioning, such that when they get too big, parts will break off and establish a new shabono, and all of the shabonos in Yąnomamö land are enmeshed in this constantly shifting web of alliances, setting up alliances between the Bisaasi-teri and the Mahekoto-teri against the Patanaowä-teri, for example, constantly setting up alliances which both serve as alliances during warfare but also as a security net, an economic security net. If you get kicked out of your shabono by an enemy village, you have somewhere to go. You can go live with your allies for a while, use some of their land to grow your crops on and so forth, and, as I've said, as military allies in the field as well.

Let me give you an example of a typical war that Napoleon Chagnon describes. This took place in 1964, when Chagnon was just starting his fieldwork, and men from one village Manau-teri, came and they stole seven women from another shabono, another village, the Patanaowä-teri. The Manau-teri come and they steal seven women, and they take them back to their own village. Stealing women is not uncommon in Yąnomamö society. They would be integrated into the new shabono they would take on husbands there and could live a pretty normal life as members of this new shabono. But such a raid cannot go unanswered, and so the Patanaowä-teri retaliate by going to Manau-teri and taking back five of these women. They go into the shabono, they raid the shabono, and they're able to get back five of the women and leave, but they're not able to get the last two.

They're not able to get the last two because they're not willing to escalate this into a killing fight. Again, remember if they kill someone, that raises things to a whole new level, and every death has to be avenged by another death. The Patanaowä-teri go to Manau-teri, they get five of these women back, but they're not willing to kill to get the other two women back, and so the Manau-teri realize that the Patanaowä-teri are a little bit scared. They backed down here, so they take advantage of this and then they raid and kill the headman of the Patanaowä-teri, and then a death has occurred, and so the Patanaowä-teri have to take vengeance on that death, and so then they raid and kill the headman of Manau-teri, and it goes back and forth, and over a year, a period of a year, eight people end up getting killed in these raids and fights.

In warfare, in working themselves up for warfare, the Yąnomamö try to work themselves into a frenzy, get themselves psyched up to go out and kill other people. They'll construct an effigy, for example, of the enemy and they'll stab it with spears and shoot it with arrows. They'll do dances until late at night and they'll sing these chants. One of my favorite chants is, "I'm meat hungry, I'm meat hungry. Like the carrion-eating buzzard, I hunger for flesh." They'll sing these chants and work themselves up into a frenzy, and then go out on these raids.

When a person, when a man kills another man in Yąnomamö society, he takes on a special status. This is called unokais, a killer; a man who has killed another person is called unokais. When they come back from a raiding expedition in which they've killed someone, they have to go through a ritual cleansing process, and they come out of this cleansing process with this honorific title of being a unokais. Unokais are very highly valued in Yąnomamö society; they have 2.5 times more wives than the common Yąnomamö man. They have three times more children than the everyday Yąnomamö person, and they're venerated in daily society. Forty percent of adult Yąnomamö men are unokais; they've killed at least once, and the more often they've killed, the higher their status in Yąnomamö society. Twenty-five percent of adult male deaths in Yąnomamö land are due to this sort of violence.

Chagnon argues that this violence reproduces itself. Perhaps there's a genetic propensity for aggression, and, if so—these men have 2.5 times more wives, three times more children—this genetic propensity would get passed on in greater frequencies to the next generation. Even if there's not a genetic propensity, they're being raised—the father figure of young boys, the children of unokais, would be this especially fierce man, and so they would learn to imitate that as well, and so this fierceness plays upon itself and builds on itself and reproduces itself over time.

There's a controversy about why the Yąnomamö are so fierce, why they go to war so often. One argument is that it's about protein, that protein is fairly scarce in this area, they highly value meat, and thus they fight over hunting grounds, for example. The main proponent of this is an anthropologist named Marvin Harris, and Harris is an arch materialist. He always looks for some protein argument to explain religion in human society. For example, he has argued in the past that Muslim and Jewish taboos against eating pork are related to the desertification of the Middle East and that raising pigs was no longer ecologically feasible, and thus the religion developed a taboo to enforce this ecological necessity.

He's also argued for the Aztecs. Building on the archaeology of Michael Harner, he's argued that the Aztecs had no big sources of protein. There were no horses; there were no cows in the New World. They had turkeys, they had dogs, they had ducks, but no big sources of protein, and the Aztec empire at its height was enormous. In the basin of Mexico, there were a million people, and so Harris has argued that the Aztecs became cannibalistic to have a source of protein, that they would go on these raiding expeditions, capture enemies, bring them back to the capital of Tenochtitlan, sacrifice them, rip out their hearts and then roll the bodies down these enormous pyramids, and neighborhood leaders would come and take these bodies and butcher them up and distribute them to people in the neighborhoods to eat. The evidence is debatable about how widespread cannibalism was in Aztec society, but I bring it up to point out that Marvin Harris is always looking for a protein argument to explain the human condition.

Harris, using Chagnon's own data, argues that the Yąnomamö have chronic protein shortages and that as a result tensions arise between shabonos, and these tensions actually arise before the protein shortages become critical and villages begin fighting one another over access to hunting grounds. Harris— this is really the neat part of his argument—he says that what this does, it creates a virtual demilitarized zone between shabonos, a no-man's land, and these no-man's lands serve as game reserves, keeping up the supply of game, of natural wildlife that can supply protein to the Yąnomamö. Harris says the Yąnomamö go to war over protein, over access to meat.

Chagnon says no, that's not the case at all, and he offers a couple of lines of evidence to support this. He says, first of all, protein intake varies a lot from village to village among the Yąnomamö, but in every village, between all villages, the overall average is well above the minimum standards established by the food and agriculture organization, the U.N. body. He also shows that high protein villages fight just as much as low protein villages, and you'd expect if they're really fighting over protein, the protein-poor villages would be much more violent. Chagnon says no, actually it's not about protein, it's about women, it's about access to women, and remember a lot of these wars start over raids to steal women from neighboring shabonos. As evidence, he uses what the Yąnomamö themselves say. He's gone back and he's asked them, "Why do you go to war? Is it because you're fighting over access to game?" and the Yąnomamö themselves say, "Well, we like meat, but we like women even better, and that's the reason that we really go to war."

Chagnon is a contrarian scholar. He's always looking for the unusual answer, proposing unusual answers. The Yąnomamö don't shift their gardens because the soils have become depleted; they shift their gardens because they don't like weeding this thorny underbrush. The Yąnomamö don't go to war over protein; they go to war over women. Establishing himself as a contrarian in the field the way he has, he's opened himself up to a lot of criticism. Recently, this criticism came to a head with the publication of a book in 2000 by a journalist named Patrick Tierney, and the title of the book was *Darkness in El Dorado*. Tierney really takes aim at Chagnon and Chagnon's ethical behavior in the field.

His most damning accusation was that Chagnon intentionally infected the Yąnomamö with measles. Chagnon had been involved in a measles eradication program. Chagnon had brought down a measles vaccine, a particular vaccine called Edmundson B, which has a live measles in it, but no one's ever gotten measles from taking this vaccine. But Tierney goes down and starts observing. He tries to correlate where Chagnon was handing out the vaccine, delivering the vaccine, and where measles broke out. He said wherever Chagnon was vaccinating people, we had these outbreaks of measles.

But, actually, we've gone back and looked at this after Tierney's accusations, and it turns out that he's making a false correlation there. Chagnon was following the measles to inoculate people against measles. He wasn't causing the measles, but Tierney paints a real conspiracy theory that Chagnon was working with a geneticist named James Neal, was receiving funds from the Atomic Energy Commission, and he believes that they were involved in some secret research, very conspiratorial theory here, some secret research trying to look at natural resistances to measles and the way in which measles are passed between individuals. But this accusation has been effectively refuted.

However, Tierney's more troublesome accusations are much less inflammatory actually, and they are that Chagnon stirred up rivalries, intentionally or unintentionally, but he stirred up rivalries by his very presence. By introducing trade goods, for example, among the Yąnomamö, he exacerbated tensions between villages. Why should this shabono get all of these metal pots and axes and all of these trade goods when we don't have anything? And so Tierney argues that Chagnon's presence exacerbated tensions between shabonos. He even argues that perhaps Chagnon staged a feast, an alliance between a couple of villages, in order for a film crew to film some of his work, a number of accusations like this.

Tierney's accusations really get at the difficulties of doing fieldwork, I think. Chagnon was in a difficult position. He could have gone down and said, "I'm going to protect the Yąnomamö from outside influence. I'm not going to bring in any outside goods; I'm not going to trade with them." But yet this is what the Yąnomamö wanted. They wanted steel axes, and you can think of the value that a metal machete and an axe would have if you're living in the jungle, if your subsistence is based on chopping down trees and burning them. They wanted metal pots, they wanted these sorts of trade items, and Chagnon was just trying to be a good human being. He says the Yąnomamö have given me so much—I've made my career studying the Yąnomamö—I want to give things back, and so this is one way to do that, is to bring trade goods down.

It's actually very paternalistic, I think, in a way, for anthropologists to think that they can protect the native people that they study from outside influences. It's really not our role to do that. On the one hand, we're romantic and we do want to protect these native ways of life. On the other hand, if they want trade goods, if this would improve their lives in some material way, who are we to say, "No, that's just for us Westerners, and you guys can't have any of it"? Tierney's accusations, the accusations of intentionally infecting the Yąnomamö with measles, have been proven to be false. However, this difficulty of doing fieldwork, the ethics of how you interact with a remote, isolated native peoples, is very troublesome.

I would also mention that we tend to romanticize native peoples in small-scale societies as being peaceful, as living in harmony with their environment. In some ways, they are; the Yąnomamö do have a much more unified spiritual view of man's relationship to nature, for example. But they also have the necessity of going down and chopping down rain forest in order to plant their gardens so that they can live, so that they can put food on the table at night. We often think of less developed, less complex societies as being peaceful, as living in harmony with nature. But my colleague Bruce Knauft actually has done a survey recently looking at homicide rates in societies around the world, and he's found that homicide rates are higher in small-scale societies even than they are in the United States. In the United States, we have a much higher homicide rate than anywhere else in the developed world. So native peoples are not as peaceful perhaps as we once thought they were, and the Yąnomamö in that sense are not as much of an anomaly as we might have thought they were.

To sum up, today we've continued talking about the Yąnomamö, the fierce people. They practice endocannibalism—they eat the bones of their ancestors in a gruel. They highly value fierceness and aggression. Unokais, killers in society, have more wives, they have more children, they have more social status than anyone else in Yąnomamö land, and whatever the material reasons for Yąnomamö warfare, whether they're fighting over protein or fighting over women, it is a culture of fierceness that gets perpetuated from generation to generation through these mechanisms of valuing unokais.

Lecture Sixteen
The Role of Reciprocity

Scope: The Inuit say, "Gifts make friends as surely as whips make dogs." Indeed, this is one of those rare cultural observations that holds true around the world, not only for the Inuit of the Arctic region but also for the Trobriand Islanders of the western Pacific, for the Kalahari Bushmen of southern Africa, and for our own culture as well.

Among many societies, reciprocity forms the very basis of the economic system. For the Dobe, all economic activity is based on reciprocity. In the Trobriand Islands, chiefs exchange symbolic valuables over long distances in a system known as the *kula* ring. In the *kula* ring, armbands travel only counterclockwise around the string of islands, while necklaces travel clockwise. Through trading in these valuables, chiefs are able to maintain and expand their political influence. Even in our own society, reciprocity oils the wheels of daily interaction.

Outline

I. Reciprocity and gift-giving are types of economic transactions that are intimately tied to cultural understandings. Reciprocity is found in all cultures, but in many smaller scale societies, it dominates economic interactions.

   A. Karl Polanyi divides economic transactions into three main types: reciprocity, redistribution, and market exchange.

   B. *Reciprocity* is the act of giving and receiving gifts; it solidifies social relationships and involves not only economic but also political and religious significance.

   1. The French sociologist/anthropologist Marcel Mauss, in his classic *The Gift* (1924), calls gift-giving a "total social phenomenon," an implicit social contract that holds small-scale societies together in the absence of contractual law.

   2. Mauss offered the case of the Maori of New Zealand and the spiritual quality they call *hau*. Gifts are endowed with *hau*, a spiritual quality that comes from the spirits of the forest and that must eventually retrace the circuit of exchange to return to their forest home.

    C. Marshall Sahlins, invoking both Polanyi and Mauss, offers a useful typology of three types of reciprocity.

        1. First is *generalized reciprocity*, usually practiced within nuclear families, that involves flows of gifts in one direction (as from parents to children) for sustained periods of time. This comes closest to notions of pure altruism.

        2. In *balanced reciprocity*, participants strive to make gifts and counter-gifts roughly equivalent, although there is often an explicit denial that accounts are kept.

        3. *Negative reciprocity* is when one party takes advantage of an implicit understanding and does not reciprocate.

II. In band-level societies such as the Dobe, generalized reciprocity forms the basis of the economy.

    A. The nomadic gatherer and hunter lifestyle does not lend itself to the accumulation of personal possessions; there is little sense of private property.

    B. The ecological circumstances in which the Dobe live also contribute to the need for extensive reciprocity.

        1. Water holes, for example, are nominally owned by a particular band, but other bands are never refused gifts of water if they are in need.

        2. The Dobe also practice balanced reciprocity through *hxaro* exchanges. These are roughly equivalent exchanges of ostrich shell water vessels, glass beads, and other goods with members of neighboring bands.

III. The Yąnomamö practice balanced reciprocity through feasts.

    A. In 1968, Timothy Asch filmed what has become a classic anthropological documentary, *The Feast*.

        1. The feast was hosted by the village of Patanaowä-teri (pop. 225), who had invited the Mahekoto-teri (pop. 125) to bury an old dispute and enter into a new alliance.

        2. During the ritualized start of the feast, both groups demonstrate their fierceness through mock battle.

3. The feast is tense because the Mahekoto-teri are fearful of an ambush, while the Patanaowä-teri worry that their generosity will not be reciprocated.
4. The feast ends with the guests demanding specific gifts from their hosts—usually a bow or poison-arrow tips but sometimes a prized possession. The hosts cannot refuse the requests.

B. Investigative journalist Patrick Tierney has sharply criticized Napoleon Chagnon and his contributions to making *The Feast*.
1. Tierney claims that Chagnon convinced the Patanaowä-teri to move to an old village site closer to the Orinoco, enticing them with measles vaccination. He compensated them with metal pots, axes, and other trade goods; Tierney sees this influx of trade goods as upsetting normal village relations.
2. After the feast, the Patanaowä-teri and Mahekoto-teri carry out a common raid on another village, resulting in the death of a woman there.

IV. The Trobriand Islanders are famous for a form of escalating balanced reciprocity known as the *kula* ring.

A. Traditionally, *kula* trading was the prerogative of chiefs and those from chiefly lineages, although over the years, more and more men from lesser-ranked lineages came to participate.

B. *Kula* trading takes place between individuals on different islands with goods whose value is purely symbolic.
1. Two goods are traded in the kula: shell armbands and necklaces.
2. The armbands travel in only a counterclockwise direction, and the necklaces travel in only a clockwise direction through the *kula* circuit.
3. Each item has a particular history associated with it; the more prestigious its former owners, the more value the armband or necklace will have.
4. *Kula* participants will have trading partners on neighboring islands in both directions. Traders try to escalate the terms of the balanced reciprocity of the *kula* system in order to possess—although only temporarily—famous items.
5. Marvin Harris, for example, has argued that the *kula* exchange is just an excuse for the trade in subsistence items that takes place off to the side of the ritual exchange.

V. Reciprocity is not confined to exotic societies—in many ways, it oils the wheels of daily social interaction in our own culture.

    A. The rules of reciprocity are most often unspoken, intentionally ambiguous. In giving Christmas or birthday presents to someone, both would deny any sort of calculation beyond a purely emotional response—but accounts are kept.

    B. Giving too small of a gift can be insulting; but giving too large of a gift can also damage a relationship by overly indebting the recipient.

    C. Marketers often employ the principles of reciprocity to sell products and foster brand loyalty.

Readings:

Arjun Appadurai, *The Social Life of Things*.

Pierre Bourdieu, *Distinction: A Social Critique of the Judgment of Taste*.

Marcel Mauss, *The Gift*.

Questions to Consider:

1. Is a gift ever given without expectations of some return?

2. Why is it impolite to bring up the political considerations that go into gift-giving in U.S. culture?

3. How do the Trobrianders use reciprocal obligations in their quest for fame?

4. Why are Yąnomamö feasts potentially dangerous events?

Lecture Sixteen—Transcript
The Role of Reciprocity

In the last few lectures, we've been filling out the bands and tribes categories in Service's bands, tribes, chiefdoms, states typology, and we've been looking particularly at subsistence and political organization and violence and cannibalism in the last lecture. Today, we're going to introduce two more typologies, typologies of economic relationships, and these fit into the Service scheme very neatly.

In this lecture, we're going to focus on reciprocity and gift giving, but first I want to introduce the scheme introduced by the economic historian Karl Polanyi. He says that we can divide all economic transactions into three main types: Those are reciprocity, or gift giving, the subject of the lecture today; the second is redistribution; and the third is market exchange. We're all familiar with market exchange; it's the system that we use in our own society. A redistributed system is one where the goods in a society go to an individual or an entity and then are redistributed by that person back out to society and we're going to talk about this more in the next lecture. But today we're going to discuss reciprocity.

The Inuit say that gifts make friends just as whips make dogs, and this is one of those rare cultural sayings that applies around the world, not only for the Inuit of the sub-Arctic region but for the Trobriand Islanders of the Pacific, for the Dobe Ju/'hoansi, for the Yanamamo, and for own culture as well. Gifts are given with at least the vague expectation that they will be returned, perhaps not right away and probably not in down-to-the-penny equivalences, but returned nonetheless. How long would you give Christmas presents or birthday gifts to someone if they never reciprocated? Such reciprocity, giving of gifts with the expectation of receiving something in the future, creates powerful social bonds between individuals. In some small-scale societies, as we'll see today, it's the basis of their entire economic system, and in our own society it often works in hidden ways, following largely unspoken rules that we probably have a hard time articulating.

The French sociologist Pierre Bourdieu one time noted that what goes without saying comes without saying. This is really true; often the most important aspects of a culture are so fundamental that they're taken for granted. There's no need to discuss or debate these things, it's just the way the world operates, and reciprocity in our own society falls into this category. It's a bit rude to make explicit the expectations of gift giving. It detracts from the extensively altruistic emotion underlying the act. We like to think of giving gifts as being acts of love, of friendship, of kindness. But calculation, economic calculation, political calculation, even emotional calculation certainly takes place. Think of the complex politics that go into deciding what Christmas present to give someone or what birthday present to give someone, or the uncomfortable position of receiving an unexpected gift and then scrambling to calculate what the appropriate return gift should be.

To give something is to indebt someone, and we acknowledge this in phrases such as "much indebted," "much obliged." There's always the idea that a gift has to be returned at some point in the future. There's no free lunch, as we say. With any gift, there are expectations, social ramifications, prices to pay down the road. In essence, a gift is an indirect delayed exchange of goods or services, and one which creates a bond, a relationship between individuals. In this, the period between a gift and a countergift is crucial. To return a gift immediately with an object of equal value is to reject the social relationship that's being offered. In turn, the longer the period before a countergift is offered creates a stronger social bond. If there's a long period between the initial gift and a countergift, this period of indeterminacy, not knowing if the gift is going to be returned or not, creates a strong social relationship between individuals.

The value of a gift, as we all know, is much more than the item's cost. A gifted object holds sentimental value, cultural associations. If your father gave you a watch, the value of that watch to you would not be what you can sell it on eBay for because there's all of the sentimental attachment tied up in that as well. Generally, the larger the gift, the stronger the bond as well, at least to a point. I remember one time when I was in college my stereo was stolen, and a good friend of mine who came from a very wealthy family, had a lot more money than I did, had just bought a new stereo, and he gave me his old stereo, and I was incredibly indebted. This was a wonderful gift, thank you so much, and yet it was too big of a gift. I couldn't repay him for that gift, at least not easily or not right away, and so it created this tension in our relationship. He was never so rude as to bring it up, but whenever we went out, deciding where to go to dinner, how late to stay out at night or in things like this, there was always in the back of my mind: Yeah, but he gave me that stereo. Can I say no? We gradually drifted apart, and I think it was because he gave a gift that was too large, and so it's just as bad to give too big of a gift as it is to give no gift at all, or to give too small of a gift.

The classic work on gift giving and reciprocity was written by a French sociologist Marcel Mauss. He's actually the nephew of the father of sociology, Emil Durkheim, and Mauss wrote a little book in 1924 titled simply *The Gift*. Mauss was very much concerned with other cultures; he was an armchair anthropologist in many ways. His research was conducted from the comfort of his Parisian study, reading travelogues and explorer accounts, but his observations about gift giving in other cultures still rings true today. Mauss called gift giving a total social phenomenon; he says that it serves legal functions, political functions, religious functions, domestic functions, economic functions. All of this is tied up in gift giving. He argues that in the great scheme of human history the gift was the first social contract. It's really what allowed alliances, communion, and peace to emerge among societies.

Mauss's most famous example comes from the Maori, the Maori peoples of New Zealand, and the Maori have a kind of concept called *hau*, and we can translate this roughly as "the spirit of the gift" or "the spirit of the forest." The Maori believe that everything ultimately comes from the forest, and if someone, if I go into the forest and I cut down a tree and I make a spear or club with that tree, part of the hau of the forest is going to live in that object. Then if I give that object away, that spirit will go through me and through this object on to the next person, but the thing about this hau, this spirit, is it always wants to go back to the forest, and so it always has to retrace its path back, and so it's a spiritual way of conceiving of the idea that every give gift has to be repaid. And, actually, the hau increases, the value of a good for the Maori increases, as it passes through more hands. If I make a spear and I give it to you and then you pass it on to someone else and he or she passes and it on to someone else, then the value of that item increases the more hands it travels through. That gift would have to follow its way back, eventually getting itself back to the forest.

Gifts, reciprocity, gift giving, Marshall Sahlins, whom we mentioned before, the anthropologist who wrote the book on the original affluent society, *Stone Age Economics*, has also offered us a scheme of different sorts of reciprocity. Recall Karl Polanyi, the economic historian, says that we have reciprocity, redistribution, and market exchange. Marshall Sahlins says we can in turn break down reciprocity into three different types, and these are generalized, balanced, and negative. Generalized reciprocity is seen best in our own society in the relationship between parents and children, where gifts usually flow in one direction for a long period of time. When countergifts do come, they may be of greater symbolic value than of material value. The more closely related people are, the more likely they are to practice generalized reciprocity, and within families generalized reciprocity is normally the rule.

Next we have balanced reciprocity, and balanced reciprocity is the preferred form in our own society, in most friendships, for example. There's no immediate return on a gift, often a denial that any balance is being kept, "No, I'm just giving this out of friendship," but there's also an implicit expectation that the value of goods exchanged will be roughly equivalent over time. This sort of reciprocity serves to establish and reinforce friendships and political alliances and generally oils the wheels of our daily interactions. We're not going to spend much time on negative reciprocity, but let me just mention that negative reciprocity is taking advantage of the expectations of reciprocity, receiving a gift and there is the implicit idea that you would return that gift at some point in the future, but receiving a gift without reciprocating, and this is negative reciprocity, taking advantage of the situation, acting in bad faith. This can range from not adding someone to your Christmas card list to borrowing money from a friend and not paying it back, all these kinds of things.

Today I would like to begin by going through each of these three types of reciprocity, but I'd like to begin with generalized reciprocity, what we like to think of as true gift giving, pure altruism. This is the sort of giving for long periods of time with no clear expectation of a return, at least not right away, and is characteristic of parent-child relationships. Again, for parent-child relationship, the generalized reciprocity lasts much longer today than it probably ever has before; it's very common for parents to support their children today until they're well into their 20s and sometimes even beyond. In most societies around the world, this is for a shorter period of time and the return is much more clear-cut. In most societies around the world, you take care of your kids when they're young and then they take care of you when you get old. Today we've sort of divorced this function from the family, but nonetheless there's still this expectation of doing something for your parents when they get old.

In generalized reciprocity, the social value of the relationship generally outweighs the economic benefits, and this is to say that the returns don't have to be in kind. They can be symbolic as well as emotional, and this really holds true for parent-child relationships in our own society. Pride in one's children, the comfort of their love, the vicarious prestige that you gain from seeing them do well, "Yes, my son's in college; he's at Harvard or

Yale or George Mason," wherever it may be, this kind of vicarious pleasure that one gets.

Outside of families, the more status difference there is between individuals, the higher the expectation that the higher status individual will engage in generalized reciprocity. It's the notion of noblesse oblige. For example, if I go out to dinner with the dean of my college, it would be rude of me to pick up the tab, to insist on picking up the tab. Of course, I would make an initial pass for the check and then expect him to take it away, and it would be rude for me to insist that I'm going to pick up the tab because he has to play the role of generous host. This is part of the social roles that we play.

Speaking of eating, food around the world is much more likely to be involved in generalized reciprocity, be governed by rules of generalized reciprocity, than any other item. I mention this because the Dobe, the very basis of Dobe economics is generalized reciprocity. You'll remember that the Dobe are gatherers and hunters. They have very few personal possessions, there's very little specialization in Dobe society, and there's a free exchange of goods between individuals, very little sense of private property. You can just walk into another person's hut and borrow whatever you need to borrow. Generalized reciprocity is really the everyday norm for Dobe society; you don't even have to ask when you're borrowing something.

The most common form of reciprocity around the world is balanced reciprocity. This is where there's an expectation of some sort of equivalence in which both parties will benefit economically or socially. The Dobe actually practice a form of balanced reciprocity with other bands and with relatives in other bands, especially in-laws, and they call this kind of exchange *hxaro*, and they'll exchange spears and arrows, knives, maybe dogs, even glass beads, which are a highly valued trade item. These are traded on visits. When one band will go and visit another band, they will have this trade in these objects, and it's used to strengthen and maintain a social security net that they can call upon in times of need.

But the best example from the ethnographic record of balanced reciprocity comes from the Ya̧nomamö. Going back for a moment to the Ellman Service scheme of bands, tribes, chiefdoms, and states, bands are characterized by generalized reciprocity; tribes, on the other hand, are characterized by a greater reliance on balanced reciprocity, and thus the Yanamamo fit in here. For the Yanamamo, as we talked about in the last lecture, maintaining alliances between shabonos is incredibly important, important to their very survival. They need to have allies in order to fight common enemies and as a social safety net for when they get attacked. The way in which these alliances are initiated, the way in which they're maintained, the way in which they're solidified, is by throwing a feast, hosting a party and what better way to show friendship than inviting people over for dinner? We do it in our own society; this is a wonderful way to show intimacy, demonstrate friendship.

This is what the Yanamamo do; they will throw feast, and these will be reciprocal feasts. One shabono will give a feast, and then after a period of time the guests will invite them to their shabono for a feast, and it will go back and forth this way. In the period between the first feast and the second feast, there's this period of indeterminacy; you never know if the other people are going to betray you, are going to be treacherous, and so there's this period of indeterminacy which can act to solidify the bonds between these two shabonos. We're tied together in this reciprocity and we haven't seen it through yet.

There was a film—Napoleon Chagnon, when he was working with the Yąnomamö, did a number of films in cooperation with a filmmaker named Timothy Asch, really some of the classic ethnographic films, and these were made throughout the late 1960s and the early 1970s. I bring this up because Asch made a film called *The Feast*, and in his own words, he says that *The Feast* is really a visual representation of Marcel Mausse's book, *The Gift*. In this film, it describes a feast that took place in 1968 between two Yanomamö villages, Patanaowä-teri and the Mahekoto-teri. These villages had been fighting for quite a while; their dispute went back a number of years, where one village had raided another and had stolen a woman, and for a number of years they had periodic raids on each other in this tense relationship. In fact, before this feast, in the year before this feast, ten people had been killed between these two villages.

They decide, "Well, this has gone on too long, we need to patch things up, we have a number of common enemies, so let's throw this feast and come back together and create an alliance." This film is remarkable because it shows the whole feast from start to finish. The guests show up at the shabono, they ritually enter the shabono, and they go around and they're dressed in their war garb. They're dressed in war paint, they're carrying spears, and they're doing war dances. The guests come in and they do these war dances all around the shabono, and, at this point, if the guests were going to be treacherous, they can attack their hosts, but they don't. This is all part of the ritual that goes along with the feast, showing, "We could attack you, but we're not. We're really fierce—look and see how fierce we are—but we're not going to follow through and attack you."

Then, in the next ritualized aspect of the same feast, the guests are shown to their hammocks where they'll stay, and these feasts will last for two or three days, and they lie in the hammocks, and then the hosts go around, again dressed in their war garb with their war paint on, with their spears, and they go around and they thrust their spears at the guests who are lying in their hammocks. The guests have to be totally stoic and not show any sign of fear at all, and again, here, if the hosts were going to be treacherous, they could kill all of their guests fairly easily, but they don't. They're showing, "We could do this if we wanted to, but we're not going to." The heart of the feast—and again these feasts last sometimes two or three days, last for a number of days, and they involve lots of eating. Everybody is fed as much food as they can possibly eat. They make plans for future raids that they will conduct together and so forth.

Then on the last day, there's a ritualized exchange of gifts. This isn't the sort of gift exchange that we would expect when guests come over to visit. The hosts don't say, "We thought about you and want to give you this small item." The guests demand what they want from the host. They've been scoping out what the hosts have the whole time during the feast, and so on this last day they may ask for some poison arrows, they may ask for a spear, they might ask for a hammock, but sometimes they ask for really nice stuff, a dog. In the film *The Feast*, the headman, the host headman, has to give up his dog, and he doesn't want to—he loves this dog—but the guests demand it. They say, "We came here, we're your guests, give us that dog," and he has to. He's obliged to fulfill this obligation, so he gives his dog up, but always keeping in the back of his mind, when I go to their village for the next feast I'm going to be sure and get something of equally important value. You have this exchange, this giving of a feast and then giving of gifts to the guests as well that creates the bond based on reciprocity, and this is a bond on which is based a political alliance, a military alliance, an economic alliance in the case of crop failures, for example, that really forms the glue that holds Yąnomamö society together.

Last time, when we talked about the Yanamamo, we mentioned Patrick Tierney and the criticisms that he raised in the book *Darkness in El Dorado* about Chagnon. One of his accusations was that the film *The Feast*, this very highly regarded ethnographic film done by Timothy Asch and Napoleon Chagnon, was staged by Napoleon Chagnon, that he had convinced the Patanaowä-teri to move from their village to a new village site closer to the Orinoco, where he was leading this measles vaccine campaign, and that the Patanaowä-teri were compensated by Chagnon with metal pots, with axes and with other trade goods, and that they created this alliance and had this feast in order to film this movie.

As a result of this alliance, the custom is to go out and form and conduct a common raid after a feast. As a result of this feast, the two groups went out and conducted a raid and killed a woman in a third, a common enemy village. Tierney's accusation is that the blood of that woman is on Chagnon's hands because he had convinced these two groups to have this feast and to solidify this alliance. But this was without intent; Chagnon didn't know what was going to happen. This alliance could have happened without Chagnon, but nonetheless there is that accusation.

So we have this example of balanced reciprocity, feeding into political and economic relationships. Another example of balanced reciprocity comes to us from the Trobriand Islanders off the coast of Papua New Guinea, where Branislav Malinowski and Annette Weiner worked and we talked about in an earlier lecture in the series. The Trobrianders are a chiefdom level of organization, and we're going to talk about them more in the next lecture, but they're known for a particular sort of trade call the *kula* trade. The interesting thing about the kula trade is they only trade two objects: They trade armbands and necklaces. The armbands are known as *mwali* and the necklaces are known as *bagi.* They're both made out of shells, and they're both purely ornamental items. They're normally not even worn; sometimes they'll be worn, but they're normally just displayed.

They're only traded in particular directions. The mwali armbands only are traded counterclockwise among a chain of islands that are off the coast of Papua New Guinea. The armbands travel counterclockwise and the necklaces only travel clockwise, so they're constantly passing one another. The way in which this trade takes place is, a Trobriand man on one island will have trading partners on islands in either direction. From one of his trading partners he'll receive these mwali armbands, and from another trading partner he'll receive the necklaces. Each of these items has a history unto itself and the history says who has owned this item in the past, and the value of these items is based partly on the aesthetics, how they look, but more important is who's owned this in the past, and the most valuable of the kula trade items are the ones that have been owned by powerful and important chiefs.

We have the system—it's sort of like the Maori system of *hau*—where the spirit of the gift follows the material object and creates social relationships between individuals, so we have this highly unusual trade in purely symbolic goods going back and forth between islands in the Trobriand chain. Marvin Harris, our arch materialist—you'll remember everything's about protein or everything's about material conditions—Marvin Harris says that the people actually conduct this kula trade just to justify trading in subsistence items, because when they take these voyages between islands to trade the armbands and the necklaces they also take along some salt, some ax blades, maybe some baby pigs, and they'll trade these items at the same time, and so Harris says that this whole structure, this whole symbolic nature of the kula trade, is just used to justify trade in the subsistence islands. But what's really important here is building up fame, the fame that gets built up by trading these items, and it can increase a chief's fame and a chief's status in his own society.

Reciprocity is at work very much in our own society today. We might deny that we keep balances when we trade gifts with our relatives or with our friends, but this sort of balance, this sort of accounting, does take place. We just normally don't talk about it; it's a bit rude to talk about. It's been used by a number of companies to their own ends. My favorite example is of Amway, the very successful multilevel marketing corporation, one of the most successful multilevel marketing corporations in the country, in the world. Amway, when it first started out was just getting by, but it wasn't very successful, but they latched onto a strategy.

What they would do is they would give the Amway agents a basket of goods, and this basket of goods they could loan to their friends and people that they wanted to sell items to. An Amway salesman would tell a friend, "Take this basket; it has some dishwashing soap, it has some laundry detergent, and try these things out, and I'll come by and pick it up in a week. If you don't like it, no problem. You've tried it out; there's no obligation, and if you like anything you can buy it." Amway sales took off and skyrocketed after they started doing this. There are a couple of explanations. Perhaps Amway makes the best dishwasher detergent in the world, maybe it's just heads and tails above everything else, or perhaps they were playing on the implicit bonds of reciprocity, that I couldn't accept this gift, even though it was said not to be a gift, without doing something in return, without paying it back some way.

You may remember the Hare Krishnas who used to be in all the airports. They had a very similar strategy. They would hand out flowers and books, and they would give these away and the people would try and give them back and they would say, "No, it's a gift, it's a pure gift. We don't want it back." Their donations took off after they started giving away these items because people didn't want to feel indebted. They would take the holy Hare Krishna book. They couldn't give it back so they would give the person $5 because I don't want to be in this social relationship with you, and then they probably walked out and threw the book in the trash can anyway, but there was this, "We're going to make this balance so that I don't feel any obligation to you."

My favorite example comes actually—the first time I bought a car it was in New Orleans. It was a hot summer day in New Orleans. M wife and I test drove this car that we liked, we decided to buy it, and we go in with the salesman into the office. As we go in, he says "Would you like a Coke? Would you like something to drink?" "Yes, a Coke would be really nice," and so he walks over, very conspicuously walks over to a Coke machine and pulls out fifty cents, seventy-five cents, whatever it was, puts it in the machine and buys me a Coke and gives it to me. They probably give out dozens or hundreds of Cokes at this car dealership every day, so why not just have a big refrigerator where you can get the Coke, but it was this act that he had given me something, and it seems silly to think that I would buy a $10,000 to $15,000 car based on a fifty-cent Coke, but actually this sort of thing works because we feel indebted to a person who gives us something. It's these bonds of reciprocity that hold society together, and this is true not only for the Dobe Ju/'hoansi but for the Yąnamamö and for ourselves as well.

Lecture Seventeen
Chiefdoms and Redistribution

Scope: In chiefdom-level societies, *redistributive exchange* underpins
both political and economic relations. Redistribution works off the
good will produced by reciprocity: A gift, be it from a friend or a
chief, entails obligation, and that obligation can be converted into
political power.

Among the Trobriand Islanders, chiefs engage in extensive and
complicated networks of yam exchanges. They place the yams
they receive as gifts in a specially built display hut to serve as a
public symbol of that chief's political clout. Annual yam
competitions are likewise politically loaded events, because the
chief with the largest yam will build political power.

The Kwakiutl Indians of the Northwest Coast also practice a form
of redistribution in their potlatch feasts. Chiefs host potlatches to
solidify the allegiance of their subjects, and they are not only
expected to give away enormous amounts of food, blankets, and
native art, but to destroy valuable goods as well. Potlatches are not
merely conspicuous consumption, however; they also serve as an
important economic security net for regions occasionally beset by
food shortages.

Outline

I. Economic redistribution occurs to some degree in all cultures.

   A. Households commonly pool resources and reallocate them in terms
   of need. Nation-states likewise practice varying degrees of
   redistribution through tax systems.

   B. Redistribution is the central economic and political organizational
   principle of chiefdom-level societies.
   1. Redistribution acts as a means of indebting subjects and
   fortifying political power for chiefs.
   2. Gaining political capital from redistribution plays into the
   tenets of reciprocity; it may be seen at work in nation-states
   through political pork barrel projects.

II. The Trobriander Islanders are a chiefdom, and chiefs build up their status through the *kula* ring, as well as various forms of redistribution.

    A. Trobriand matrilineages are ranked in status; a chief or nobleman inherits his position not from his father but from his mother's brother.

        1. Rank and eligibility for chiefdomship is ascribed, determined by one's matrilineage of birth and standing within that lineage.

        2. Within the limitations of kinship, however, there is a great deal of room for jockeying for power.

        3. Chiefs nominally own all coconuts and pigs; thus, any consumption of these savored items is symbolically a gift from the chief.

    B. Yams are a staple of the Trobriand diet and at the symbolic heart of Trobriand society.

        1. Noblemen maintain two types of gardens: one to eat from and one to trade from. Trobriand men spend a great deal of time cultivating yams.

        2. Yams are symbols of wealth, power, and prestige. Chiefs build elaborate open-front yam huts to hold their bounty and prove their political worth.

        3. But the yams on display cannot be grown by the chief himself. They must be received as gifts from relatives—from members of his own matrilineage and his wives' matrilineages.

    C. Politically ambitious men need to get relatives to give them yams, which they will display and redistribute.

        1. Malinowski recorded that a man primarily received yams from his wife's brother. He saw this as symbolic compensation by a child's matrilineage to his paternal progenitor.

        2. Annette Weiner found that yams do indeed come from a man's wife's matrilineage but that these are given *through* the wife, building up an obligation from the husband.

        3. This obligation has to be paid back in gifts from husbands of women's wealth: banana-leaf bundles and skirts.

        4. Annette Weiner also argues that the *kula* trade is best understood as a "quest for fame"; ambitious chiefly aspirants try to make their symbolic fortunes.

        5. Pierre Bourdieu distinguishes between economic capital and symbolic capital (which includes social and cultural capital).

In societies such as the Trobriands, the value of symbolic capital eclipses that of economic capital.

6. With the yam gifts, a husband is able to redistribute these to villagers and, thus, build up his political base.

D. The Trobriand preoccupation with yams comes to a climax during their harvest festivals in July and August.

   1. Known as *mwasawa* (the "time of play"), a centerpiece of the festivals are yam competitions between chiefs.

   2. Competition yams are known as *kuvi*. They are decorated and may be up to 12' long.

   3. The chief with the biggest yam wins the competition and increases his prestige as a great man.

III. The Kwakiutl are a chiefdom-level society of the Northwest Coast region.

   A. First studied by Boas, the Kwakiutl today are best known for their totem poles (actually chiefly genealogies) and masks (especially the spectacular transformation masks).

      1. An anomaly for a chiefdom, their economy is not based on agriculture but rather "gathering," inasmuch as salmon fishing may be considered gathering.

      2. The natural abundance of salmon, which can be smoked to last all year, was sufficient to sustain the large population densities that give rise to chiefdom-style political organization.

      3. The Kwakiutl are mostly matrilineal, although some groups practice cognatic descent.

      4. As with the Trobrianders, chiefs claim the right to their positions through inheritance, yet within the confines of kinship, a great deal of political maneuvering for position takes place.

   B. Kwakiutl chiefs must continually solidify their support and expand their base to stay in power. They do this largely through feasts called *potlatches*.

      1. Hosting a potlatch feast requires months or years of saving and preparation. Guests from neighboring villages are invited and feted for several days.

2. In the course of the potlatch, guests are given gifts of art, fish oil, berries, and blankets. Chiefs will also sometimes destroy canoes or pieces of art.
3. Following contact and the great demand for pelts by the Hudson Bay Company, the Kwakiutl saw huge inflation in the expectations for a successful potlatch. The potlatch was eventually outlawed and has only recently reemerged among Kwakiutl communities.
C. Since Boas's day, the potlatch has long intrigued anthropologists.
   1. Boas saw the potlatch as the product of a particular history. Boas's student Ruth Benedict expanded on this notion, arguing that it was a cultural pattern pushed out of control by Western contact.
   2. Others argue that it serves a material function by increasing productivity all around and providing an economic safety net.

Readings:

Ruth Benedict, *Patterns of Culture.*

Bronislaw Malinowski, *Argonauts of the Pacific.*

Annette Weiner, *The Trobrianders of Papua New Guinea.*

Questions to Consider:

1. How does redistribution build up political power?
2. What is the purpose of destructive consumption, such as in the potlatch?
3. How do yams (which are men's wealth) play into the economy of females?

Lecture Seventeen—Transcript
Chiefdoms and Redistribution

Karl Polanyi said that we can divide up all economic transactions into three main types, and those are: reciprocity, and reciprocity is most characteristic of band-level societies and tribal-level societies, although we find it in chiefdoms and states as well; redistribution, and this is going to be the focus of the lecture today—redistribution is characteristic of chiefdom-level societies; and market exchanges. The examples that we're going to use in the lecture today to talk about redistribution are the Trobriand Islanders, who we've talked about before, and the Kwakiutl, who live on the northwest coast of North America.

Redistribution occurs in some degree in all societies. At the most basic level, redistribution occurs within households. Members of a household will pool their resources, and those resources will then be allocated to members of the household according to need. All nations, all states, also serve a redistributive function. These vary along a continuum. On the one hand, we can talk about the Soviet Union and the radical redistribution, and on the other hand we could talk about countries like the United States, which are much less redistributed but nonetheless function to gather up resources from everyone and then redistribute it back out to the population. But redistribution is especially prevalent among chiefdoms, and for chiefdoms it is a way of solidifying their political power, a means of fortifying political power, and it's related in some important ways to the indebtedness of reciprocity that we discussed in the last lecture.

In a chiefdom, for example, giving tribute to the chief is an obligation. Among the Trobriand Islanders, for example, the chief nominally owns all of the coconuts and all of the wild pigs on the island. When you take coconuts or when you catch a wild pig, you give the chief some tribute, and that is your obligation, to give the chief his tribute. However, when the chief redistributes what is given to him, that's generosity, that's his generosity which incurs all of these social debts, which can solidify his political position in society. The same works with politicians in our own country. Think about pork barrel politics, politicians coming back home to proclaim what they've brought, what portion of the federal budget they've been able to allocate to their home districts, and then using that to get reelected. It's the same mechanism that provides the basis of political power for chiefs.

I'd like to start by discussing the Trobriand Islanders, again off the coast of New Guinea, a chiefdom-level society, a matrilineal society, and one based on horticulture, hunting and gathering, and fishing. There's a little bit of pig raising that goes on, but not a whole lot. In terms of their subsistence basis, this is much more characteristic of a tribal-level society, gardening, hunting and gathering, and chiefdoms are supposed to practice intensive agriculture. But because of the relative abundance of natural resources on the Trobriand island, the aquatic resources, plenty of fish—the soils are very fertile— they're able to maintain these population densities characteristic of a chiefdom, even though their subsistence basis is more like that of a tribe.

As chiefs, they have ascribed authority rather than achieved authority. Trobriand chiefs inherit their position, and, since they live in a matrilineal society, they don't inherit their position from their father but rather from their mother's brother, who is the other male in their matrilineage. All lineages in the Trobriand Islands are ranked. There are chiefly lineages, there are noble lineages, and there are commoner lineages. One is born into a particular lineage, and this is going to determine in important ways the role that one will play in society. Young men tapped to assume the role of the head of a matrilineage will go and live with his mother's brother, and this is called avunculocal residence, go and live with his uncle, with his mother's brother because they're related, as we've discussed in a lecture earlier in this course, they're related matrilineally, and it's through these matrilineal ties, even in matrilineal societies, it's men who hold the formal positions of power, and they get their position of power by being related through women, but a young man will inherit the position from his mother's brother.

Given these kinship limits, a man inherits chiefly status, but within these limits there's still quite a bit of room for maneuvering and jockeying for power. We're going to talk about those in just a moment. Chiefs in Trobriand society, materially they live pretty much like everyone else. Nobody really goes hungry; they eat the same things. Yams are the staple of the diet, so materially their conditions are pretty much the same. Chiefs do have a few prerogatives. They wear special decorations; there are special sorts of necklaces the Trobriand chiefs will wear, special headdresses. They have certain food taboos; they're not supposed to eat stingrays or boned fish or certain sorts of garden greens. There's also a notion that chiefs have to be respected, so you're not supposed to look a chief directly in the eye. Commoners always sit below a chief, physically below a chief, but beyond that they live pretty much like everybody else.

In Trobriand society, yams are at the heart of the Trobriand diet and at the heart of Trobriand spiritual life and symbolic life. They're symbolically and materially the heart of Trobriand life. If we had to make a comparison, we could say it's sort of like the bread of life or like bread for our own culture, but there's not really a good comparison for U.S. culture. For Japan, we could say rice is the heart of the diet and symbolically at the heart of the meal as well. For the Maya in Guatemala, we could say that corn and corn tortillas are materially and symbolically the heart of their life, and for the Trobriand Islanders it's yams. Men spend a great deal of time cultivating yams to give away, and there are two main types of yam gardens. There's one that a family will eat from and one that a family will trade from.

Men spend a great deal of time cultivating yams, and they'll have several different garden plots. The garden plots that they eat from, they just use for the subsistence of their family. Yams last a pretty long time, so they can store them for months at a time and they can provide food throughout the year. From the other plots, they have to give the yams away that they grow on these plots, and the yams that are grown on these other plots are already destined to a particular person, namely, mostly his sister and his sister's family. Remember that this is a matrilineal society, so a husband is always an outsider to the group. The yams, these exchanges of yams, tie him through reciprocal bonds to his wife's family.

Now Trobrianders live in huts that are elevated off the ground. They have thatched roofs made from wooden sides, and in front of their huts chiefs will have a separate little house, and this is a yam house. What chiefs try and do—yams are a symbol of wealth and political power—they try and get as many of their relatives as they can to give them yams. They display these yams in the yam huts in front of their houses, and the fuller the yam hut, the more prestige and the more power a chief will have. The only equivalent I can think about in our own society would be if you put your annual salary in big letters out in front of your house, for example, to sort of display to the world how much money you make. It's fundamental that a chief cannot fill up his own yam hut. If he grows the yams and puts them in the yam hut himself, that doesn't count. They have to be received as a gift to count.

Politically ambitious men try and get their relatives to give them yams because even if they come from a chiefly lineage, even if they're destined to take on the role of a chief, they need to accumulate these yams so they can move up and maybe not just be head of their matrilineage but head of their hamlet or head of their village or head of the whole island or paramount chief of all of the Trobriand Islands, and to do that they have to share their political power by having the yams to display. The most important source of yams for a man is his wife's brother and his wife's father.

Malinowski, who was working on the Trobriand Islands in the 1910s, said that a man receives yams from his wife's brother, his wife's father, also from his sons sometimes, sometimes from his younger brothers, sometimes from his sisters' sons, so there are various different sorts of sources of yams, but the most important come from the wife's brother and the wife's father. Malinowski said the reason why a man will give his sister's husband yams is to compensate that person for reproducing their lineage. This is a matrilineal society; a man's children are members of his wife's family, his wife's matrilineage. They're related to his wife's family in a way that they're not related to him. Malinowski said that the man receives yams from his wife's family as payoff. Thanks for reproducing the lineage. Thanks for reproducing all of these kids. Here are some yams and this is your payment and you should be happy with that.

Annette Weiner, a woman, went back and studied the Trobriand Islanders in the 1970s, and she noted an interesting aspect of this that Malinowski missed. She said that yams are not given directly by a woman's brother to her husband; they're given to her, and then she gives them to her husband. This may seem like a fine line, a small semantic point, but it's actually very significant. A man will give yams to his sister, who then gives them to her husband. The significance of that is the woman is giving something to her husband, and so debt, again back to reciprocity, debt is being built up. A man feels obligated to his wife because she's the source of most of his yams that he needs to display in his yam hut in order to increase his political power and his social standing in society.

Interestingly enough, the men have to pay this back, but they don't pay it back with yams. There's a particular form of wealth that's unique to women, women's wealth, and this is composed of banana leaf bundles and woven skirts made from banana leaves, these elaborate, dyed red, very beautiful skirts, banana leaf skirts, and so a man has to keep his wife supplied with banana leaf bundles and banana leaf skirts, which increases her prestige, and so it's this cycle of circulating yams and banana leaf skirts that builds up prestige for everyone.

Here I would like to invoke a distinction made by the French sociologist Pierre Bourdieu, who distinguishes between two main types of capital. There's economic capital, which is money or machinery—it's what Karl Marx would have called productive capital, capital that makes something else, what we would generally call capital in our own society—and symbolic capital. Symbolic capital, Bourdieu divides into two main types, social capital and cultural capital. He says social capital are one's networks, one's family and friends and acquaintances and contacts. You can be born into a situation where you have a lot of social capital or you can go out and create networks of friendship, which can then provide you with social capital. Cultural capital, Bourdieu says, is one's cultivation, your artistic knowledge, your educational credentials, social graces, vocabulary, all of these things that can allow a person to prosper in society, given the dominant culture of the society.

What Bourdieu shows is that we might think of these as being two very different kinds of capital. We have economic capital, or real productive capital, and then these two forms of symbolic capital, which are cultural and social. Bourdieu shows that these are convertible, one into the other. If a man in an agricultural society spends a lot of time building up social capital and cultural capital, at some point in the future that prestige that he's built up, he can convert that back into material capital. In an agricultural society, you have very intense labor needs at certain points of the year and very low labor needs at other points of the year. At harvest time and at planting, you need lots of hands out into the field to help you. While the crops are growing, just to weed and fertilize and so forth, you don't need a lot of help, and then at harvest you need a lot of helping hands as well. What Bourdieu argues is that by helping other people out, by building up social debts and building up social capital, you can then use this prestige when you need some help.

It's like, "OK, I helped you with your harvest. I helped you to do all of these things. Now it's time for you to come and help me as well." By using this distinction between economic and symbolic capital, it helps us understand what motivates the Trobriand Islanders in these exchanges. They're not trying to get more yams because they want to eat more than everybody else. They're trying to get more yams because it builds up their social capital and their cultural capital, and it displays to the world how other people think about them. It also ties into the kula trade that we talked about that the Trobrianders enter into. Why do they trade bracelets and arms shells? It's not the material value of those goods that is so important, it's the symbolic value, and by building up the symbolic capital, the social capital, this cultural capital, they're able to elevate themselves in society and become greater and greater chiefs, more and more important chiefs.

The Trobriand men spend quite a bit of time trading in pigs and trading in banana leaf skirts in order to keep their wives happy so that their wives' families will give them yams that they can display in their yam huts. What do they then do with these yams? They redistribute them back out to the commoners and use them to pay for common goods: building trade canoes; they use them to compensate religious specialists for conducting rituals and so forth. They redistribute this back out, and in redistricting it back out, they build up debt from their subjects which then increases their power, and it becomes the cycle of increasing power.

Talking about yams, let me mention a couple of other things before we move to our next example. A lot of this yam exchange takes place in the months of July and August, and this is a period that the Trobrianders call *mwasawa*, and this is two months of play that follow the harvest period. During this period, they'll trade yams, and they also have yam competitions. The chiefs will either grow themselves or have commissioned enormous yams, and it's a special kind of yam called the kuvi yam that will grow to sometimes 10 or 12 or 15 feet long. They compare them, they have a yam length contest, so all of the chiefs lay out their yams and they see who has the biggest yam of all. The chief with the largest yam wins the competition and gains all of this prestige. The Freudian connotations here are obvious, but it's interesting the way in which they use this to build up symbolic capital.

It's also interesting that during these celebrations, during this mwasawa, months of play that the Trobriands engage in after harvest every year, it used to be a time of these incredibly lascivious dances, very sexual dances that would go on for hours and hours, men and women dancing together, and then occasionally couples would pair off and go into the woods or into the forest for a tryst. When the English missionaries and colonial officials showed up, they were outraged by this; it was scandalous. I can't believe you're having these dances. We've got to stop this right away. And what can we do to divert the Trobrianders' attentions away from having these lascivious dances, these yam competitions, this yam trading, all of this? They said, "Let's introduce cricket. What's a more staid game than cricket?"

They taught the Trobrianders cricket. The Trobrianders picked up cricket and began playing it, but they reinterpreted it. They would predetermine the outcome of these cricket games. They would decide which chief's team was going to win based on which chief had the more prestige; the more prestigious chief had to win, and so they would determine the outcome of these games ahead of time. They would insert these dances in the middle of the cricket matches, so they would still do their lascivious sexual dancing. They would just intersperse it with playing cricket as well, not quite what the English had in mind.

Talking about redistribution and building up political power, I want to turn for a bit to the Kwakiutl, and the Kwakiutl are a group, a chiefdom, living on the northwest coast of North America, made famous by Franz Boas, the father of American anthropology. The Kwakiutl are best known for their totem poles, which are actually elaborate chiefly genealogies. There are spectacular transformation masks that they have, really wonderful artwork. Like the Trobriand Islanders, they're a chiefdom, but they're not a chiefdom that practices intensive agriculture. This points us again to the limitations of typologies such as bands, tribes, chiefdoms, and states. Here we have a chiefdom level of political organization, but it doesn't quite fit in that category.

The reason why is they're gatherers, they're really hunters and gatherers, but what they gather is salmon. They're on the northwest coast of North America. They have seasonal abundance of salmon, enough salmon to catch when they're running to last them all year long, and they'll smoke some of them and they'll save some of them and eat some of it fresh, but they have this abundance of natural resources that allows them to maintain these population densities and the political organization of the chiefdomship.

They're matrilineal, like the Trobriand Islanders are, also. Chiefs inherit their position, as among the Trobriand Islanders, and there's jockeying for power between chiefs to determine who will be the better chief, the more powerful chief, the paramount chief of the region. The way in which chiefs compete among the Kwakiutl is through a custom called potlatch feasts. These potlatches are feasts given by chiefs, and they may require months and very often years of saving, and chiefs will build up reserves in order to throw just the best potlatch that they've ever had. They'll invite everyone from their own village and then people from neighboring villages to come for this feast that may last for several days. When they get there, they're plied with food, all the salmon that you can eat, all the fish that you can eat, given as much food as they can eat.

They're also given gifts. They're given fish oil and blankets and berries, and these things will last for days and days at a time, and the chiefs will even, to show how generous they are—and again they're showing their generosity to build up their political capital; "I deserve to be chief because I'm throwing this wonderful feast and giving you all of this good stuff"—to show how generous they are, they even get into what we could call conspicuous destruction. They will take canoes out and sink them. They'll take pieces— they engrave copper pieces of art—they're very famous for the coppers—they'll chop these up and throw them into the water or give them to people.

During the early contact with Westerners, and particularly with the Hudson Bay Company in the 16th through the 19th centuries, the Kwakiutl became fairly affluent by trading skins for blankets, Hudson Bay blankets, the famous Hudson Bay blankets. This led to an incredible period of inflation in the potlatch, so successful potlatch chiefs would give everybody a mountain of blankets when they came to their potlatch, but they would also build up these literal mountains of blankets and set them on fire and burn them, and again just showing, "I'm so generous, I'm so incredibly wealthy, that I'll just burn this stuff, and it doesn't mean anything to me." By doing this, by destroying things and by giving these away, they're able to build up their political and their social capital.

So why potlatch? Why have these feasts? Franz Boas said that it's just the product of a particular historical tradition, and Boas, who was one of the first to work with the Kwakiutl, was content just to document this tradition. Boas's student, Ruth Benedict, said that each culture has its own temperament, its own ethos. It's sort of like a personality writ large, and she says that the Northwest coast Indians like the Kwakiutl, their cultural temperament, their cultural ethos is Dionysian. It's highly competitive, it's egocentric, it's almost megalomaniacal and that it's this personality writ large that produces potlatch. Interestingly enough, Benedict in her book, *Patterns of Culture,* contrasted this with the Zuni living in the Southwest, the U.S. Southwest, which she said was a very cooperative and Apollonian culture, so she set up these two ideals, the Apollonian Zuni and the Dionysian Kwakiutl living in the Northwest.

Marvin Harris, and you'll remember Marvin Harris from our earlier discussions, this arch materialist, says that it's not really about building up symbolic capital. It does that; chiefs are able to show how powerful they are. They're able to buy the allegiance of their own villages and of neighboring villages through these potlatch feasts, but Marvin Harris says that what's really going on here is that it's a social safety net, that sometimes when the salmon are running there's abundance for everybody, there's plenty of food to go around, plenty of food to last all year long if you smoke it, but sometimes the salmon don't run, and in those years Northwest coast Indians are in a hard position.

He says that the potlatch serves a couple of functions. First of all, by having this competitive feasting, it increases productivity all around. All the chiefs want to have the most efficient, the most productive village of all so that they can have the best potlatch feasts. Secondly, it serves a social safety net function. When one village has a rough year, when there's a bad year, there's always a potlatch coming up, and they can go to this potlatch, and not only will they be fed for two or three or four days but they'll be able to take home as much food as they can carry, so it serves this important social safety net.

Redistribution, chiefdoms, chiefs depend on their political power by redistributing goods back out to their subjects. This is based on the obligations that are entailed that we talked about with reciprocity. The subjects have to give the chief tribute—this is an obligation—but when the chiefs in turn go back and redistribute these same goods that they've been given to the same subjects, maybe not in the same proportions but to the same subjects, they are being generous and incurring the social debt, and so they're able to build on the obligations implicit in relationships of reciprocity to increase their political power. For chiefs, as in tribes, you'll remember we said that the headmen of tribes, their material circumstances are the same as everybody else's. This is mostly true for chiefs as well. It's this almost paradoxical function that actually the more they give away, the higher their prestige. In our own society, it's the more a person accumulates, the higher their prestige, but among chiefdoms they have to demonstrate their generosity and continually redemonstrate their generosity to maintain their position, and they do this through redistribution.

Cultures, Economies, and Western Expansion
Lecture Eighteen
Cultural Contact and Colonialism

Scope: State-level societies have large populations, market economies, and standing armies. Western states have used their military and economic might to expand their influence. Early contacts between Westerners and natives were often wrought with cultural misunderstandings. The arrival of Cortés in 1524 played into existing political instability in the Aztec empire and to popular beliefs about the return of the god Quetzalcoatl from the west. Similarly, Captain Cook was taken for Lono by the Hawaiians and ultimately murdered as a result.

Western contact brought not only goods and ideas but also disease and devastation for many native peoples. In the New World in particular, disease and, to a lesser extent, warfare wiped out a large percentage of the native population. At the same time, Europe's hunger for gold and silver, tea and sugar, and other exotic and valuable goods led to the push to create colonies around the world. We look to the rise of the rubber trade in Brazil and the enormous wealth it created in the middle of the Amazon—and to the market's devastating collapse. We also examine the role of "drug foods" in creating markets for European traders, especially the opium-for-tea trade that led to the outbreak of war between England and China.

Western contact has also led to new forms of consumerism among native peoples. Although we may lament the loss of traditional ways of life, we must keep in mind that this is often what the natives want. We conclude by considering the peculiar case of cargo cults that arose in Melanesia following World War II.

Outline

I. The history of contact between the Western nation-states and the rest of the world has been fraught by cultural misunderstandings.

A. Hernán Cortés set sail from Cuba in 1519 and landed on the coast of Veracruz, where he met representatives of the Aztec emperor Montezuma.
   1. At the time of Spanish contact, the Aztec empire had expanded to the point where internal tensions were beginning to threaten its stability.
   2. In the decade before Cortés's arrival, there had been a number of evil omens that were interpreted as foretelling the fall of the empire.
   3. The mythology of the god Quetzalcoatl—a white being supposed to return one day from the east to reclaim the Aztec empire—played into Cortés's arrival, so that many saw him as a god.
   4. Cortés was able to communicate with Montezuma through two translators: Jeronimo de Aguilar, a shipwrecked Spanish sailor who learned Mayan, and La Malinche, an Aztec woman who also spoke Mayan.
   5. With just a small number of troops (significantly, with horses), Cortés was able to defeat the grand Aztec empire.

B. A similar misunderstanding resulted from Captain James Cook's encounter with the Hawaiians.
   1. At the time of contact, Hawaiian political organization was a highly developed chiefdom led by King Kamehameha.
   2. Kings were considered to be semi-divine, and royal families practiced incest to keep the blood lines pure.
   3. Two primary deities for the Hawaiians were Lono, the god of fertility, and Ku, the god of war. In the decades before contact, Ku had ascended in importance as the Hawaiian empire expanded through subjugating neighboring groups.
   4. Lono remained an important deity, and he was the focus of elaborate annual rituals to ensure the continuation of the agricultural cycle.
   5. In 1778, Captain James Cook arrived from Tahiti around the time of the Lono celebrations, and many took him to be Lono or one of the god's emissaries.
   6. In January of 1779, Cook returned, again during the Lono festival. When he left, a mast broke and he was forced to return in February, at a point in the ritual calendar when Ku

usurps Lono's power. Cook was killed, serving as a proxy for
Lono.

II. Western contact also brought devastation to many native peoples as
they tried to cope with new diseases and new economic relations.

    A. In the process of conquest, disease was often just as effective as
war and brute subjugation. This was especially true in the New
World, where native populations were decimated.

    B. Out of the colonial encounters also emerged a situation of
economic dependency.

        1. World system theory sees the global colonial economy as
composed of the core countries of Western Europe and the
United States and the peripheral countries of the Southern
Hemisphere.

        2. Peripheral countries—which sell raw materials—are seen to
develop a dependency on core countries—which make value-
added products from the imported materials.

        3. The 19th-century rubber boom in Brazil illustrates the
precarious position of relying on one primary export.

            a. By the late 18th century, novelty rubber products had
begun to trickle into Europe from Brazil. In the early 19th
century, cottage industries along the Amazon were
producing small quantities of erasers and rubber shoes.

            b. In 1844, Charles Goodyear discovered the process of
rubber vulcanization, making it resistant to freezing and
cracking. This greatly expanded the usefulness of rubber,
and demand from Europe began to rise. John Dunlop's
1890 invention of the pneumatic tire opened further
markets.

            c. Natural rubber comes from the *Hevea brasiliensis*, and
demand was met by legions of tappers. Great wealth was
created—the Amazonian city of Manuas was a
showcase—and by 1910, 40 percent of all of Brazil's
export earnings came from rubber exports.

            d. However, in 1875, Henry Wickham smuggled rubber
seeds and seedlings to London's Kew Gardens. The
plants were adapted to the climates of Britain's Asian
colonies, and production in Malaysia began in the 1890s.

      e. In Brazil, rubber plantations were made impossible because of the South American leaf blight. Thus, the Southeast Asian producers were able to vastly undersell the labor-intensive Brazilian producers. Brazilian rubber exports virtually disappeared by the 1920s.

III. Western expansion also brought with it capitalism and a rise in consumerism.

    A. Following World War II, a number of independent but very similar messianic movements emerged on once-inhabited islands. These are known as *cargo cults* because of their emphasis on Western material culture.

    B. During the war, these cultures witnessed an almost unimaginable influx of goods in occupied areas, which, once the war ended, was gone as quickly as it arrived.

    C. Melding this experience with traditional millenarian religious beliefs, cults emerged that attempted to call back the cargo planes and ships that had left. Model airplanes, runways, and telegraphs were constructed for use in the ceremonies.

    D. The most famous of these was the John Frum cult of the New Hebrides, centered on the U.S. army uniform of one "John Frum."

Readings:

Sidney Mintz, *Sweetness and Power*.

Matthew Restall, *Seven Myths of the Spanish Conquest*.

Marshall Sahlins, *Islands of History*.

Questions to Consider:

1. How has Western contact changed native societies for good or bad?

2. What do people from other cultures find so compelling about Western goods?

3. How did events in other parts of the world affect rubber production in Brazil?

Lecture Eighteen—Transcript
Cultural Contact and Colonialism

We've been talking about Elvin Service's bands, tribes, chiefdoms, and states continuum. We discussed bands, the Dobe Ju/'hoansi; we discussed tribes, the Yanamamo. We've talked about chiefdoms with the Trobriand Islanders, and today we're going to turn our attention to states. States are distinguished primarily by their large size, and their large size gives rise to a lot of the other elements that we consider to be distinctive of states. States also practice intensive agriculture, they have market economies, and significantly they have socioeconomic classes. These socioeconomic classes, they may be hereditary or not. It may be a meritocracy system like we have in our own country, but the important thing is that there are classes of people that enjoyed different material standards of living.

This is really distinctive of states having socioeconomic classes. In bands, in tribes, in chiefdoms, you have people with higher status sometimes, a chief or a headman, but their material circumstances of life are about the same as everybody else's. But with the advent of states, we get permanent classes that have different access to material resources. Perhaps related to this is the fact that states also have centralized authority, the rule of law, and they have an army or a police force to enforce this rule of law as well, the army for conflicts with the outside world and the police force to maintain internal conflicts.

States first arose in Mesopotamia, the famous city-states of Sumeria, around 3500 B.C. City-states take many different forms, and they've developed in different ways over the years. We have kingdoms, we have modern nation-states, and here let me mention that a lot of times we use nation and state as synonyms, but in anthropology they mean two very different things. A nation implies a group with a shared common heritage, a group that considers itself to be related to one another in some fundamental way, a common history, sharing a common history. A state is simply a form of governmental organization characterized by the points that we just outlined. Nation-states, often we talk about nation-states, and nation-states are a very recent addition to human history. They're a product of Western civilization, Western Europe, that arose in the 18th century. Nation-states have become very expansionist, and, in fact, everybody in the world today virtually lives in a nation-state, but nonetheless they are this fairly recent addition to human history.

Western states, even before they became nation-states, Western states have been historically very expansionist. This has led to situations of cultural contact around the world, sustained cultural contact, especially starting in the age of discovery and exploration, when the Europeans were setting out around the world and discovering all of these native peoples that they had no idea existed before. In these situations of cultural contact, there's often a clash of cultural models, different ways of looking at the world, and if you'll remember from earlier lectures, we talked about cultural models as being shared mental models, shared ways of looking at the world. We tend to interpret new data, new situations and new events that we encounter in the light of these established cultural models that we already hold. What I'd like to do today is talk about a couple of situations of contact between the West and other non-Western states and the way in which cultural models have clashed.

To do this, I would like to begin by talking about Spanish contact in the New World and the story of the Aztecs and Cortés. When Cortés showed up in Mexico in 1519, he encountered a state-level society. The Aztecs were a state-level society, a rather large state. They had only begun—the capital of the Aztecs, Tenochtitlan, had been founded in 1345, so it was a rather young empire, less than 200 years old, rather young as these things go. When Cortés showed up and he saw Tenochtitlan, he was taken by the city. This was a huge city; there were about 200,000 residents in the city itself, about a million residents in the metropolitan area in the basin of Mexico. This was five times larger than London of the time, and so he is very much taken by the size of the city but also what the city looked like. Some of the people accompanying Cortés called it the Venice of the New World because it was traversed by canals.

The Aztecs used a particular kind of agriculture called *chinampa* agriculture, where they would build up soil from the bottom of these canals and make raised beds, which were extremely fertile, that they would use then to plant their gardens on to supply the city with produce and so forth. Cortés shows up in 1519, not very many troops; he brings a few hundred troops with him, crucially brings horses with him, and discovers this incredible city in this vast empire, and he was very much taken by it. As an aside, let me mention there was always a problem of communication and contact between Western states and these native societies. The way in which Cortés got around that, the way in which he was able to communicate with Montezuma, who was the Aztec emperor at the time, was by using two translators.

When Cortés landed on the coast of Veracruz, he very soon took into his service a woman named Marina. She was baptized as Marina, and she's known popularly in Mexico today as La Malinche. She was a woman who had been born to an Aztec noble family, but her father had died, and when her mother remarried her stepfather had sold her into slavery, and she had been shipped down from central Mexico, Mexico City, which is where Tenochtitlan was, down to the borderland between the Aztec empire and the Mexican empire of the Yucatan peninsula, and so she had lived with Maya-speaking peoples and had learned Maya, so she spoke Nahuatl, the language of the Aztecs, as well as Maya, and she entered into Cortés' service, but this wasn't enough to translate. She still didn't speak Spanish.

However, some years earlier, in some of the early Spanish explorations off the coast of Mexico, there had been a shipwreck, and one of the survivors of the shipwreck made it to the shore and had been living with Mayan peoples in the Yucatan Peninsula for a number of years, and so he spoke Spanish and Yucatec Maya, a Mayan language, and so Cortés was able to communicate with the Aztecs by speaking in Spanish to this man, whose name was Jeronimo de Aguilar. And when he had heard that Cortés showed up, he made his way up to join the Spaniards as well; so Cortés could speak in Spanish to Aguilar, Aguilar could speak in Maya to La Malinche, and La Malinche could then translate that into Nahuatl.

La Malinche became Cortés's consort; Cortés had a child by La Malinche, and she is a particularly powerful figure in the Mexican imagination today, on the one hand venerated as the mother of Mexican culture, having the first mestizo, or mixed blood child, with Cortés, but also reviled by some as being a traitor to her race, as helping Cortés in his conquest of the Aztecs. Cortés shows up; he employs the services of La Malinche and Jeronimo de Aguilar in order to be able to communicate with the Aztecs. When he showed up, the Aztec empire was at the height of its expansion. Perhaps it would have continued expanding for several more hundred years, but at the time that he showed up the Aztecs had taken over all of central Mexico and they had trading outposts even farther south throughout Central America.

As part of this Aztec expansionism, there had been a change in Aztec ideology. There were two primary gods. One was Huitzilopochtli, and this was the god of the sun or the god of warfare, and the other was Quetzalcoatl, and Quetzalcoatl was the god of fertility, the god of creation, and the god of literacy. Quetzalcoatl was very often represented as a feathered serpent, but he was also sometimes represented, and this is very common for Meso-American gods to have different representations, different aspects, he was also sometimes represented as a light-skinned man, and this was very crucial.

During the years of Aztec expansionism, what had happened was the importance of Quetzalcoatl as a god had decreased, and the importance of Huitzilopochtli, the god of war and the god of the sun, had increased. Huitzilopochtli required blood sacrifice in order to continue the cycle of existence, and so this ideologically underwrote the Aztec expansionism, capturing prisoners, bringing them back to Tenochtitlan and then sacrificing them and perhaps, as we mentioned in an earlier lecture, perhaps practicing cannibalism to some extent, or not. We're not really sure the extent of Aztec cannibalism, but there had been this rise in human sacrifice and in blood sacrifice.

In addition, in the years before Cortés showed up, there had been a number of strange omens. Perhaps this is hindsight. Perhaps people are looking back; perhaps the Aztecs after the conquests looked back and said, "Oh, yeah, all of those weird things that were happening before Cortés showed up," so it's hard to separate hindsight here from what was really going on before Cortés showed up, but there had been these bad omens, and the emperor Montezuma was a bit worried. His empire had been stretched to its limits, by some accounts. People that the Aztecs had subjugated were becoming unruly, and so his grasp on the empire as a whole was a bit tenuous. Then these omens occur, and then these rumors start circulating that perhaps Quetzalcoatl is going to return and reestablish the order that he intended for the Aztec empire.

It's in this context that Cortés shows up, and the story goes, the most common interpretation of this is, that the Aztecs mistook Cortés for Quetzalcoatl, and they welcomed him willingly into their capital city because this was the god, this was Quetzalcoatl returned, and, in fact, in most accounts, we see that Montezuma prostrated himself in front of Cortés when he first showed up, which would lead us to believe that perhaps he was taken as a god. On the other hand, perhaps these stories are a bit overplayed. The historian Matthew Restall, in a recent book, *Seven Myths of the Spanish Conquest,* says it's actually very ethnocentric of us to think that the Aztecs thought that the Spaniards were gods and it sort of plays into this European notion of "We're inherently superior in some way. Of course the native peoples think we're gods because we are so exceptional."

Some stories say that the Aztecs believed that the Spaniards riding on horses were a single beast, and this probably isn't the case. White-skinned people don't look that much different than Native Americans, for example, so it's probably a bit of a stretch for us to say that the Aztecs were so naïve and so gullible as to mistake the Spaniards for gods or mistake Spaniards on the backs of horses as being gods. But, nonetheless, there was probably still some indeterminacy there. There had been these omens, there was this myth that Quetzalcoatl would return at some point in the future and so perhaps there was some. Maybe Cortés is a god, maybe he's not—we're really not sure—but nonetheless Montezuma welcomed Cortés into Tenochtitlan and expected him, even if he didn't believe that Cortés was a god, expected him to follow a model of expansionism that was familiar to the Aztecs and to the Meso-Americans.

They would come in; perhaps they would become the new rulers. The Aztecs would begin giving tribute to the Spaniards and they could continue their life pretty much the way it was, just passing tribute up one more level in the rung. However, of course, it didn't work out this way. Cortés's demands for gold increased and increased, and after a couple of years—he showed up in 1519—and after a couple of years, through various acts of treachery, he was able to actually pretty handily defeat the Aztecs, which happened in 1521, and instituted this whole period of Spanish conquest and colonialism in the New World.

A similar story takes place in the Hawaiian Islands in the contacts between the native Hawaiians and Captain Cook, Captain James Cook. The Hawaiians were a state as well, a state system or somewhere between a chiefdom and a state; again these categories are not hard and fast, and so it's hard to place particular societies as a chiefdom or a state. The Hawaiians fell somewhere between chiefdoms and states; it was a society with extreme stratification, social stratification. There were three distinct classes: There were the nobles—there were about ten ranked lineages of nobility; there were the dwellers on the land, the commoners; and then finally there were what we could translate in English as the pariahs, and this would be similar to India's untouchable class, so you had these three stratified classes in Hawaiian society.

The king owned all of the land, and he administered the rights to the land through a vast bureaucracy. Here we see a little bit of the chiefdom aspect of native Hawaiian civilization; the king owns all the land, and through his benevolence he allows the commoners to work on that land, and so just by making a living, they owe something to the king. They're indebted to the king because it's his land. The Hawaiians also believed that their kings were related to gods, physically related to gods, and they were really godlike in some way. This led to one of the few instances in the world of sanctioned incest; brother-sister marriage was allowed among the nobility to keep these godly bloodlines pure.

In the 1770s, the king of Hawaii, King Kamehameha, was uniting all of the political units of the various islands under his rule, and this was a process that was completed in 1796. This centralization, like with the Aztecs, this centralization had religious overtones, and it was played out in a conflict between Ku, who was the god of war, and Lono, who was the god of peace, and again very similar, Ku very similar to Huitzilopochtli and Lono very similar to Quetzalcoatl. In the process of conquering neighboring islands, Kamehameha really began to emphasize the importance of the god of war, Ku. This makes sense: An expansionist state, they're conquering and subjugating other peoples; the god of war is going to take on more importance than Lono, the god of peace.

It's in this context that Captain James Cook shows up. Cook, as we all know, was a famous voyager. He made three main voyages between 1769 and 1779, probably added more to geographical knowledge than anyone else had ever done at the time. He explored and he mapped Tahiti, New Zealand, Australia, part of the Antarctic, and on his last voyage, his third and last voyage, which took place from 1776 to 1779, he first went to New Zealand, then he went back to Tahiti, which he had visited before, and from Tahiti he makes the voyage up to Hawaii, so Cook is coming from Tahiti to Hawaii. This is significant because the Hawaiian origin myths say that the Hawaiians originally came from Tahiti, and this may or may not be the case, but this is what the Hawaiians say was their origin myth.

Cook shows up in Hawaii on January 18, 1778, but he doesn't stay for very long. He stays for a little while, and then he runs up the coast of North America to the Bering Strait, but when he came January 18, 1778, when he came, this was during the period in which Lono is supposed to make an annual return to the Hawaiian islands, and the god of fertility returns every year to ensure fertility for the years to come. He comes, stays for a few weeks, they have a number of ceremonies for Lono, and then Lono leaves, and of course this is all symbolic, but then Cook, this unusual white man, shows up around the same time that Lono is supposed to show up, stays for a while, leaves, runs up the coast of North America, explores part of the Bering Strait, and then he comes back to Hawaii.

He comes back to Hawaii in 1779, around the same time, around one year later from his first arrival. This fits into the Hawaiian model of what Lono is supposed to do. Lono comes back year after year; Cook shows up in January of 1778, shows up again in January of 1779, and a number of interpretations, mainly by Marshall Sahlins, have argued that the natives welcomed Cook as the returned god Lono and that this fit perfectly into their model, their ritual calendar of what Lono was supposed to do. However, on Cook's second visit, he comes to Hawaii, they do a number of ceremonies in which it seems like he was venerated as Lono, or these ceremonies to offer sacrifice to Lono, and then toward the end of January of that year the Hawaiians start getting anxious for him to leave and start encouraging him to leave. This is when Lono was supposed to leave: You've been here for a while already. Isn't it about time that you packed up and set sail?

Cook finally does that. He sets sail, but when he leaves Hawaii, the Hawaiian Islands, one of his masts breaks. The mast breaks, and so he's forced to return, and he's forced to return at a point in the Hawaiian ritual calendar in which Ku, the god of war, kills Lono, the god of fertility. Lono is going to be regenerated year after year, but this is part of the ritual calendar. The god of fertility comes, the god of war kills the god of fertility, and then the god of war, the god of practicality, the god of governmentality, takes over for the year and allows the Hawaiians to continue their expansionist politics. Cook shows back up and gets killed. He's killed, and Marshall Sahlins argues that he's killed because he was seen as Lono. Lono has to be killed, and the Hawaiian king at the time, Kamehameha, was fearing for his power. If Lono comes back and takes over power, then I'm going to lose my own power.

There's a wonderful book that Marshall Sahlins has written called *Islands of History*, in which he sets it up like a murder mystery. Who killed Captain Cook? He winds up with the conclusion that one of Kamehameha's courtly noblemen killed Cook in order to save the reign of Kamehameha. This is one of those instances where it's the opposite of Cortés and the Aztecs, actually, so the European here gets killed, and the Europeans get expelled, and the Hawaiians are able to keep their reign for some time longer. Of course, it didn't last forever, although the Hawaiians are a case where they were able to maintain native rule for quite some time under British protection. In 1898, Hawaii of course was annexed by the United States.

In these processes of contact between the West and the rest of the world, we very often play up this idea of the Europeans being taken for gods and the misunderstandings of native peoples about European intentions. It's useful, however, to note that the same process worked the other way around. The

Winnebago of the Great Lakes region tell a story of the French showing up in the 17th century and seeing a Winnebago man smoking tobacco. The French had never seen anyone smoking tobacco before and they think that this man is on fire, so they dump water on him to put out the fire. But he wasn't on fire at all, of course, and so this is a case of the French misunderstanding what is going on, so these processes of misunderstanding, it's important to point out, go both ways. We have better documentation for the natives' misunderstanding, but there are these stories like that of the Winnebago.

The process of colonization and Western expansion wreaked havoc on native societies around the world. Disease, the native peoples did not have resistance to diseases. There was warfare; there was subjugation; there were these long periods of colonial rule that established racial hierarchies, many of which continue to this day. It's also been argued that during the period of European expansion an economic system emerged in the world, which continues to this day.

This idea is most associated with two scholars, Emmanuel Wallerstein and Andre Gunder Frank. And they developed a line of theory that we know as world systems theory, or dependency theory. They argue that in the early days of colonial expansion what happened was all of the countries in the world got divided into two main categories. We have core countries—and this would be Western Europe; today we could expand it out to say Western Europe, the United States, and maybe Japan—and peripheral countries, and this would be everywhere else, but mostly talking about the Southern Hemisphere, so core countries and peripheral countries. These overlap more or less with what we would call colloquially first world and third world countries, the first world being core countries and the third world being peripheral countries.

Wallerstein and Frank argue that what happened was the colonial powers instituted an economic system whereby peripheral countries would export raw materials to core countries, and these raw materials would then be converted into commodities in the core countries and then sold for a profit. That profit would remain in the core countries and be reinvested in technology, which would keep the core countries economically, technologically advanced and keep the peripheral countries underdeveloped. We could talk about cotton in India, for example, as a great example, cotton being exported back to England, being converted into textiles and then sold for a profit, which would then be invested in technological developments and keeping the first world ahead. Wallerstein and Frank argue that this system of dependency that emerged between core countries and peripheral countries actually continues to this day. It got established during the colonial period, but it still marks global economic relations to this day.

The best example of this probably comes from the rubber trade in Brazil. Rubber was something unheard of in Europe in the 17th, 18th, even in the 19th century. By 1800, there were a few products trickling into Europe, rubber balls, shoes, erasers, a few manufactured products, but mostly novelties. But the Europeans were very much taken by rubber at the time, but the market for rubber didn't take off until 1844, when Charles Goodyear developed a technique of vulcanization, of flash heating rubber which would make it resistant to becoming brittle when it got cold. This expanded the market for how people could use rubber. But even then it wasn't until some years later, in 1890, when John Dunlop developed the pneumatic tire, using this vulcanized rubber, that rubber really took off, and this was around the time of course in which car production was taking off at the same time, so there became this enormous market for rubber, and most of the rubber at the time was coming from Brazil.

To give you a bit of background, rubber naturally comes from the *Hevea brasiliensis* tree; there's a lot of synthetic rubber today, but natural rubber comes from *Hevea brasiliensis*, and the process of harvesting rubber was done by rubber tappers in the Brazilian Amazon. Rubber trees naturally are actually quite dispersed in the forest; you might find two per acre or something like that, and rubber tappers would make paths through the Brazilian Amazon forest. They would find rubber trees, they would tap those trees, leave a little cup there, and they would have a path that might take them days or even weeks to follow along to get enough rubber trees to really have a big chunk of rubber. The tappers would periodically follow their trails through the forest, gather up the rubber that had been collected in a cup, and at night they would melt it into a big ball, and then they would take it down to the port towns on the Amazon River and sell it to traders, and then it would be shipped back to Europe.

During the boom years of rubber, and this was really the late 19th and the very early 20th century, rubber production in Brazil took off, and there were thousands and thousands and thousands of tappers being employed by the rubber trade. To give you an idea of the volume of this trade, in 1850 there were 638 metric tons of rubber exported from Brazil. This is in 1850, right after Goodyear had developed vulcanization, 638 metric tons. By 1912, this had risen to over 31,000 metric tons, so this is a booming market going on in Brazil, and it introduced a lot of wealth into the Amazon region.

A couple of cities—the main cities along the Amazon are Belen and Manaus, and they became as wealthy as their European contemporary cities, Manaus famously. Manaus is located right about in the center of the Amazon River in Brazil, in the middle of nowhere, and Manaus became the showcase city. They built an opera house, which was supposed to be as nice as any opera house in Italy, and in fact there are apocryphal stories that Caruso once sung there; so in 1896, Manaus opened this opera house, and they were trying to be as nice of a city as one would find in Western Europe. However, what happened was the rubber trade bottomed out some years later. An Englishman by the name of Henry Wickham had smuggled rubber seeds out of Brazil back to London. They had been cultivated in the Kew gardens, the royal gardens in London, and then the English had set up rubber plantations in Malaysia.

It turns out that in Brazil there's an endemic disease, the South American leaf blight, that affects rubber plants, and so you cannot set up rubber plantations in Brazil; it just doesn't work. However, the English had been able to develop these hybrids that they could use on plantations in Malaysia, and so the Malaysian market overtook the Brazilian market in just a number of years, and the Brazilian rubber trade completely bottomed out. As a result, what this shows us is the danger of putting all of a country's eggs in one basket. Brazil, at the height of the rubber trade, was getting 40 percent of their export earnings from this one product. But then, from competition from England and English colonies in Malaysia, they lost this whole market and they lost out, and this is really the danger of this kind of dependency, dependency on a single product in the world economy.

Colonialism involved not just production but also consumption; practices of consumption changed rather dramatically as native peoples came into contact with Western societies. The most fascinating example of this came from cargo cults. Cargo cults emerged in Melanesia following World War II. What had happened in this area was the Japanese and American forces had come to these small islands and set up these bases, virtually overnight set up whole cities, bringing in airplanes, setting up airstrips, setting up stores and houses, and setting up virtual little cities. The native peoples were quite taken by this, obviously, but then, at the end of World War II, the Japanese and the Americans pack up and they leave, and so the natives had experienced this period of extreme prosperity, but for just a short period of time, and then it was gone.

They interpret this, in terms of their native millenarial religious beliefs, that there is a golden age going to come at some point in the future and save us from our conditions of material poverty. They began to venerate the soldiers who had left, and there are a number of cults that emerged in Melanesia, and we call these cargo cults, the most famous of which is the John Frum cult. John Frum was evidently an American soldier whose uniform had gotten left behind, and the native peoples in the New Hebrides made an effigy of John Frum, began worshiping him, and they also built fake airstrips. They built fake telegraph and radio huts, and their rituals would be to light all of the lights along the airstrip and to do fake telegraph calls to the Americans to come back and bring back all of this prosperity. "We don't know why you left, but it is our fate, it's our millennial fate, to have these great loads of goods coming in." Some of these still continue to this day.

In state-level societies, because of their size, they have an unparalleled ability to marshal resources and to be expansionist, to spread around the world, through colonialism, through coercive trade, and the responses to these have been quite varied, ranging from outright surrender and colonization, as with the Aztecs and the Hawaiians, and also a reinterpretation, putting this contact, putting this new data into established cultural models, such as we find with the cargo cults.

Lecture Nineteen
Cultures of Capitalism

Scope: Capitalism, which first arose in England in the 18th century, has become the dominant mode of economic organization around the world. The spread of capitalism has also brought about fundamental cultural changes. A Marxist perspective defines capitalism as when labor comes to be treated as a commodity that can be bought and sold in the market.

In cultural anthropology, we employ a concept of *hegemony* that is at once more precise and more ambiguous than common usage (synonymous with "political domination"). In anthropology, *hegemony* refers to the ways that domination can be achieved through cultural indoctrination rather than brute force. Karl Marx argued that culture—in the form of ideology—can blind individuals to their own self-interests (think of his famous characterization of religion as an opiate of the masses). This notion was expanded by the Italian scholar Antonio Gramsci, who introduced the concept of hegemony to explain how control over education and the mass media promulgate prevailing ideologies. Yet, from an anthropological perspective, hegemonic is a problem concept because it assumes that we (the observers) know better than the people we study.

In this lecture, we discuss the nature of state-level power. We also examine cultural strategies and the ways groups with little power use such "weapons of the weak" to pursue their ends. For example, Malaysian peasants resist trends toward agricultural mechanization by dragging their feet, spreading gossip, feigning ignorance, and other forms of non-confrontational resistance.

Outline

I. The emergence of capitalism, first in England and Europe, then spreading across the world, has been a long-term process, going back to the 18th century.

   A. Karl Marx defines capitalism in a very particular way: when labor becomes a commodity.

1. Marx presents a scheme in which commodities (C) and money (M) are traded. In the simplest form of trade, *barter*, one commodity is exchanged for another: $C—C^1$; money may them emerge as an intermediary in this equation: $C—M—C^1$.
2. The age of exploration and global trade brought about what Marx termed *mercantilism*: $M—C—M^1$. Here, the abstraction of money replaces the concrete utility of a commodity as the goal of exchange.
3. Finally, *capitalism* emerges when part of C = labor (that is, when labor is treated as a commodity).

B. Developments in the production of cotton cloth in the 18th century played a major role in England's industrial revolution.
1. Woolen textiles were long important products of England, Ireland, and Scotland, produced by cottage-industry artisans. This was also the model for early production of cotton textiles.
2. However, starting in the 1730s (with John Kay's invention of the flying shuttle) and throughout the 18th century, technological developments (including Eli Whitney's 1793 cotton gin) led to enormous increases in efficiencies.
3. By 1810, one spinner could produce as much cotton as 200 spinners were capable of in 1740, but production was concentrated in water (and, later, steam) mills.
4. This increase in efficiency came at the expense of the independent lifestyle of artisan producers, who could not compete on price with the big mills and were eventually forced to work in the mills.

C. Marx argued that these changes in the economic base produced novel forms of social organization—including the heightened alienation of workers and consumers.
1. In capitalist forms of production, workers do not control the means of production but are free to sell their labor to whomever they please.
2. Furthermore, workers become alienated from the fruits of their labors, no longer feeling the close artisan connection with their products that was the norm for most of human history.

II. Marx saw society and culture as often obfuscating the material circumstances of individuals, inducing people to act in ways not in their own self-interests.

  A. In his 1852 essay "The Eighteenth Brumaire of Louis Bonaparte," Marx develops his notion of "hidden" or "false" consciousness.

    1. He saw the French peasants as being duped by Louis Bonaparte's Napoleonic rhetoric and efforts to conjure up the image of his benevolently regal uncle, Napoleon Bonaparte.

    2. But his policies encouraging private property forced peasants to mortgage their patrimonies to the emergent banking class.

    3. Elsewhere, Marx argues that religion is an opiate of the masses, submerging class-consciousness.

  B. The Italian scholar Antonio Gramsci, whose writings survive from scraps smuggled out of his prison cell in the 1920s, developed Marx's idea of false consciousness into the concept of *hegemony*.

    1. *Hegemony*, in Gramsci's words, is "the 'spontaneous' consent given by the great masses of the population to the general direction imposed on social life by the dominant fundamental group." This is to say that hegemony occurs when dominant classes leverage their privileged access to mass media and national discourse to foment support for the system that privileges them.

    2. In this light, hegemonies are particular ideologies— representing particular class interests—that come to be seen as "natural" or "common sense"—taken for granted and unquestioned.

    3. Gramsci argued that war is a breakdown of hegemony– hegemony mutes and co-opts opposition, thus removing the need for bare-faced domination.

III. Much recent anthropology that looks at power relations adopts a Gramscian-style critique of hegemonic systems. Documenting resistance to hegemonies has become a hallmark of modern cultural studies.

  A. This owes much to the political scientist James Scott.

    1. Scott conducted fieldwork in the 1970s in "Sedaka," a small agrarian village (of a few hundred residents) in Malaysia.

      2.   The green revolution techniques of fertilizer and mechanization were beginning to be implemented in local rice farming.

      3.   The new techniques brought higher yields but also resulted in the success of a few larger farms over the vast majority of small-holding farmers and fueled incipient class tensions.

B. Scott found that overt opposition to the changes was effectively squelched by Malaysian authorities, but the farmers of Sedaka had developed a number of "weapons of the weak" they used to fight the new hegemony.

      1.   Weapons of the weak can be very effective because they are hard to combat. They may include foot dragging, feigned ignorance, false compliance, gossip, and others forms of covert action.

      2.   They offer resistance without overt opposition.

C. Despite its utility as an analytic tool, anthropologists have problems with the concept of hegemony.

      1.   We tend to privilege the words of our informants, while critiques of hegemony often see them as being duped by an ideology.

      2.   Often, the power at stake in hegemonic formations is ambiguous. For example, the tremendous rise in breast implant surgeries may be seen as a form of male hegemony in the United States or as a form of female empowerment.

Readings:

Antonio Gramsci, *The Prison Notebooks*.

Karl Marx, *The Eighteenth Brumaire of Louis Bonaparte*.

James Scott, *Weapons of the Weak*.

Questions to Consider:

1. Can someone be oppressed without realizing it?

2. How do political ideologies shape the modern American cultural landscape?

3. Is elective plastic surgery empowering or an example of hegemonic duping?

Lecture Nineteen—Transcript
Cultures of Capitalism

Last time we looked at the contact between state-level societies of the West and other cultures, and today we're going to turn our attention to another aspect of states, the market economy and capitalism. We're going to look at capitalism as a culturally specific model that developed in Western Europe and expanded throughout the world, and we're going to look at Marxist critiques of capitalism. Discussing Karl Marx often invokes a negative reaction. My father, for example, whenever I say "Marx says," he sort of rolls his eyes and looks away. It's this idea of how can we take Marx seriously after the failure of the great communist experiment in the Soviet Union. But it's useful to distinguish between Marx the scholar, who was a political economist, a political philosopher, not unlike Adam Smith in many ways, and Marx the activist.

Social scientists, we're very poor at prediction, although economists, some economists anyway, would like to think otherwise. We're very poor at predicting the future; we're very good at explaining what happened yesterday, last year, last decade, or whatever it may be, but we're poor at saying what's going to happen tomorrow. Human behavior is just too variable to make those sorts of predictions. But this is where Marx went astray, is when he moved from social analysis to political prediction and his ideas about the inevitability of a Communist revolution. In this lecture, we're going to focus on Marx the scholar, and I'm going to show that you don't have to be a Communist to find value in his analysis of early capitalism. Indeed, as we're going to see in a later lecture, recent management theorists have taken a page from Marx's writings about worker alienation to develop their theories of business management.

We're going to start with a look at Marx's view of capitalism, then we're going to look at the Marxist literature on hegemony, or state domination, and we're going to conclude with the often subtle ways in which power is exercised and resisted in state-level societies. Let me begin by saying that capitalism is neither good nor bad. It's a system of production. We have to treat it in a culturally relative sense, just as we do hunting and gathering and other forms of production as well. Capitalism, it's a system of production, and an incredibly efficient one. Capitalism has created more wealth in the world than any other system. It's been incredibly successful. We have global capitalism today; it is the basis of the world market. In Marx's defense, in his critiques of capitalism, he was observing it in its cruelest infant stages, the infamous working conditions of the 19th century, this move from bucolic village life to urban squalor and poverty and hunger and working in these early factories.

Marx, in his writings on capitalism, distinguishes between different types of exchanges. He says the most basic sort of exchange is barter. You take one good and you trade it for another. "I've got a pound of rice and I would like to have a pound of salt, and so we can trade these two items." Marx says that what's crucial here is that the end of the gain is a use value. "I've got a pound of rice, but I need a pound of salt, and so will trade my rice for salt to get this material utility of salt." The end of the gain is use value. Marx, when he was writing about this, used a number of equations, and so for barter he would use the equation C converts into C prime. One commodity is exchanged for another sort of commodity.

He said markets began to be more efficient when they started to use money to mediate these exchanges. "I've got a pound of rice, and I need a pound of salt, but maybe I can't find anybody who has extra salt who needs rice, and so it's much more efficient for me to sell my pound of rice for money and then go and use that money to buy a pound of salt." We could represent this, or Marx represented this in his equations as C, which stands for commodity, gets converted into M, which stands for money, which is then converted into C prime, which is another commodity. The end of this is likewise use value. "I'm looking to get the utility of a pound of salt, or a pound of sugar, or whatever it may be."

Marx says that in the age of exploration there was a fundamental shift, and he calls this phase mercantilism, where people would start out with money and they would go abroad and buy a product, let's say, ivory in India, and then bring that back to England or Western Europe and sell it for a profit. He would represent this in his equations as starting with M for money, using that money to buy a commodity, C, and then selling that commodity for more money, which he represents as M prime, so we have M to C to M prime. He says what's crucial about this is that the end of the gain is not use value, but exchange value; it's making more money. Of course, the money that's going to be made can be converted into commodities that we can actually use that have some material utility, but he says the crucial thing here is a mindset that is not trying to get a pound of salt because you need that for your food but trying to get more money and to accumulate more money over time.

I mention this to lead up to Marx's definition of capitalism. Marx says that capitalism occurs using the same sort of equation of M to C to M prime, money to commodity to more money, when labor starts being treated as if it were a commodity, when people start selling their labor as if it were a commodity. We take this to be the natural state of things. We all sell our labor; we might sell it by the hour, we might sell it by the month, given our salary structure, whatever it may be, but we sell our labor, and this seems to be the natural state of things, but Marx pointed out that this is very particular to capitalism and that it has far-reaching social and cultural implications. Once again, to emphasize this—this is an important point— Marx defines capitalism when labor becomes a commodity, when labor can be bought and sold with money.

To give you a specific example about how this played out, let's look at textile production, cotton textile production in England. Wool and textiles were long an important product of England and Ireland and Scotland, and cotton was introduced in the 17th century. At first, cotton cloth was produced along the same cottage industry model as woolen goods. But the guilds were less restrictive with cotton. They were really based around wool production, and so the guilds were less proactive in terms of cotton production, and this opened up the door to introduce labor-saving devices. Throughout the 18th century, a number of labor-saving devices were introduced into the cotton textile production process.

Let me just list a few. In 1733, John Kay invents the flying shuttle, which allows a single weaver to do the work of two weavers, increasing demand, doubling the demand for cotton yarn. In 1764, the spinning jenny was invented, which has several spindles instead of just one, and this allows one person to do the work of three or four people. In 1769, water-framed spinning machines were developed; in 1790, steam-powered spinning machines were developed. In 1793, Eli Whitney famously invented his cotton gin, which separated the cotton from the seeds. Before Eli Whitney invented the cotton gin, one worker could produce one pound of cotton per day. After the cotton gin, one worker could produce 50 pounds of cotton per day. These are incredible labor-saving advances, technological advances, in the cotton production process. By 1820, power looms had taken over from handloom weavers, and, all in all, over this 100-year period cotton production became 200 times more productive than it had been before.

This is a great success story of capitalism, producing more cloth much more cheaply, bringing up everybody's standard of living. This points to the fact that economics doesn't have to be a zero-sum gain; we can create entirely new wealth. If one person's labor, a day's labor can produce 200 times more than what they could produce before, this is going to increase everybody's standard of living by lowering the prices.

What happened in this process of technological advances in cotton cloth is that it forced women, women and men, who had once worked in their homes as independent artisans, as independent workers, their own bosses, it forced them to start migrating to cities to work in factories. They just couldn't compete with the efficiencies of factory production. Who's going to buy this expensive hand-woven cloth when cheaper, and at the time higher quality, cheaper higher quality machine-made cloth is available? Nobody's going to do it, and so this really forced all of these artisans out of business. These former self-employed artisans began having to sell their labor, sell their labor as a commodity to the factories. There's an analogy in society today, the conflict between Wal-Mart and these big box stores and mom and pop operations. A lot of people romanticize the mom and pop hardware store, but, when push comes to shove and they go to buy their hammer and they want to save $1 on it, they go to Home Depot or to Lowe's or somewhere, and it's the same process that was working that put all of these early cotton artisans out of business.

These artisans began having to sell their labor as a commodity, and this resulted in really different cultural models, different ways of thinking about time, for example. Before the Industrial Revolution, the calendar had really been the hallmark of time, and then after the Industrial Revolution it became the watch and the clock, because time needed to be broken down into smaller units. If you're selling your labor, how do you sell that? It's by time, by the hour, for example. Discipline began to be introduced in the work place that was unknown before. Coffee and tea and sugar, for example, in the European factories, in the early English factories, began to replace beer breaks, and coffee and sugar and tea is the perfect proletarian food source. It's high in calories, it's cheap, and it provides caffeine as well, and so factory owners began, rather than supplying their workers with beer, supplying their workers with coffee and tea.

All of this played into a number of other developments that were going on at the time, iron production, the development of water-powered machinery, then the development of the steam engine and steel, and all of this came together to form England's Industrial Revolution in the 19th century. But what I want to focus on here is the alienation, what Marx called alienation, which is inherent in the capitalist production process. Marx used "free labor" always in an ironic sense. He said that workers in a capitalist system are free to sell their labor to whomever they want, but they're only free because they've been denied the form of production that they're used to, being their own bosses, being independent entrepreneurs and artisans and so forth, so they're free to sell their labor, but only within the system that denies them other alternatives.

Marx saw this as being a devastating shift in the cultural ethos. Whereas people before were independent artisans, they began selling their labor, and that by not controlling their means of production, and means of production are just what you need to make a living— for a farmer it's hoes and land and seeds; for a weaver it would be a loom and fabric and so forth—Marx said that by removing this connection between workers and their means of production the workers become alienated. Workers want to be their own bosses, Marx said—they want to control their own destinies in some fundamental way—and the early capitalist system removed that possibility. They began having to work for others because it was factory-based labor that was realizing in all of these efficiencies, and individual artisans couldn't build these large textile factories.

Interestingly enough, as a sideline, I read recently a survey of Fortune 500 company executives, and something like 75 percent of them said that one day they would like to set out on their own. I think this is echoes of Marx's idea of alienation, that these executives, they're being very well compensated, but they don't want to work for this large company. In an ideal world, they would work for themselves; they would control their own means of production and thus have control over their own destiny in some way.

Marx said that capitalism involved two forms of alienation. The first is alienation of workers from their means of production. They have to work; given technological advances and the inability of workers or artisans to buy these new technologies, they're forced to sell their labor. The second is the alienation of workers from the fruits of their labor. They're no longer artisans. In pre-capitalist societies, there's usually a social relationship between the producer and the consumer. The object that gets traded has all of these social meanings. If you buy a piece of jewelry from a silversmith that you know, it carries all sorts of different meanings than if you just went to a chain store and bought an industrially produced piece of jewelry, for example. Marx says that workers get alienated from what they produce. They're no longer vested in that product in the same way, and the social relationships that used to be transmitted through products get diminished as well.

We're going to turn to Marxist notions of alienation in a later lecture, but here I would like to continue by talking about hegemony and false consciousness. The idea of hegemony is often invoked in contemporary political discourse, and it generally is used as a synonym for political domination. In anthropology, however, it traces its origins back, the word hegemony traces its origins back, to the work of Antonio Gramsci and Karl Marx, and particularly Marx's writings on hidden or false consciousness. Marx was a bit wary of the masses; just as he called for a workers' revolution, at the same time he was a bit wary of the masses. He believed, for example, that religion acted as an opiate of the masses very famously, that people could be duped into buying into a system that exploited them, into actively supporting a system that exploited them.

We see this most clearly in one of my favorite essays of Marx's, which was published in 1852, and it's titled "The Eighteenth Brumaire of Louis Bonaparte." In this essay, he's looking at the rise of Louis Bonaparte, Napoleon Bonaparte's nephew, in France. Louis Bonaparte was trying to ride on the coattails of his uncle, that I am the torchbearer of the Napoleonic tradition. But what Marx said was that whereas Napoleon Bonaparte had protected the interest of peasants in many ways, his nephew Louis Bonaparte was selling out the interest of peasants. Louis Bonaparte was very much caught up in the interest of the emergent merchant class of his day, and so Louis Bonaparte was encouraging what we would call today privatization of lands.

This was sold to the French peasants as a good thing. You can buy your own land and then you don't have to work in these feudal conditions. You don't have to have a lord lording over you. You can buy your own land and be the master of your own destiny. But people were buying their land with mortgages, so they were taking out mortgages from this emerging class of merchant bankers and really enriching this very small segment of society. Marx saw this. And the French peasants supported Louis Bonaparte. They said, "Yes, this is great for us. We're going to own our own land. This is really realizing the dream of Napoleon Bonaparte." And Marx said the French peasants were duped by the Napoleonic rhetoric into buying into this project. He writes famously—let me quote here from *The Eighteenth Brumaire of Louis Bonaparte*:

> The mortgage debt burdening the soil of France imposes on the French peasantry an amount of interest equal to the annual interest on the entire British national debt. Small holding property in this enslavement by capital, toward which its development pushes it

unavoidably, has transformed the mass of the French nation into troglodytes. Sixteen million peasants, including women and children, dwell in caves, a large number of which have but one opening, others only two or three, and, as you know, windows are to a house what the five senses are to the head. The bourgeois order, which at the beginning of the century set the state to stand guard over this newly emerged small holdings and fertilize them with laurels, has become a vampire, which sucks the blood from their hearts and brains and casts them into the alchemist cauldron of capital. The code Napoleon is now nothing but a codex of the strengths of foresales and compulsory auctions.

Marx goes on to ponder why, and this is again quoting from him, "why a nation of 36 million can be surprised by these swindlers and taken to prison without resistance," and he observes wryly that "a nation no more than a woman is excused for the unguarded hour in which the first adventurer who comes along can do violence to her." Marx sees the French peasants as being duped by a political rhetoric into supporting a program of privatization which acts against their best interests, acts as an opiate of the masses, getting them to support a project which exploits them. Why would people act against their own self-interests? It doesn't make much sense. The Italian scholar Antonio Gramsci, who was a Marxist, who actually went to prison for being a Marxist—he was writing in the early part of the 20th century, in the 1920s and 1930s—developed Marx's notion of false consciousness, or hidden consciousness, this idea of being duped by a dominant ideology into what we call today hegemony, this modern concept of hegemony.

Let me mention that Gramsci, Antonio Gramsci, is very much invoked in social science literature these days, but his writings, what we have of his writings, were mostly smuggled out of this Italian jail cell on scraps of toilet paper and little pieces of paper and folded up, so it's a very telegraphic sort of writing; it's not a clear narrative. But what Gramsci argues is that hegemony, false consciousness, what he called hegemony, is a spontaneous consent given by the masses of a population to the general direction imposed on social life by the dominant fundamental group. This is to say, that dominant classes in a society are able to leverage their privileged access to mass media, to national discourse, to public education. They're able to use their privileged access to these means of communicating with the public to foster a system that continues to support them, continues to support them in their position of privilege.

Gramsci argues that hegemony emerges when a particular ideology representing particular class interests comes to be seen as natural or common sense. It's unquestioned, and in this, Gramsci argues that, for example, war is a breakdown of hegemony. We often hear hegemony invoked in the context of American expansion, for example, American hegemony in the world, and the United States is sending out its troops to impose its hegemony on Iraq—fill in the country of your choice there—but Gramsci argues that this isn't hegemony at all. War only emerges when hegemony breaks down. A hegemonic system gets people to support that system willingly, actively support the system, even if it is exploiting them, and so hegemony really removes the need for barefaced domination. It co-opts opposition in this way.

Hegemony is not unique to Western society. Earlier in the course, we talked about female circumcision in African societies, for example, very often supported by women themselves. Many would argue that this is a case of hegemony, of women buying into a patriarchal system that exploits them, that does harm to their own bodies, and actively supporting that system in some way. It's too easy to say that we're duped, and anthropologists have a complicated relationship with this concept of hegemony. On the one hand, it can be liberating to uncover hegemonies and show how people are being duped. On the other hand, as anthropologists, we place a lot of value in what people say and what people believe. We go there to study them and to record what they say, and we place a lot of value in people's views themselves.

It puts us in a difficult position, an ethnocentric position, to say, "You guys, you're blinded by ideology, you're blinded by this opiate of the masses, you're blinded by religion or political rhetoric, and we know better because we're anthropologists and we have some stranglehold on the objective truth, and we can take these blinders off of your eyes and show you how you're being exploited." Anthropology has a complicated relationship with the concept of hegemony, but the way in which we've explored it in recent years is looking at resistances to hegemonies, the way in which people resist the order which actively exploits them. This is mostly associated, most clearly associated with the work of a political scientist, James Scott, a political scientist, but a political scientist who has done ethnographic fieldwork, a political scientist who we could really consider to be an anthropological brother in some ways.

In 1987, he wrote a book called *Weapons of the Weak: Everyday Forms of Peasant Resistance*. He was working in a village that he calls Sedaka in Malaysia—this is a pseudonym he calls Sedaka in Malaysia—and he was doing his fieldwork there in the 1970s, following mechanization of agriculture, the rice agriculture in this village. What he finds in this village is a tension between peasants who used to be farmers and own their own land, who were then having to sell their land and work for people who had enough money to buy the machinery for mechanized agriculture, had enough money to buy fertilizer, had enough money to buy hybrid seeds and so forth. He found a lot of class tensions between these haves and the have-nots, the former peasant farmers who were having to work for this emergent class of agricultural capitalists.

There were a lot of tensions there, but this was also in Malaysia, a state with a history of severe state repression. The peasants who were having to give up their farmlands were very unsatisfied with this situation, but they didn't feel free to protest it, at least not overtly, because they would be thrown in prison, perhaps tortured by the authorities and so forth. What Scott argues is that they developed these techniques that he calls weapons of the weak, and these are ways at getting back at authority without overtly resisting that authority. Some of these examples would be foot dragging, feigned ignorance. The plantation owner tells a peasant to go and fertilize the fields and the peasant says, "I'm just an ignorant peasant. I don't really know how to mix the fertilizer. I'm not sure if I can do that," and so by feigning ignorance is able to get back in a little way at his boss, or false compliance, "Yes, I'm going to go do that, no problem at all," and then not carry through, and foot dragging, just moving as slowly as one can.

These are techniques that are used today by workers in industrial settings and in commercial settings. The best example of weapons of the weak, of foot dragging, I can think of is actually the deli lady at my neighborhood grocery store, who moves incredibly slow when I ask for a pound of sliced ham, for example, and this is her way of getting back at the system. "I'm being paid minimum wage, I'm not appreciated in my job, and so I'm going to move as slowly as I can, and this is a way for me, a disempowered person, to exercise authority over you, the consumer." There are a number of ways in which people employ weapons of the weak. We've mentioned foot dragging, feigned ignorance, false compliance, gossip—telling gossip about other people—pilfering, petty sabotage, ways in which workers are able to resist their bosses without seeming to resist.

An interesting aspect of this idea of hegemony here, or part of the problem with this idea of hegemony for anthropologists, boils down to the notion of can people be oppressed without realizing it. Can people be oppressed without realizing it, or do people know? Who knows best about these things? One example, to illustrate this, is the case of breast implants in the United States. Today, about 200,000 women a year in the United States have breast augmentation surgery. This is something that's really just taken off since the late 1970s, and the effect has been so dramatic that bra sizes have gone up in the United States. They jumped from a 34B to a 36B in 1991, and they jumped in the year 2000 to a 36C, and this cannot be accounted for just with natural growth rates. Yes, we're all getting a little bit bigger, but the breasts are getting even larger, at least based on bra size.

Why do women get breast implant surgery? We can look at this in one of two ways. One is that it's a form of empowerment for women. This technology has allowed women to take control over their bodies and actually change their bodies in a way in which they see fit, a very empowering thing. Or it could be a case of hegemony. It could be that women are duped into buying into a dominant male fantasy about breasts that exploits them, exploits them as objects. The anthropologist Laura Nader has written on this, and she notes that in the late 1970s and early 1980s there was a glut of plastic surgeons in the United States and that these mostly male plastic surgeons made a conscious effort to expand their markets.

Let me read here—this is from an article where she's quoting from the past president of the American Society of Plastic and Reproductive Surgery: "There is a substantial and enlarging medical knowledge that these deformities (and here he's referring to small breasts), that these deformities are really a disease which results in the patient's feelings of inadequacy, lack of self-confidence, distortion of body image, and a total lack of well being due to a lack of self-perceived femininity. Enlargement is therefore necessary to ensure the quality of life for the female patient."

What is breast augmentation? Is it a form of female empowerment or is it a form of hegemony? It's hard to say, but it comes back to this notion of who knows better, the native person, the person who is experiencing this reality that we're talking about, or the outside observer. Sometimes there's wiggle room here. It doesn't have to be either-or. Each offers a unique perspective, and this is part of the value of anthropology, combining various perspectives on the same topic to get at some notion of truth, or as close to truth as we can ever come.

Lecture Twenty
Is Economics Rational?

Scope: Culture and economics are intimately related, even if disciplinary boundaries too often separate their study. Economics may be defined as the study of how scarce resources are allocated toward specific ends. From the Greek root for "household" (*oikos*), economics originally referred to the ethic of household provisioning. In modern usage, it has come to refer to the science of economic decision making. Yet it is a science that rests on a number of big assumptions about rationality.

In this lecture, we examine economic rationality from the perspective of different cultures. We find that symbolic values (rather than strict material utility) motivate economic transactions among the Dobe, the Trobrianders, and even in contemporary U.S. culture. We thus place economics in cultural context, recognizing its valuable contributions to understanding human behavior but also acknowledging that economic logics vary across cultures. Finally, we turn to recent findings from experimental and behavioral economics, especially the "prisoner's dilemma" and "ultimatum games," showing how cultural notions of equitability often trump strict rational self-interests, even in our own culture.

Outline

I. Economics is the study of how limited resources are allocated.

   A. From the Greek *oikos* ("household") and *nomos* ("law"), economics was originally concerned with managing households. During the 20th century, it moved from a more philosophical and humanistic approach to a more scientific orientation.

   B. Economics studies the production, distribution, and consumption of goods. This includes not only how we produce the goods we consume but also the social relations they involve.

II. Economic anthropologists take a different approach to the economy than do economists. The discipline of economics has adopted a *formalist* paradigm that attempts to isolate human behavior. Economic anthropology takes a *substantivist* approach, seeing all economic relations as embedded in particular social contexts.

A. In economics, there has been a move from the study of political economy to *econometrics*—that is, toward mathematical models of behavior.

    1. Much economic modeling rests on the assumption that everyone acting in his or her own best self-interest advances the self-interests of all (Adam Smith's *invisible hand*).

    2. Economic models tend to assume strict rationality and universal applicability.

    3. Image advertising campaigns pose a problem for rational models.

B. In contrast, a substantivist approach is more culturally relative, seeing all economies as culturally embedded.

    1. Max Weber took a substantivist approach in his *The Protestant Ethic and the Spirit of Capitalism* (1904), showing how capitalism developed in the Protestant German north but not in the Catholic south.

    2. Substantivists argue that many of the assumptions of economic models may work in Western cultures but often do not apply in native societies.

    3. Marshall Sahlins has shown how even the U.S. food industry is based as much on cultural consumption as material necessity.

III. Economics, anthropology, and psychology have converged in recent years with the burgeoning subfields of experimental and behavioral economics.

A. Experimental economics tests the expectations of rationality through actual behavior.

    1. The "prisoner's dilemma" is a classic example of an economic experiment—and one in which the optimal solution for both parties is not the most individually rational.

    2. The "ultimatum game" pairs two individuals. Player A is given a sum of money (x), a percentage of which he must offer Player B. If the offer is accepted, the money is split as offered, but if the offer is rejected, neither player gets any money.

    B. Behavioral economics likewise looks at actual (not ideal) behaviors; it is much more anthropological in that it seeks to build theory from observable behavior.

        1. The concept of *bounded rationality* is a central theme in behavioral economics, looking at how knowledge, context, and cognition affect one's rationality.

        2. Full knowledge is crucial to making rational choices, but as Joseph Stiglitz and others show, real-work economic transactions often involve asymmetrical access to information.

    C. Behavioral and experimental economics can help us explain a number of rational anomalies in our everyday behavior.

    D. Proximate knowledge (information that has recently come to our attention) carries a disproportionate weight in our decision-making processes that is often irrational.

IV. Recent work in developmental economics has also turned toward anthropology.

Readings:

Michael Kearney, *Reconceptualizing the Peasantry.*

Joseph E. Stiglitz, *Globalization and Its Discontents.*

Richard H. Thaler, *The Winner's Curse.*

Richard Wilk, *Cultures and Economies.*

Questions to Consider:

1. Are there situations where one acts more (or less) rationally than at other times?

2. What would your offer be in an ultimatum game?

3. Do you place the same monetary value on opportunity costs as on other financial outlays?

Lecture Twenty—Transcript
Is Economics Rational?

We concluded last time by talking about hegemony and this notion of outside views versus inside views of culture and economic exploitation. Today, we're going to take an anthropological view of economics. From this perspective, it's very useful sometimes to have an outsider, an anthropologist, look at this discipline of economics and so we can combine an outsider's view with an insider's view of what's going on and offer a cultural perspective of the discipline of economics. This is going to critique some of the fundamental premises of economics, and let me say from the outset that I find value in the discipline of economics. Some of my best friends are economists, if I can say that, and, indeed, after we critique some of the assumptions of economic rationality and self-interest, we're going to turn to what I consider to be some of the most exciting work in social sciences today, which comes from economics, experimental economics and behavioral economics, the sort of economics that has taken a page from anthropology.

Let me begin by talking a bit about economics. The term economics itself comes from the Greek roots *oikos,* or household, and *nomos,* or law, and so economics originally referred to the law of the household, managing a household and considering a household as an economic unit. In this sense, it's more of an ethic than a science. How can we take care of everybody in our household? How can we provision our household with what it needs to survive? But economics over the years has converted into a science in many ways, a social science, but a social science that stresses the scientific part of that equation over the social part of the equation. There's a beauty to mathematical models of the economy. Mathematical models of economics have really taken off since the mid-20th century to today and have become the predominant paradigm in economics, mathematically modeling the economy. But we have to recognize the limitations of these models as well. We can appreciate their beauty, we can appreciate the parsimony of the models, but we have to realize the limitations at the same time.

The study of economics, an economist would say, is allocating scarce resources toward unlimited ends. We have unlimited wants and we only have scarce resources, and we have to figure out how to allocate those. But economics in some sense has moved beyond this even to become an ideology or a cultural mindset, a cultural model, a way of looking at the world, which very often seems to be the natural state of things. Free markets are the natural state of things; unfettered markets are the way things are supposed to be, so we're going to critique these notions of economics. To do that, let me begin with a distinction that's made by the economic historian Karl Polanyi, who we've talked about before in the class. Polanyi says that we can break up views of economics into two main perspectives: substantivist economics, which we would call cultural economics, a cultural perspective; and formal economics.

What he calls formal economics is the formal discipline of economics, what gets taught in economics departments and universities around the country. Formal economics, as Polanyi points out, and others as well have noted, formal economics today is based on two assumptions: the assumption of rationality, that humans are basically rational and intend to act rationally; and an assumption of self-interest, that we act rationally in our own self-interest. In the move, what used to be political economy, which would unite Marx and Adam Smith and Keynes and many others, has really moved to econometrics, mathematical modeling of the economy in the latter part of the 20th century.

The idea behind self-interest and rationality harkens back to the work of Adam Smith and Smith's notion that when an individual pursues his or her own self-interest, they're simultaneously pursuing the best interest of the society as a whole. This is the moral justification that Adam Smith in 1776 in his classic *Wealth of Nations* provided for the discipline. Smith, like Marx, is often caricatured in popular perceptions. He wasn't really this radical free trader; he saw a role for government and government intervention in the economy. But, at the same time, he pointed to this notion of pursuing one's self-interest works in the self-interest of society as a whole.

Let me read a quote from the *Wealth of Nations*: "It's not from the benevolence of the butcher, the brewer, or the baker that we expect our dinner but from their regard for their own self-interest. We address ourselves not to their humanity but to their self-love, and never talk to them of our own necessities but of their advantages. Nobody but a beggar chooses to depend chiefly on the benevolence of his fellow citizens." He goes on to say that "Every individual generally neither intends to promote the public interest nor knows how much he is promoting it; he intends only his own gain, and he is led by an invisible hand to promote an end which was no part of his intention." This is Adam Smith's famous invisible hand; if we all pursue our own individual self-interest, it's going to make the economy work more efficiently and produce more wealth for society as a whole.

The assumption of rationality, the assumption that rationality is universal and that there is some sort of universal rationality is obviously very problematic to anthropologists. We show that different cultures have different cultural logics. There are different rationalities at work in different societies around the world, and so an economic assumption of there being a single rationality, a single self-interested rationality, is problematic at best, the notion that humans are rational and that they act to maximize returns. They act to maximize returns on their investment, their investment of time, their investment of money, they act to maximize—utility, in the way economists would talk about it—but this is one of those nebulous concepts that encompasses so much cultural stuff that it really becomes useless.

Utility is the usefulness of an object to you, or to you or to you, but that utility is defined by you, so a utility of a cup is apparent. The utility of this cup is that it holds my water; it holds my coffee. The utility of a pen is that I can write with it, but what about the utility of a movie, for example? That's going to vary substantially from person to person and cannot be boiled down to these nice, neat, rational choices. Utility is defined differently between cultures. This is really what substantivist or cultural economics points out, so formal economics rests on these two pillars, these two assumptions of rationality and self-interest.

Substantivist economics, anthropological economics, holds that economies are culturally embedded, that economies arise from cultures, that particular circumstances of economies differ from society to society and we cannot have universal rules that apply around the world. We can look back to the work of the German sociologist Max Weber, who wrote a classic text in 1904, *The Protestant Ethic and the Spirit of Capitalism*, in which he really captured this notion of substantivist economics. What he did in *The Protestant Ethic and the Spirit of Capitalism* was compare the prosperous Protestant northern Germany, in which capitalism had taken off, with the less developed Catholic south of Germany, and he says that the Protestant ethic of saving money, of living austerely, led to the development of people to save money and the development of capitalism because people had money that they could invest, whereas in the south of Germany the Catholics were always having festivals and they were spending their money on wine and having a good time and capitalism couldn't develop in that context. What Weber is arguing is that capitalism emerged from a particular social, religious, cultural context.

We can think of a number of counterexamples to the economic assumptions of rationality and self-interest, things that we've talked about in this course so far. The Dobe Ju/'Hoansi, for example, the idea that there are unlimited wants and that we have to allocate scarce resources to unlimited wants, it doesn't hold up for the Dobe. They don't have unlimited wants, and accumulating lots of stuff, as we discussed, would actually be maladaptive for the Dobe. The Trobrianders likewise; the Trobrianders spend a great deal of their time trading in yams, and even in these kuvi yams, those huge 10 to12 feet long yams, they can't be eaten because they're too fibrous. Their value is symbolic. Or think about the Trobriand kula trade, where they trade these shelled necklaces and armbands.

There's very little material utility to these objects. Their utility is symbolic, and so the economies of trade are embedded in those particular cultural systems. It's important that we take into account not only economic capital but what Pierre Bourdieu called symbolic capital, honor, prestige, these social debts that can be built up by loaning someone something, for example, that can then get converted back into real capital, as we discussed in Lecture 16. The anthropologist Marshall Sahlins has argued that really what anthropologists need to do is turn economics on its head. He argues that it's a symbolic logic that organizes demand and not the other way around.

To illustrate this, he turns to the meat trade in the United States. He says, Why in the United States do we eat cattle and pigs and not horses and dogs, for example? He says it would make just as much economic sense for us to raise horses for meat. In fact, it would probably be more efficient to raise horses for meat. What do we use horsemeat for in the States these days? It's for dog food, cheap dog food, so we could raise horsemeat in the United States on the Great Plains incredibly cheaply, but we don't do this because we have a symbolic system that places horses and dogs as being somehow closer to humans. It would be almost cannibalistic to eat a dog. But of course this is a culturally specific notion. In many Asian cultures around the world, it's perfectly fine to eat a dog. It would be more acceptable to eat a horse because they're not quite as humanlike as dogs, but nonetheless that would still be a bit taboo. Even cultures as closely related to us as the French commonly eat horses, and so there is a cultural logic that organizes the economic demands for these products.

Sahlins in the same work also points out that this notion of distancing what we eat, cows and pigs, from being cannibalistic, from eating humans or dogs or horses, in doing this we play these linguistic games. What is cow meat? It's beef. We have this synonym that removes it from the physicality of eating meat. What do you call horsemeat? It's horsemeat, but we have separate words—we have beef and pork for cattle and pigs—but we don't have separate words for dog meat and horsemeat, for example. He also points out, just as another aside here, that if the laws of supply and demand are universal and apply in all contexts, then why isn't tongue, for example, cow tongue, more expensive than filet mignon? There's much more filet, there's much more steaks on a cow than there is tongue, and yet tongue has been encoded culturally as being a food of poverty. But there's much less of a supply of it, so why aren't prices actually higher for tongue?

We can think of these examples, and I can go on and on with examples of cultural exceptions to these presumed laws of rationality and self-interest, but what I would like to do now is turn to an emergent field in economics, or two interrelated fields in economics, experimental economics and behavioral economics. This is the work of a group of economists, and among them are John Nash, who won the Nobel Prize, Vernon Smith, Daniel Kahneman, and others who have decided to take a behavioral approach. Let's not construct these abstract models of how people should act if they were acting rationally, how people should act if they were producing their own self-interest. Let's see what people actually do and try and construct our models out of that, a very anthropological approach to the study of economics.

Experimental economics, one of the classic cases in experimental economics is a hypothetical game called the prisoner's dilemma. This really raises the question, Was Adam Smith right that acting in one's own self-interest always works for the greater good? Was Smith correct, pursuing your own self-interest also advances the self-interest of the group? To answer this question, let's consider this prisoner's dilemma. Put yourself in this context, put yourself in this mindset, and consider what you would do in this circumstance. Pretend that you're a criminal, first of all; pretend that you and an accomplice have committed some crime together and that you've both been arrested, but the police don't have enough evidence to convict both of you, so they've arrested you, and they've put you in separate interrogation rooms. You've not been able to talk with your accomplice, so you haven't been able to work out a common story.

Your interrogator, the police officer, walks in and offers both of you a deal. If you refuse to talk to the police, and you know that they don't have enough evidence, if you and your accomplice both refuse to talk to the police, you'll be convicted on a lesser charge and serve two years each in prison. If you don't talk to the police, if you cooperate with your accomplice and keep your mouth shut, you'll be convicted on a lesser charge and serve two years in prison. If you confess and your accomplice does not confess—so if you turn on your accomplice, if you defect in the language of this game, if you confess and your accomplice does not confess, you will go free and he or she will serve five years in prison. Conversely, if you don't confess and your accomplice confesses, you will serve five years in prison and the other person will go free. Finally, if you both confess, you will each serve four years in prison.

To review this very briefly, if both of you refuse to talk to the police, you'll be convicted of a lesser charge and each serve two years. If you confess and your accomplice does not, you'll go free and he or she will serve five years. And if you both confess you'll each serve four years. What would you do? It's always in an individual's best self-interest to confess. In the language of this game, that's called defecting, because you're not cooperating with your accomplice. It's always in your best interest to defect, and why is that? You're always going to serve less time in prison. Your accomplice can do one of two things; they can hold out or they can confess. You can do one of those two things as well. If you confess, if you defect, and the other person does not, you go free and that person serves jail time. If you both confess, then you're going to serve four years in prison versus five years in prison, so the best solution for an individual is always to defect, always to confess, because you're going to serve less time in prison no matter what your accomplice does.

However, the best solution for both of you is not to confess, to cooperate with one another. If you both cooperate and hold out, then you're going to serve a total of four years in jail, whereas, any of the other solutions, you would either serve five years or eight years in jail in total jail time between the two of you. Collectively, it's better for you to hold out, but individually, self-interestedly, it's always better to confess, so there's this disconnect between the two. What this proves is that sometimes self-interest can work against the common good. This was John Nash's great realization, and this can be used to radically modify Adam Smith's notion of self-interest.

Let's consider another hypothetical situation; this one is called the tragedy of the commons. There's a village that keeps a common pasture, and this common pasture is big enough for every household to keep one, let's say sheep, in the pasture without degrading the quality of the pastureland. Everybody can keep one sheep on the pastureland, and they can be sustained forever. But individuals may think, "Who's going to notice there's just one extra sheep up there? I can just put two sheep and nobody will really notice, and I get to freeload off of the good will of the whole village. I'll just put one extra sheep up there." But then if everybody does this, if everybody thinks this, if everybody pursues their own individual self-interest, the pasture land is going to become degraded and isn't going to be able to support anyone, so pursuing one's own individual self-interest again in this sort of situation can produce a common bad rather than a common good, if you will.

My own work in economic anthropology has pursued this line in recent years, and what I've been doing is playing games with people, with Maya peoples in Guatemala. I've also played these games with my students here in the United States and a little bit in Germany. The game I've been using most often is the ultimatum game. This is a game that you play with real money, and the notion is to see how people react, if people react rationally when they're playing a game with real money. Again, if you would, put yourself in this circumstance. I'm going to set up this game, and think about what you would do. I'm going to give you—in Guatemala I play with just a few dollars, but to make it more significant here in the States, let's say $100.

In this game you have two players, Player A and Player B. They don't know each other; they don't know who each other are, but they know that they're teamed up with another player. You're going to be Player A. I go around and I give you $100 in cash. You're Player A; you have $100 in cash. You're going to be able to make one move in this game. Your move is you have to offer a percentage of that $100 to Player B. You can offer $1, you can offer $20, you can offer $50, you can offer $75, $80, whatever you would like, but you have to offer some percentage of that $100 to the opposite player. That's your one move in the game. I will then take your offer over to Player B and I will say, "Player A has offered 'x' amount," $20, $50, $75, and then Player B either accepts that offer or rejects it. If Player B accepts the offer, you divide up the money as it's been offered. If Player B rejects the offer, all of the money gets returned to the central pot and neither player gets any money at all. How much would you offer, what percentage of this $100 would you offer to an anonymous Player B?

The most rational choice is to offer the smallest percentage possible, to offer $1, for example, because you're going to maximize your returns, and if Player B is acting rationally, Player B will accept $1. One dollar is better than nothing, but, in fact, and in this game, Player B knows how much money Player A has gotten. In fact, when I play this game with my students, my university students for example, I get a bipolar distribution. I get a lot of people, mostly economics majors, offering $1 or $2, a very small percentage, but then I get another large number of people offering $50. More people in fact offer $50 than any other amount.

This would seem irrational. Why would people offer more than $50? And if I interview these participants, they'll say, "It just seems fair to offer half of it. It's extra money that I'm getting, and I'm afraid the other person would turn down an offer for less than $50." In fact, that is the case. People turn down offers of $1 or $2 or even $10 or sometimes even $20. Why would they do that? It doesn't make rational sense. Why turn down $10? You're either going to have $10 or you're not. But it's because it offends their sense of equity, of fairness. Why should the other person get $90 and I'm only going to get $10? I'm going to reject that offer, and I'm going to show that person how they should act. In economic terms, what Player B, if Player B let's say rejects an offer of $10, what they're doing is paying $10 to punish the other person. In economic terms, if you reject an offer, it's called opportunity cost; if you reject $10 it's just like paying $10, so Player B is willing to pay $10 to punish Player A for not being fair.

These games, they really get at this notion that cultural ideas, cultural models of equality, equity and fairness, can trump pure economic rationality in these cases. Interestingly enough, in the U.S. the average offers are about 30 to 35 percent. When I played this game with Maya peoples in Guatemala, the average offers were about 51 percent. They're hyper-generous offers, and the idea is because there's a strict notion of economic equality among the Maya, and when I would interview people, "Why would you offer more than half, for example?" they would say, "The other person probably needs it more than I do, and I just want to help them out," so a very different notion of economic rationality. This gets at the idea or gets at this notion of actual behavior differing significantly from expected behavior.

Let me give you a couple of other examples that come from the field of behavioral economics. A psychologist by the name of Daniel Kahneman has come up with this idea of bounded rationality. He says, in fact, all of these anomalous cases, yes, that's all true, but we do act rationally sometimes, but our rationality is bounded. In certain contexts, we act rationally; in other contexts we do not. And this is a very useful notion for understanding economics. Sure, we're all rational, at least we are all rational some of the time, but we're not all rational all of the time.

Richard Thaler, the economist who has done more than anyone else probably to popularize this field of behavioral economics and has a wonderful collection of essays called *The Winner's Curse*, looks at a variety of economic anomalies and tries to explain those in terms of cultural conceptions of equality and fairness, and a number of things, one thing that he calls status quo bias, and this is the idea that people are not very willing to accept extra risks. To get at this notion, what he did was he offered people two alternatives, and again this is a hypothetical situation. Put yourself in these circumstances. You've come down with a disease; you've just been diagnosed with this disease and your doctor says, "I have a vaccine that can cure you, and you have a one in a thousand chance of dying a painless death in two weeks with this disease," a one in a thousand chance of dying a painless death.

"But we've got this vaccine, so how much would you be willing to pay for a vaccine that would remove this one in a thousand chance of dying a painless death in two weeks? Think about that. How much would that be worth to you? Now, consider an alternate scenario. How much would you be willing to accept to participate in a study in which there was a one in a thousand chance that you would die a painless death? What would that figure be?" For most people, the second figure is several times what the first figure would be. You would have to pay me a whole lot to take on this extra risk, but if I already have the risk I would only be willing to pay so much to alleviate this risk.

Thaler also points to the importance of proximate knowledge, that we act on knowledge that we've learned recently weighs more heavily in our decision-making process. This can cloud our pure rationality. For example, after there's a big win in the lottery, lottery ticket sales go up. The pot is going to be smaller, so it's really not rational, but people have it in their minds that I could actually win—somebody just won—so I'm going to buy a lottery ticket, or driving more safely after seeing an accident. People tend to drive very carefully in the hours, days, and weeks after they've seen a very bad accident. Their chances of getting into an accident themselves is the same as it was before they saw the other accident, but we weigh proximate knowledge, knowledge that we've learned recently, more heavily than we do other sorts of knowledge. In this way, all of these cultural elements, these quirks of behavior, we might call them, play upon our rationality and cloud our rationality.

Human beings, when we act economically, sometimes we react rationally. When we buy toilet paper, for example, we probably act very rationally, because we go to the grocery store, we can very easily compare all of the different kinds of toilet paper, the qualities of toilet paper, the price of each of those different toilet papers, and make what economists would consider to be a very rational decision. On the other hand, when we buy something really big, like a house, we often act irrationally. What's another quarter percentage point of interest? It's only going to add $25 a month to my mortgage bill or something, and yet $25 a month for 30 years is a lot of money, and so we act irrationally in these contexts where we have less information to play on.

Likewise, a person might be willing to drive all across town, drive for 45 minutes to save $10 on a clock radio, let's say. And yet that same person would not be willing to drive across town to save $10 on a big screen television, for example, because the $10 seems like less in comparison to the sum that's going to be paid, so it's all relative in this sense. It's the same $10. If you're going to save $10 on a clock radio, that's the equivalent of saving $10 on a big screen TV. But we don't see it that way because of the particular context in which it's set.

What anthropologists have to offer to the study of economics is actually looking at what people do. It's very important to make these models of rational choice, and economists have been very successful at doing that, but just as important are constructing new sorts of models that reflect how people actually live and work in the world, and this is what anthropology has to offer economics and something that in behavioral and experimental economics they've picked up on in recent years.

Lecture Twenty-One
Late Capitalism—From Ford to Disney

Scope: The late 20th-century U.S. economy was a period termed *late capitalism*. Late capitalism may be dated to the early 1970s and the launch of the first communication satellites. Since that time, communication technology has increased and prices have dropped dramatically, making the world a virtually smaller place. Transportation costs have likewise dropped.

Industrial capitalism is marked by *Fordist* forms of production— namely, assembly-line mass production. In contrast, the post-industrial era of late capitalism has moved toward what is termed *post-Fordism*. Post-Fordist strategies simultaneously move toward outsourcing production while attempting to reduce the alienation inherent in capitalist production. The experimental venture of General Motors to produce Saturn cars illustrates the post-Fordist trend.

It has been argued that as the American economy has moved away from industrial production, it has become increasingly symbolic. We look to advertising strategies, the new urbanism movement, and Las Vegas and Disneyland to show how symbolic values drive the American economy.

Outline

I. Adam Smith shows the collective benefit of trade and specialization that allowed capitalist production to expand.

   A. This was especially clear during the move to industrialization and mass production.

   B. Antonio Gramsci describes the processes of *Taylorism* and *Fordism* that led to increasing specialization of tasks and alienation of workers.

   C. After Henry Ford opened his assembly-line factory, the price of a Model T fell from $780 in 1910 to $360 in 1914.

II. Late capitalism has been around since the early 1970s, although the pace of change greatly accelerated in the 1980s and 1990s.

- **A.** Late capitalism is marked by post-Fordism: post-industrial production; decentralization; and greater mobility of capital, labor, and ideas.
    1. In the late 20th century, the U.S. economy transformed from a factory-based industrial model to a service-based economy. Increasingly, production takes place overseas.
    2. This system has been enabled by greater mobility of capital, commodities, and people.
- **B.** The best example of post-Fordist production comes from Saturn, a subsidiary of General Motors formed in 1985 to rethink the process of industrial organization. The first Saturn cars rolled off the Spring Hill, Tennessee, assembly lines in 1990.
    1. Saturn employs a post-Fordist style of labor-management relations that stresses teamwork, empowerment, and responsibility.
    2. The early ads emphasize this style, arguing that the company's workers are no longer alienated in the same way Marx envisioned.
    3. Saturn also tries to recreate the bond between consumer and producer, as seen in later ads.
- **III.** In the late-capitalist marketplace, symbolic values have, in many ways, come to replace material values.
    - **A.** There is increasing investment in *fictitious* capital (versus productive or *real*) capital; fictitious capital may include image, brand maintenance, intellectual property, art, and other such intangibles.
        1. Soft-drink and tennis-shoe ads attempt to sell images of authenticity.
        2. Neighborhood-style chain restaurants, micro-brews, and single-malt scotch likewise appeal to a quest for something "real."
        3. Yuppie coffees, artisan chocolates, and other such gourmet fare attempt to recapture a presumptively lost authenticity.
    - **B.** Simultaneously, there is a trend in American culture to recapture the "real" that has seemingly been lost. The French philosopher Jean Baudrillard argues that just as we have come to define ourselves more by what we consume than by what we produce, we also seek authenticity more than ever.

1. Baudrillard introduces the concept of *hyperreality* in his examination of contemporary U.S. culture.
2. Hyperreality attempts to be more real than the real thing, where the meticulous copy becomes more meaningful than the original. Reality television and Starbucks illustrate this phenomenon.

IV. Examples of hyperreality may be found in the entertainment economy of the United States.

   A. Disneyland has recreated a Louisiana swamp tour, mini-exhibits of foreign capitals, and other better-than-the-original copies.

   B. The theme casino-hotels of Las Vegas similarly copy the grandeur of New York or Paris or Venice.

   C. An architectural movement called the *new urbanism* attempts to recapture aspects of community that were lost in the process of suburbanization.
      1. Disney's planned community outside of Orlando--Celebration, Florida--employs alleys, sidewalks, and front porches to conjure up neighborly spirit.
      2. Some residents have resisted the strict conformity such a project in social engineering requires; they protest by placing pink flamingos in their yards.

   D. The painter Thomas Kinkade further blurs the boundary between original and copy with his retouched lithographs.

Readings:

Jean Baudrillard, *Simulation and Simulacra*.

Setha Low, *Behind the Gates*.

David Remnick, ed., *The New Gilded Age*.

Questions to Consider:

1. Why is "authenticity" so important in American consumer culture?
2. Can Marx's notion of alienation provide useful insights for management strategies?
3. How does hyperreality try to capture an idealized past?

Lecture Twenty-One—Transcript
Late Capitalism—From Ford to Disney

Last time we discussed cultural critiques of economic rationality and self-interest, showing that we're not always as rational as we sometimes think we are. Today we're going to look at the interplay of culture in our own economic system, which is sometimes called late capitalism. We're going to begin by defining two new concepts, Taylorism and Fordism, that come to us from Antonio Gramsci, and we're going to wind up looking at the way in which recent management theories have come to terms with Marxist notion of alienation that we introduced earlier. Let me begin with the concept of Taylorism, and this is something that was introduced from Antonio Gramsci. You'll remember he's the man who introduced the idea of hegemony in his writings from prison, from an Italian prison, where he was imprisoned for being a Marxist.

Taylorism comes from the work of Frederick Taylor, who in 1911 published *The Principles of Scientific Management*, which was really the first real management text published in the United States and probably anywhere in the world. Taylor's great contribution was devising a means of detailing a division of labor and breaking down the production process to its smallest possible component in time and motion studies based around performance. The idea was, don't have an artisan assemble a whole stove, but let's have one person put on the side panel, another person screw in these screws, another person put on the knobs, and so forth, breaking the production process down to its smallest possible components and releasing businesses from the need to hire skilled labor, to hire artisans. You can hire unskilled labor if all they're going to be doing is screwing in bolts and so forth. This was Taylor's addition to the management theory, or his pioneering work in management theory.

Taylor's ideas were really taken by Henry Ford and put into practice in his model of mass production in the assembly line for the Model T. Ford started making Model T's in his factory in Highland Park, Michigan, in 1914, and he was able to, by employing an assembly-line model, by breaking down the production process into its smallest components. Whereas before he would go in to an automaker and order a custom car, after Ford instituted the assembly line, he could make thousands of cars, tens of thousands of cars based on the same model and sell them for a much lower price. The assembly line model, in breaking down the production process into its smallest components, realized incredible efficiencies in economics. This is best seen in the price of Model T's, which cost in 1910, a Model T cost $780. In 1914, after the assembly line had been instituted, it cost $360, less than half the price that it cost the year before.

This is really the promise of capitalism; greater efficiencies in the production process create more goods that can be sold for lower price and thus making them available to a wider swath of society, more stuff for everybody. Also involved in the process of assembly-line production and Tayloristic or Fordistic production is uniformity. The products have to be alike in order to realize these efficiencies. Ford was famous for saying, "You can have a Model T in any color as long as it's black," and this was part of—the increase in efficiency was realized through uniformity.

As part of this process, Antonio Gramsci took these two ideas and called them Taylorism and Fordism, and he critiqued them for increasing alienation. He said that Fordism displaced a predominantly craft-based production, in which skilled laborers exercised substantial control over the conditions of their own work, and then reduced it to these smallest possible components and switched from skilled labor and artisanal laborer to unskilled labor. What this does is it increases alienation; it increases the alienation of workers from the fruits of their labor. If you're building a whole car, the producer would feel vested in that car, would feel a personal connection to that car. If you're just screwing in a bolt on the wheel, and you're doing that thousands of times a day, you don't feel that same investment in the product that you're building. There's not that personal connection between the worker and the product that's being created.

It increases the alienation of workers from the products that they're building. It also invokes alienation of workers from the means of production. They don't control their means of production; they have to sell their labor and work for large companies. This increased alienation. Ford was able to minimize the effects of this, the psychological, the emotional effects of this, by paying his workers well. There's a tradeoff; you're not going to be the craftsman or the artisan that you once were perhaps but you're going to be paid enough, and Ford famously said that he was going to pay all of his workers enough that they would be able to buy his own cars.

This Fordist model of production, of mass production, of assembly-line production, really took off in the early part of the 20th century in the United States. It was applied to lots of different models, and not just cars. Hilton made a fortune, for example, building hotel rooms that were exactly alike in cities around the world. There was this appeal of uniformity. McDonald's building, you can buy the same Big Mac in Beijing or Kuala Lumpur or in Paris or in the United States, so there was this uniformity of products that went along with this. This was really the commodification of products. Commodification means making a product not unique.

Original artwork is an anti-commodity; an original piece of artwork cannot be reproduced in itself. We can make lithographs, we can make copies of it, but the value of an original piece of art is related to the relationship of the artist to that work. An individual made this piece of work, so art is the anti-commodity. Commodities, when Ford turned cars into commodities, they became alike. A commodity is essentially alike. A ton of steel is a ton of steel is a ton of steel—it doesn't matter where it's made. Part of the process of Fordism and Taylorism was a move toward commoditization of products, making things less original, less personal and more uniform. They're cheaper if they're uniform, but you lose some of the personal qualities as well.

I introduce these concepts of Taylorism and Fordism that we get from Antonio Gramsci really to talk about what we call today post-Fordism, forms of production that have arisen over the last 20 years or so in the United States that take into account Marxist critique of alienation, that take into account Gramsci's notions of Fordism and Taylorism and the problems that that entails for workers in trying to incorporate this into management theory to make places better places to work. The best example of post-Fordism comes from the Saturn Car Company. Saturn's logo is "A different kind of company, a different kind of car." Saturn is a subsidiary of GM. The company was formed in 1985, and the first cars rolled off the assembly line in 1990 at their plant in Spring Hill, Tennessee. At Saturn, what they've tried to do is reduce worker alienation through new styles, post-Fordist styles of labor-management relations, changing the culture of the work place in order to change the economics of production.

What happens is at Saturn, they form groups into teams, and so rather than having a person just screw in one screw on a dashboard, they'll assign a team to do the whole dashboard assembly, for example, and these teams are empowered in very significant ways. They act like little companies within the plant. They'll make contracts with the production team behind them on the assembly line and the production team in front of them on the assembly line, and they're able to decide how many cars a day they're going to be able to put the dashboards on. They're even able to decide their working hours. They have flextime, and they can decide whether they want to come in at eight in the morning or nine in the morning.

They're given quite a bit of flexibility in doing these things, and this empowers the workers to feel more invested in the company they're working for. This is allowed by a unique memorandum of understanding that was signed between the U.A.W., the autoworkers' union, and GM to establish Saturn. This gave the ability—this gave teams a lot of independence—the ability for them to act like little independent businesses. It allowed shop floor workers, blue collar workers, to sit in on management meetings. It allowed them to participate in marketing decisions. It allowed them to participate in major purchasing decisions. It really integrated management and labor in a new sort of way.

The tradeoff for all of this power given to workers, what the workers agreed to do was to take a large portion of their salary in profit sharing based on profitability and the efficiency of their teams. Interestingly enough, in 2003 this memorandum of understanding was rejected, was revoked by the union. With the economic downturn of the early 2000s, the profit sharing just wasn't profitable for the workers any longer, and so they decided to go back to an old-style union contract. Bu, nonetheless, in the early days of Saturn up through 2003, there was this new form of management, of post-Fordist management, and trying to get workers invested in new sorts of ways in the company that they worked for.

This is best seen in a number of early ads that Saturn developed, and it's stressed that workers are no longer alienated. At the Saturn plant, workers are no longer alienated in the way in which Marx envisioned it. If I can, let me read some of the text of one of these ads, an ad that showed a car worker who had moved down from Detroit to Spring Hill, Tennessee, to start working in the Saturn plant because he wanted to work for a company that embodied the values of artistanship and workmanship that he wanted to reclaim.

He says, "It used to be I saw the product that I was making, but that was just one part of the thousands of parts that went into the makeup of a car. There was no way I would ever see the cars that when into it. The way things were done, I just wasn't involved. No one ever asked me what I thought. Then I heard about Saturn building a whole new car in a whole new car plant. They figured out a new way of running things, too. No one else in the world had done it this way, not that I know of, not since the Model T, anyway. Raw material comes in the back door and a car comes out the other end. Seems to me that when you see where your part fits into the bigger picture, it means a lot more. That's my perception anyway."

It's this notion of workers once again being invested in the product that they're building. "I'm not just screwing on a bolt; I'm not trying just to do as little as I can to get through the day and clock out and go home and drink my beer. This is more than just a job to me; it's a way of life, and I want to build a quality car because building Saturn cars is what I'm about." This has real emotional, psychological, cultural implications for workers, the way in which they feel about themselves and the way in which they feel about the company that they work for, but it also realizes real quality improvements for companies. If workers aren't employing the weapons of the weak that we talked about in an earlier lecture, trying to get by, pilfering and foot dragging and feigning ignorance, and all of these ways in which workers can resist the authority of management and do as little work as possible, they're not involved in that culture of resistance between labor and management anymore, and it creates a better product.

Saturn is trying to reduce the alienation of workers from the product that they're building. Saturn also very consciously tries to create a tighter bond between the producers of products and the consumers of products. In pre-capitalist societies, you would have had a very close relationship with your butcher, with your baker, with the silversmith, the people you bought products from. You would have social relationships as well, and it would have been hard to divorce the social relationships from the economic relationships. We've lost a lot of that. We lost a lot of this during the height of Fordist production, with the uniformity of commodities that were being produced and the anonymity of large corporations. But Saturn is trying to recapture this, and one of the ways in which they've represented this is through a series of ads, one ad in particular, where a schoolteacher writes in and describes what she expects her Saturn car to be like. Let me read a section from the letter that she wrote that was featured in one of the television ads,

"Dear Saturn team members who are building my car: My name is Judith, and I'm a third grade teacher. Last week, I placed an order for a Saturn after reading about it in a magazine article. I like the whole idea of what Saturn was about. It's one of those things I try and instill in my kids, so I hope it's true. It reminds me a bit of a mom and pop operation in the old days, where you made a car for this person and this person was happy with the car they got. I just wanted you to know that you were building that Saturn with the blue-green exterior and the gray interior for me. So you know who I am, I'm enclosing my school picture. I am looking forward to my new car. I'm sure if everything I've read is true, I won't be disappointed."

Then in the ad, what they do is they take this letter and they attach the photograph to the letter and they put it on the chassis as it's going down the assembly line, as the car is being built. All of the workers look at this and they read the letter and they see who this car is for, and so it's creating, perhaps just virtually, but it's creating a relationship between the producers and the consumers, something that's lost in mass-produced industrialized commodified production. This is very important; it's a very important marketing tool for Saturn to have this sort of relationship. They've also had very successful Saturn Days during the summer, where thousands of Saturn owners come to the plant and meet the workers who are building their cars, reestablishing a personal relationship between consumer and producer, something that again is lost or was lost during the height of industrial capitalism.

Part of what this does is it acts to decommodify products. The schoolteacher, she's not buying just any Saturn; she's buying a Saturn that was built especially for her. Sure it's on the assembly line, sure it's just like lots of other Saturns, but there was a personal touch. The workers knew who they were building this for, and there was a personal relationship there which acts to decommodify the product. Again, think about original art being the ultimate anti-commodity. This is like a little piece of original art, the workers doing personalized touches to the Saturn to make it just for our schoolteacher Judith. We've seen a move in what is called the late capitalist economy, and this really starts in the 1970s and accelerates during the '80s and '90s with the advent of globalization. In late capitalist consumption, we see more customization, companies targeting smaller niches, more precise consumer demographics, and really stressing the affective values of products that they're trying to sell.

Some have argued, the anthropologist Jonathan Friedman, for example, has argued that in this late capitalist economy, symbolic values have come to replace or outweigh utility values, material utility values. Friedman argues that this is a very ephemeral base for us to ground our identity in. We're consuming these products. In consuming these products, we're building up part of our self-identity, but, in doing so, Friedman argues that this is a very ephemeral base to ground our identity in, and thus we start searching for products that are more unique, less commodified, and in some way more real or more authentic.

As a result, we find all of these ironies—for example, transnational corporations like Nike selling an idea of authenticity. Just do it, just be yourself by buying a sneaker that was made in Taiwan in a sweatshop and marketed here in the United States. Selling an image, Nike is a great example of this. If you see sneaker ads on television, tennis shoe ads on television, and not just Nike, Reebok and others as well, they're not telling you anything about the product at all hardly, and a rational view of economics says that advertising is supposed to tell us about the price, it's supposed to tell us about the quality, it's supposed to help us make rational decisions when we go shopping. But lots of ads these days, especially tennis shoe ads, don't include anything about the product. They're selling an image, they're selling an idea, they're selling a lifestyle, and this is what Friedman is talking about when he says that symbolic values have come to replace material values very often in this late capitalist economy.

As part of this, we seem to have this search for authenticity. We can see it in neighborhood restaurants, or restaurants that pretend to be neighborhood restaurants, TGI Friday's, Applebee's, and places like this that are part of large chains, but they try and individuate themselves. It's just like the corner restaurant that we used to have in the good old days. The problem with saying this, with this claim that symbolic values are more important than material values is that it's very often hard to separate the two. We could see the surge in interest in microbrewed beers, for example, in recent years as a quest to reclaim the authentic. I don't want to have a mass-produced beer; I want to have something that's made in small batches, that somehow is unique, that when I drink it can say something about me as a person having this refined taste.

But we can't separate the symbolic values here from the material values. Maybe the microbrewed beers taste a lot better, so maybe there's a material reason, a real utility reason why we would choose those, but you can't separate that from the fact that drinking a particular microbrew also represents you in some way to the rest of the world. You're consuming a symbolic value at the same time you're consuming a material value. Maybe microbrews or single malt scotches, the same argument would apply to single malt scotches. There's a lot of cultural capital involved in knowing just exactly what scotch you want to drink, what part of Scotland it's from, how much peaty taste is in there, how much salt water taste.

Or wine, the same thing goes for wine. There's a lot of cultural knowledge behind choosing a particular kind of wine. Some wines taste better than others objectively, but of course we learn taste as well. This is part of our cultural capital. We learn the more sophisticated tastes that we may exhibit to the rest of the world. It's hard to separate consuming symbolic values in wine, microbrews, or in scotches, whatever it may be, from consuming the material values of those objects as well.

A great example of the decommodification of products comes from coffee. Coffee started out as a drink of the elites in Europe in the early days. When coffee was first trickling into Europe, it was the drink of aristocracy, of royalty, and then over the years it filtered down to the masses, becoming what Sidney Mentz has called the ultimate proletarian hunger killer, a great drink for the masses who are working in factories, a little coffee and sugar or a little tea and sugar. It's cheap, has a lot of calories, and it has caffeine to keep the workers going. What started out as an elite beverage, a decommodified beverage if you will, a luxury product that was unique in many ways, and then it became a mass product of workers.

Over the years, consumption of coffee increased up through about the 1950s, and in the 1950s coffee consumption leveled off and then began to decline slightly in the 1960s. Production during this time was highly industrialized, and coffee became highly commodified. Coffee was coffee was coffee; a few big companies controlled the market— General Mills, Procter & Gamble, Nestle, and so forth—and they would blend different sorts of coffee together to create a blend that was palatable to the widest segment of the markets, so not having unique coffees, but trying to make the blandest or the most acceptable coffee for everybody.

And then by the early 1980s, smaller coffee roasters had come back on the scene, and retailers were trying to distinguish types of coffee, to decommodify it. Coffee isn't coffee isn't coffee; now you can go to your neighborhood coffee store and you can buy Kona or Blue Mountain or Kenyan AA. You can buy organic coffee or whole coffee or fresh coffee. You can buy different styles of coffee, and in doing this we've tried to decommodify the coffee market. I don't just drink the coffee; I drink a double Kenyan latte, or whatever the language is that they use at Starbucks these days. It's decommodifying this product that was at one time a perfect example of a homogeneous commodity. The same thing has happened in other markets as well, with chocolate, with wine, and so forth.

I would like to conclude by applying some of these to contemporary U.S. culture and U.S. cultural economics through the eyes of a French scholar, the French scholar Jean Baudrillard, and he has said that in the late capitalist system of the United States that substance is nothing and image is everything. He goes back to this observation by Friedman that symbolic values have become more important than material utility values. Baudrillard argues that in late capitalism we define ourselves more by what we consume than what we produce—generations ago, we would have defined ourselves by what we produce ourselves, and today we define ourselves more through consumption—and that this leads us to try and consume authentic and real products, not just the mass-produced homogeneous products of the industrial age.

In this process, Baudrillard argues that we've come to value reality so much that we produce products that he calls hyperreal. Hyperreal products are things that are more real than the real thing. What does that mean? For example, reality television: reality television isn't really reality, but in watching it and consuming it, we take it to be reality, and we want it to be representative in a way that reality often isn't in real life. It's the same way with Disneyland. Take Disneyland, for example: you could go to Disneyland and take a swamp tour instead of going to southern Louisiana and taking a swamp tour.

You go to south Louisiana, the weather might be hot, the mosquitoes might be out, you could see an alligator, you might not see an alligator—there are all of these chances that you take in the real world to experience a swamp tour. You go to Disneyland, and you take their swamp tour, and it's going to be perfect every time. The alligator is going to jump out of the water at just the right moment so that you can snap a photo to take home. It's more real than the real thing because it's able to fit in all of the iconic elements that we associate with a swamp tour into the perfect swamp tour, more real than the real thing. Las Vegas is another great example—all of the New York, New York and Paris and all of the new sorts of casinos—theme casinos that are being built in Las Vegas.

We can also see the architectural, the urban planning movement called new urbanism as representing this as well, as trying to recapture a romantic view of what communities used to be like way back when. Perfect examples of this are Seaside, Florida, for example, where they filmed the movie *The Truman Show*, Celebration, Florida, which is a wholly owned development of Disney outside of Orlando, Florida. They're very strict, and in these new urban developments they have alleyways in the back, sidewalks in the front of the houses, every house has a front porch, and it's mixed use. You can walk to the grocery store. There's a town square. In Celebration, Florida, for example, you can walk to the grocery store, you can walk to the chemist's shop, whatever it may be. The idea is that we can recapture a sense of community that we've lost in this country by creating these very often gated communities that combine front porches and sidewalks, and the kids can be out front playing around and all of these things. They're more real than those communities that they're mimicking were; they're creating something that's hyperreal.

Finally, I could raise the example of artwork and the commodification and decommodification of artwork as seen in the work of Thomas Kinkade, who calls himself the painter of light. Thomas Kinkade sells original artwork, and you'll remember original artwork is the opposite of a commodity, but what he also does is he reproduces his art. He makes lithographs of his original art, so you would start out with a non-commodity, original art, and then you would make a commodity by making reproductions of this. But then Thomas Kinkade makes this more complex still because he employs teams of whom he calls illuminators, and they'll go back through, and on the reproductions they will touch up with oil paint sections of the reproductions, and so then it makes it not a commodity anymore.

You started off with an anti-commodity original art, you commodified it by making reproductions of it, and then by highlighting them, you take it back out of this commodity chain as well. Kinkade has been very successful at selling these illuminated pieces of art because they're unique, and he even sent out his illuminators to his stores to customize art for customers, and so you can tell someone, "I really like this print here, and I'll take it, but I want you to touch it up, add a little bit more red to the sun, or add a little bit more white to the wispy smoke coming out of the house," or whatever it may be.

It's too easy and it's too elitist to simply critique modern American consumption patterns. We should see these as being culturally relative, just like we've looked at cannibalism and other aspects of culture in other places around the world, and it's important to keep in mind that this is morally no better or no worse than other forms of consumption. It's easy to take potshots at this kind of hyperreality, but if people are enjoying it, it's fine, and this is just a reflection of American society the way it is today. In the moment of consumption, there's a sincerity to these acts that we have to take seriously and not be ironically distanced from. This is applying this notion of culture relativity that we've applied to other cultures around the world to ourselves here at home.

Ethnic Identities in a Globalized World
Lecture Twenty-Two
The Maya, Ancient and Modern

Scope: The Maya are best remembered for the grandeur of their classic-era (A.D. 250–900) civilization—the impressive temples and cities built in the rainforest, their hieroglyphic writing, the blood sacrifice. But there are more than 8 million Maya living in what is today Guatemala, Belize, and southern Mexico. In this lecture, we look at the modern Maya and the ways their culture has been shaped over the centuries. We look at ancient Maya calendrical systems that are maintained today by Maya shamans and the unique patterns of dress and language that set the Maya apart. We also look to the effects of Guatemala's brutal civil war of the early 1980s on Maya communities and what this can tell us about violence and terrorism.

The Maya case illustrates many of the themes discussed in this course and shows how cultures can change yet retain a sense of continuity at the same time.

Outline

I. Classic Maya civilization flourished from about A.D. 250 to around A.D. 900.

    A. It arose in the quasi-rainforest region of lowland Central America.

        1. Grand city-states, such as Tikal, Copán, and Dos Pilas, were constructed in the jungle and ruled over by kings and priests. Elaborate webs of trade, kinship, and political alliance linked these polities.

        2. Dense populations were supported by maize farmers, who employed raised fields and other techniques to produce crops in the relatively fragile soils of the region.

    B. The classic Maya had highly developed bodies of astronomical, mathematical, and calendrical knowledge.

        1. Maya calendars were used for ritual purposes, as well as recording the absolute dates of historical events.

> **2.** The Maya were the only New World culture to develop a fully functional writing system, and in recent years, great advances have been made in decoding the Maya hieroglyphs. The texts can be used to corroborate archaeological data.
>
> **3.** There was no division between science and religion, and numerology and astrology were central to the Maya belief system. Blood sacrifice was also practiced to ensure continuation of the cycle of life.

> **C.** Around A.D. 900, classic Maya civilization collapsed: The Maya stopped building grand temples, writing hieroglyphic texts, and maintaining their key calendrical system. Increasing warfare and ecological stress led to the collapse.

II. The Maya did not mysteriously disappear at the collapse, however; they simply stopped living in their previous cities. Post-classic Maya civilizations (A.D. 900–1524) arose in the highland region of Guatemala and Chiapas, Mexico.

III. Today, about half the population of Guatemala is made up of Maya Indians.

> **A.** Guatemala is a relatively small country (about the size of Tennessee) with a population of about 12 million.
>
> > **1.** More than 21 separate Mayan languages are spoken in Guatemala today; these are further divided along town-specific dialects.
> >
> > **2.** Traditional dress is the most visible marker of Maya identity for indigenous women. The hand-woven skirts and blouses are patterned on community-specific styles.

> **B.** Guatemala has an extremely high poverty rate; more than half of the population lives in poverty and over 16 percent, in extreme poverty. Guatemala ranks among the worst in Latin America for life expectancy, infant mortality, literacy, and other measures.

> **C.** Guatemalan society is divided between the indigenous and *ladino* (or non-Indian) populace. Indians suffer the highest poverty rates in the country and widespread discrimination.

> **D.** Tecpán Guatemala is a Kaqchikel Maya town located in Guatemala's western highlands, where I have conducted long-term fieldwork.

1. Tecpán is located in *tierra fría*, 7,000 feet above sea-level, alongside the Pan-American Highway.
2. It was the site of the pre-contact Kaqchikel Empire and the first Spanish capital in Guatemala.
3. Today, there are some 10,000 residents in the town proper, about 70 percent Indian and 30 percent *ladino*.
4. The town is famous for its large Thursday market, which attracts buyers and sellers from the whole region.

E. The Maya of Guatemala have retained many of their distinctive customs over the centuries.

IV. Since the time of contact, the Maya have periodically suffered from violent repression. This reached a peak in the early 1980s, a period known as *la violencia*.

A. Marxist guerrillas emerged in the Maya highlands of Guatemala in the mid-1970s. The Guatemalan military dictatorship responded with overwhelming force.
1. From 1978 to 1981, Guatemala was ruled by General Romeo Lucas Garcia, who promoted a policy of draining the sea of Indians in order to catch the Marxist fish. The violence further escalated from 1981–1982 under the rule of General Efraín Ríos Montt.
2. Tens of thousands were killed in massacres; the vast majority of the violence was carried out by the army against indigenous villagers.
3. Although peace accords were signed in 1996, violence still plagues Guatemalan society.

B. Tecpán suffered enormously through the violence.
1. In 1976, Tecpán was hit by a devastating earthquake, and the whole town was destroyed.
2. In 1981, a Catholic priest was murdered, the town hall was bombed, and the army set up a garrison off the central plaza. At least 20 clandestine graves have been identified in the area.

V. Distinctive patterns of religious beliefs—some Western and some indigenous—also characterize Maya peoples.

A. Traditionalist Maya religion invokes the pre-Columbian sacred covenant between gods and humans. Religious specialists called "day-keepers" (*aj q'ij*) perform rituals and curings to combat the work of evil spirits and malevolent sorcerers.

B. About 60 percent of Tecpánecos are at least nominally Catholic and practice a hybrid form of Catholicism and native worship.

Readings:

Robert Carmack, *Harvest of Violence.*

Edward F. Fischer and Carol Hendrickson, *Tecpán Guatemala: A Modern Maya Town in Local and Global Context.*

Rigoberta Menchu, *I Rigoberta Menchu, an Indian Woman.*

Victor Monetjo, *Testimonio: Death of a Guatemalan Village.*

Questions to Consider:

1. How are the modern Maya of Guatemala related to classic-era Maya civilization?

2. Did the civil war in Guatemala fail because it was class-based rather than ethnic-based?

3. How did the culture of terror in Guatemala affect traditional Maya culture?

Lecture Twenty-Two—Transcript
The Maya, Ancient and Modern

In the last few lectures, we discussed the expansion of Western societies, the development of capitalism as a mode of production that spread around the world, and the interplay of culture and economy in our own society. In this section of the course, we're going to turn to globalization. We're constantly reminded by media pundits, academics, business leaders that the world is a much smaller place than it once was.

As proof, we simply have to look around us. Overnight delivery and e-mail have accelerated the pace and expanded the possibilities of social and commercial interaction. The Internet has spawned long-distance friendships and collaborations that seamlessly span continents and time zones. Much of our clothing and other consumer goods are assembled abroad. We have a good idea about what all of this means to us, but what does it mean to them, those people who live at the periphery of the globalized economy? And what can we learn from anthropology about this rapidly changing world?

Today we turn to a particular case study, our last case study of the course, and one that's very close to my heart, and that is of the Maya of Guatemala, where I've done most of my fieldwork as a cultural anthropologist. We're going to use the Maya to illustrate a number of topics that we've discussed in the class thus far, from physical anthropology and archaeology to linguistics, but, more than anything else, the Mayan case demonstrates the malleability and the resilience of culture. Maya culture is certainly not the same as it was 1,000 years ago. Culture is constantly changing; this is the one great rule of culture, but through such change runs threads of continuity as well, and that's what we're going to focus on today.

When you think about the Maya, the image that probably first comes to mind is of the ancient Maya, the temples rising up out of the lowland rain forests of Central America, those grand city-states Tikal, Copan, Palenque, Dos Pilas, and others, and this is the Maya of the Classic era, and the Classic era lasted from about A.D. 250 to about A.D. 900. This was when Mayan civilization really flourished, ancient Mayan civilization really flourished, and they demonstrated all of these grandiose elements that really capture the Western imagination, notably, hieroglyphic writing. Mayan civilization was the only civilization in the new world to develop a fully developed writing system, and it was a mix of ideographic symbols and syllabic symbols. The Maya also were adept astronomers: they kept eclipse charts; they knew Saturn; they kept charts of Saturn's movement. They were very well developed astronomers and also mathematicians.

The Mayan developed the concept of zero before it was developed in the West, before it was developed in India, and they also kept elaborate calendrical systems that were related to their religious beliefs. A couple of the important calendrical systems—first of all is the long count system, and this provides an absolute date, an absolute date just as our own dating system does, of the 5th of July, 2004, for example, and because we've been able to decipher Mayan hieroglyphs, and there's been an explosion of decipherment in the last few years, because we've been able to decipher Mayan hieroglyphs and this calendrical system, we've converted what was once a prehistoric civilization into a historic civilization. Using Mayan calendrical systems, we can date when particular kings took the throne, when city-states fought with each other, and so this is one of those fascinating cases where a prehistoric civilization has become, for archaeologists and anthropologists, a historic civilization. The Maya had the long count calendrical system. They had another calendrical system that we call the calendar round, and this was a 260-day calendar, and 260 days, interestingly enough, approximates the human gestation period. This calendar round, this 260-day calendar, was used for divinational purposes.

The ancient Maya practiced blood sacrifice as part of their religious practices, not quite as bloody as ancient Aztec civilization but, nonetheless, blood sacrifice is an important part of Mayan religion. Maya peoples thought that they had to offer blood to the gods in order to continue the cycle of creation. Some of the sacrifice occurred with enemies. Soldiers would be captured from enemy city-states, taken back to temples, and then sacrificed to the gods, but the best sort of blood sacrifice came not from enemy soldiers but from the Maya royalty themselves.

The Maya believed that the kings were related to the gods, physically related to the gods, and so the best sort of blood sacrifice would be this royal blood, this almost godly blood. There are images from ancient Mayan hieroglyphic text of queens, for example, Mayan noble women, running strings with spikes on them through their tongue and collecting the blood below to offer as a sacrifice. As gruesome as that sounds, the male nobility had it even worse. Maya kings would perforate the foreskin of their penis with a stingray spine and collect the blood that way and offer it to the gods. This is obviously symbolic of firtility, the blood coming out of the penis and being collected and then offered up to the gods.

Something happened around A.D. 900; we call it the Maya collapse. Some anthropologists would say we should avoid the term collapse; it gives the wrong impression. The Maya didn't disappear, but they did stop building these grand city-states. They even stopped living in these city-states. They stopped erecting monuments with hieroglyphic text. They stopped using the calendrical system, so they stopped using a lot of these elements that we consider to be characteristic of classic Mayan civilization. But the Maya didn't die out; they were still around, and in fact there was another flourishing of Mayan civilization in what we call the post-classic period. The post-classic period begins around A.D. 900, around the time of Mayan collapse, and ends around 1524 with the arrival of the Spaniards. Classic Mayan civilization was concentrated in the lowland areas of Central America, Guatemala, and Mexico and Belize. Post-classic Mayan civilization was concentrated in the highland areas of this region, and it is a very militaristic civilization with fortified city-states.

I'm going to jump over the 300 years of Spanish colonial rule, of independent civilization and move to the modern Maya of Guatemala, which is where I work today. Today, over half of the population of Guatemala are Mayan Indians, and this is a country about the size of Tennessee, about the size of the state of Tennessee, with a population of about 12 million, and half of the population are Mayan Indians. It's a country of striking contrasts, of geographic contrasts, dramatic mountain peaks and valleys, a very verdant area, with volcanoes and mountains and so forth. It's also a country of striking social contrasts. It's not a poor country, and yet it's rife with poverty. Almost half of the population of Guatemala live in poverty, and this is according to World Bank figures, which mark poverty at $2.00 a day, living at under $2.00 a day. This figure jumps even higher if we look only at the Mayan population in Guatemala, only at the Indians. About 68 percent of the Indians live in poverty, and about 20 percent live in extreme poverty, meaning that they don't earn enough even to supply their basic subsistence needs.

A physical anthropologist, a colleague, Barry Bogin, has looked at the height of the Maya, and for a long time the Maya were considered to be the pygmies of Central America, and this was seen to be a genetic basis to their height. However, Bogin has looked at Mayan immigrants to the United States and has found that once they arrive in the States their height goes up, and the height of their children goes up dramatically. In fact, they're not the pygmies of Central America; it's a function of poverty and not a function of their genetic heritage. It recalls the studies of Franz Boas that we talked about in the early part of the class, where he looked at Italian immigrants to the United States in the early 20th century and proved that they were not inherently inferior to native Americans, they just didn't speak the language, and they didn't have the nutritional resources that native Americans had.

Guatemala is a country, not a poor country, but a country divided by access to wealth, with some very rich people and lots of very poor people, and this is related to access to land. In Guatemala, 95 percent of landowners, and these are mostly peasants, mostly Mayan peasants, 95 percent of landowners own 20 percent of the land, and two percent of landowners own about 69 percent of the land. There's a vast inequality in access to land, and this is an agricultural society, and so this shows the extent of poverty. Guatemala has one of the highest genic coefficients in the world. The genic coefficient is a measure of inequality. It ranges from zero in hypothetical situations of perfect equality, where everybody in a country or society makes exactly the same amount of money, to one in hypothetical situations of perfect inequality, where one person earned all of the income in the country and everybody else earned nothing. In Guatemala, this genic coefficient is 0.58, and that places it right up there with Brazil and Sierra Leone, with the most unequal countries in the world.

This inequality has ethnic correlations, and we have two main ethnic groups in Guatemala, the Maya and who we call the Ladinos. The Mayan Indians, the Indians are descendants of the ancient Maya, the native peoples, and they're characterized by a number of different traits. Maya peoples generally speak a Mayan language, and there are 21 different languages spoken in Guatemala, again, a country the size of Tennessee, 21 separate languages, and this doesn't include the dialectical variations as well, so there's quite a bit of linguistic diversity, which is related in part to the geographic diversity of the country. Mayas speak a native language; they generally wear traditional dress, particularly the women. Lots of men have stopped wearing their traditional dress; the women still wear traditional dress, which you've probably seen before, these elaborately colored and hand-woven *huipiles*, or blouses, and skirts as well. The Maya generally practice a hybrid form of Catholicism and indigenous religious practices, and this is something that we're going to come back to later in the lecture.

In Guatemala, about half the population are Mayan Indians, speaking a native language, wearing traditional dress, practicing this hybrid form of religion. The other half of the population we characterize as Ladinos, and this is a word that they don't use themselves to characterize themselves. They just would call themselves Guatemalans, but Ladinos see themselves as being the bearers of the Spanish tradition. We define them generally negatively in relation to the Mayan. They don't speak a Mayan language; they speak Spanish. They don't use traditional dress; they wear Western-style clothes. They're generally Catholic, although there's a growing population of Protestants as well. There are poor Ladinos and there are rich Ladinos, but the richest people, the most powerful people in Guatemalan society, are never Indians, they're always Ladinos, so Ladinos are associated with power and wealth in Guatemala, even if there are a number of poor Ladinos.

In Guatemala you often hear elites talk about the "Indian problem" of their country. Of course, this is a problem not for the Indians but for the Ladinos, and the Ladino see the Indians as being a bit backward, a bit stupid, a bit ignorant, a barrier to development. We could become a nation-state like France or Spain in this model of Western Europe except we have this backward, ignorant, savage Indian population that's holding us back from realizing our development potential. As a result, we have a high level of discrimination in Guatemalan society. Indians will walk into stores and be ignored. In government offices they'll be called upon last when they're waiting in line, for example. They're very often treated as children. In Spanish, we have two pronouns for the second person singular, the formal pronoun *usted* and the informal pronoun *tu*, and very often Ladinos, even Ladino children, will call Mayas, even Mayan elders, by the informal pronoun, whereas they expect to be referred to by the formal pronoun, and this is a form of putting Indians in their place. They're childlike; they can be treated with this *tu* form, this informal pronoun form.

I've done most of my work as a cultural anthropologist in a town in highland Guatemala called Tecpan, Tecpan Guatemala. It's a Kaqchikel Maya-speaking town, Kaqchikel is one of the 21 languages in Guatemala, and it's located in the western highlands of the country, about 7,000 feet above sea level, what they call *tierra fria*, the cold land, because it's eternally chilly at this altitude. It was the site of the pre-contact Kaqchikel empire, which was located on the site of Iximche right outside of the town of Tecpan, and it was also the first Spanish capital of Guatemala, where Pedro de Alvarado, Cortes's lieutenant who was sent down from central Mexico to conquer the Maya, established his first capital at Iximche.

We've talked about the archaeology of the ancient Maya, and for Tecpanecos, archaeology has a very personal meaning, with Iximche, the site of the pre-Columbian Kaqchikel empire, as being a point of pride. We lived in the home of the ancient Mayan empire; we were the site of the first

Spanish capital. And Tecpaneco farmers are always picking up pottery shards and sometimes even complete vessels in their fields, and they treat these with a form of reverence and respect, even if they sometimes sell them on the black market, but there's this connection with their archaeological heritage, and they feel like this is part of who they are.

Tecpan is a fairly small town, about 10,000 residents, mostly Indians, 70 percent Indian, and to the casual observer it appears as a typical Mayan town. However, in the region, it's known as a very affluent and progressive place. I was struck when I first moved to Tecpan to do my fieldwork in the early 1990s by the fact that they had two beauty pageants, and I should have expected this, knowing the history of discrimination in Guatemala between Ladinos and Indians, but being from the south I'm very sensitive to racial segregation. I was surprised that in Tecpan they have two annual beauty pageants, one to elect a Ladino queen and one to elect a Maya queen. This just sort of gives you an idea of the extent of discrimination; having two beauty pageants is seen as being a very progressive thing. "We have a Maya queen, we let them have their own ceremony, and so we're being very open and progressive by doing that."

Maya peoples, because they suffer discrimination, sometimes pass as Ladinos. This is possible because there's been so much intermixing, so much racial mixing over the centuries, that physically lots of Maya could pass for being Ladinos, for being Spaniards, and so if they learn Spanish really well, if they drop their native language and learn Spanish, they stop wearing traditional dress and start wearing Western clothes, and if they move from their natal communities, particularly if they move to a big city, they can virtually pass as Ladinos and then not suffer this discrimination in the university, in the work place, or whatever it may be. There's still a glass ceiling; they can't make it up to the very upper echelons of society, but, nonetheless, passing as a Ladino can provide them with some level of upward mobility.

Guatemala suffered greatly from a period known as *la violencia* in the late 1970s and early 1980s. Guatemala had had a period of military dictators leading up to this time, but repression had never been a fact of daily life. However, in the late 1970s, Marxist guerrilla groups emerged in the Maya-dominated highlands of Guatemala, and the army came out and decided that we have to stamp out these Marxist guerrillas at all costs. They were supported in this by the United States, and of course this was a period in which there were civil wars raging in Central America. The Sandinistas had taken over in Nicaragua, there was civil war going on in El Salvador, and the fear was that if the Marxists are successful in Guatemala, if they take over Guatemala, then they're right there in Mexico, and Mexico's always been sort of suspiciously leftist anyway, and then if it were able to move up to Mexico, they would be right here at the border of the United States and pose an imminent threat to our own national security.

In the late 1970s, a new general came to power, General Romeo Lucas Garcia, and he was followed by General Efrain Rios Montt, and under their rule the violence really stepped up. This was a period of kidnappings, of tortures, of secret jails, of razed earth policy, coming in in helicopters and destroying whole Mayan villages, burning down houses, burning down crops, expelling people from their native communities, and so forth. The idea was that Mayan Indians, being a little bit stupid, being a little bit ignorant, they're very vulnerable to the silver-tongued oratory of these Marxist guerrillas who will come into their towns and try and convert them to their cause, and also the Maya are by far the poorest members of Guatemalan society, so they would be the natural constituency for a Marxist revolution. The idea was, what we need to do is drain the pond in order to catch the fish. This is a great opportunity, this war against Marxist rebels, to get rid of our Indian problem once and for all. If we can wipe out the Indian population, then we will wipe out the base of support for Marxist guerrillas and also create an ethnically homogeneous society, which will allow us to develop in the way in which we want.

Guatemala was extremely affected during the violence. We speak a lot about terrorism these days, but this is the sort of terrorism that's hard for us to imagine. I recall recently I was talking with a friend of mine from Tecpan and he was describing what it was like living there in the early 1980s, lying in bed at night and hearing the soldiers walk by, and wondering if they were going to stop at his door and bust in and rip him out of bed and take him down to the local garrison for questioning, questioning from which people normally didn't emerge, at least not alive. Their bodies might be found a few days later by the side of the road, with cigarette burns or missing limbs or fingers as a sign for what might happen if one was considered to be a subversive.

This period of violence, the U.N. truth commission, which was established after the peace accords which were signed in 1996, looked at the massacres that happened in Guatemala. We're talking about tens of thousands of people being killed, hundreds of thousands of people being kidnapped and tortured, and hundreds of thousands, perhaps even millions of people being expelled from their homes, communities. The U.N. truth commission determined that this was actually a case of genocide, that the Mayan population had been intentionally targeted to wipe them out. The peace accords were signed in 1996, formally ending this period of violence. The violence had actually died down in the late 1980s, although you'd still have periodic guerilla attacks plaguing Maya communities.

Today, as an aside, I would mention that there is a Guatemalan forensic anthropology team doing some wonderful work, digging up these massacre sites from Mayan villages and trying to reconstruct what happened, this history that was never written, that was hidden intentionally by the military of what they did. This is very important work in the way in which physical anthropologists are able to use the techniques of physical anthropology and archaeology to reconstruct very recent history in a politically important way.

I would like to conclude the lecture today by talking about cultural resilience and hybridity. I mention religion, that most Mayan peoples and the Mayan peoples of Tecpan practice a hybrid form of Catholicism and native religion. Most people are nominally Roman Catholic, but this is a Roman Catholicism that's been infused over the centuries with native religious beliefs and practices. Much like the Fulbe, whom we discussed earlier in the course with Islam, the Maya have adopted Catholicism, but they've really made it their own, and most still practice some form of native Mayan religion.

Mayan religious practices were especially open to adopting new elements when the Spaniards arrived. The Spaniards said, "You have to worship at the cross." It turns out that a cross was a very important icon in ancient Mayan religions, so the Maya said, "Worship at a cross? That's fine, we can do that." The Spaniards said, "You have to participate in communion, this blood sacrifice," and the Maya said, "Yes, we can understand that, sacrificing blood to continue the cycle of creation," and so there was a melding in the early years of contact and the centuries of contact since between Roman Catholicism and native Mayan religions.

In native Mayan religious beliefs, there's a blurry boundary between the material world and the spiritual world. They believe the two are intimately related in a way in which we see as being very separated in the Western tradition. They also believe that there's a covenant between humans and the gods, a reciprocal relationship. Humans have to give sacrifices and praises to the gods in order to continue the cycle of regeneration. Also very important in native Mayan beliefs is a notion of balance, of physical balance and metaphysical balance. They have various forms of the soul, but they believe that the soul needs to be planted and centered. In fact, after a birth, they will plant the umbilical cord of the infant in order to plant that infant's soul and ground them in the earth in what's important.

A lot of Mayan religion revolves around maintaining this metaphysical balance of forces acting on the human soul, and this is related to conceptions of illness. There are hot illnesses, for example, and cold illnesses. If you suffer from a hot illness, you would drink cold fluids, for example, to counteract that and bring your metabolism back into balance. One woman told me a story one time that she was pregnant, and she was walking out to the well in her garden, and she saw a poisonous snake crawl in front of her. She went back inside and she urinated in a cup and she threw the urine on the snake. Pregnancy is considered to be a very hot state, and by throwing this urine, this hot urine on the snake, it killed it instantly. Interestingly enough, while pregnancy is considered to be a very hot state, fetuses are considered to be cold, and there's a whole series of rituals that goes around heating up the fetus in the womb.

We can conceive of Mayan religious practices in terms of cultural models that we talked about earlier in the class. The Maya believe that there are various kinds of souls, but the most important soul is called *koosh*, and this is the heart soul. They speak about people in terms of how this heart soul is, this *koosh* is. One could have a hard heart or a happy heart, and what everybody wants is a balanced and grounded heart. But one's heart is shaped and molded through one's life experiences, and this can change over time. There's a story—a man I know in Tecpan was shanghaied by the army some years ago during the violence and taken off and put through this incredible basic training, this incredibly brutal basic training.

They were given a puppy when they started their basic training that they had to carry with them all the time, feed him—they couldn't leave this puppy at any point during the day— and at the end of basic training they had to slit the dog's throat and ritually drink a little bit of the blood to inoculate them against the horrors of such violence. Before he left, before he was shanghaied by the army, this guy was a wonderful man, a wonderful father, a wonderful son, an active participant in the politics of the local community, but he comes back and he drinks a lot. He started abusing his wife and his family. They eventually left him and his life really disintegrated, and the way in which Tecpanecos talk about this is that his heart, his *koosh*, was changed. It became uncentered through this horrible process that he suffered through basic training.

The Maya have different sorts of religious specialists. Their primary shamans are called *aj q'ij*, and this literally means day-keepers, and they maintain a sacred calendar. In fact, although the ancient Maya stopped practicing the long count, the absolute dating system, they've continued to practice up until this day, continued to maintain the calendar round, the 260-day calendar that helps people divine spiritual illnesses. These *aj q'ij*, these shamans, these day-keepers, will use this calendar to diagnose illnesses, spiritual illnesses and physical illnesses in people and prescribe particular rituals to cure them. There are also malevolent shamans who are called *aj q'ijts,* malevolent witches, and these are almost inevitably really antisocial people in town. One man I know who's accused of being a witch in Tecpan, he doesn't shave, he's never gotten married, he lives alone, he reads funny sorts of books and so forth, and he doesn't participate in the rituals of daily life. As a result, he's accused of being a witch, and this is very common, not only in Mayan society but in other societies around the world, accusations of witchcraft.

The staple of Mayan subsistence is maize agriculture, what we call milpa agriculture, maize and beans grown together as staple crops. Maize and beans are almost a perfect diet actually, supplying when eaten together all of the essential amino acids. I'm going to talk more about Mayan agriculture in the last lecture of the course, but I wanted to mention here the fact that the Maya feel very tied to the land, and it's related to this idea of souls having to be grounded, having to be centered in some way. Even as Mayan society has been changing through the processes of modernization and globalization, this connection to the land has remained.

I remember one time some friends of mine from Tecpan, the town in which I worked, had moved out of town and had started living in Guatemala City, the capital. They had gone to the university, they had gotten good paying professional jobs, and they were raising their children in the capital. Nonetheless, they maintained their milpa lands, their maize plots in Tecpan, and they would go back periodically to check on these, and they would use the maize that was harvested for their daily needs. In fact, they would say, "It's not really filling to eat maize that's not from one's own land. It doesn't taste the same. It doesn't physically nourish us in the same way." This couple, Pical and Rosa, would hire a person to cultivate their land for them, and they would split the crop at the end of the day, a sharecropping arrangement.

One day when I was living in Tecpan, they came in from the capital and they said, "Let's go out to our fields. The harvest is just over. Why don't we go out and check on the fields?" We drive for about an hour, we walk for about another hour, and we finally reach their fields, which are located in a remote hamlet on the outskirts of town. We spend all day long going around and picking up the pieces of maize that had been left behind from the harvest, and we end up filling about two nets, and they collect maize in nets, two nets full of maize. At the end of the day, we carry this back and put it in the truck and drive back into town, and I start thinking, "This is an incredible waste of time. You guys make good money in the capital, and yet you've taken a day off to come here and to harvest the little bit of maize that you could have easily bought with just a few hours of your labor when you were selling it."

But that was missing the point really, because what was important was not the material value of the corn that they had salvaged from the harvest but the fact of not letting any of the sacred corn go to waste. The Maya origin myths say that humans are made from corn. They're men of corn, people of corn, and so in this way it was important for them to come back and salvage even a little corn kernel that was left on the ground. It was important not to be wasted, and this was for spiritual reasons as much as material reasons.

The Maya, to conclude, the Maya have this glorious history of the ancient Maya and developing calendrical systems and mathematical knowledge and astronomical knowledge. They suffered over the centuries from Spanish colonialism and more recently this period of violence in the late 1970s and early 1980s, and yet, nonetheless, they're able to retain these spiritual bases of Mayan culture that give their life meaning.

Lecture Twenty-Three
Maya Resurgence in Guatemala and Mexico

Scope: *Ethnicity* is a slippery term. In some ways, it has come to replace *race* as a socially acceptable way of categorizing people, and it is often used as a synonym for *cultural heritage*. Some view ethnicity as ingrained and innate. But in this lecture, we look to ways that cultural elements can be strategically used in building ethnic identity—the ways that ethnicities are constructed and deployed as political tools. Various identity markers—including language, dress, and cuisine—create boundaries that define in-groups and out-groups. In Guatemala, such markers have historically been the focus of discrimination against indigenous peoples, but in recent years, the Maya, like indigenous peoples around the world, have begun to revitalize their cultural traditions and take pride in their ethnic identity. In this lecture, we examine their efforts and their surprising successes. We also look to the Zapatistas of Chiapas, Mexico. The Zapatistas have taken a more revolutionary and confrontational approach, forging strategic links with international organizations. The leader of the Zapatistas, Subcomandante Marcos, is not himself an Indian, but he has become a powerful symbol of Maya resistance.

Outline

I. Ethnicity as a social category encompasses key aspects of race, language, and culture. Ethnicity implies a common origin for the ethnic group.

   A. Despite its putative genealogical and biological connotations, ethnicity is also something that is actively constructed, performed, and improvised on.

   B. We use various markers to help us identify ethnic origins, but these can be misleading.
      1. Language is a useful ethnic marker because it is not easily adopted or shed and reflects sustained socialization.
      2. Clothing is a very visible, yet easily adapted, marker of identity.
      3. Racial features are the most common ethnic markers.

II. Out of the ashes of the Guatemalan holocaust has emerged a pan-Maya movement that seeks to revalue indigenous culture.

    A. The pan-Maya movement seeks to unify the disparate Maya ethno-linguistic groups and communities to exert influence in the Guatemalan democratic process more effectively.

    B. Pan-Maya leaders have strategically emphasized that their work is with cultural and linguistic rights to avoid deadly political repercussions.

        1. A number of young Maya leaders have been trained in linguistics, and among their first efforts were to have Mayan languages officially recognized and to develop a unified alphabet.

        2. These native linguists are adding new words to the vocabularies of Mayan languages so that speakers need not resort to Spanish when speaking about technology or business.

        3. Female pan-Mayanists have also developed new styles of traditional dress that crosscut historic town-specific designs.

    C. Pan-Mayanists glorify the Maya past with a vision of a more pluralistic future Guatemala.

        1. They portray classic Maya civilization as learned and largely peaceful, downplaying blood sacrifice.

        2. They have resurrected hieroglyphic writing and ancient calendrical systems to use in their publications.

    D. Given the repressive atmosphere of Guatemalan national politics, the pan-Maya activists have had surprising success. They were able to work many of their key demands into the 1996 peace accords.

III. Just over the border in Mexico, Maya activists have taken a different stance. There, Zapatista rebels are leading an armed conflict to extract legal and economic concessions from the government.

    A. The Zapatista rebellion began on 1 January 1994, when armed and masked rebels took over the city of San Cristóbal and a number of other communities in Chiapas.

        1. Chiapas is the poorest state in Mexico and, with its high density of Maya peoples, is much like Guatemala.

        2. Most Maya communities in Chiapas depend on *milpa* agriculture, which has been threatened in recent years by large-scale farming.

B. The 1 January 1994 initial uprising was timed to correspond to the initial implementation of the North American Free Trade Agreement (NAFTA).

    1. The Zapatista movement is firmly anti-globalization and has made alliances with other anti-globalization movements. Ironically, they have used the Internet and other globalized technologies to press their claims.

    2. The Zapatistas especially oppose NAFTA-led efforts to privatize communal lands.

    3. The Zapatista Army of National Liberation takes its name from the Mexican national hero Emiliano Zapata.

C. The Zapatistas are led by Subcomandante Marcos, who has become a Mexican pop icon. Marcos often writes his revolutionary communiqués in poetry or as fables. He always wears a black ski mask and is usually smoking a pipe.

    1. Marcos has been identified as Rafael Guillén Vicente, a former university professor who moved to the southern Mexican jungle in the mid-1980s.

    2. Marcos is not Maya. He is the son of an upper-middle-class furniture store owner in Tampico.

    3. But, hiding behind his mask, Marcos refuses to be categorized. Indeed, he blends indigenous Maya, Spanish Mexican, and Western cultures into a new, postmodern form.

Readings:

Edward F. Fischer and R. McKenna Brown, eds., *Maya Cultural Activism in Guatemala.*

Matthew Gutman, *The Romance of Democracy.*

Subcomandante Marcos, *Our Words Are Our Weapons.*

Questions to Consider:

1. Does it matter that Subcomandante Marcos is not Maya?

2. How have the Maya of Guatemala used their cultural heritage as a form of social capital?

3. What are the most reliable markers of ethnic identity? Have you ever been mistaken when assuming someone's background?

Lecture Twenty-Three—Transcript
Maya Resurgence in Guatemala and Mexico

There's been an explosion of ethnic identity movements around the world at the turn of the 21st century. Today, we're going to continue discussing the Maya of Guatemala, as well as the Maya of southern Mexico, to look at the resurgence of ethnic identity and the practice of identity politics in the modern world. We're going to look first to the burgeoning pan-Mayan movement in Guatemala and its culture-based and nonviolent approach to working for indigenous rights, and there we're going to turn to the Mayan Zapatista revolution in Chiapas, Mexico, that emerged in 1994.

But first, let me say a few words about ethnicity. Ethnicity, I think, today is very often used as a code word for race. We generally consider it in anthropology to be the expression or the presentation of cultural differences. It overlaps in some important ways with the social category of race, but race has become a little bit impolite to invoke in conversations, and so often today where we would have not that many years ago talked about race, today we talk about ethnicity. A good definition of ethnicity is simply a system of social classification that creates meaningful groups based around certain cultural features. We call these cultural features ethnic markers.

Let me just go over a few ethnic markers to give you an idea of what they are, primarily language. Language is an incredibly important ethnic marker. It's not easily adopted, it's not easily shed, and so it can reflect very well one's cultural origins. It can tell a lot about a person's heritage, at least to the extent that language and culture overlap. We have language; dress is also an important ethnic marker, and dress is more easily adopted. We can think of different sorts of dress ethnic markers: Afghan headdresses, Muslim women's veils, and Mayan dress. Mayan dress both marks people as being Indian, as opposed to Ladino in Guatemala, and it marks regional differences and even town-specific differences. In Guatemala, every town has its own particular style of native Mayan dress. You can look at a *huipile*, a blouse, and you can say that's from Tecpan or that's from Patzun or that's from Comalapa.

We have language, we have dress, and we also have phenotypic features, race, what we would generally consider to be race. Racial features are less useful as indicators of cultural heritage, especially in this day and age, in which we have people living in different parts of the world and so many immigrants in our own country that race can often mislead us about one's cultural heritage. Sociobiologists would say that ethnicity is useful as a shorthand for determining or estimating probable genetic relatedness and that we're more likely to help out people from our own ethnic group because it would be helping our own gene pool, but from a cultural standpoint ethnicity is the presentation of one's cultural identity. It's not much of an issue in small-scale societies. Among the Dobe Ju/'Hoansi, ethnicity is not much of an issue because they're the only people in their society, but in multicultural societies ethnicity becomes very important.

A crucial point about ethnicity, and this is something that was brought home by the anthropologist Frederick Barth, is that what's more important than the cultural stuff of ethnicity, these markers, are the boundaries that ethnicity creates. This is really the purpose of ethnicity, to create in-groups and out-groups and to distinguish between the two. Ethnicity is always contextually defined. It depends, we can invoke different aspects of our identity in different circumstances, and this is true with ethnicity as well, and this is most clearly seen in immigrant populations, so Mayan Indians in Guatemala, for example, are Indians, Indihinas, Indios, but when they come to the States they become Latinos or Hispanics, given this different sort of context, and so ethnicity can change depending on the context. There are also two versions whether ethnicity is imposed from the outside, Indians coming up from Guatemala to the States, and we as a society say now you're Latinos, for example, imposed from the outside, versus self-identity, self-identity ethnicity.

Ethnicity has become especially important in recent years as a vehicle for identity politics. Identity politics is just what the term implies; it's the use of certain cultural elements, elements of identity, toward political ends. You'll recall we discussed earlier in the course the distinction that Pierre Bourdieu makes between economic capital and symbolic capital, or cultural capital. Identity politics is really using cultural capital, leveraging cultural capital for political advantage. Given this context, I'd like to talk a little bit about Mayan resurgence in Guatemala.

Amazingly, out of the ashes of the Guatemalan holocaust of the late 1970s and early 1980s emerged an ethnic revitalization movement among the Maya. They are promoting cultural revitalization that they hope will bring about a pan-Mayan unity. Remember the Maya are half the population in Guatemala, and yet they're divided by language—they speak 21 different languages. Each community has its own particular dialect as well. They're divided by dress, they're divided by geography, they're divided by local ties. Most Guatemalan Maya primarily identify themselves with the town that they were born in. Who are you? I'm a Tecpanecos, I'm a Patsunero, I'm a Komolapeno, or whatever it may be.

What the pan-Mayan activists, what these cultural activists want to do, is unites the Mayan people, culturally have them identified first and foremost as being Indians and not being from a particular town or being speakers of a particular language but being Indians. If they're able to do that, since they make up half or more than half of the population, they can exert their political influence through the democratic process and bring about changes in society. These pan-Mayan activists very much glorify the ancient Mayan past. They point to the literacy of classic Mayan civilization, they point to the scientific advances of classic Mayan civilization, and they say, "We don't need to be embarrassed about being Maya; we don't need to be ashamed. Our ancestors created this wonderful, glorious civilization that we should be proud of rather than being ashamed of being modern Indians."

They glorify the ancient Mayan past with a vision toward a more pluralistic future in Guatemala. What they're really doing is seeking political power, socioeconomic equality through cultural revitalization, and they're looking for a peaceful solution to Guatemala's many ills, not an armed revolution, and this is significant. Coming off of this history of violence, they're not saying we want to overthrow the Guatemalan state; rather, they're focusing on cultural issues. We want to preserve Mayan languages, we want to record Mayan religious practices, we want to encourage Maya people to wear traditional dress, and these are actions or requests or demands that are seen as being especially palatable to the powers that be and not being threatening in a way that would get the leaders of this movement killed, and it wasn't that long ago, and even to this day, political assassinations are not out of the question in Guatemala.

The Maya have focused on these cultural issues, and specifically linguistics in the early days of this pan-Maya movement in the 1980s and 1990s, focusing on linguistic issues which are non-threatening to the powers that be and in doing so combating entrenched Ladino racism against Indians. The Ladinos in Guatemala, for example, very often call Indian languages dialects. It's just a *dialecto*; they don't really speak a language, it's just a dialect, but of course they are real languages and they're not lacking in contrast to Spanish. By revaluing Mayan languages, they're able to promote cultural equality. As part of this process, they've been developing new words, neologisms that are used to expand the vocabulary of Mayan languages and show that they can express just as complex ideas as Spanish can.

For example, whereas not too many years ago, there was just one word in Kaqchikel Maya for all things metal, a bicycle, a typewriter, whatever it may be—it was *ch'ich*. This was just metal thing, and you would have to understand from the context what was being referred to. But today they've expanded the vocabulary of this native Mayan language to include things like computation, and it's interesting. In doing this, what they do is they call on salient cultural metaphors from Mayan society and then transpose these metaphors into new domains. For computing, for example, they call computers *kematz'ib*, which means weaver of writing, weaving a very salient process in Mayan towns and culture, and so they're able to take this model of what weaving is and then transpose it into this new domain of computation, and it's something that's very familiar to people, familiar and new at the same time, so computers are weavers of writing, computer programs are the warp of writing, computer archives are woven writing, and so forth.

They've also been working to unify the alphabets used to write Mayan languages. Hieroglyphic writing died out centuries ago, but they've adopted Latin characters to represent modern Mayan languages. But in doing so, missionaries who did most of this work developed different alphabets for each language group. One missionary would go work with the Kaqchikel Maya, another missionary would go and work with the Kiche Maya, and they would develop different alphabets for each of these languages. The Mayan activists see this as further dividing, dividing and conquering the Mayan people, and so these Mayan activists said if we can come up with one alphabet to represent all 21 Mayan languages in Guatemala, this will increase literacy and also allow Mayan groups from one language area to understand more or less what is being written about in another Mayan area and so promote pan-Mayan unity in the process.

They're also using a lot of symbols from ancient Mayan culture. They've resurrected hieroglyphic writing actually and use this on book covers and pamphlet covers, for example. Most Mayan people in Guatemala are illiterate in the first place, so they don't even understand Latin-based Mayan writing. But the power of the hieroglyphic symbols still means something to them. It still represents this grandeur of ancient Mayan civilization. I had mentioned that the long count calendar, this absolute dating system had died out centuries ago, but again pan-Mayan activists in Guatemala have reactivated this. They've learned from Western scholars such as myself how this ancient system works and then reclaimed it as their own, and they've started to use this long count dating system on the cover of books and pamphlets once again, and most people can't read it, like the hieroglyphic writing, but it still makes an important symbolic statement about the literacy and the grandeur of ancient Mayan civilization.

They've also been tweaking cultural elements such as dress. I mentioned earlier that each town has its own specific dress, but in recent years Mayan women have begun to mix and match pieces from different towns. It's part of a stylistic thing, fashionable. "There's no reason why I have to just wear the dress from my own town; I really like the blouses from the neighboring town, so I'll wear those." But it's also making a political statement. It's saying, "I'm not going to be confined to just being a person from my own town. I am a Mayan woman, and so wearing any sort of Mayan dress is perfectly valid and reasonable," so making a political statement through their dress.

These might seem like pretty mild reforms, introducing new words into a language, promoting a unified alphabet, promoting new forms of dress, and so forth, but through these incremental cultural changes the Maya have been able to affect real political changes as well. In 1996, peace accords were signed between the Marxist guerrillas and the army, and the Maya were at the negotiating table and were able to gain a number of concessions, concessions to protect their languages, concessions to protect sacred sites where they conduct their religious rituals, and so forth, very important concessions, and a number of important government posts have gone to Mayan peoples in recent years. Demetrio Cojti, a friend of mine from Tecpan who had gotten a scholarship from a Belgian priest who was stationed there to go and study at the University of Belgium and ended up getting his Ph.D. in Belgium, has come back and was appointed the Vice Minister of Education. The Minister of Culture is a Mayan woman who was likewise educated abroad. They've made significant gains in Guatemalan society, incremental, nothing dramatic, nothing revolutionary, but bit by bit changing the attitude of Ladinos toward the Maya.

I'd like to contrast this with the case of the Zapatista movements in Chiapas, Mexico. Chiapas is the southernmost state in Mexico. It borders Guatemala, and in many ways it's culturally continuous with Guatemala. It's a highland area. There are mostly Mayan Indians living there. It's the poorest state in Mexico in terms of poverty. It's very much like Guatemala. They speak different Mayan languages there than they do in Guatemala, but nonetheless the basic cultural patterns are the same.

Before I talk about the Zapatistas, let me mention one thing about the Mexican Revolution. The Mexican Revolution is the defining moment in modern Mexican history, and this happened from 1910 to 1917. You're probably familiar with that great hero of the Mexican revolution, Emiliano Zapata, and he was a leader of Indians and peasants, and he said, "We need to rise up and take over the government and break down this colonial system and redistribute land to everyone in the country." His rallying cry was "Tierra y Libertad," land and liberty. Using this base of support from peasants and Indians, he marched into Mexico City and was an instrumental figure in the Mexican Revolution, which established the government which lasts to this day and the constitution which lasts to this day, so Emiliano Zapata, we're going to come back to him in just a moment.

In 1994, January 1 of 1994, a movement occurred, broke onto the world stage rather dramatically in Chiapas Mexico, and this is the Zapatista movement. The Zapatistas are the Zapatista Army of National Liberation. On January 1 1994—this is also the date in which NAFTA, the North American Free Trade Agreement, began its first implementations—these rebels, these Mayan rebels, the Zapatista rebels took over a number of towns in Chiapas, including San Cristobal de los Casas, the state capital of Chiapas and a minor tourist center, and were able to control a large portion of the state of Chiapas and declared a revolution against the Mexican state. "We're going to take over, we're going to stand up for Indian rights, we're going to stand up for peasant rights, and we're going to fight globalization, especially NAFTA." The Zapatistas saw and see NAFTA as being a real threat to their way of life. NAFTA enforces the privatization of communal lands, for example, which are very close to the heart of many Mayan communities. The Zapatistas say, "We have to fight NAFTA, we have to fight these forces of globalization which are eroding the economic bases of our communities."

The rank and file of the Zapatista movement are overwhelmingly Mayan Indians from Chiapas. Their leader is a man named Subcomandante Marcos. It's interesting that he calls himself the sub-commander, *Subcomandante*. He says, "I'm not really the leader of this movement; the Mayan Indians are the leader of this movement, and I'm just following their lead. I don't want to be the figurehead, so I'm going to be the sub-commander rather than the commander of this movement." Subcomandante Marcos is an interesting character. He wears a ski mask, he smokes a pipe, he's generally pictured in army fatigues and wearing a uniform, and he's become a national icon in Mexico, this black ski mask, smoking a pipe, and delivering really compelling speeches.

He never takes off his ski mask, and for a long time nobody knew who Subcomandante Marcos is, but due to the work of the government and some investigative journalists, it's been discovered that he's a man, Rafael Guillan Vicente. He was born in 1957. His parents were middle-class furniture storeowners. He studied philosophy in the national university in the 1970s, actually went to Paris for a while and studied philosophy, and came back and became a philosophy professor. Then in 1984, he gave it all up. He gave up his life, his reasonably comfortable life as a philosophy professor, moved down to the jungle regions of Chiapas bordering the highland areas of Chiapas, and started organizing a revolution. He was very much inspired by Marxist ideology, and he went to the Mayan jungles hoping to foment a Marxist revolution among the Maya.

Much to his credit, he was able to respond to the Mayan concerns themselves, and they said, "Yes, these class-based revolutions, that's all well and good, but we're poor, not because we're of a poor class; we're poor because we're Indians. We're poor because we suffer discrimination. We're poor because of our ethnicity, and that's a battle that we need to fight." A traditional Marxist ideology would say that ethnicity clouds the mind, it disguises real class relations, and you have to raise people's consciousness up so that they realize where they sit in the class structure, and then they will be willing to lead a revolution. But Marcos and his compatriots were open enough to revise this and say that's not working: Let's lead an ethnic based revolution. Let's respond to what these Mayan people themselves want and lead this as a revolution.

That's what he did, and he spent ten years in the jungle organizing this movement, and then on January 1, 1994, they break onto the world stage, take over a number of towns in highland Chiapas and make this dramatic statement not only to the Mexican state but to the world as a whole. Since that time, they've lost a lot of this territory although there are still dozens of Zapatista Mayan villages. They're in a détente with the Mexican army. There's a demilitarized zone; the army has set up a perimeter around the Zapatista zone, but they've been going for more than ten years, maintaining their autonomy in Chiapas.

The Subcomandante Marcos has become a pop icon in Mexico. If you go to Mexico City you can buy Subcomandante Marcos T-shirts; they look sort of like Che T-shirts. You can buy little dolls of Subcomandante Marcos, you can buy Zapatista music from street vendors, and so forth, and he's become a real sex symbol as well. Lots of young Mexican girls look up to Marcos as a beefcake figure. What he's able to do, Marcos, his miraculous quality is that he's able to blend Western and Mexican and indigenous traditions into a political philosophy which is palatable not only to the Maya but also to non-Mayan supporters in Mexico as well, and his supporters abroad. He's found quite a bit of support from Italy, especially from southern Europe, but also from northern Europe as well and a little bit from the States.

But he's not an Indian, he's not a Maya, and so in the early days of the revolution this led the Mexican state and the Mexican press to accuse him of just being an outside agitator, of someone coming in and trying to stir up rebellion among the Maya when they wouldn't have rebelled on their own. But Marcos, one of his geniuses is he's able to resist easy categorization. Using the mask, for example, he says, "I don't want to personalize this movement. I don't want to be the figurehead of this movement; I'm just representing the Mayan people and so I'm always going to wear this mask."

At one point, there's been quite a bit of fascination with Marcos's sexuality, and I think there's sort of a natural human tendency to be fascinated with the sexuality of politically powerful people. At various times he's said to have multiple wives in different towns that he visits periodically, or multiple lovers, and at one point he was accused in the press of being gay. As a response, he wrote a poem, and Marcos writes a lot of his political communiqués and manifestoes in poetry, or in parables or fiction. He writes this poem to respond to accusations of being gay. Let me read a little bit of this. He writes about himself in the third person usually.

> Marcos is a gay in San Francisco, a black in South Africa, an Asian in Europe, a Chicano in San Isidro, an anarchist in Spain, a Palestinian in Israel, an indigenous person in the streets of San Cristóbal, a Jew in Germany, a sexist in the feminist movement, a woman alone in a Metro station at ten at night, a retired person standing around in the Zocalo, a peasant without land, a dissident against neoliberalism, a writer without books or readers, and a Zapatista in the Mexican southeast. In other words, Marcos is a human being in this world. Marcos is every untolerated, oppressed, exploited minority that is resisting and saying 'Enough!'

Enough is their symbol, *Ya basta*! Enough already is the slogan of the Zapatista movements. Marcos here is able to turn this accusation "Marcos is gay" and turn this around and say, "Yes, I'm gay and I'm black and I'm

Jewish and I'm Palestinian and I'm all of these things, and because I wear this mask, you can read into me your own political agendas." This has been the secret to his success, his popularity, not only in Mexico but abroad as well. The environmentalists love him because he talks about the Indians living in harmony with the environment. The leftists love him because he's seen as a new form of leftist possibilities. The Spanish anarchists love him because of this revolutionary potential.

In doing so, in this poem about Marcos being all of these different people, he's also able to combine a very Mayan sensibility about the multiplicity of the self. We're not just one thing, we all encompass multiple selves. He's able to represent that and also include a very fashionable, these days, postmodern theoretical concern which says the same thing, that says we cannot be reduced to any one category. I'm a white male, but I'm more than just a white male. I'm also a father, I'm an anthropologist, I'm a Southerner, and we all encompass thousands probably of such identities that we have to juggle all of the time, and probably more so today than ever before, given the wide range of cultural resources that are at our disposal. By writing his political manifestoes in poetry and sometimes in parables, he's able to convey the complexity of his position, the ambivalence that's often lost in political discourse that seems to break down into black and white, right and wrong.

All of these people love him, the environmentalists, the Indian rights activists. All of these people see in Marcos a project that they can project their own political projects onto him, onto what he represents. He's also not anti-Mexican. This is part of his appeal as well. He says, "The name of the movement itself, the Zapatistas, we're trying to get Mexico to go back to its founding principles, tierra y libertad, just like Zapata said back in 1910. We're not against the Mexican state; we're just against the corrupt Mexican government that we have right now," so he's very effective in playing this as well, "I'm not anti-patriotic, and in fact I'm more patriotic than the congressmen who sit in parliament in Mexico City and pretend to be Mexican." If you'll indulge me, let me read a passage from one other point that conveys this complex patriotism that Marcos feels; this was a communiqué of Marcos's called *Problems*.

> This thing that is one's country is somewhat difficult to explain, but it's more difficult to understand what it is to love one's country. For example, they taught us that to love one's country is, for example, to salute the flag, to rise upon hearing the National Anthem, to get as drunk as we please when the national soccer team loses, to get as drunk as we please when the national soccer

team wins, and a few other etceteras that change little from one presidency to the next. And, for example, they didn't teach us that to love one's country can be, for example, to whistle like one who is becoming ever more distant, but behind that mountain there is also part of our country where nobody sees us and where we open our hearts because one always opens one's heart when no one is watching, and we tell this country, for example, everything we hate about it and everything we love about it and how it's always better to say it, for example, with gunshots and smiling.

He's able to answer political attacks with this kind of poetry that subverts the attack that was initially made. He's saying "I'm not against Mexico; I love Mexico. I want Mexico to be the country that it can be, to live up to the promise that's included in the Mexican constitution." The Zapatistas had quite a bit of success early on. They were able to garner international support, partially and ironically by using the Internet. They have their own Internet sites, they have their own e-mail system, and so they were able to call international attention to their plight at the same time that they made demands against the Mexican state. The Mexican army is powerful enough that they could have gone down and wiped out the Zapatistas, and that's not out of the realm of possibility. But international attention was so focused on them at the time of the revolution that that would have been politically untenable.

They were able, early on, to make a number of important political gains, especially on the international stage, and at one point in 2001 they marched on Mexico City, and 100,000 people came out to see Marcos and the other Zapatistas, more people than came to see the Pope last time he was in Mexico. He's a pop icon, he's like a pop rock star in Mexico City, and all the young women were out shouting "Marcos, Marcos," and the young men as well, but Marcos during this march on Mexico City wouldn't speak. He ended up speaking a little bit because the crowd was calling for him, but again he was playing this "I want to stay in the background. I'm Subcomandante Marcos. This is the Maya movement, I'm just trying to support them, and so I don't want to be the center of attention here."

We've seen two very different forms of Mayan ethnic activism, both equally authentic, both based on the realities of modern Mayan culture but shaped by the particular histories of Guatemala and its recent state violence, and Mexico in this revolutionary Zapatista heritage. Both are based on Mayan culture, but very different interpretations of Mayan culture. The Zapatistas stress a millenarian future, while the pan-Mayans stress the virtues of a distant past. But both are able to leverage the cultural capital of being indigenous and being Maya to fight for political gains today. The Zapatistas are more grassroots and more revolutionary in many ways, but the pan-Mayanists have arguably achieved more sustainable results. These cases point us toward the malleability of culture and ethnicity and the creative ways that it can be employed in a globalized world. This is a topic we'll continue with in the next lecture.

Lecture Twenty-Four
The Janus Face of Globalization

Scope: Globalization has affected native peoples in ways both positive and negative. In this lecture, we look at the increasingly close contact remote peoples have with the outside world. We look at the effects of gold mining in Brazil and the devastating impact on Yąnomamö communities—from disease and heightened violence to breakdowns in traditional community structures. We then turn to the case of the Kayapo, who live farther south in the Brazilian Amazon, and the ways in which they have been able to capitalize on their native identity in ventures with The Body Shoppe, associations with Sting, and the mobilization of resistance to large dam projects. We also look to modern Maya farmers in Guatemala, who are turning to growing exotic crops, such as broccoli and snow peas, for the U.S. market.

Globalization is making the world a more homogenous place just as it foments greater cultural diversity and ethnic strife. In this lecture, we explain this paradox. Looking at McDonald's in Japan and China, we see how even the most emblematic of American cultural imports is interpreted in locally specific ways. We also follow the global chain of the bluefin tuna trade, from New England fishermen to Tokyo wholesalers to San Francisco sushi bars, to see the way that a single commodity takes on many social meanings as it passes through different hands.

Outline

I. Globalization is nothing new. Indeed, the world was a very globalized place over a century ago. What has changed around the turn of the 21st century is the speed and intensity of interconnections.

    A. It is useful to distinguish between globalization as empirical reality and globalization as ideology.

        1. In the last half of the 20th century, there was a dramatic drop in the cost of transportation and communication. This has resulted in a virtual collapsing of time and space distances.

        2. What was once the privy of the jet set is now within the reach of the masses. Falling telephone costs and the rise of the

Internet have enabled diaspora communities to maintain close contact with their homelands and has given rise to novel sorts of virtual communities.

    3. Predictions that globalization would make the nation-state obsolete were overplayed.

B. Some critics fear that the forces of globalization are destroying cultural diversity (the McWorld scenario), while others point out that globalization has strengthened some religious and cultural associations (the *jihad* scenario).

C. Most of the clothes we wear, the toys we buy, and the electronics we use are made overseas, connecting us in hidden ways to people around the world.

    1. The trade in bluefin tuna connects New England fishermen to Tokyo traders and, ultimately, to sushi eaters around the world.

    2. Even when cultural goods are exported (by Hollywood or McDonald's), they are always adapted by local populations.

II. Often, the most detrimental effects of globalization can be seen among the remote, small-scale societies, such as the Yąnomamö.

A. Since the 1960s, the Yąnomamö have come into increasing contact with the outside world. For example, Salesian missionaries have set up health clinics, schools, and economic cooperatives at a number of mission posts in Yąnomamö territory.

B. This contact has brought a variety of major lifestyle changes to the Yąnomamö.

    1. Trade goods, introduced by the missionaries, government workers, and anthropologists, have changed social relations based on reciprocity. Access to shotguns has made traditional Yąnomamö conflicts even more violent.

    2. Clustering around Salesian missionary outposts, Yąnomamö village structure has been upset. New villages are often made of separate houses that allow for more privacy.

    3. On the Venezuelan side, the government has tried to incorporate the Yąnomamö into national life, appointing a number of young bilingual Yąnomamö to act as government agents. On the Brazilian side of the border, the Yąnomamö have been granted a 36,000-square-mile reservation and a degree of formal autonomy.

      4. The traditional power structure that valued elders and mediational skills has been supplanted by government-appointed officials.

  C. Gold was discovered in Brazilian Yąnomamö territory in the 1980s, leading to an illicit gold rush.

      1. As many as 40,000 miners invaded Yąnomamö territory, setting up hundreds of clandestine airstrips.

      2. Their crude strip-mining techniques polluted rivers, and their airplanes and helicopters scared off game, strangling neighboring communities.

III. In contrast, the Kayapo of Brazil have faired much better in dealings with the outside world.

  A. The Kayapo, are a GΛ-speaking group who live along the upper tributaries of the Xingu River in the Amazon region of Brazil. They number about 4,000, living in 14 villages.

      1. The Kayapo received large formal land reserves (semi-autonomous territory) from Brazil in the 1980s and 1990s.

      2. They practice slash-and-burn agriculture, as well as hunting and gathering.

      3. Like the Yąnomamö, they have headmen (with achieved status and little formal power).

  B. One of the world's largest gold mines is located in Kayapo territory.

      1. The neighboring Kayapo village of Gorotire is the largest and wealthiest Kayapo settlement.

      2. Kayapo villages have set up shortwave radios in villages to maintain contact. They have also bought video cameras, televisions, and generators.

      3. With earnings from gold-mining concessions, residents of Gorotire have bought airplanes and hired Brazilian pilots to police their territory for illegal loggers and miners.

  C. The Kayapo have established relations with The Body Shoppe, the rock star Sting, and various international environmental organizations.

      1. They supply The Body Shoppe with the Brazil nut oil used in a bestselling line of hair conditioners.

2. "Chief" Ropni (or Raoni) established relations with Sting to work on environmental issues and has even gone on tour with him.
3. Using such international connections, the Kayapo have been able to halt a World Bank–funded government dam project that would have flooded Kayapo lands.

IV. In the modern globalized world, cultures are in increasing contact and are changing with increasing velocity (sometimes for the better, sometimes for the worse). Maya farmers around Tecpán, for example, are increasingly growing broccoli for export to the United States.

Readings:

Arjun Appadurai, *Modernity at Large.*

Theodore C. Bestor, *Tsukiji: The Fish Market at the Center of the World.*

Geoffrey O'Connor, *Amazon Journal: Dispatches from a Vanishing Frontier.*

Questions to Consider:

1. Is globalization threatening the cultural diversity of the world?
2. How have ethnic groups been able to leverage their cultural capital to gain concessions from governments?
3. What is the role of culture in the global world?

Lecture Twenty-Four—Transcript
The Janus Face of Globalization

In this last lecture of the course, we're going to turn to a topic that we've touched upon in the last few lectures, and that is globalization. What is globalization exactly? It's so often invoked in the social sciences and the popular media. What is it exactly, and what does it mean for theories of culture and human nature that we've put forth in this course, in this series of lectures? I'll argue that globalization itself is neither good nor bad. We're going to look back at the Yąnamamö, we're going to return to the Maya, we're going to introduce the case study of the Kayapo of Brazil, and we're going to use these to illustrate the various ways in which indigenous peoples interact with the global system and the multiple possibilities of globalization on indigenous peoples.

But first, what is globalization? What is it exactly? We can point to reduced communication and transportation costs. What was in 1930 a three-minute phone call from New York to London cost the equivalent in today's dollars of about $300. Today the cost of that same call approaches zero; it's much less than ten cents if you look for a good deal. The cost of transportation has likewise fallen, and equally dramatically. What was once the purview of the jet set is available to a wide swath of American society today. This results in a virtual collapsing of time-space distances. It's not as far. Of course, we're not literally collapsing geographic distances, but the virtual distance in time and space, because of these lower communication and transportation costs, is much greater.

We also see a reduction in tariff barriers and opening up of markets, the establishment of a free trade area such as the European Union and the North American Free Trade Agreement. This has led some people to argue that in this age of globalization national boundaries are less important than they once were, that nation-states are less important than they once were. Especially during the heydays of the late 1990s, it was thought that the nation-state was going to end, the end of the nation-state, the demise of the nation-state. That hasn't turned out to be the case, but nonetheless the forces of globalization reduce the importance of nation-states in fundamental ways.

There are increasing flows of goods around the world but also increasing flows of ideas. Incredibly, some 85 percent of world box office receipts go to Hollywood movies, so we're not just exporting goods but we're exporting ideas and concepts and culture as well. Some people have set up a dichotomy of globalization and we can call this the McWorld versus jihad dichotomy. This comes from a book by the political scientist Benjamin Barbour, who writes along the same lines as another political scientist, Samuel Huntington, who's written *The Clash of Civilization.* The idea is that there are competing forces in globalization.

On the one hand, the world is becoming a much more culturally homogeneous place. You can go to McDonald's in Beijing or Paris or Kuala Lumpur. You can go to Starbucks in any of those places. As I just mentioned, 85 percent of world box office receipts go to Hollywood movies, so the world is becoming a much more culturally homogeneous place. Yet, at the same time, the world is becoming more factionalized along ethnic and religious lines. Religious fundamentalism in particular has been a source of division in the world in recent years. As goods travel around the world with increasing velocity, they touch people's lives and they change their social circumstances. One way to look at this change in culture is to trace particular goods as they flow around the world through this global economy.

In this vein, I would like to start by discussing the case of bluefin tuna, and the anthropologist Ted Bestor, who's at Harvard, has written a fascinating ethnography tracing the commodity chain of bluefin tuna. Atlantic bluefin tuna, they're big fish. They range from 200 to 600 pounds, sometimes as much as 1,000 pounds, and they take a long time to reel in. This is a battle to reel in these fish, sometimes four or five hours it'll take a fisherman to haul in one of these bluefin tuna. This has developed a machoesque culture among New England fishermen who fish for bluefin tuna. It's man against nature; it's us against the sea. We have to go out and conquer the ocean and bring back in these huge tuna to sell, and so there's this whole cultural complex that revolves around fishing for bluefin tuna.

When these New England fishermen catch these bluefin tuna and they bring them back to the dock, they sell them more often than not to Japanese buyers. To the New England fisherman, the Japanese buyers are a bit inscrutable. They don't really understand the criteria. Weight is one, and that's an obvious criteria, but beyond that the cosmetics of the fish are very important to these Japanese buyers, and the New England fishermen talk about it in terms of the inscrutable Japanese and what are their criteria really for buying these fish. The Japanese buyers on the docks are on their cell phones, talking back to Tokyo, seeing what the latest market prices are for bluefin tuna, and then they'll offer a price. They'll buy this tuna, and they'll buy it for $3,000, sometimes as much as $10,000. They ice them down, take them normally to JFK—take them to an international airport— ship them to Tokyo and to the world's largest fish market, the *tsujiki* fish market in Tokyo, where they will be sold mostly for sushi.

The New England fishermen view the Japanese buyers as having these odd criteria. The Japanese, however, see these bluefin tuna, the cosmetics of this bluefin tuna, as very important because they see raw food, sushi, raw fish as being natural and pure in some fundamental way. In this sense, the cosmetics are very important, and so the Japanese buy these tuna, they ship them back to Tokyo, they're sold to the fish market in Tokyo, and then they're shipped out to sushi bars, either in Japan or sometimes back into the States, particularly along the West Coast. The nicer sushi bars in San Francisco and Los Angeles are going to buy their bluefin tuna from Tokyo.

We have this product that has all of these different cultural meanings. It means one thing to New England fishermen who catch it, and it ties into their culture of man against the ocean. It means another thing to these Japanese buyers, who are looking for a cosmetically perfect fish that can be sold raw and embody this purity of raw food. It means another thing to people eating sushi in Japan and another thing still to people eating at the sushi bars in San Francisco, and all the cultural meetings that we've attached to eating sushi in this country. This is a wonderful example of how transnational trade and products link people together in very opaque ways and embodies all of these different sorts of cultural meanings.

In this way, globalized products are always made local. This is a critique of the McWorld hypothesis, that the whole world is becoming culturally homogeneous. The best example comes from the work of an anthropologist, James Watson, and his colleagues, who have conducted studies of McDonald's experiences in Asia. He published a book called *Golden Arches East*. American and Japanese notions, they point out, of mealtime behavior are very different. The Japanese, especially older Japanese, see rice as being fundamental to having a meal. It's not a real meal unless you've eaten rice, and so they view McDonald's not as a place to go for a meal but as a place to go for a snack in between meals, very different than the way Americans view McDonald's.

They also believe that sharing food is fundamentally important as well, and so they will group together all of their fries in the middle of the table, for example, and then share that just as they would share a bowl of rice. It's impolite in Japanese society to eat with one's hands, and so they'll cut up their hamburgers and eat them with toothpicks, for example, so this epitome of cultural homogeneity, exporting McDonald's around the world and making everybody the same, it actually gets localized everywhere it opens. McDonald's in Japan is different from McDonald's in Los Angeles, which is different from McDonald's in Beijing or elsewhere. It's not the same.

Of course, making the world palatable to local cultures is not always possible. I would like to give a couple of different examples of the effects of globalization and the effects of modernization on modern peoples. First, indigenous peoples: first, I'd like to turn back to the Yąnamamö, who we've talked about before, who live in southern Venezuela and northern Brazil, who live in these shabonos with 100 or 200 people, practice traditional shamanistic religious practices, are shifting agriculturalists—practice swidden agriculture—and are hunters. In recent years, the Yąnamamö have come into increasing contact with the outside world, with missionaries, particularly Catholic Silesian missionaries who have made inroads in the Yąnamamö land trying to convert them to Catholicism, some Protestant missionaries as well and government incursions as well, the Venezuelan government trying to incorporate this Amazonian part of their state and these Yąnamamö peoples into national society.

The effects have been rather devastating for the Yąnamamö in contact with the outside world. When the missionaries set up a post, they encourage Yąnamamö to move to around this post, and they encourage them to do this by setting up health clinics, by giving away trade goods, and so forth. This has led the Yąnamamö to abandon their shabono style of living, with an open area in the front where you can see everybody that you live with, everyone living together, and they've adopted what they call long houses, but are really much more Western style of houses. They have walls, there are individual family units, and they'll still group these houses around the plaza so it looks a little bit like a shabono, but, crucially, people can go into their home and close the door and no one can see them. This has had dramatic impact on the way in which the Yąnamamö interact with one another.

You'll recall their fierce egalitarianism, their envy; if someone has something that other people don't have, there's this envy that gets expressed through this fierce egalitarianism of "give me that." But now, if you can hide your stuff in your home, it both allows people to accumulate things that they couldn't have accumulated before, increased private property, and also increases suspicion of having more stuff and increases envy within these communities and has broken down the social bonds within these communities in many ways, the transparent way of life. Grouping people together also increases the transmission of diseases, and so the Yąnamamö have suffered this way from malaria and measles and other things.

And, as part of this process of civilizing the Yąnamamö, civilization comes from *civitas*, of living in the city, and so by bringing the Yąnamamö together and creating these new sorts of cities, this has also allowed the Venezuelan government to incorporate them more into the state. The way in which they do this is they look for the young Yąnamamö who are learning Spanish, and they appoint them to government posts, the equivalent of a policeman or the mayor of these towns. What this has done is turned upside down the Yąnamamö system of political leadership, which is based on elders being respected, which is based on headmen having to constantly reaffirm their authority by giving stuff away back to the community, but here we have young upstart Yąnamamö, who are appointed by the outside government to be the leaders of their community, and the elders, who used to be the most venerated people in society, are pushed to the side.

We've had these devastations, these ill effects of contact with the outside world, in Yąnamamö culture in Venezuela, in Brazil as well, and you'll recall the Yąnamamö live in both southern Venezuela and northern Brazil. In Brazil, gold has been discovered in Yąnamamö land, and we've had this modern gold rush, illegal gold rush, because prospectors aren't supposed to enter onto Indian reservations, and the Brazilian government has given the Yąnamamö a reservation in northern Brazil. However, this doesn't stop the prospectors. They will come in. They'll fly in first in helicopters and scope out areas where they suspect there to be gold. Then they'll cut down an airstrip in the forest, start flying in small planes, set up a little village, and start strip mining, this incredibly devastating, environmentally devastating, form of mining.

They just pump water out from the river and hose down cliffs and then remove the gold from the wash-ff. It releases mercury into the environment. First of all, the helicopters and the airplanes scare off all of the game, so the surrounding Yąnamamö villagers don't have game that they can hunt like they used to. Second, this releasing mercury into the environment kills fish, it destroys the natural environment, and so a number of Yąnamamö villages in Brazil have been reduced to begging from gold miners to make a living. They can no longer hunt, they can no longer grow their crops on the fields that have been polluted, and they've effectively become beggars. The Yąnamamö present a case of the devastating potential effects of globalization on a native group.

To look at the other side of the coin, the flip side, the up side of globalization for native peoples, I would like to turn to the Kayapo Indians who live in Brazil, who live in the heart of the Amazon along the Xingu River in Brazil. The Kayapo are a fairly small group; their population in the 1990s was about 4,000 individuals living in 14 different villages. In the 1980s and 1990s, they received huge reservations from the Brazilian government, semi-autonomous territories, and the Kayapo today have lands equivalent to the size of Austria, and this is a group of 4,000 people with this immense span of land. They practice slash-and-burn agriculture, as well as some hunting and gathering. In many ways their subsistence practices are like the Yąnamamö, and, like the Yąnamamö, they are tribes. They have headmen—they don't have chiefs in society. This is achieved status. No formal power gets passed down from generation to generation.

In the late 1980s, gold was discovered in Kayapo land, and in fact one of the largest gold mines in the world is located very near to a Kayapo village, Goro-tiri. As a result, the Kayapo have been able to claim royalties from this gold mining, and some of these Kayapo villages, Goro-tiri in particular, have become immensely wealthy. They have money managers in Sao Paulo, who control these trust funds and to which the gold royalties flow. With some of this money, they've been able to buy Western technologies to fortify their own culture. For example, they've bought shortwave radios that they put up in Kayapo villages, so, whereas before they might have to walk a day or even two from one village to the next, now they have shortwave radios and can communicate with one another.

At one point, the BBC came down to film a documentary about the Kayapo, and the Kayapo became fascinated with their video technology, so they bought video cameras and they bought VCRs and they bought televisions and they bought generators, and now they send video postcards from one village to another village, and they use this to create political unity among these disparate Kayapo villages as well. They've also used some of these gold earnings to buy airplanes and to hire Brazilian pilots to patrol their territory, to look for illegal loggers who are coming onto the reserve lands and taking away trees, to look for illegal gold miners, and, when they find them, they call the Brazilian federal police to come in and kick these people off of their lands. It's an indigenous air force in some ways, and this is allowed through these gold earnings. The Kayapo have benefited from the earnings from the gold mines on their territory, and they've been able to employ these technologies, shortwave radios and video cameras and so forth.

They've also established relationships with The Body Shoppe. The Kayapo have the distinct advantage of being very photogenic, of being what we would consider to be real Amazonian Indians. They wear face paint, they have elaborate headdresses, and so forth, and The Body Shoppe started buying Brazil nuts from the Kayapo to use in a best-selling line of hair conditioners that they have and then using the Kayapo images to appeal to the target audience of The Body Shoppe and saying, "We're able to save the Amazonian rain forest. We're paying Kayapo to not cut down the forest and plant new things but to go around and harvest Brazil nuts which are already growing there." The Kayapo have been able to play off of their indigenousness this in this way.

Perhaps, most famously, the Kayapo have connected with the rock star Sting, and one Kayapo in particular, who's called Chief Ropni, and it's interesting to call him chief. They're a tribal-level society in the anthropological typology; they have headmen and not chiefs, but the whites who come and encounter these indigenous groups always want to be taken to the chief, "Take me to your leader." And so the Kayapo headmen have begun calling themselves chiefs and adopting this language of the outside world. Sting was doing a tour of Brazil at one point and became very much enamored with the cause of saving the Amazonian rain forest, and he visited the Kayapo, and from one day to the next he says he was converted. He saw that the rain forest is the patrimony of all of humanity that needs to be saved, and the way in which we can save it is by encouraging groups like the Kayapo, who live in harmony with their environment, albeit this is a romanticized view of how the indigenous peoples live with the environment, but Sting said the Kayapo live in harmony with their environment and so we have to help them out, and he even took Chief Ropni on a world tour with him one time.

The Kayapo have been able to use their indigenousness as leverage to convert it to economic capital and to convert it into political capital as well. At one point, the World Bank was going to fund dams being built along the Xingu River, where they live, and this would have flooded a number of Kayapo villages. What they were able to do is they sent out video crews to other dams that had been built in Brazil, videotaped what had happened, interviewed native peoples who had been displaced by these dams, compiled all of this, brought it back to the Kayapo villages, showed these films and had community meetings to decide whether this is something that we should support or something that we should oppose. They decided to oppose it, and they set up a meeting between World Bank officials, Brazilian officials, and themselves in Alta Mira, a town in the Amazon.

At this meeting, they also called in the international press, and it was a real coup for the Kayapo because they entered in with their feathers, their body paint, their spears, and really presented themselves as being the indigenous people who are protecting the environment. The international press ate it up, and they were able to stop this dam project from being built. Public opinion changed so much after this that the World Bank removed its funding and the dam was never built. They were able to leverage their cultural capital of being Indian and convert it into these political gains as well. One has to wonder what would happen if the Kayapo weren't so photogenic. Would they have been able to make these same sorts of gains? Just being Indian isn't enough; it has to be the sort of Indian that we white people, Westerners, want to see. It has to fit into our stereotypes.

As a final example, I would like to go back to the Maya of Guatemala and economic changes that have been going on in Maya lands. I mentioned last time that milpa agriculture, maize and bean subsistence plots, are really at the heart of Tecpan and Mayan subsistence, and also at the heart of symbolic life. Its food serves as a powerful ethnic marker, just like language and dress, and the Maya say that if we don't eat corn we're not really full, and really if we don't eat corn from our own villages or our own plots it doesn't really fill us up the same way that other food does. About half of the adult males in Tecpan are full-time farmers, but they've suffered some changes in recent years, particularly the opening up of markets, Guatemala signing trade agreements with the United States.

They've gotten rid of price controls on basic foodstuffs, corn, beans and wheat, and they've been reducing their tariffs so that foreign goods come in, and before in Tecpan Mayan farmers grew corn and beans, and they would shift this periodically with wheat, and wheat that they would sell on the national market in Guatemala. However, with the dropping of tariff barriers in Guatemala, all of this really cheap U.S. wheat has been flooding into the country, and it's totally wiped the market out. Nobody in Tecpan, for example, grows wheat anymore, hardly.

But the wheat has been replaced by other nontraditional crops. Today, in Tecpan, in the area around Tecpan in highland Guatemala, lots of Mayan farmers are growing broccoli and snow peas and blackberries and raspberries and other exotic produce for export to the United States. These are mostly grown by small-holding Mayan farmers. These are very labor-intensive crops. They don't grow well on plantations, the plantation model of agriculture in Guatemala, which is very exploitative, but these crops don't fit into that very well. It's better grown by smallholding Mayan farmers, who can bring the whole family out and apply the herbicides and the pesticides and do the weeding, do all of this intensive care that these crops require.

In an interesting way, in adopting these crops which pay a pretty good price, the Maya have been able to continue with their traditional agrarian way of life and yet make a bit of extra money in these crops that pay a bit more. They still employ family labor. At planting time, the whole family goes out. At harvest time, it's not just the father of the family, but the wife and the children and the cousins go out as well. They're able to fortify this communal form of labor, which has historically been very important to Mayan communities, but do so in a new way, do so growing broccoli instead of maize, do so growing cauliflower instead of corn, and so forth.

This is tied to an increase in broccoli consumption in the United States. Broccoli consumption in the U.S. has increased about a thousand percent over the 1980s and 1990s. It's become a staple crop or staple food, a cheap green food. Going to the store, you might think, "I need to get some vegetables. I need to get something green. I'll get some broccoli and I'll get some lettuce." It's become a standard, a staple of the American diet and an icon of healthy eating in many ways. Most people don't realize that a good portion of our broccoli comes from Guatemala, that a good portion of our broccoli is grown by these impoverished small-holding Mayan farmers, so, once again, like the bluefin tuna, there are opaque connections that connect Mayan farmers in Guatemala with supermarket consumers in the United States.

The result has been an influx of money into Tecpan, and Tecpan has seen rapid development over the last ten years because of the money coming in from broccoli and other sorts of exports. Whereas before, when I was living in Tecpan in the early 1990s, there were about three phones in town, three phones, none of which hardly worked, today, almost every house in town has a telephone, and lots of young men walk around town with cellular phones. There's even an Internet café that's opened up in this small highlands Mayan village. They have an Internet café, and I have Mayan friends who have their own Hotmail accounts, and they're able to communicate with relatives who have immigrated to the States, with me, and with other friends in Guatemala. Little movie houses have opened up selling and renting bootleg Hollywood action movies. There's been a fascination with Pokemon and other symbols of global pop culture.

335

Through this influx of money, they've both been able to fortify traditional agricultural relations but introduce all of these new cultural things as well into the local economy, in the local culture. It would be easy to lament the loss of culture in this way. Isn't it a shame that the Tecpanecos are watching Hollywood action movies? Isn't it a shame that their native culture is being diluted by all of these cultural imports from the United States? I feel that way myself, to be honest, in some ways, and yet it's a patronistic point of view. We can't protect the Maya from what they themselves want. If they think it makes a better life for them to adopt elements of Western culture, who are we to say, "No, that's just for us, that's just for gringos, that's just for North Americans or Westerners, and you can't have that"? It's a very patronistic view to take.

Anthropology is a unique discipline in taking an inclusive view of the human condition. It's an interdisciplinary discipline, and we've seen the wide range of topics that anthropologists study in this class. We started off by looking at the biological bases of human culture and then we moved on at looking at language and the way in which language can encode cultural knowledge. We've looked at cultural models and mental models, the way in which emotions are expressed, religion, cannibalism, and even of economics. We've looked at patterns of marriage and kinship. We've looked at political and economic organization, and then we wound up this course with an anthropological critique of economics, presumptions of rationality, and the effects of globalization on native peoples around the world.

Despite the vast differences of all of the case studies that we've looked at, the Maya, the Kayapo, the Yanamamö, the Trobrianders, despite the vast differences between each other, and from us, they're as much like us as they are different from us. Cultures are always changing, sometimes for the worse, sometimes for the better, but in the process of change itself there's an element that we can celebrate and not lament. A friend of mine in Tecpan told me recently that globalization is an economic current. The fact is it's a worldwide economic torrent; nobody can halt or stop this flood. It's like the Rio Grande; you can't stop it. The problem is we don't understand the source of this river. Where is this river coming from? What purpose does it serve? When we understand the source and causes of this river, we can use it to our own advantage.

This is really the advantage of anthropology. It's a different way of looking at the world; it forces us to reconsider things that we take for granted. We've looked at kinship terminologies; we've looked at emotions. Is mother love natural or is it something that we've learned? Is affluence the same around the world or is it something that's unique to particular cultures? By comparing other ways of looking at the world, other ways of doing things with our own ways, it allows us to critically examine elements of our own culture that we take to be given or natural or inevitable. This doesn't mean that we have to reject our own culture, it doesn't mean that native peoples are better than we are or vice versa, but it does help us make informed decisions and can even spur on creativity in ourselves by revealing the relativity of culture.

Maps

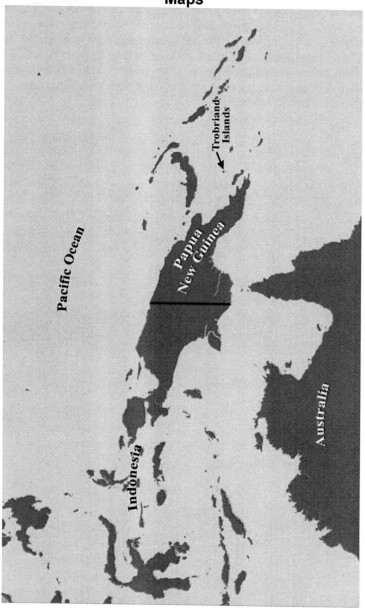

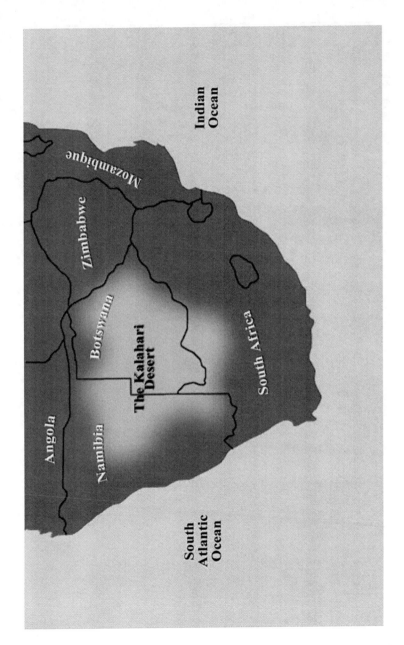

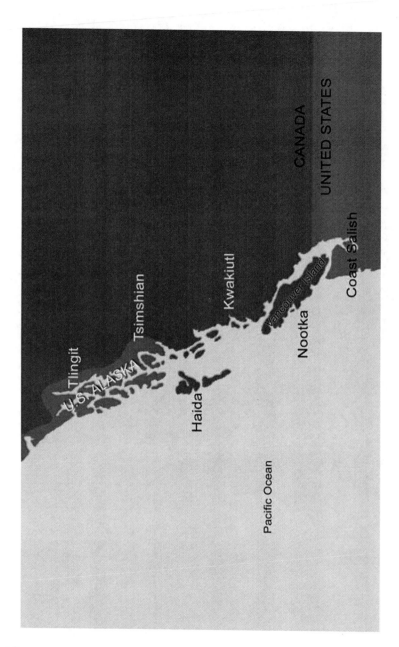

Tlingit
Tsimshian
Kwakiutl
Nootka
Coast Salish
Haida
U.S. ALASKA
CANADA
UNITED STATES
Vancouver Island
Pacific Ocean

340

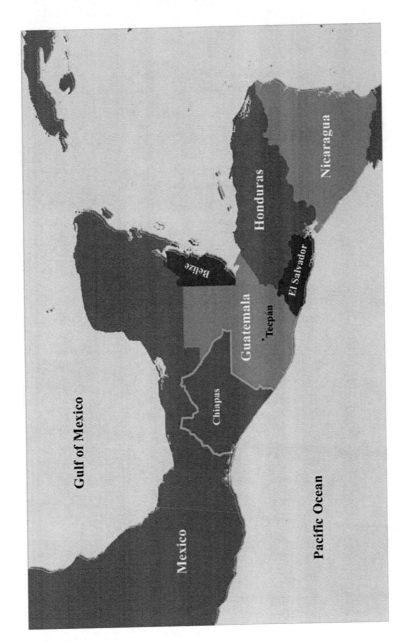

341

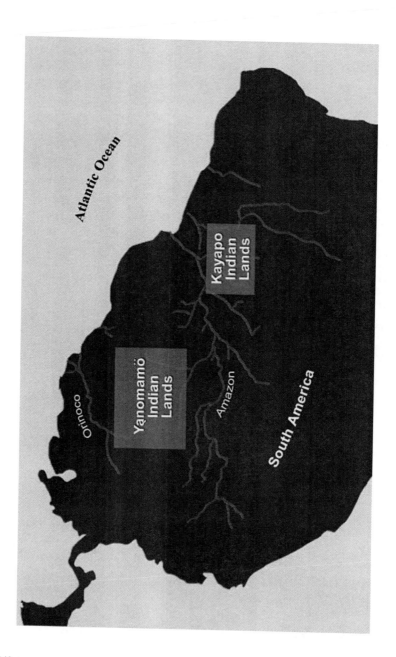

Atlantic Ocean

Kayapo Indian Lands

Yanomamö Indian Lands

Orinoco

Amazon

South America

342

Glossary

achieved authority: political positions that must be earned through demonstrating one's worthiness (for example, headmen).

affine: a relative by marriage.

animism: a belief in souls.

ascribed authority: inherited political positions.

Australopithecine: early hominids (human ancestors) that walked upright, although they had relatively small brains.

balanced reciprocity: gift-giving with the expectation of receiving a counter-gift of comparable or better value.

bands: social groups of less than 50, without formal political positions, based on gathering and hunting economies; for example, the Dobe Ju/'hoansi.

berdache: third gender in North American Pueblo and Plains societies; men who dress and live as women.

bounded rationality: the idea that humans are more rational in certain contexts than in others.

chiefdoms: social groups with thousands of members, a political system based on hereditary authority; for example, the Trobrianders.

cognate: a word with the same root as the word under study.

cognitive models: mental models of how the world works; may be more or less idiosyncratic (personal models) or shared (cultural models).

communitas: the sense of community solidarity produced by collective passage through a state of liminality.

consanguine: a blood relative.

cross-cousin: children of opposite-sex siblings; one's cross-cousins would be one's father's sister's children and one's mother's brother's children.

cultural capital: a form of symbolic capital based on cultural competencies, including, for example, artistic knowledge and educational credentials.

cultural models: mental models of the world and how it works that are widely shared by members of a culture.

cultural relativism: the notion introduced by Boas that each culture should be considered on its own terms, rather than judged by the cultural standards of another.

ebene: the hallucinogenic snuff used by Yąnomamö shamans.

Erklärung: German, used by Max Weber to denote explanation and functional understanding, as opposed to the more subjective *Verstehen*.

emic: the view from within a culture; a cultural insider's explanations; contrast with etic.

endocannibalism: ritualized consumption of the remains of one's dead relatives.

endogamy: rule mandating marriage within a variably defined group (for example, marrying within one's religion or ethnic group).

environment of evolutionary adaptation (EEA): the early Pleistocene of East Africa, where human ancestors first evolved.

ethnocentrism: the (usually implicit) belief that one's culture is superior to others; that one's own cultural customs are "natural."

ethnography: the process of gathering data from fieldwork and writing it up; cultural descriptions of other societies.

etic: an outside perspective on cultural customs; contrast with emic.

exocannibalism: ritualized eating of one's enemies.

exogamy: rule of marriage outside a variably defined group; to marry within that group would be incest.

fa'fa'fines: third gender on Samoa; men who dress and live as women.

Fordism: mass production based on the assembly line model popularized by Henry Ford.

formalist economics: the study of universal laws of economics that are not bound by cultural context (compare with substantivist economics).

gender: the social category associated with a particular sex.

generalized reciprocity: in which gifts flow in one direction for long periods of time.

hau: the Maori concept of the spirit of a gift.

headman: political position in tribal-level societies; the headman must lead by example and constantly reaffirm his right to lead.

hegemony: as developed by Anotonio Gramsci, the notion that cultural forms can induce people to willingly accept subjugation and exploitation.

hekura: microscopic spirits that inhabit the Yąnomamö world; can steal one's soul; can also be manipulated by shamans.

historical particularism: the notion introduced by Boas that each culture is the product of its own unique history; opposed to the unilineal evolution of 19th-century theorists.

hxaro **exchanges**: balanced-reciprocity exchanges practiced by the Dobe Ju/'hoansi, often involving glass beads and other trade goods.

hyperreality: term used by philosopher Jean Baudrillard to denote a copy that is, seemingly, more "real" than the original.

inclusive fitness: combines direct fitness (number of an individual's offspring that survive to reproduce themselves) with indirect fitness (the number of an individual's genes, carried by that person and his or her relatives, that are passed down to the next generation); used by sociobiologists to explain nepotism and altruism.

kinesics: the study of body language.

Ku: Hawaiian god of war.

kula: the exchanges of the Trobrianders, in which armbands and necklaces made from shells are traded through a large ring of islands.

late capitalism: stage of capitalist development that started in the 1970s and accelerated in the 1980s and 1990s; characterized by post-industrial knowledge and service economies, economic globalization, and post-Fordist production techniques.

liminality: concept introduced by Victor Turner to denote a temporary state in which normal social strictures are dropped; an inversion of normal social order associated with carnival and rites of passage.

Lono: Hawaiian god of fertility.

magic: belief that the supernatural world can be controlled through rituals; as compared to the belief in an omnipotent supreme being (religion).

milpa **agriculture**: maize and beans agriculture traditionally practiced by the Maya.

mwasawa: Trobriand period of "play" in the two months after harvest.

natural selection: the mechanism for evolution introduced by Darwin; certain variations among individuals may be favored by natural conditions.

negative reciprocity: taking advantage of the implicit expectations of gift-giving by accepting a gift but never reciprocating.

parallel cousins: cousins of same-sex siblings; one's mother's sister's children and one's father's brother's children.

phoneme: the minimal unit of sound; phonemes vary from culture to culture.

polyandry: marriage of one woman to more than one man.

polygyny: marriage of one man to more than one woman.

potlatch: feasts thrown by Kakiutl chiefs that involve massive redistribution, as well as conspicuous destruction.

post-Fordism: flexible production techniques adopted by Saturn and a number of other companies in the 1990s.

prisoner's dilemma: a foundational problem in experimental economics: two individuals are arrested for a crime they committed, but the police do not have enough evidence to convict them both of the crime. They are interrogated separately and each made the offer that if both refuse to confess, they will be convicted of a lesser charge and serve two years each; if both confess they will each serve four years; and if only one confesses, that person will go free while the accomplice will serve five years.

	Player B: cooperate	Player B: defect
Player A: cooperate	2 yrs./2 yrs.	5 yrs./0 yrs.
Player A: defect:	0 yrs/5 yrs.	4 yrs./4 yrs.

proxemics: the study of physical distance as a form of communication.

pulaaku: the Fulbe code of conduct that stresses stoicism.

Quetzalcoatl: a primary Aztec deity, usually represented as a feathered serpent, but also said to take the form of a light-skinned man (and, thus, perhaps initially confused with Cortes).

r and K selection: a species' reproductive strategies may be placed on a continuum from r (favoring a large absolute rate of reproduction—many offspring) to K (favoring a low rate of reproduction but investing heavily in those offspring).

Rashomon effect: from the 1950 Japanese film *Rashomon*, the effect of different observers perceiving the same event in very different ways.

sandbadham **marriage**: fluid marriages between Nayar (India) women and one or more "visiting husbands."

Sapir-Whorf hypothesis: the proposition that worldview and culture are at least partly dictated by grammar and language structure.

shabono: the Yąnomamö village made of a circular palisade, a thatched roof living area, and a large open plaza; may have between 40 and 300 inhabitants.

shaman: a religious specialist who acts as a mediator between the spirit world and the material world.

sim-pua **marriage**: a traditional Chinese form of infant betrothal.

social capital: networks of family, friends, and acquaintances that serve as important assets.

social Darwinism: line of thought developed by Herbert Spencer that attempted to apply Darwin's natural selection to human societies.

substantivist economics: the view than economic systems are culturally embedded, that there are no universal economic laws (compare with formalist economics).

swidden agriculture: also called slash-and-burn, the technique of cutting down and burning trees and vegetation on a plot before planting; swidden plots are usually farmed for several years, then a new plot is cut down.

symbolic capital: forms of non-material capital, such as social capital or cultural capital, that may be converted into material resources.

tali-**rite marriage**: a temporary and ceremonial marriage performed with young Nayar (India) girls, marking their passage into womanhood.

TAT: Thematic Apperception Test, a psychological test that shows subjects pen-and-ink drawings of various scenes and asks them to describe the scenes.

taupu: ceremonial virgins on Samoa, daughters of chiefs.

Taylorism: developed by Frederick Taylor, a method of production in which each process is broken down into its smallest components to reduce the need for skilled and artisanal labor.

Tenochtitlán: the Aztec capital city; today, the site of Mexico City.

traje: traditional Maya dress.

tribes: social groups with hundreds of members and a headman form of political authority, based on a horticultural economy; for example, the Yąnomamö.

ultimatum game: an experimental economics game that pairs two individuals. Player A is given a sum of money (x), a percentage of which he must offer Player B, who can either accept or reject the offer. If the offer is accepted, the money is split as offered, and if the offer is rejected, neither player gets any money.

unokais: honorific given to Yąnomamö men who have killed.

Verstehen: the German word used by Max Weber to denote a subjective understanding, as compared with the more functional *Erklärung*.

waiteri: the valued Yąnomamö personality quality of fierceness.

weapons of the weak: concept introduced by James Scott to denote the ways in which subjugated and disempowered peoples can exert resistance.

world systems theory: view of the global economy that sees less developed countries as dependent on more developed countries.

Cultural Sketches
(Biographical Notes)

Dobe Ju/'hoansi

The Dobe Ju/'hoansi are a hunting and gathering group living in small bands on the northwest edge of the Kalahari Desert in Botswana and Namibia. The Ju/'hoansi follow game and harvest cycles throughout the year, staying within areas defined by water holes. Their camps (which consist of grass huts set around an open plaza) are usually occupied for only a few months.

The Ju/'hoansi (who are also known as the Kalahari Bushmen, the San, and the !Kung) are a classic band-level society (as illustrated in Lecture Thirteen). They have are no formal positions of political authority, relying instead on situational leadership. Although we often think of hunters and gatherers as impoverished, studies have shown that there is actually very little hunger among the Ju/'hoansi and that the average workweek is only about 20 hours. In addition, the vast majority of their calories come not from meat but from gathered foods. The Ju/'hoansi also have little notion of private property and practice a generalized form of reciprocity (see Lecture Sixteen).

The Dobe Ju/'hoansi are one of the most thoroughly documented societies in the world, thanks to the work of Richard Lee, Irven DeVore, Marjorie Shostak, and others who worked on the Harvard Kalahari Project starting in 1963.

The Ju/'hoansi speak a San (or "click") language (discussed in Lecture Six). The / represents a dental click, a sound not unlike "tsk," as in a scolding ("tsk, tsk"). The *J* is pronounced as in the French "je." An alternate spelling is Zhu/wansi.

Fulbe

The Fulbe (also known as the Fulani) are an ethnic group spread out across West Africa. Numbering as many as 10 million people, the Fulbe all speak varieties of the Fulfulde language and are (at least nominally) Muslim. They trace their dispersed origins back to early 19th-century *jihads* that spread the faith westward across Africa.

Traditionally, they have had a chiefdom-style political organization, although sustained contact with colonial powers and modern African states has diminished the importance and power of chiefs. Most Fulbe are cattle herders, although the Fulbe of northern Cameroon studied by Helen Regis are farmers.

As discussed in Lecture Nine, the Fulbe have melded Islamic teachings with traditional beliefs. Koranic scholars (*Mallums*) are called upon to interpret scripture and to heal illnesses brought about by cannibal witch attacks and soul-stealing river spirits. There is a strict division between women and men in Fulbe life, but women have more power than in many other Islamic societies. They may divorce, for example, if their husbands do not adequately provide for them with annual gifts of batik cloth. The Fulbe also highly value stoicism; their code of conduct (*pulaaku*) calls for strong emotions to be muted.

The Fulbe also practice an important rite of passage for males (see Lecture Ten). Boys are taken to a temporary camp, where they are forced to eat unclean foods and learn secrets associated with manhood. They are then circumcised and return to the village as men.

Kwakiutl

The Kwakiutl are one of a number of related ethno-linguistic groups living along the northwest coast of North America, from British Columbia up to the Inuit territories of the sub-Arctic. The Kwakiutl were made famous by Franz Boas and his extensive studies of almost all aspects of native life, from language and arts to history and body measurements (see Lecture Three). The Kwakiutl and other northwest-coast groups are also known for their totem poles and spectacular masks (such as those in the collections of the American Museum of Natural History and the Chicago Field Museum).

Kwakiutl subsistence is based around salmon, which are seasonally abundant and can be dried for eating year-round. The Kwakiutl have a matrilineal society with a chiefdom style of political organization. Kwakiutl chiefs compete with one another to build their power through potlatch feasts (see Lecture Seventeen). During potlatch feasts, which would last for several days, hosts ply their guests with food and gifts. In addition, there are displays of conspicuous destruction—with canoes, artwork, and blankets sunk or burned. Potlatches were incredibly costly, and chiefs would often have to save for years to throw one, but a successful potlatch would secure valuable political allegiances. Some have argued that the potlatch also served as a form of insurance—if the salmon did not run one year, neighboring chief's potlatches could provide needed food and supplies. Potlatches were banned in Canada for many years as irrational acts of destruction. Recently, they have been revived by a new generation of Kwakiutl reclaiming their heritage.

Maya

When one thinks of the Maya, the first images to come to mind are likely of Classic-era Maya civilization (A.D. 250–900) that flourished in the lowland forests of Central America. Yet there are more than 6 million Maya people living today in southern Mexico, Guatemala, Belize, and Honduras. In Guatemala, the Maya make up over half of the population.

The Maya of Guatemala are concentrated in the thousands of small, rural communities spread throughout the western highlands. Because of rugged terrain and social isolation, this is an area of great linguistic diversity; 21 separate Mayan languages are spoken in Guatemala alone. Just as Spanish is the *lingua franca* of Guatemala, Catholicism is the common religion, but here, too, we find significant variation. Native shamans still maintain sacred ancient calendars and perform rituals, and Protestant missions are making significant inroads.

The vast majority of Maya in Guatemala are subsistence farmers, growing the staple crops of corn and beans. Guatemala is a country of stark inequalities, and the Maya suffer disproportionately from lack of land and poverty. During the late 1970s and early 1980s, they also suffered from military campaigns against communist guerrillas (a period known as *la violencia*). In Lecture Twenty-Two, I call on my fieldwork in the town of Tecpán Guatemala, to show the lasting impact of the violence on traditional lifeways.

It is easy to see the modern Maya as victims, but we must not lose sight of the fact that they take an active role in constructing their lives. Maya farmers around Tecpán, for example, have begun exporting snow peas and broccoli to the United States, using their traditional skills to increase their earnings by tapping into a global market. As we see in Lecture Twenty-Three, Maya activists in Guatemala and Mexico have also been successful in recent years in pushing for indigenous rights reforms.

Sambia

The Sambia are an Anga-speaking group in the New Guinea highlands. *Sambia* is a pseudonym used by Gilbert Herdt, the anthropologist who has worked with the Sambia since the late 1960s. Herdt used a pseudonym to protect the isolated Sambia from unwanted attention following the publication of his work.

The Sambia are a patrilineal chiefdom-level society. There is a stark division between men and women. Men view women as potentially polluting and try to keep contact to a minimum. Sambia houses have separate areas for men and women, and there are even separate male and female paths through their villages. Menstruating women are required to move out of their houses and into a menstrual hut located outside the village proper. Men, for their part, spend much of their early lives living in the village men's hut.

As discussed in Lecture Ten, the male initiation rites are the most dramatic aspect of Sambian society. The Sambia believe that males are not born with a supply of semen. Thus, to turn them into men, prepubescent boys are required to drink the semen of older boys. They learn this secret ritual through an intense initiation ceremony, after which they will live in the men's hut and practice ritualized homosexuality until they get married in their early 20s. After the birth of their first child, men are no longer supposed to have sexual contact with other males. Yet a fear of females as depleting a man's semen supply keeps men suspicious of their wives.

With increasing contact with the outside world (led by Seventh Day Adventist missionaries), the Sambia today are abandoning many of their former customs—moving into Western-style houses, going to church, and rarely conducting male initiations.

Trobrianders

The Trobrianders are a matrilineal chiefdom located on a string of small islands off the coast of Papua New Guinea. They were first studied by Bronislaw Malinowski during World War I (see Lecture Four) and have since become a classic case study in cultural anthropology. Annette Weiner conducted an important restudy of the Trobrianders in the 1970s, focusing on a number of aspects of women's lives that Malinowski missed.

As discussed in Lecture Twelve, the Trobrianders are a matrilineal society with four ranked clans. Although descent is traced through female lines, men hold the formal positions of power (inherited from the mother's brother). Contrary to the expectations of Freud's Oedipal complex, adolescent Trobriand boys have tensions, not with their fathers, but with their mothers' brothers. Malinowski used these data to argue against the universality of the Oedipus conflict. Malinowski also wrote that a young man is obliged to marry his father's sister's daughter (a cross-cousin); Weiner found that although this may be a cultural ideal, in practice, men most often do not marry a cross-cousin. High-ranking Trobriand males often have several wives, which increases their kinship ties and political prestige.

A great deal of political maneuvering goes on between Trobriand chiefs jockeying for power. The material circumstances of chiefs are much as they are for everyone else—there is not much variation in standards of living. Wealth is more symbolic than material, and a key symbol of wealth and power is yams, displayed in yam huts in front of chiefs' houses. A full yam hut is a clear sign of political prestige; the catch is that these yams must be received as gifts. Men receive yams through their wives (from a wife's brothers, in particular). Weiner shows that this practice puts Trobriand men in debt to their wives, an obligation that must be repaid with women's wealth (banana-leaf bundles and woven skirts). For upwardly mobile chiefs, redistributions of yams serve as a means of building up political power (see Lecture Seventeen).

The Trobrianders are also known for the *kula* trade ring, an elaborate system of balanced reciprocity, as discussed in Lecture Sixteen. In the *kula* ring, men have trading partners on islands in either direction. To these partners, they trade armbands (which move only counter-clockwise through the ring) and necklaces (which travel only clockwise); both are made of shells, and each item has a particular history of ownership associated with it. To possess a famous item brings prestige, although the items are not hoarded and constantly circulate.

Yąnomamö

The Yąnomamö live in the rainforest at the border between Venezuela and Brazil. They number about 20,000, spread out over a large territory and living in villages called *shabonos* of between 40 and 300 people. They are best known from the long-term fieldwork of anthropologist Napoleon Chagnon, who worked primarily in the village of Bisaasi-teri in Venezuela.

In many ways, the Yąnomamö are a classic patrilineal tribal-level society (see Lecture Fourteen). Rather than hereditary chiefs, Yąnomamö *shabonos* have headmen who earn their positions through networking and leading by example. The Yąnomamö practice a slash-and-burn style of agriculture, growing plantains, manioc, taro, sweet potato, and tobacco. Using poison-tipped arrows, they also hunt pigs, monkey, deer, and armadillos.

The Yąnomamö live in a world filled with mischievous and malevolent spirits. Shamans use hallucinogenic snuff to contact and manipulate the spirit world. At death, the Yąnomamö cremate the bodies of their dead relatives, crush up the bones, and drink the mixture in a gruel—symbolically rejuvenating their lineage.

As discussed in Lecture Fifteen, the Yąnomamö are also an especially violent society, with frequent raids and warfare between *shabonos*. Men who have killed take on the status of *unokais* and generally have more wives than other men. Anthropologist Marvin Harris argues that the Yąnomamö fight because of chronic protein shortages, but Chagnon counters that, in fact, they are fighting over women.

The journalist Patrick Tierney has published a scathing critique of Chagnon's work with the Yąnomamö—accusing him of intentionally infecting the Yąnomamö with measles as part of a secret experiment. While the genocidal allegations have been disproved, Chagnon's work raises important questions about the impact of anthropologists (and the trade goods they bring with them) on native communities.

Bibliography

Films:

The Ax Fight. Timothy Asch and Napoleon Chagnon. Documentary Educational Resources, 1975. Multifaceted view of violent conflict between two Yąnomamö villages.

The Gods Must Be Crazy. Jamie Uys. Columbia TriStar, 1980. The fictional story of an isolated Kalahari band and their fateful encounter with a Coke bottle that falls from a passing airplane.

Books:

Appadurai, Arjun. *Modernity at Large: Cultural Dimensions of Globalization*. Minneapolis: University of Minnesota Press, 1996. An anthropologist's account of the processes of cultural and economic globalization.

————. *The Social Life of Things*. Cambridge University Press, 1988. Collection of essays examining the cultural biographies of commodities; see especially the essays by Appadurai and Kopytoff.

Barfield, Thomas. *The Dictionary of Anthropology*. Oxford: Blackwell Publishers, 1997. A useful basic source for definitions of terminology and concepts in anthropology.

Bass, Bill, and Jon Jefferson. *Death's Acre: Inside the Legendary Forensic Lab—the Body Farm—Where the Dead Do Tell Tales*. Putnam Publishing Group, 2003. A fascinating account of forensic anthropologist Bill Bass's work establishing the "Body Farm" at the University of Tennessee.

Baudrillard, Jean. *Simulation and Simulacra*. University of Michigan Press, 1995. Leading French philosopher's treatise on *simulacra* (copies with no original) and simulation in the modern economy; discusses hyperreality in the United States.

Benedict, Ruth. *Patterns of Culture*. Mariner Books, 1989. A seminal text written by one of Boas's early students. Benedict compares the Zuni, Kwakiutl, and other cultures in terms of core psychological traits.

Bestor, Theodore C. *Tsukiji: The Fish Market at the Center of the World*. Berkeley: University of California Press, 2004. An anthropologist looks at the world's largest fish market in Japan and the dense web of supply that keeps it stocked.

Boas, Franz. *Race, Language, and Culture.* University of Chicago Press, 1995. A collection of important articles written by the father of American anthropology in which he outlines his concept of cultural relativism by looking at race, language, and culture.

Bourdieu, Pierre. *Distinction: A Social Critique of the Judgment of Taste.* Harvard University Press, 1987. An important analysis of different forms of capital—not just economic but social and cultural as well—by one of France's leading contemporary theorists.

Brown, Michael. *The Search for Eve.* HarperCollins, 1990. Account of the recent research combining analysis of mitochondrial DNA with archaeological evidence to postulate a common human ancestor in East Africa about 200,000 years ago.

Burridge, Kenelm. *Mambu: A Melanesian Millennium.* Princeton, NJ: Princeton. University Press, 1995. Study of Melanesian cargo cults and millenarian religious beliefs in Melanesia.

Carmack, Robert. *Harvest of Violence.* Norman: University of Oklahoma Press, 1992. A collection of essays by anthropologists working in Guatemala on the effects of the violence in that country.

Chagnon, Napoleon. *The Yąnomamö.* International Thomson Publishing, 1992. Ethnography of the Yąnomamö of the Venezuelan rainforest.

Conklin, Beth. *Consuming Grief.* University of Texas Press, 2001. A moving account of death, grieving, and the practice of cannibalism among the Wari of the Brazilian Amazon.

Dawkins, Richard. *The Selfish Gene.* Oxford University Press, 1990. An important early text in sociobiology, arguing that humans are best seen, from an evolutionary perspective, not as individuals but as containers for selfish genes.

Diamond, Jared. *Guns, Germs and Steel.* New York: W.W. Norton & Company, 1998. Popular account of the rise of Western dominance.

Donner, Florinda. *Shabono.* San Francisco: HarperSanFrancisco, 1992. An impressionistic account of life among the Yąnomamö, focusing on spiritual beliefs and the roles of shamans.

Fagan, Brian. *People of the Earth: An Introduction to World Prehistory.* Prentice Hall, 2003. A comprehensive overview of archaeology and world prehistory.

Ferraro, Gary. *Classic Readings in Cultural Anthropology.* Wadsworth Publishing, 2004. A collection of seminal essays in cultural anthropology.

Fischer, Edward F. *Cultural Logics and Global Economies: Maya Identity in Thought and Practice*. Austin: University of Texas Press, 2001. Examination of economic and political globalization and their effects in a Maya community in Guatemala.

Fischer, Edward F., and R. McKenna Brown, eds. *Maya Cultural Activism in Guatemala*. University of Texas Press, 1997. Collection of essays examining the resurgence of Maya culture in Guatemala in the 1990s.

Fischer, Edward F., and Carol Hendrickson. *Tecpán Guatemala: A Modern Maya Town in Local and Global Context*. Westview Press, 2002. Ethnographic study of a Kaqchikel Maya town in highland Guatemala.

Fisher, Helen. *Anatomy of Love: A Natural History of Mating*. Ballantine Books, 1994. A biological perspective on human attraction and mating.

Friedman, Jonathan. *Cultural Identity and Global Process*. London: Sage Publications, 1994. Insightful essays on culture in an age of globalization.

Geertz, Clifford. *The Interpretation of Cultures*. Basic Books, 2000. A widely cited collection of essays on the meaning of culture; includes a classic analysis of the Balinese cockfight.

Goldstein, Melvyn C. "When Brothers Share a Wife." *Natural History*, March 1987, pp. 39–48. An analysis of fraternal polyandry among the ethnic Tibetans living in the Nepalese Himalayas.

Goody, Jack. *The Development of the Family and Marriage in Europe*. Cambridge University Press, 1983. A wide-ranging study of changing customs of marriage and the family in Europe of the last centuries; includes a detailed discussion of incest taboos as defined by the Catholic Church.

Gramsci, Antonio. *The Prison Notebooks*. Internal Publishers Company, 1971. Reflection on the concepts of hegemony, Fordism, and culture, written while the author was in prison in Italy.

Gregor, Thomas. *Anxious Pleasures*. University of Chicago Press, 1987. A study of the Mehinaku of the Brazilian Amazon, focusing on sexuality and psychology.

Gutman, Matthew. *The Romance of Democracy*. University of California Press, 2002. A sensitive ethnography looking at the complexities of democracy in a barrio of Mexico City.

Hall, Edward T. *The Silent Language*. Anchor, 1973. An analysis of language and nonverbal communication.

Harris, Marvin. *Cannibals and Kings: Origins of Culture.* New York: Random House, 1977. A lively materialist interpretation of a wide range of cultural traditions, from Aztec cannibalism to Muslim pork taboos.

Herdt, Gilbert. *Sambia Sexual Culture: Essays from the Field (Worlds of Desire).* University of Chicago Press, 1999. Ethnographic study of the Sambia of Papua New Guinea, looking at their unusual sexual customs.

Jankowiak, William. *Sex, Death and Hierarchy.* Columbia University Press, 1992. Rich ethnographic account of life in an Inner Mongolian city.

Kearney, Michael. *Reconceptualizing the Peasantry.* Westview Press, 1996. A pioneering look at peasants in a globalized world. Calls on the author's fieldwork in Oaxaca, Mexico, and with Oaxacan immigrants to California.

Lakoff, George, and Johnson, Mark. *Metaphors We Live By.* University of Chicago Press, 2003. Linguistic analysis of key metaphors in American English.

Lee, Richard. *The Dobe Ju/'hoansi.* Harcourt Brace, 1993. Ethnographic study based on long-term fieldwork among the Dobe Ju/'hoansi of Botswana.

Lévi-Strauss, Claude. *The Raw and the Cooked.* University of Chicago Press, 1983. The first in a series of books that analyzes the structure of myths of native American groups.

Lizot, Jacques. *Tales of the Yanomami.* Cambridge University Press, 1991. Engaging study of Yąnomamö oral traditions and daily life.

Low, Setha. *Behind the Gates.* New York: Routledge, 2003. An ethnographic analysis of life in an American gated community.

Malinowski, Bronislaw. *Argonauts of the Western Pacific.* Waveland Press, 1984. Malinowski's study of the Trobriand Islanders, focusing on the *kula* ring.

———. *The Sexual Lives of Savages.* Routledge, 2001. Malinowski's account of kinship, marriage, and sexuality among the Trobriand Islanders.

Marcos, Subcomandante. *Our Words Are Our Weapons.* SevenStories Press, 2002. Writings from the poetic and charismatic leader of Mexico's Zapatista revolution.

Marx, Karl. *The Eighteenth Brumaire of Louis Bonaparte.* Internal Publishers Company, 1963. A biting critique of French peasants who supported Louis Bonaparte.

Mauss, Marcel. *The Gift*. W.W. Norton, 2000. Classic treatise on the nature of gift-giving.

Mead, Margaret. *Coming of Age in Samoa*. Perennia, 2001. Mead's best-selling account of the sexual lives of adolescent Samoan girls.

Menchu, Rigoberta. *I Rigoberta Menchu, an Indian Woman*. London: Verso Books, 1987. Nobel-prize winner's autobiographical account of life in Guatemala during the violence.

Mintz, Sidney. *Sweetness and Power: The Place of Sugar in Modern History*. New York: Penguin, 1990. A fascinating study of how demand for sugar in England influenced production on plantations in the New World.

Monetjo, Victor. *Testimonio: Death of a Guatemalan Village*. Curbstone Press, 1987. A moving account by a Maya anthropologist of the Guatemalan army's raid on the village where he taught school.

Morris, Desmond. *The Naked Ape*. Delta, 1999. An early sociolobiological perspective on humans as animals.

Murphy, Yolanda, and Robert Murphy. *Women of the Forest*. Columbia University Press, 1985. Sensitive portrait of gender relations among the Mudurucu of Brazil.

O'Connor, Geoffrey. *Amazon Journal*. Plume Books, 1998. A journalist's gripping account of social and environmental change in the Amazon region.

Pinker, Steven. *The Language Instinct*. Perennial, 2000. Provocative overview of recent research on language and the way the mind works. Pinker argues that language is a human instinct.

Rathje, William. *Rubbish! The Archaeology of Garbage*. Harper Perennial Library, 1993. An overview of Rathje's ongoing archaeological excavation of modern garbage dumps.

Regis, Helen. *The Fulbe of Northern Cameroon*. Westview Press, 2002. Ethnographic account of the Fulbe of northern Cameroon.

Remnick, David, ed. *The New Gilded Age*. New York: Random House, 2000. Insightful essays from the *New Yorker* on the culture of the 1990s economic boom.

Restall, Matthew. *Seven Myths of the Spanish Conquest*. Oxford University Press, 2003. This erudite and highly readable study debunks a number of common preconceptions about Spanish contact in the New World.

Sahlins, Marshall. *Islands of History*. University of Chicago Press, 1987. Sahlins's interpretation of the clash of cultures between Captain Cook and the Hawaiians, in which he attempts to solve the mystery of who killed Captain Cook.

———. *Stone Age Economics*. Aldine de Gruyter, 1972. Important text in which Sahlins argues that gathers and hunters are the "original affluent society," as well as an analysis of reciprocity across cultures.

Scheper-Hughes, Nancy. *Death without Weeping*. University of California Press, 1992. Moving account of life in an impoverished Brazilian shantytown.

———. *Saints, Scholars and Schizophrenics*. University of California Press, 2001. Psychological analysis of social life in a small community in western Ireland.

Schultz, Emily, and Robert Lavenda. *Cultural Anthropology*. McGraw-Hill Humanities/Social Sciences/Languages, 2000. Useful general introduction to cultural anthropology; a college textbook.

Scott, James. *Weapons of the Weak*. Yale University Press, 1987. A political scientist who has conducted fieldwork in Malaysia writes about the subtle ways in which disempowered individuals resist domination.

Shore, Bradd. *Culture in Mind*. Oxford University Press on Demand, 1996. Clear and well-written introduction to cognitive models.

Soshtak, Majorie. *Nisa: The Life and Words of a !Kung Woman*. Harvard University Press, 2000. The fascinating oral history of a Dobe Ju/'hoansi woman and the trials and tribulations she faces in love, marriage, and motherhood.

Stiglitz, Joseph E. *Globalization and Its Discontents*. W.W. Norton & Company, 2003. Nobel-prize winner's critique of economic globalization and misuses of economics.

Tannen, Deborah. *You Just Don't Understand: Women and Men in Conversation*. Quill, 2001. A sociolinguistic analysis of speech differences between men and women.

Thaler, Richard H. *The Winner's Curse: Paradoxes and Anomalies of Economic Life*. Princeton: Princeton University Press, 1994. A prominent economist explains irrational behaviors.

Tierney, Patrick. *Darkness in El Dorado*. New York: W.W. Norton & Company, 2002. An investigative journalist's scathing critique of Chagnon's fieldwork among the Yamomamö.

Turner, Victor. *The Ritual Process*. Aldine de Gruyter, 1995. Important contribution to the study of ritual that introduced the concepts of liminality and *communitas*.

Watson, James. *Golden Arches East*. Stanford, CA: Stanford University Press, 1997. A collection of essays looking at how McDonald's has been localized in Asian countries.

Weiner, Annette. *The Trobrianders of Papua New Guinea (Case Studies in Cultural Anthropology)*. International Thomson Publishing, 1988. Study of the Trobriand Islanders based on fieldwork in the 1970s; updates many of Malinowski's observations.

Whorf, Benjamin. *Language, Thought, and Reality*. MIT Press, 1964. Collection of essays outlining the Sapir-Whorf hypothesis.

Wilk, Richard. *Economies and Cultures*. Westview Press, 1996. A useful introduction to economic anthropology, covering both formal economics in the Adam Smith tradition and Marxist approaches.

Wilson, E. O. *On Human Nature*. Harvard University Press, 1988. Manifesto of a preeminent scholar of sociobiology.

Wolf, Arthur. *Sexual Attraction and Childhood Association*. Stanford University Press, 1995. Study of sexual attraction that supports the idea that sustained early childhood association mutes sexual desires. Field data from ethnic Chinese of Taiwan.

Wright, Robin. *The Moral Animal*. Vintage, 1995. A journalist's well-written synthesis of recent sociobiological work, focusing on the biological bases of morality.

Young, Michael. *Malinowski's Kiriwina*. Chicago: University of Chicago Press, 1998. Collection of photographs taken during Malinowski's fieldwork in the Trobriand Islands.

Internet Resources:

The Anthropology Tutorials. Dr. Dennis O'Neil, Palomar College. http://anthro.palomar.edu/tutorials

The Gorilla Foundation. http://www.koko.org/

Notes